PAUL
SIMON

ALSO BY ROBERT HILBURN

Johnny Cash: The Life

Corn Flakes with John Lennon:
And Other Tales from a Rock 'n' Roll Life

Springsteen

PAUL SIMON

THE LIFE

ROBERT HILBURN

SIMON &
SCHUSTER

London · New York · Sydney · Toronto · New Delhi

A CBS COMPANY

First published in the United States by Simon & Schuster, Inc., 2018
First published in Great Britain by Simon & Schuster UK Ltd, 2018
A CBS COMPANY

1 3 5 7 9 10 8 6 4 2

Simon & Schuster UK Ltd
1st Floor
222 Gray's Inn Road
London WC1X 8HB

www.simonandschuster.co.uk
www.simonandschuster.com.au
www.simonandschuster.co.in

Simon & Schuster Australia, Sydney
Simon & Schuster India, New Delhi

Paul Simon lyrics courtesy of Paul Simon Music

A CIP catalogue record for this book is available from the British Library

Hardback ISBN: 978-1-4711-7417-9
Trade Paperback ISBN: 978-1-4711-7418-6
eBook ISBN: 978-1-4711-7419-3

Interior design by Joy O'Meara
Printed in the UK by CPI Group (UK) Ltd, Croydon, CR0 4YY

CONTENTS

Prologue   1

PART ONE

The Boxer   7

PART TWO

The Sound of Silence   51

PART THREE

Bridge Over Troubled Water   119

PART FOUR

Still Crazy After All These Years   187

PART FIVE

Graceland   247

PART SIX

Questions for the Angels   319

Epilogue   387

Acknowledgments 393
Bibliography 397
Notes 403
Photo Credits 418
Index 419

PROLOGUE

Ever since his debut on *Saturday Night Live* in 1975, Paul Simon looked forward to walking the narrow hallway to the stage at NBC Studios in Midtown Manhattan. Whether alone, or with Art Garfunkel, or with the high-stepping, show-stopping South African vocal group Ladysmith Black Mambazo, he enjoyed the well-wishes of the cast and crew as he made the walk—their smiles, shouts of encouragement, and even pats on the back.

This time—the night of September 29, 2001—it was different.

As soon as Simon stepped into the hallway, he saw a row of New York City firefighters and police officers, their heads bowed, still mourning the deaths of more than four hundred of their comrades in the World Trade Center terrorist assault eighteen days before. It made Simon wonder whether this tribute to the victims of the 9/11 attacks—some nine thousand killed or wounded—wasn't premature. Many in the *SNL* cast of comedians asked themselves the same question. Would people really be ready for jokes?

Simon had already joined nearly two dozen musicians—including Paul McCartney and U2—in performing on a September 21 telethon that was broadcast around the world and raised more than $200 million for families of the victims. In one of the show's emotional highlights, he sang his most famous composition, the gospel-edged "Bridge Over Troubled Water." But that night wasn't quite the same. The telethon was designed as a worldwide expression of solidarity and support. Artists performed on candlelit stages with no studio audiences, giving the event an intimacy that was somber and inspiring.

For *SNL*, Lorne Michaels, the creator of the culture-defining series, wanted to aim directly and unmistakably at the residents of New York City—opening with Mayor Rudy Giuliani standing with some thirty fire and police personnel who had just come off duty at ground zero, the dust of the site still visible on their uniforms. The plan was for the mayor to say a few words about the glory and resilience of New York and then have Simon sing a song, which would serve as a crucial step in Michaels's goal of lifting the city's spirits.

Michaels believed Simon was the perfect choice—the only choice. He was one of the all-time great American songwriters, inducted into both the Rock & Roll Hall of Fame (twice) and the Songwriters Hall of Fame, and the only artist to receive Album of the Year Grammy Awards for records made in three separate decades. His tunes had been recorded by a treasure chest of vocalists, from Elvis Presley and Frank Sinatra to Barbra Streisand and Ray Charles.

Simon was also a New Yorker whose career reflected the triumphs and struggles of the city itself. He had come out of the borough of Queens with his schoolboy chum Art Garfunkel to enjoy superstar status around the world, and then exhibited the guts to walk away from the duo at the height of its popularity in 1970 to follow his own musical dreams. The first solo decade proved to be an even more creative period for him than the 1960s, thanks to his wider musical range, and the 1980s were equally commanding, including his masterpiece, *Graceland*. At the same time, Simon had felt the sting of defeat. He'd never been forgiven by a lot of Simon and Garfunkel fans for breaking up the partnership. He had also gone through two divorces and had failed in his ventures into movies (*One-Trick Pony*) and Broadway (*The Capeman*).

To Michaels, Simon had one other vital link to this special evening: he had been in the city on 9/11, and he knew the fear that gripped it. On that morning, he had walked two of his children—Adrian, eight, and Lulu, six—to school, about fifteen minutes along Central Park West. It was a lovely day with just a trace of prefall chill in the air. By the time he returned to his apartment just after nine o'clock, his wife, Edie Brickell, was at the door with the news that an American Airlines plane had crashed into the North Tower of the World Trade Center.

As Simon stared at the television screen, his first thought was that it was a tragic accident—only to watch in horror as a second plane, this one from United Airlines, smashed into the South Tower. There was now no question that the city was under attack. In panic, he raced back to the school to bring home Adrian, Lulu, and the children of some of his friends. To keep the kids calm, Paul and Edie turned off the television so they could play without hearing the frightful details of what was happening downtown, just a few subway stops away.

President George W. Bush soon confirmed the attack, and city officials closed the bridges and tunnels leading into and out of the city. Within minutes, a plane attacked the western façade of the Pentagon, and yet another crashed in a field in Pennsylvania. By the end of the day, there was a strange smell in the air in New York—not a normal smoke smell but all the chemicals from the crashes. "It was like we were all trapped, all helpless," Simon said. "You wanted to help, but what could you do?" Days later, he got his answer with requests to perform on the two broadcasts.

Even with his concern about the timing of *Saturday Night Live*, there was no way Simon would turn down Michaels, who was one of his closest friends and whose judgment he trusted implicitly. Plus, Simon had been around the *SNL* set so much that he was like an honorary member of the cast. Still, it was daunting. As soon as he stepped into the hallway, he began to worry about maintaining his composure. Simon had sung at funerals and memorial services for friends and musicians, and he knew how difficult it was to look at grieving faces.

Giuliani, as solemn as the fire department and law enforcement officers at his side, opened the show with a statement about the city's resolve: "Our hearts are broken, but they are beating, and they are beating stronger than ever. New Yorkers are unified. We will not yield to terrorism. We will not let our decisions be made out of fear. We choose to live our lives in freedom."

As he finished, the TV audience heard a few gentle guitar notes, and the camera slowly panned from the mayor to Simon. Dressed in black and wearing an FDNY cap, Simon stood in front of a huge American flag as he began singing the song Michaels had chosen for him: not "Bridge Over Troubled Water" but "The Boxer," a story of Simon's own struggle and resilience, complete with New York City references.

Though recorded more than thirty years earlier when Simon was just twenty-seven, "The Boxer" was a song of remarkable craft and depth, its early verses written in the first person, but its final verse shifting dramatically to the third person to add a compelling ring of universality. That final verse:

> In the clearing stands a boxer
> And a fighter by his trade
> And he carries the reminders
> Of every glove that laid him down
> And cut him till he cried out
> In his anger and his shame
> "I am leaving, I am leaving"
> But the fighter still remains
> Lie-la-lie . . .

The audience remained silent during the first two choruses, giving the moment an added poignancy. As Simon ended that final verse, however, scattered members of the audience whispered the "Lie-la-lie" chorus with him, adding to the emotion in the studio. Fifteen years later, Lorne Michaels called Simon's performance the most moving musical moment in the history of *Saturday Night Live.*

"I was so proud of Paul and the show and the city," he said, acknowledging his own tears that night. "The strength he showed with that song—standing in front of those firefighters and law enforcement officers and knowing what they had gone through, what the city had gone through—was just incredible. Even after all this time, I think he's the only one who could have done it. He is as much a symbol of the show and of New York as there is."

It was a defining moment for Simon because it underscored what had long been one of his quintessential qualities as a songwriter. Like "The Boxer," so many of his songs moved past any inherent darkness to express consolation, optimism, and even faith. In a rock 'n' roll world forged by rebellion, his music—from "America" and "Mrs. Robinson" to "American Tune" and "The Boy in the Bubble"—was founded on empathy.

Despite melancholy and self-doubt at points in his personal life, he avoided despair or hostility in his songs. "If all I have to say is how disappointed I am about whatever there is in life, then I don't see what the contribution is," Simon said. "There's already plenty of that out there. I really don't believe philosophically that's my job. But I'm not lying when I go the other way. Love is amazing, and like I say on the *You're the One* album, it's something you want so desperately that it can make you laugh out loud when you get it. It's like medicine for us."

Indeed, Simon's first great song was born during a period of trauma when he was in need of comfort himself. After years of toiling at the lower levels of the music business trying to write teen pop hits largely by copying what was on the radio, he felt in the fall of 1963 that he was at a dead end. Inspired by the emergence of the folk movement in New York's Greenwich Village, he vowed to reach inside to find out if he truly had anything of his own to say in a song. If he was going to be a failure as a songwriter, he told himself, he was going to be a proud failure.

As he often did, Simon took his acoustic guitar into the family bathroom, where the tile made the sound all the more alluring, and he turned off the lights so that he could relax and feel totally at one with the music. "Ever since I was thirteen or fourteen, songwriting has always been a great place of security and comfort," he said. "Songwriting never turned around and stabbed me in the back. I remember times when I was really sad, and I'd sit and play an E chord for a half hour. I wasn't writing a song. I was just comforting myself with this instrument I loved."

Night after night in November, he sat in the bathroom with his guitar, alone with his music and his future. Then his world changed with the assassination of President John F. Kennedy. Simon, who'd just turned twenty-two, was on his lunch break from his job at a publishing company in Manhattan when he heard the news. His mother, Belle, remembered that he spent hours despondent in his bedroom.

Not long after the tragedy, Simon returned to the bathroom, switched off the lights per his custom, and started softly fingerpicking on the guitar. It was around then that he hit some warmly evocative notes that he played over and over again. Slowly, he began reflecting on thoughts that had been nagging at him for months: the way people ignored the words of those, from musicians to religious leaders, who preached against injustice and excess materialism.

As he sat alone, these words eventually burst forth: "Hello darkness, my old friend."

For the next five-plus decades, Simon wrote with such ambition and craft that it looked easy from a distance. He'd deliver a prized album, tour, and then largely disappear for the three or four years it took to write and record another collection. Through it all, he rarely shared his personal story in interviews or engaged in the tabloid-ish episodes that contribute to many artists' personas, which rival their music in the public eye. Yet Simon, too, had to deal with the struggles and challenges of a life in the pop world. He wasn't a born songwriter. He spent six years writing one mediocre song after another until, through a series of pinpointable events, he finally became the artist who wrote "The Sound of Silence." This evolution makes Simon an ideal case study of pop music excellence and longevity—how true artistry is achieved and how you then need to protect it against distractions such as fame, wealth, drugs, marriage, divorce, ego, rejection, changes in public taste, and fear of failure. Simon wasn't immune to any of them.

PROLOGUE

PART ONE

The Boxer

CHAPTER ONE

The first sound Paul Simon fell in love with was the crack of a baseball against a Louisville Slugger, preferably one swung by a member of his beloved New York Yankees. He could even tell you the moment: the summer of 1948 when, at age six, he sat down with his father to listen to his first baseball game on the radio. Lou Simon was a professional musician, and he was out a lot, especially in the evenings, so Paul loved any chance to spend time listening to the radio with him, regardless of the program.

But this time was special. Paul immediately got caught up in the excitement of the announcer's voice (most notably, the ebullient Mel Allen) and the cheers of the Yankee Stadium crowd. He later became enthralled by the team's illustrious history of legendary players and more World Series championships by far than any other franchise. His allegiance was so strong that when his grandfather Samuel Schulman took him to see the rival Brooklyn Dodgers play at Ebbets Field, Paul wore his Lone Ranger mask as a disguise—on the outside chance that if he ran into anyone he knew, he didn't want them to think he was a Dodgers fan. The games had such a powerful effect on Paul's mood that his mother had to listen in to the afternoon broadcasts to keep track of the score. If the Yankees lost, she knew there was no point in defrosting a steak, because Paul would be so upset he wouldn't eat.

One thing Paul loved as much as the games themselves was the Topps baseball cards that came five to a package, along with a stick of bubble gum. Each card featured a color photo of a major leaguer on one side and the player's game statistics and personal data on the other. Where most youngsters cared only about the batting or pitching stats, Paul focused on another piece of information: the player's height. He knew by junior high school that his dream of playing for the Yankees was threatened by an issue that would haunt him for years: his size. Thumbing through the cards, he hoped to find players close to his own height to give him hope that he might indeed be able to play pro ball—if he just got a big growth spurt. Paul was around five feet tall at the time, and the shortest players he could find were Yankees shortstop Phil Rizzuto and Philadelphia Athletics pitcher Bobby Shantz, both five foot six.

Paul was still so short his senior year at Forest Hills High School that the baseball coach, Chester (Chet) Gusick, wouldn't let him try out for the team until some of the other kids told him that Paul was a terrific player. Given a turn during batting practice, Paul made the team by hitting a home run. Despite his size, he batted over .300 and showed enough speed on the basepaths to be put in the leadoff spot in the batting order. He was even named to the league all-star team.

His greatest moment on the field came on May 13, 1958, with the Forest Hills Rangers trailing Bayside High by a run in the seventh inning. Paul was on third base when he noticed that the opposing pitcher was taking his full windup rather than pitching from the stretch. In that instant, he knew he had a chance to pull off one of baseball's rarest and most exciting plays: stealing home. After getting the go-ahead from the coach, he took off as soon as the pitcher began his windup, and he slid across home plate just before the catcher applied the tag. Two innings later Paul contributed a bunt single to a four-run rally, which gave the Rangers a 7–3 win. But it was the steal that Paul would always remember. The headline in the *Long Island Press* said it all: "Simon Steals Home." Sixty years on, a reproduction of the article is still displayed on a wall in Paul's Manhattan office.

As it turned out, that steal was Paul's last hurrah in baseball. When he tried out for the team at Queens College the following year, he knew after a few days of practice that there was no way he could compete against college pitchers, many of whom stood over six feet and threw with blazing speed. "The coach didn't say anything, but I realized I was done," Simon said. The moment wasn't as devastating as it might have been, because Paul, by then, was consumed by a new sound: rock 'n' roll.

Simon was not a child prodigy who astounded the rest of the family by playing sonatas on the piano at age three or writing dazzling poetry in his grade-school notebooks, his lifelong pal Bobby Susser pointed out. Paul had little interest in pop music as a child—certainly not the bland mainstream hits that were on the radio in the early 1950s. Even when his father tried to stir an interest in music with piano lessons, Paul resisted.

It wasn't until the summer of 1954 that Paul, quite by accident, discovered his calling. As he did each game day, Paul sat down to listen to the Yankees on WINS. But on this day, the radio was tuned to another station: one playing the mainstream pop that bored him. As he reached to change the station, the DJ's remark caught his ear. "He said something like, 'This record is becoming a hit around the country, but I think it's the worst record I've ever heard,' " Paul said a half century later. "Now, that was interesting—the worst record he'd ever heard. I had never heard anyone say that on the radio." Sure enough, DJs were always praising records; there was no point in saying they didn't like the next record because it might encourage listeners to tune out. Curious, Paul kept listening and soon heard a doo-wop expression of romantic infatuation by the Crows, a black rhythm-and-blues group from Harlem. Called "Gee," the record felt fresh and alive. The song's giddy lyrics (supposedly written in ten minutes) were catchy, and the group's lead singer, Daniel (Sonny) Norton, moved up and down the notes with acrobatic ease.

"Ohh-ohh-ohh, gee-ee," Simon recalled, singing one of the tune's open-ing lines. "The record sounded so young, and it had a good beat, and the lyrics were simple. I even liked the name of the group: the Crows. Imme-diately, I felt, 'That's my music.' It's not those big ballads you heard on the radio back then: things like 'See the pyramids, along the Nile,' and all that."

Wanting more of this new sound, Paul turned the dial endlessly in the coming weeks, hoping to find a station that played it regularly. As it turned out, he didn't need to turn the dial at all. Alan Freed, a disc jockey who had popularized rock 'n' roll in Cleveland earlier in the 1950s, moved his show to WINS, the Yankees station, in September 1954. Paul began looking for-ward to Freed's show with the same passion as the ball games. When he would say again and again over the years that he knew he wanted to be in music by the time he was thirteen, Paul was speaking about the lure of "Gee" and a handful of other extraordinary R&B songs he heard that year, including the Moonglows' "Sincerely" and the Penguins' "Earth Angel."

He got so caught up in the sounds that he asked his father to buy him a Stadium acoustic guitar for his thirteenth birthday that October and teach him some chords. Lou, who played upright bass, didn't care for this primi-tive doo-wop sound, but he was pleased his son was finally interested in some kind of music; it'd be a good hobby, ideally leading him to something more sophisticated, such as jazz or Broadway show tunes.

It wasn't long before Paul wanted more. To capture the harmonies of the records, he needed another singer. He didn't need to look far. Thanks to one of life's wondrous twists of fate, Paul's parents had moved into a home just two blocks from a family named Garfunkel.

Paul Fredric Simon was born on October 13, 1941, at Beth Israel Hospital in Newark, New Jersey, but the Garden State ties were short-lived. Before his second birthday, he was calling New York home—which is where fate comes in. Belle's brother's wife, Goldie, died on May 23, 1943, and Belle's brother Lee Schulman, a graphic artist who lived in Kew Gardens Hills, Queens, asked her to stay with him for a while to help care for his young son, Jerry. Belle's family was tight knit, and she didn't hesitate, even though it meant that she and Paul would have to leave Lou behind temporarily in Newark, where he played bass on a music show that aired weekday mornings on radio station WAAT.

The move not only introduced the Simons to Kew Gardens Hills, which would be Paul's home for the next two decades, but it also led him to his future singing partner. Lee Schulman lived on Seventy-Second Avenue, almost directly across the street from Jack and Rose Garfunkel, whose second son, Arthur, was born on November 5, 1941. Despite the proximity, there is no evidence that the children actually met until grammar school.

Kew Gardens Hills—adjacent to prestigious Forest Hills, home for years of the US Open tennis championship—was in the 1940s a picturesque middle-class neighborhood. To young couples, the rows of mostly attached or semiattached houses represented a coveted piece of the American dream. Yet there were moments of anxiety for Paul, including living in a house where a mother had just died and not having his father around except for occasional weekends. Looking back years later, Paul wondered if his long history of violent dreams wasn't triggered by living in his uncle's home. The dreams, which would become more frequent over the years, could be very gory and upsetting. Without ever finding a reason for them, he simply learned to accept them.

After a year or so of separation, Lou rejoined the family when he got a job playing bass on radio station WOR in New York. He and Belle rented an attached house at 141-04 Seventy-First Street, close enough to the Schulmans for Belle to walk over there to watch Jerry until Lee got home from work. "It was happy times again," Paul said. "Dad was back."

When the Simons' second son, Edward, was born on December 14, 1945, Lou and Belle needed a larger place, and they bought their first home: an attached residence at 137-62 Seventieth Road. By this time, Belle no longer needed to help her brother because Lee had remarried. To make the Simon family reunion even more joyous at the time of Eddie's birth, the nation was still caught up in celebrating the end of World War II.

———

In a photo of Paul standing in the driveway of the family's two-story house—the same driveway where as a youngster Paul and his dad often played catch—the Simon house looks identical to the one next to it. If the camera had provided a wider view, we would see that every other house up and down the long block looked the same. This cookie-cutter approach caused Lou endless frustration. "My father used to drive into the wrong driveway all the time," Paul said. The story is special to Paul because it's one of the few times he heard his mother or father complain about anything. Paul's acquaintances from those days agree: this was a loving family.

"Paul was such a good, happy baby," said Beverly Wax, whose husband, Harold, played accordion at the Newark radio station with Lou, and who first saw Paul when he was just a week old. "He fit in perfectly with his mom and dad, who were the nicest people you could find." Paul and Eddie enjoyed each other's company so much that they eventually gave up their separate bedrooms to share what was Paul's upstairs room. It was a bonding that continued into adulthood, when Eddie would eventually comanage his brother. "We all know people whose lives have been very much molded by trauma, but that wasn't our case," Eddie said. "If you were ever in trouble, my mom and dad would help you. They made it so you were not fearful. In his career, Paul's never been afraid to move on."

Fittingly, Paul's parents met through music. While on a weekend getaway in the Berkshires with girlfriends in 1937, Belle Schulman met Lou, who was playing in a band. They began a courtship that led to their marriage on September 15 of the following year in Newark. Both were native-born Americans, children of immigrants who had come to the United States separately between 1882 and 1909. Paul's father's family came from small towns in the Austro-Hungarian Empire, in territory that is now part of Ukraine, while Paul's mother's family came from small towns—shtetlach in Yiddish—in Lithuania, which was then a province of Imperial Russia.

Paul's paternal grandfather was born Pinkas Seeman, but he changed his first name to Paul before arriving in the United States in 1909, and he adopted the last name Simon before Paul's father was born in 1916.

Seeman/Simon was a successful tailor until he lost his business in the Great Depression, and subsequently opened a small deli in Newark. Belle's father, Samuel Schulman, was for years a commissioned salesman at Phillips Clothing Company, a retail store in Manhattan. His future wife, Ettie Marcus, worked across the street in a clothing accessories store. They were married in 1902, and Paul's mother was born in 1909, the last of two sons and two daughters in the family.

While Paul's grandparents immigrated to the United States primarily in search of a better life, they were fortunate to leave Eastern Europe before anti-Semitism led to the butchery of the Holocaust. George Schulman, Paul's cousin, traced his family roots to Lithuania, where he said bullet holes in a churchyard wall in the town of Trishik were still visible. In the early summer of 1941, Nazi SS troops rounded up seventy to eighty Jews, almost certainly including some of Paul's relatives, and opened fire. Soon the Nazis moved through other cities, including Kalvarija and Vilkaviskis, where more relatives lived. Jewish men were typically rounded up and shot, and women and children were murdered within weeks.

In the safety of America, Lou, under the stage name Lee Simms, led his own dance band every Thursday afternoon for nearly twenty-five years at the landmark Roseland Ballroom in Manhattan's theater district. He also did periodic dates with Lester Lanin, the society bandleader whose elegant dance music was featured at hundreds of parties for some of the world's wealthiest and most celebrated people, from actress Grace Kelly's engagement to Prince Rainier III of Monaco in 1956 to the sixtieth birthday of Queen Elizabeth II in 1986. On top of it all, Lou also played several seasons in the house orchestra for CBS-TV shows hosted by personalities such as Jackie Gleason, Arthur Godfrey, and Garry Moore. Paul and the rest of the family would watch the programs at home, hoping to get a glimpse of Dad.

That résumé, however, made Lou's musical world seem more glamorous than it was. Aside from the freelance dates at CBS, he spent most of his time in music performing at social gatherings, weddings, and bar mitzvahs. The jobs didn't pay all that much, and they were irregular, forcing Lou to spend almost as many hours lining up gigs as playing them.

The stress may have contributed to his lifelong health problems, including numerous heart attacks.

One of Paul's favorite childhood memories was accompanying his father to the radio station when he was around four and watching a live broadcast. As the musicians played, they read the notes from sheet music on a stand and then tossed away the top page to see the next one. Paul thought one of the musicians had thrown the paper by mistake, so he raced over, picked up the sheet music, and placed it back on the stand, causing everyone in the room to break out in laughter—a moment so embarrassing that Paul recalled his discomfort decades later.

While Paul didn't respond to the piano lessons, Eddie enjoyed playing classical piano, especially when his father accompanied him on bass. What impressed Eddie was how his dad, even in the informality of their home, took the music seriously. There was nothing casual about his playing: he played in perfect tune, from the start of the duet to the end, and Eddie thinks Paul picked up on that dedication. Music was something to be treated with respect. Bobby Susser, his friend, also believes Paul embraced Lou's dedication. "Lou always wanted to be a notch or two above the rest no matter what he was doing, and he wanted the same for Paul. With regard to music, there was no such thing as mastering it. The goal was always to get better—never settle."

The Simon home on Seventieth Road was in such a new development that construction of the local elementary school, PS 164, wasn't finished until Paul was ready for the third grade. That meant he attended kindergarten at PS 117 in the fall of 1946. That school was in Jamaica, Queens, just two miles away across the Grand Central Parkway, but any separation from his mother was difficult. When the bus pulled up for the first day of school, Paul refused to get on unless Belle came with him. She gamely climbed aboard for the short ride along Main Street.

Things went fine that day, and Paul stepped on the bus by himself the following morning. In the coming months, he adjusted well to school, and he received high praise from his teachers during his three years there—

though one of them would later describe him as especially sensitive, noting that he tended to cry easily. Belle, too, remembered Paul's sensitivity when he befriended a neighborhood boy with Down syndrome and accompanying speech problems. On his way home from grade school, Paul would often stop by the boy's house and play catch with him. It got to where the boy would start shouting, "Paul! Paul!" whenever he saw Paul coming down the street. That was, Belle said, the first word the youngster learned.

Simon also had a tremendous imagination, said Beverly Wax, the family friend from the New Jersey days. "He was always making up games or stories. Even when he was little, I thought that he might become a writer. He was always observing things and then describing them in an original, thoughtful way. Even when he was ten or eleven, he spoke like an adult."

Helene Schwartz Kenvin, who also attended PS 117 and PS 164, recalls Paul being well liked. She and Paulie, as she called him, were class president and vice president, respectively, for several semesters. She also believes Paul benefited from the high academic standards of his grade school, which required students to complete a three-year study program of the nation's historical documents, including the Bill of Rights, the Gettysburg Address, and Patrick Henry's speech to the House of Burgesses—papers crammed with complex legal and philosophical language. Kenvin said, "Can you imagine nine-year-old children reciting 'on States disseyered, discordant, belligerent . . . on a land rent with civil feuds'—from Daniel Webster's reply to Senator Robert Y. Hayne—and understanding what they were saying? We all became exceptionally literate, and I think that it shows in the poetry of Paulie's lyrics."

Despite getting high marks, Paul's teachers sometimes mentioned to his mother that he could do even better if he paid attention rather than stare out the classroom window and daydream. But Belle, herself a popular elementary schoolteacher for years, defended her son. "I think she understood that the ones who are looking out the window are sometimes your best students, not the ones who always raise their hand and want attention," Paul said. "I always thought that was embarrassing. I wanted attention, too, but I didn't want to be seen as wanting it. I wanted it to come naturally, by doing something that warranted it, rather than me manipulating people to look at me." Onstage years later, Paul tended to follow that same guideline. He wasn't interested in being a showman; all he cared about was playing the music.

Whatever his manner in the classroom, Paul was placed into a special progress program at Parsons Junior High that enabled him to go through the school in two years rather than the normal three. If Paul needed any further assurance about his own intelligence, the word passed down in his family was that Lou, during high school, registered the highest IQ score in the state of New Jersey. "I went to two Ivy League universities, and I've often said I never met any group of people as smart as the kids I knew when I was a child," said Kenvin, who would later teach advanced criminal-constitutional law and litigation at Rutgers Law School in Camden and handled several celebrated constitutional-law trial cases as an attorney.

The Simons belonged to a synagogue, but their lives didn't revolve around religion, and the boys received different signals from their parents. Although Lou wasn't religious, Belle came from a religious background, and she'd go to the synagogue by herself during the high holidays. They eventually agreed for Paul and Eddie to have their bar mitzvahs and then be free to decide their own religious paths. Paul didn't embrace organized religion, but he developed a deep spirituality that was reflected in many of his songs, including occasional Christian imagery.

"I'm not religious, but I believe in God—at least I'm getting there—and I believe in spiritual powers," Paul said. "I believe that the nonscientific and the nonrational world exists, and it's powerful and valid. The thing I'm comfortable with is that if there is a God, and He created this planet and everything on it, I've got to say an incredible 'Thank you so much—great job. I'm really grateful to be here in this marvelous setting.' If it turns out there's no God, I still feel the same way. I'm really grateful to be here. What a beautiful planet."

Paul remembers first seeing Garfunkel in 1951 at an assembly at PS 164 when they were both in fourth grade. Artie, as Paul grew to call him, sang "Too Young," a ballad that had been a hit for Nat "King" Cole, and Paul was struck by two things: the loveliness of Art's voice and the strong impression he had on the girls.

Their actual friendship, however, didn't begin until the closing weeks of sixth grade when they both performed in the school's production of *Alice in Wonderland*. Oddly, Paul was cast in the main singing role, the White Rabbit, while Art, with that spectacular voice, played the nonsinging Cheshire Cat. During the weeks of rehearsal, they enjoyed each other's company. They were both clever and shared a sense of humor that was a touch irreverent. They both loved *Mad* magazine, a new, wildly satirical look at popular culture. They also both liked baseball. There was no sense of competition over who was the better singer. In fact, it'd be a year before they even got the idea of singing together. While at PS 164, Simon's world revolved almost exclusively around baseball.

Eager to do more than listen to games and daydream about playing in the majors, Paul, at the age of ten, began searching neighborhood playgrounds for pickup games. Hearing that a bunch of kids would gather almost daily during the summer to play softball at PS 165, he rode his Schwinn bicycle a mile or so to the paved school yard, where he first met Bobby Susser.

"Paul was the new kid, and some show-offs wanted to test him," Susser recalled. "We were all wearing jeans, and Paul was wearing short pants, and someone said, 'Oh, so Mommy made you wear short pants today.' Paul got off his bike, just as cool as could be, and said back to this guy, 'No, my mom didn't force me to wear these pants. I chose to wear them. It's a hot day, you'll notice, and these pants are a lot more comfortable than your jeans. You ought to try it sometime.' " Susser thought, "Wow, this is a smart kid. No one is going to push him around." From that moment, Bobby wanted to be on Paul's side.

Susser, too, would become a songwriter, specializing in children's songs. His albums have sold more than five million copies. He was also such a good pitcher that he was named the most valuable player in the New York City Baseball Federation League in 1957. One of the highlights of Bobby's all-star season was striking out Joe Torre, the future Hall of Fame catcher and Yankees manager, twice in one game. It was all the sweeter because Torre and some of the other rival players—who'd laughed before the game when they saw how short Bobby was—walked over to Susser after the game and shook his hand.

Paul and Bobby would play pickup games two or three times a week at the school yard and invariably cap the afternoon by going to the Honeycomb luncheonette for tuna sandwiches or egg creams. They later had a bittersweet moment when their team went to the regional finals in the five-foot-and-under softball league, but Paul was disqualified on the day of the championship game. The opposing team's coach complained to a league official that Paul was too tall—and, indeed, he had grown to five foot one.

Paul enjoyed competition so much that he and Eddie designed a series of games to play at home, especially on rainy days or when their parents were away. Though four years younger, Eddie was a scrappy kid who exhibited much of the raw skills and drive of his brother. As the contests grew in number and complexity, Paul and Eddie began calling them their personal Olympics. They ranged from bedroom basketball, where they'd turn a pair of socks into a tight round ball, to a version of baseball in which they'd swing a tennis racket at one of the fuzzy dice that teens in those days liked to hang from car rearview mirrors. Years later, Bobby Susser saw Paul approach music the same way he approached the games. "Whatever it was, Paul would outwork you, outthink you, and outpractice you," he said. "He had this passion to be the best at whatever he was doing."

Paul and Art were attending Parsons Junior High School when Paul heard "Gee" on the radio. Doo-wop, with its mostly sweet, wistful harmonies, is a long way from the rawness and ache of the blues or the bravado and fury of hip-hop, but it was a central step in the evolution of black pop in America and one of the kick starts of rock 'n' roll. Though the records usually had musical accompaniment, it was really the vocals that mattered, making the music tailor-made for the streets of New York. Soon doo-wop groups sprang up on street corners—mostly in black neighborhoods, but also in Italian and Jewish ones—where they would try to re-create the vocals from the records.

Though they didn't sing on street corners, Paul and Art did get together regularly to sing into magnetic wire recorders, the primitive devices that stored sounds on thin steel wires—the forerunner to the much more efficient magnetic tape recorders that became popular in the 1950s. The teens would listen to their vocals on the recorder to measure how well their voices blended. They soon felt good enough about their music to take it public by singing "Sh-Boom," an R&B hit popularized by the Chords and the Crew-Cuts, at an assembly in 1954. The response was encouraging, and they began working even harder on their harmony. As Paul got more comfortable on the guitar, he and Art raised their ambitions again by trying to write their own songs—almost always patterned after something they had heard on the radio, which is how most young songwriters begin. After school each day, Paul couldn't wait to get home to listen to the radio, and he was rewarded during the fall term with several marvelous tunes, including the Spaniels' "Goodnite, Sweetheart, Goodnite," the Drifters' "Honey Love," the Charms' "Hearts of Stone," and the Clovers' "Your Cash Ain't Nothin' but Trash." Still, Paul couldn't convince his father that the music had any merit. When he played "Earth Angel" for Lou, his father deemed it "awful," Simon said much later, and it hurt.

A year later, Paul and Art wrote a doo-wop song, "The Girl for Me," that they felt was as good as most things they heard on the radio. They even sang the engaging song at a talent show at Forest Hills High School. Lou boosted their confidence when he registered it with the Library of Congress. They were encouraged, too, by Charlie Merenstein, the father of one of Paul's baseball chums and, more importantly, the head of Apollo Records, an indie label with an emphasis on doo-wop, gospel, and jazz. Merenstein was so impressed by Paul's ability to spot hits that he frequently played records for him just to get his opinion. He urged Paul and Art to take their songs to some of the record companies in Manhattan. "We didn't go to any of the big places; they wouldn't have let us in," Simon said. "We just looked up the addresses of these little companies in the phone book, and we'd knock on the doors. Sometimes someone would listen to our song. Mostly they were too busy."

The pair spent the rest of 1955 trying to write another tune as promising as "The Girl for Me." When Paul brought new tunes to his dad, Lou was always honest. He saw no value in false praise, even if it sometimes upset Paul. "That was the only time Paul was obstinate," Belle said. "My husband would say to him, 'What are you doing there? You can't put five notes into that sequence; there's only four to that phrase, Paul.' And Paul replied, 'It's my phrase, Dad. I'm gonna put as many in as I want.' His dad would reply, 'No, Paul, you're driving me crazy. You can't do that and call it music.'"

Some observers over the years have suggested that these early confrontations are what caused Paul to devote himself to music with such intensity—yet another example of a young musician obsessed with winning his father's approval. But Paul's story doesn't fit the stereotype. Bobby Susser believes that Paul's relationship with Lou was, indeed, a defining thread in Paul's life, but it was more complex than simply wanting to win his dad's approval. Susser spent a lot of time with Lou because he had communication problems with his own father and found in Lou the love and counsel he wanted so badly.

"Paul always wanted his father's approval, but that wasn't what drove his writing," Bobby said. "He had this unending passion for the music. I think he realized that Lou's early criticisms were right—that the songs weren't very good, and Lou was trying to help him, and that honesty stuck with Paul. When he was working with people years later, he felt it was always important to be honest." Unquestionably, Lou's comments toughened Paul. "My father was very judgmental," Simon said years later. "And I became judgmental, too." Whatever his father's comments, Paul maintained his search for exciting new records, and he was rewarded in the early days of 1956 with someone who would become his first real musical hero.

Elvis Presley's dynamic young voice on the car radio, both sensual and immediate, reached through the speaker with the song "That's All Right" and grabbed Paul as he sat in the backseat of the family car—a Buick or a Ford, he recalled—in the parking lot of the Grand Union supermarket in Queens. His parents were inside shopping, but Paul, as usual, preferred to remain in the car, checking out the latest sounds on the dial. It was the most transforming musical moment for the teenager since "Gee." Paul was fourteen.

Fueled by a remarkable combination of physical and vocal charisma, Elvis arrived at precisely the moment that a restless, questioning generation of teenagers was looking for a defining figure. Overnight, millions of teens fell under his spell. Characters from youth-oriented movies had already been speaking to that emerging demographic. Marlon Brando's edgy, rebellious tone as the motorcycle gang leader in the 1953 film *The Wild One* was one early touchstone. His character, defiant in his black leather jacket, summarized teen frustration and impatience in words as forceful as any in a rock record in the 1950s. Asked what he was rebelling against, Brando sneered, "Whaddaya got?"

Two years later, James Dean reflected the youthful Zeitgeist even more as a deeply troubled, misunderstood teen in *Rebel Without a Cause*. Young moviegoers identified with his memorable observation "If I had one day when I didn't have to be all confused and I didn't have to feel that I was ashamed of everything. If I felt that I belonged someplace. You know?" The case can be made that Brando and, especially, Dean warmed up the teen audience for Elvis as much as any Fats Domino or Bill Haley recording.

Though Elvis's fame would be ignited later in 1956 by "Heartbreak Hotel" and his other RCA recordings, Paul responded most to the music Elvis made earlier with visionary Memphis record producer Sam Phillips on Sun Records. Elvis was only nineteen when he recorded "That's All Right" in 1954, and he blended country and blues in a way that seemed at once mysterious and irresistible. Paul's favorite of the Elvis Sun singles was "Mystery Train," and echoes of the song's seductive rhythm would show up decades later in "Late in the Evening" and "Graceland."

"All I knew was I wanted to be this guy," Simon said. "I wanted to be Elvis." But reality hit when Paul was one of sixty million viewers who saw

Elvis perform "Hound Dog" and "Love Me Tender" on Ed Sullivan's television variety show that September. In an instant, he knew he couldn't be
Elvis, who was six feet tall, strikingly handsome, had this amazing voice,
an exotic name, and hailed from a magical place in the South: Tupelo,
Mississippi. "I realized I had to get as far from what Elvis was doing as I
could with my music," he said. "I wasn't going to compete with him because I knew I couldn't beat him. But I still felt I could make it. I just had
to go softer. Besides, it was very important to me that I not be an imitator
of anybody. I wanted my own parade. That's a competitive drive I had, for
whatever reason, whether it was in my nature or it came from my family
or from my neighborhood—probably a father thing.

"When people asked me if the competitiveness is because I'm short,
I'd say, 'No.' Simply wanting to make the best music can make you competitive. You have no idea how competitive John Lennon was around Paul
McCartney. When I first met them, I felt like someone had taken all the
oxygen out of the room. I almost couldn't breathe, they were so competitive, and that's what made them so great. They wouldn't settle for just
good. That was me, too."

CHAPTER TWO

Paul's search for a new sound to jump-start his writing arrived on the family radio one morning in May 1957 in the form of the Everly Brothers' "Bye Bye Love," a fresh, potent mixture of country, pop, and rock. As much as Paul loved doo-wop and Elvis, he had been content to listen to them on the radio. Records were expensive: nearly $1 for a single, or roughly the cost of twenty packs of baseball cards or ten comic books. But he didn't want to have to wait until "Bye Bye Love" came on the radio. He wanted his own copy, and he rode two busses for nearly an hour to Tri-Boro Records in Jamaica, Queens, to get it.

Returning home, Paul put the 78-rpm record on the family's phonograph player and listened to both sides, but chiefly "Bye Bye Love." He had been playing the record for almost an hour when he accidentally scratched it with the needle. He immediately headed back to Tri-Boro Records to buy another copy. Careful not to scratch it again, Paul played the record constantly. Lou and Belle went along with it, still pleased that their son was into music but also continuing to remind him that he should think of music only as a pleasant pastime, not a real career like, say, law.

Art, too, was caught up in the exquisite two-part harmony. He and Paul soon began trying to duplicate the Everlys' vocals themselves. Eddie had a front-row seat at the practice sessions. "I'd be sitting in the kitchen with them, and Artie would be hitting the backbeat on a telephone book, and Paul would be playing guitar, and they'd be singing those Everly Brothers songs," he said.

Nothing explains Paul's enthusiasm for this new direction better than the fact that he was willing to sell the bulk of his beloved baseball card collection to help pay for a $200 magnetic tape recorder. The new machine was a huge improvement over the wire recorder they had been using, and it led to even more intense practices. They'd sit nose to nose, looking right at each other's mouths to copy diction, Garfunkel has said. He wanted to know exactly where Paul's tongue would hit the top of his palate when he'd sing a certain letter or word to know exactly how to get the harmony right. Paul and Art both enjoyed singing so much that they rarely had an argument over it. "We would sometimes have a disagreement over something, but we had this thing we'd do where we would say, 'Let's just drop it,' and we would," Simon said. "We would just completely drop it. I don't think there was any sense of competitiveness."

Another source of inspiration was Alan Freed's raucous rock 'n' roll concerts at the Brooklyn Paramount Theatre. Paul would spend an hour on the subway to see stars such as Chuck Berry, Frankie Lymon, Jerry Lee Lewis, Bobby Darin, and the house band featuring jazz saxophonist Big Al Sears. Those shows contributed to Paul's lifelong love of working with a well-trained, world-class band. In fact, he loved everything about those shows, including the clothes—notably the wild jackets. He thinks Art may have gone to one of the shows with him.

Starting in the fall of 1956, Paul joined some twenty million other eager rock 'n' roll fans all over America who watched *American Bandstand* weekday afternoons on ABC-TV to see the biggest recording stars of the day, from Buddy Holly and Chuck Berry to the Everlys—mostly artists who, like Elvis, came from the southern United States. In fact, Paul was so enamored of Elvis and his new musical heroes that being from the South was part of his rock 'n' roll fantasy.

But it's wrong to think that Paul and Art were so single-minded in their pursuit of music that it squeezed everything else out of their lives. Paul took special delight in applying his baseball skills to stickball, a popular game played in the streets that used a rubber ball and a broomstick or pole. Kids played one another for neighborhood bragging rights or, in some cases, for money. Paul enjoyed going to adjacent neighborhoods, where his baseball feats weren't known, and luring unsuspecting opponents into games by pretending he wasn't very good, and then outscoring them and collecting on the bet. He also worked in the stockroom for a Kitty Kelly shoe store. In letters to friends from summer camp in Bellport, Long Island, in 1957, Paul also seemed very much a regular teenager. On August 9 he wrote Art, who was at another camp, and told him at length about the tomfoolery of his job as a waiter and his pursuit of girls:

"I swear I've never pulled so many weird stunts in my life as I've pulled up here. This place could be a sanitarium for the way we act . . . Now on to the girl situation. This topic is so confusing and crazy that's it's best left alone. I'll just say that I've gone steady thrice (dig this crazy language, man). Right now I like a girl named Elaine." In a PS, he also noted, "I've written a new song called 'Bobbie.' I think it's real good. See ya."

"Wake Up Little Susie," written by Felice and Boudleaux Bryant, the same married couple who wrote "Bye Bye Love," was a novelty about a teen boy and girl getting into trouble when they came home hours late from a date. Within days of hearing the song that September, Paul and Art wrote "Hey, Schoolgirl," the story of a boy asking a girl in class to get together after school, complete with the Everlys' opening guitar hiccup licks. To brighten things further, Paul tacked on some fractured, nonsensical syllables— "who-bo-a-boo-chi-bop"—like the ones in Little Richard's "Tutti-Frutti"; words that somehow reflected the exuberance of 1950s teens. Believing again they had a chance at a hit, Paul and Art made another run at the small Manhattan record companies, but no one was interested. Undaunted, they decided to make a sample record themselves to better demonstrate to labels how the song would sound. After class on Wednesday, October 16, they went into Sanders Recording Studio on Seventh Avenue in Manhattan, where for $10 they made a temporary acetate copy. It was three days after Paul's sixteenth birthday.

As it happened, Sid Prosen, who owned a record label named Big, was at Sanders that day. When he heard "Hey, Schoolgirl," he must have figured he had found his own Everly Brothers. Prosen, whose chief claim to fame was writing one of pop singer Teresa Brewer's biggest hits, "Till I Waltz Again with You," told Paul and Art that he wanted to release the song on his label. Big was really a small company, but Paul and Art weren't about to say no to any deal. Because they were both under eighteen, Prosen met with their parents two days later at his office in the Brill Building, the music business citadel that was home to numerous music publishers and labels.

Less than a month after first hearing "Wake Up Little Susie," Paul and Art watched excitedly as their parents signed the contract, which was for one year with two one-year options. They would be paid two cents per record sold in the first year. The next day, Prosen took the duo into another recording studio, Beltone, to record "Hey, Schoolgirl" again. Unknown to Paul at the time, Beltone was the same studio where the Crows had recorded "Gee" four years earlier. "My dad drove us into the city, and he played bass on the record," Simon said. "I think we also had a drummer and a second guitarist. It was probably a three-hour session because that was the minimum amount of time you could book, but it didn't take us long to do the song and the flip side (another original titled "Dancing Wild")."

One thing Prosen didn't like about his new recording team was their names: neither Paul and Art, nor Simon and Garfunkel. He came up with Tom & Jerry, drawn from the popular MGM cat and mouse cartoon characters. For last names, Art (aka Tom) chose Graph, a whimsical nod to his fondness for making elaborate graphs that listed the titles of that week's best-selling records. Paul picked Landis, after Sue Landis, a girl at school he had a crush on.

Not revealing the pair's real names, a three-page bio offered some personal touches about Tom & Jerry. "Despite their sudden success, the two sixteen-year-olds . . . continue to lead normal teenage lives. They attend their regular classes at school, go out on dates, and hold down after-school jobs. [Tom] plans to study liberal arts at Princeton following his graduation from his school. Jerry is looking forward to going to Harvard Law School." That last line surely brought a smile to Lou and Belle's faces. The bio was accompanied by a press photo of Paul and Art posing proudly in their new flaming-red jackets and crew cuts—huge grins on their faces.

"Hey, Schoolgirl" was a hit—at least on the East Coast, where Prosen proved to be a tireless promoter. A review in the November 25 issue of *Billboard*, the leading music trade publication, predicted big things for the single and even compared Tom & Jerry to the Everlys. Paul delighted in this first rush of success. "If you were on the high school baseball team, you were famous in school and the whole neighborhood—the same went for basketball and football teams," he said later. "To be on radio and television with a hit song . . . was beyond what anyone could have possibly imagined. It was overwhelming!"

The first in a series of thrills was hearing the record on Alan Freed's radio show—thanks, the rumor was, to Prosen's having slipped him $200 in payola, the widespread practice of paying DJs to play a song. Prosen told Paul and Art what day Freed was going to start playing the record, and they kept listening until, sure enough, it came on. Their hearts raced again when they heard "Hey, Schoolgirl" on Dick Clark's *American Bandstand*, the nationally televised teen dance party. They watched kids dance to their record and give it a near-perfect score of 95 because it had a "good beat" and was "fun to dance to."

The ultimate was when Tom & Jerry appeared on *American Bandstand* on November 22, 1957, and lip-synched "Hey, Schoolgirl" as well as met wild Louisiana rocker Jerry Lee Lewis, who was also on the show that day. Viewers got a chance to step inside Paul's rock 'n' roll fantasy when Clark asked Jerry (Paul) where he was from. Remembering his heroes all came from the South, he looked straight into the camera and replied: "*Macon, Georgia.*"

"I was just living out my Elvis fantasies," Simon said years later. "I didn't know if I'd ever get another chance to be on national TV. Macon just popped into my head, probably because Little Richard was from there." Another thrill came a few weeks later when "Hey, Schoolgirl" climbed to no. 49 on the national pop chart, the same week the Top 10 included Elvis's "Jailhouse Rock" and Buddy Holly's "Peggy Sue."

The single would have gone higher if Prosen had the money to promote it around the country the way he did in the New York area, where most of the single's reported hundred thousand sales were made. For all the excitement, "Hey, Schoolgirl" didn't do well enough to land the duo a spot on the multiact rock shows that toured the country in the late 1950s. But Tom & Jerry did perform a few live dates, including a promotional radio-sponsored show in Cincinnati, a music industry convention in Chicago, and a big-name concert at the State Theater in Hartford, Connecticut, headlined by LaVern Baker, the future Rock & Roll Hall of Famer best known for the R&B novelty hit "Tweedle Dee." However, the fun didn't last long.

The first time Paul and Art broke up was in the spring of 1958. The split caused a wound so deep in Art, apparently, that it would never heal fully. The break started innocently enough with Sid Prosen asking Paul if he had any songs for the second Tom & Jerry single. Most of the tunes Paul played for him were in the bright rockabilly vein of "Hey, Schoolgirl," but some were closer to Elvis. Prosen got an idea: How about Paul recording a couple of the Presley-like tunes on his own? That would be in addition to another Tom & Jerry record.

Caught up in the excitement of the moment, Paul agreed. He and Prosen went into the studio with Paul's father again on bass to record the lively "True or False" and a ballad, "Teenage Fool," neither of which was close to noteworthy. But Paul's vocals were colorful enough in an age of

Elvis mania to explain why Prosen would think the single had a chance to make the charts. To avoid confusion with Tom & Jerry's next record, Prosen wanted to use a new name for Paul: True Taylor.

The mistake Simon and Prosen made—and it was a massive one—was that they didn't tell Art about their plan. He was crushed when he found out; Art felt that Prosen and Simon had betrayed him. Art knew he had a wonderful voice, but he also knew he was dependent on Paul for songs, which meant that Paul had all the power. Art realized he would always be in danger of being tossed aside. Some twenty years later, Art was still expressing privately his hurt and resentment about the Big Records experience in a long, heartfelt letter to Paul. Eventually he would express his hurt publicly. According to Belle, Art's father tried to get Lou to sign a second contract, this one stipulating that Paul wouldn't sing or record with anyone except Art. Lou's response, Belle said, was, "Do you think I'm stupid? Why would I do that? Why would you be so sure that Paul could take care of your son for his whole life? Maybe Paul will do better on his own. Of course I wouldn't sign anything like that!"

Big Records released the True Taylor and new Tom & Jerry singles early in 1958. Both songs flopped. Results were no better in May when Prosen issued a third Tom & Jerry single. By the fall, Tom & Jerry were history, personally and professionally. Though they would cross paths occasionally, Paul and Art wouldn't have a meaningful conversation for five years.

Garfunkel enrolled in Columbia University to study architecture, his music career largely shelved. He even said over the years that he had never fully bought into the notion that music was a serious career option. Not so with Simon. He began classes that fall at Queens College. But Simon's attendance at the college, located just two miles from the Simon house, was largely to please his folks. He had no doubt music was going to be his life.

For someone who would be described as "controlling" in the recording studio, Simon had a surprisingly casual approach when it came to college. In a move reminiscent of his choosing the stage name Landis, he picked

English as his major in the fall of 1958 partially because he liked a girl who had that major. He did take time during his four and a half years at Queens College to join Alpha Epsilon Pi, an international Jewish fraternity, and although he was popular enough to be elected president, he said his only interest in the fraternity was the chance to write songs for the organization's winning entries in the college's annual *Follies* variety show competition.

Simon's real day began midafternoon when classes ended, and he'd hop the subway into Manhattan. He marched from one indie label or publisher to another, taking advantage of whatever opportunity arose, whether it was trying to get his own songs recorded or singing on demonstration, or "demo," records. The latter were designed to showcase new songs for record companies that were seeking material for their artists. "I loved to go into the studio and make demos," Simon said. "I was learning all the studio stuff, how to overdub, how to sing harmony with myself, how to play bass, how to imitate other voices so that the record would appeal to whatever artist they were trying to get to sing their song. All that was an enormous help years later when I started making my own records."

Burt Bacharach, the composer–record producer who was in the early stages of a hugely successful career with lyricist Hal David, said Simon stood out among the demo singers. "There was nothing casual about his approach," Bacharach said. "He cut a demo for me on a song called 'Gotta Get a Girl,' which was intended for Frankie Avalon, and you could see right away he was going somewhere in the music world. I made a point of trying to get him again whenever I needed another demo." The song was the B-side of a modest 1961 hit, "Who Else But You."

Because he could play guitar and sing, Simon often collected $50 for a demo and sometimes did two a week, which was good money for a college side job. It's not surprising that Simon's grades at Queens College suffered that first semester, with an A in music offset by a D in math.

Simon spent hours upon hours in recording studios either making his own records, usually as Jerry Landis, or, mostly, demoing other writers' songs. Hard-core Simon fans have spent decades trying to track down all that music, hoping for unreleased gems. But their energy was wasted; little of what Simon did was worth finding. There was no twinkle of future greatness in any of it. Even he called it mostly "crap." The titles of the demo songs alone suggested their place in generic teen pop, such as "Two Hearts on a Chain" and "Teen Age Blue." When he would complain to Lou when his latest tune didn't receive any attention, Lou didn't try to sugarcoat things. Recalled Simon, "He'd go, 'Let me tell you something, Paul. They don't give an A for effort. You win some, you lose some. If you lose, you can't complain. This is the real world. Get back to work.' "

During this period, Simon certainly knew a good song when he heard one. Years later, he would look back and express great admiration for Chuck Berry and the team of Jerry Leiber and Mike Stoller, who wrote rock and R&B classics such as "Jailhouse Rock," "Kansas City," and "Yakety Yak" for the likes of Elvis Presley, Wilbert Harrison, and the Coasters, respectively. "I loved Chuck Berry's great use of language, the way words just tumbled out so effortlessly and contained all sorts of surprising images," Simon said. "He didn't just use a lot of youthful vernacular, but he made up words himself, like in 'Maybellene,' where he wrote, 'As I was motorvatin' over the hill.' And Jerry and Mike were also great songwriters and great record makers: white guys from Los Angeles who went into black culture and absorbed it and wrote about it on a very high level. They were absolute geniuses."

Through it all, however, Simon's own songs showed little if any of those writers' influences. He kept writing in the style of the latest pop hit, however lame. That's not to say all his time was wasted. Writing even bad songs helped him pick up pointers about the songwriting process. Mainly, the studio experience taught him the mechanics of making a record. In his mind, each recording was a learning experience. That apprenticeship also educated him in the business of music, including the importance of songwriters retaining the copyright on their songs. In the 1950s and 1960s, it was a common practice for publishers to pressure budding artists into giving up half their future songwriting royalties, or else no deal. The latter practice was a holdover from the prerock days when most songwriters needed publishers to get their songs to the attention of recording stars such as Bing Crosby and Frank Sinatra. Even Bob Dylan and Lennon-McCartney started their careers with the old-fashioned publishing deals, thus surrendering their publishing royalties. Simon was one of the first songwriters to recognize he could publish his own songs and save, literally, a fortune. By retaining his publishing, he received 100 percent of the royalties on his songs, starting with "The Sound of Silence." Over the course of his career, that simple but significant move would earn him tens of millions of dollars. By maintaining ownership, he also controlled use of his songs in commercials and films.

During a demo session his freshman year, Simon met another talented young singer and songwriter, Carol Klein, who was also a first-year student at Queens College. She had already recorded two singles under the name Carole King, but neither did much. At Queens, the teens became friends, and King even helped him with one of his math classes. In the spring of 1959, they worked together on a demo for "Just to Be with You" by a songwriter named Marvin Kalfin. Their vocals gave the doo-wop song enough charm to catch the ear of Jim Gribble, a manager whose white doo-wop group the Passions enjoyed a modest hit with it that fall. King recalled, "We didn't go, 'Oh, I wish that was us on the radio.' We were proud our demo led to a hit."

By the time of the single, King had met and married songwriter Gerry Goffin, a night student at Queens College. She was so caught up in the songs they were writing that she quit school to concentrate full-time on music. Her daring was rewarded a year later when the Shirelles' version of the pair's composition "Will You Love Me Tomorrow" became the no. 1 song in the country. They went on to become one of the most successful songwriting teams of the rock era. "I was glad for her, but it was also incredibly frustrating," Simon admitted. "They were making big hits, and I was still trying to get a record deal or just make another demo. I kept asking myself, 'How did they do that?' "

Yet remaining at Queens College was one of Simon's wisest decisions. According to Mort Lewis, who would later manage Simon and Garfunkel, Simon most likely would have kept pursuing the path of teen pop hits if he had followed Carole King out the door. At best, he would have joined the ranks of songwriters who supplied the hit makers of the day with songs. But that was largely a dead end. "The arrival of Bob Dylan and the Beatles made almost of all those writers obsolete," Lewis added. "The best of the new singers and bands wrote their own songs."

Even without his college classes, the summer of 1959 was busy. Besides watching the Yankees struggle through a rare mediocre season, Simon followed two very different stories in the news.

Like much of young America, he fell under the spell of Massachusetts senator John F. Kennedy, who was launching a bid to become the Democratic Party candidate for president. Just as Paul and other young people wanted to define themselves through their music, they also wanted new voices in politics. A leader. Kennedy offered a dramatic contrast from the old order as symbolized by President Dwight D. Eisenhower, who was born all the way back in 1890. For Simon, seeing Kennedy at the podium was a little like seeing Elvis onstage or the Yankees' Mickey Mantle on the field. There was in each case a massive adrenaline rush. Decades later, Simon would cite Kennedy, Mantle, Presley, and comedian Lenny Bruce as the four great heroes of his teen years. "I was very, very taken with Kennedy," he said. "I liked everything about him. He was like a rock star: sunglasses, drove a convertible, and he was progressive in his politics." With his interest kindled, Simon embraced issues that were being championed on college campuses, including anxiety over escalating Cold War tensions and the increasingly urgent civil rights movement. Simon would rarely write overt protest songs in the future, but his youthful, compassionate, liberal leanings would eventually find their way into many of his tunes.

In a different way, Simon was fascinated by the unlikely account of Salvador Agron, a Puerto Rican teenager who came to New York City with his parents and got involved with a street gang, the Vampires. Searching for a rival gang to retaliate against after one of the Vampires was beaten up, Agron stabbed two innocent boys to death. Agron's case was tabloid fodder for weeks, all the more intriguing because the sixteen-year-old was wearing a long red-lined black satin cape during the crime. Hence, the nickname "Capeman." The story—including a lengthy trial and Agron's subsequent repenting in prison—continued to intrigue Simon for years, leading him to think from time to time about possibly telling the story in a song.

In the midst of all this, Simon also was drawn that summer to a new, energetic sound that was beginning to be championed on college campuses and mainstream radio: folk music. The Kingston Trio was the hottest thing in pop since Elvis, thanks to a bright, accessible style of folk, which appealed chiefly to college students who had outgrown the narrow teen focus of fifties rock 'n' roll. To discerning young listeners, however, the trio's sound felt more like a slick reproduction of folk music than the real thing—and it would take a second wave of more challenging and original folk artists to ignite a movement among young fans. Meanwhile, Simon continued to go around in circles.

Simon's first single after leaving Big Records came out in August 1959 on MGM Records. The 45, still under the name Jerry Landis, featured two Simon compositions, "Anna Belle" and "Loneliness," but it was another flop. Despite the setbacks, there was some good news that fall. Like millions of young people during the Cold War, Simon was living under the shadow of the military draft. When he registered soon after his eighteenth birthday, he learned that he was 4-F; he was deferred. Doctors found a heart murmur, which continued to be detected for around ten years before it simply disappeared.

It was around that time that Simon bought the car of his dreams with his $2,000 in royalties from Big. "Paul didn't know anything about cars," Bobby Susser said, "but he bought a shiny, red 1958 Chevrolet convertible that had this feature every kid went crazy over: *triple* carburetors. It was just the coolest thing. He would use any excuse to drive around the neighborhood, usually with the radio tuned to the rock station. I'd often ride with him, and you just felt like every eye was on us. You couldn't get any cooler than that."

Unfortunately, Simon had only a few months to enjoy the car. He was cruising around the neighborhood with Bobby one day when he heard a strange noise from underneath the chassis. When Simon saw sparks, he pulled the convertible to the curb, and he and Bobby got out just in time to see flames engulfing the Chevy.

"What happened next tells you a lot about Paul," Bobby added. "People around us are all excited: 'Look at the car! Look at the flames!' But Paul is very quiet—even though he loves this car. When someone finally asks him what he's going to do, Paul replies, as calm as anything, 'I'll call the insurance company in the morning.' It was typical. Paul saw there was nothing he could do about the car, so he didn't anguish about it—at least not on the outside. He just figured out his next step."

Simon got a break in January 1960 when Jim Gribble, the Passions' manager, asked him to sing on a record with the Mystics, another of his young groups. The white doo-wop outfit's lead singer had quit even though the Mystics had a Top 20 hit with "Hushabye."

"Our manager was always looking for that diamond in the rough," Al Contera, the Mystics' bass player, said. "So on any given day, there would be dozens of guys and girls hanging out in his office, hoping to be put on a record. When the Mystics had to find a new lead singer, we tried a million guys. Nobody could sing the way we wanted, and then someone noticed little Jerry there in the corner."

One of the songs Simon recorded with the Mystics, a ballad called "All Through the Night," almost made it to the *Billboard* Hot 100 in the early weeks of 1960. Despite liking Simon's voice, the other members of the Mystics felt he didn't fit in with the group's "tough-guy" sensibilities. "We were from the streets of Bensonhurst, Brooklyn. We were tough guys, and here was Jerry, this nerdy little guy from Queens with a guitar as big as he was, leading us," Contera continued.

Besides his height, Simon was now worrying about another aspect of his appearance: his thinning hair. He would eventually turn to various devices to try to camouflage the hair loss, before scaling back. "I know some people who don't give a damn about their hair," Simon said, "but I had these big rock 'n' roll role models: Elvis, the Beatles, Mick Jagger. They were all skinny and tall, and they had a lot of hair. That's what rock 'n' roll was, and it was a big thing with me. I once had this conversation with John Lennon, and he really wanted to know how I knew enough to keep my own publishing rather than give half of it away like the Beatles did. I told him I grew up around the music business and saw how all the companies would take your publishing, which alerted me right away that there must be something valuable in that publishing. Then I asked him, 'Who ever told you how to comb your hair like that?' "

Back in a solo role, Simon, still as Jerry Landis, made two singles for Warwick Records in 1960, the most notable being a novelty inspired by a Connie Francis hit, "Lipstick on Your Collar." The new song, "I'd Like to Be (the Lipstick on Your Lips)," was written by Hal David and Sherman Edwards—the same Hal David who also teamed with Burt Bacharach. As Simon settled into his fall classes at Queens College, he was 0 hits for 4 singles. At nineteen, he wondered if he wasn't a has-been in the music business. It was at that precise time that Simon's career began to turn around.

Allen Toussaint, the respected New Orleans arranger-producer-songwriter who would become friends with Simon, believed that millions of musicians had talent, but few of them ever evolved into genuine artists who produced a unique body of work. To achieve that level of accomplishment, he felt, a person needed a "trigger" in his or her life that set high, unyielding standards. For Simon, that trigger came in three stages—the first of which was in the classrooms of Queens College.

CHAPTER THREE

Dr. Rosette (Rose) C. Lamont taught comparative literature and French at Queens College, and played an invaluable role in Simon's creative development. A one-woman ambassador of the arts who was born in Paris, she loved spreading her joy of reading and performing, and Simon was an ideal pupil: intelligent and eager to learn. In turn, it's easy to see how he would fall under the spell of someone so charismatic and sophisticated. The first class he took from Lamont, in the fall of 1960, was "19th and 20th Century French Literature," during which he read major existential figures, including Albert Camus and Jean-Paul Sartre, and sat through lectures by Lamont that made the works come to life for him.

From that point, Simon began responding to other literature classes, delighting in the words and craft of Robert Frost, James Joyce, T. S. Eliot, and Emily Dickinson. His courses included "Major American Writers," "The Bible as Literature," and "Pope to Blake" on the English lit side, and "Around the World in Song," "American Ballad and Song," and "20th Century Opera" on the music side. All of a sudden he was stepping into new worlds, trying on identities, the way adolescents do to see what fits. Simon started reading the literary journal *Granta* and even took a couple of acting classes. Years later, he would list Frost and W. B. Yeats as his favorite poets from the first half of the twentieth century and Philip Larkin, Seamus Heaney, W. H. Auden, Anne Carson, Stanley Kunitz, Paul Muldoon, and Billy Collins from the second half.

Simon was still bored with what was passing for rock 'n' roll. The music that once excited him had turned into a wasteland. Many of rock's greatest talents were, in essence, missing in action. Buddy Holly died in a 1959 plane crash. Elvis was in the army from 1958 to 1960. Jerry Lee Lewis was ostracized after the scandal of his marriage to his thirteen-year-old cousin. Chuck Berry faced criminal charges of having sexual relations with a fourteen-year-old girl and eventually served a year and a half in prison.

"By the end of the fifties, rock had run out of genuine creative stuff, and it was stupid," he said. "The records I was making were stupid. They were just gimmicky, and I gradually lost interest in it. When I started taking those literature classes, I began to feel, 'That's who I am.' I discovered it there." Despite his feelings, Simon continued to write tunes in that vapid teen pop style as if his college experience and recording gigs were totally different parts of his consciousness. It would take another trigger or two to fully redirect him.

In early 1961 Warwick Records released another Jerry Landis single, and it was quickly forgotten. The next time the name Jerry Landis appeared on a single was that fall when Canadian American, another small indie label, released two more of his ballads, "I'm Lonely" and "I Wish I Weren't in Love." His record as a solo artist was now six singles, zero hits.

Around this time, Simon's friends, and even his parents, started noticing changes in his personality. The generally upbeat preteen on the playground at PS 165 had become moodier or, some would say, melancholy. "We'd often hang out on the weekends, and everyone would be having a good time, and you'd look over and see Simon off by himself, sort of staring into space," Bobby Susser said. "Eventually he'd come over and join in, but you felt a part of him was somewhere else."

Simon acknowledged a personality change, but he didn't trace it to a single moment or event. "There was always something about me, about my face and my expressions," Simon said. "When I was an infant, my aunt Roselynd said they used to call me Cardozo"—after Benjamin Nathan Cardozo, a Supreme Court judge with a dour look—"because I looked so serious. When I was nine or ten, people would ask me all the time, 'What's wrong?' Even my mother once asked me, 'What happened? You used to be so happy, and now you look sad.' All I know is that this feeling of melancholy entered into my personality somewhere in adolescence. Artie says I was angry about height, but I wasn't angry. I was melancholy. But nothing happened, except whatever happened chemically—a hormonal change that brought something out of me. Adolescence is kind of a moody time anyway."

With his solo aspirations sinking, Simon stepped back from the performer role in hopes of moving ahead by writing and producing a hit for a group. Stopping by the old Honeycomb luncheonette that spring, he noticed three teens singing doo-wop on the street. "He comes up to us and says he wanted to make a record and wondered if we were interested—just like that, very direct and businesslike," said Marty Cooper, the leader of the trio. "We didn't know who he was, but we jumped at the chance. He was really into it. He bought me stage clothes and had professional pictures taken by Bruno of Hollywood." Simon had not only a song for the trio but also a name: Tico and the Triumphs. Tico was the name of his favorite Latin music label, and Triumph was a line of motorcycles; Marlon Brando rode a Triumph Thunderbird 6T in *The Wild One*. The song, "Motorcycle," had two things going for it commercially: motorcycles were a big part of the rock 'n' roll rebel imagery, and Simon used the actual roar of a motorcycle on the record to better catch the ear of radio listeners. He found a minor label, Madison, willing to release the record in the fall of 1961, and the motorcycle roar caught on with DJs on the East Coast. But Madison folded suddenly, and the single was switched to Amy Records, where it was lost in the shuffle.

Throughout their time together, Cooper marveled at Simon's drive. "He was constantly monitoring the radio, looking for new ideas, and he was always talking about something he had heard," Cooper says. "One day he'd tell us about the gentle way that the leader of the Fleetwoods [Gary Troxel] sang, and then he'd play us a new record by the Tokens, 'The Lion Sleeps Tonight.'" The song, best known for its "Wimoweh" chant, was an early indication of Simon's interest in world music. Soon after mentioning the record, Simon showed up at rehearsal with a song, "Wildflower," that combined elements of his old rockabilly interests with a new, exotic, international feel highlighted by a series of Hawaiian lyrics. The song went on to be the Triumphs' second single, but it failed to catch on. Neither did a third single, "Get Up & Do the Wobble," which was a flagrant attempt to create a new dance craze.

Simon's final attempt at making a pop hit as Jerry Landis came in the fall of 1962. It was a novelty titled "The Lone Teen Ranger," which was inspired by the 1958 hit single "Western Movies," a great, goofball record by the Los Angeles vocal group the Olympics. In his song, Simon complains that his girlfriend is obsessed with the masked Lone Ranger, a hugely popular Western radio-TV hero. To get her back, Simon vows to put on a mask of his own, ride a horse, and carry a six-gun, hence the Lone Teen Ranger. He threw everything into the recording, including the sounds of ricocheting gunshots, galloping horses, and even the vocal gibberish that worked on "Hey, Schoolgirl." It was probably the catchiest record Simon made since "Hey, Schoolgirl"—and the Amy single got enough airplay to push the record to no. 97 on the pop chart in January 1963, but no higher.

Simon's spirits continued to languish. Fortunately, Arthur Yale, the head of Amy Records, offered him a job that gave him time to regroup. All he had to do for $75 a week was come into the office and listen to the stacks of demo tapes from publishers or songwriters who hoped to interest the label in recording the songs. Simon knew the chances of anything good arriving at Amy's doorstep were minimal. If someone had a good song, it'd be sent to the big labels. Freddy DeMann, who joined Amy Records in 1962 as national promotion director and went on to manage

Madonna, recalls meeting Simon and thinking he had an awful lot of self-confidence for someone who hadn't had much success in the music business. Beneath the brash exterior, however, Simon was feeling increasingly insecure. "I was still confident in my ability to hear a hit," he said later. "But I had begun to lose faith in my ability to write a hit."

By this time, new developments in folk music helped redirect Simon's thinking, notably Joan Baez, whose records touched him on two levels: the beautiful, angelic quality of her voice and, perhaps most of all, the striking presence on the album of the acoustic guitar. Since "Hey, Schoolgirl," Simon had been playing mostly electric guitar on sessions because that was the instrument of choice in the teen pop world. But the Baez records made him yearn for the intimacy and warmth of the acoustic sound. He was also drawn to folk music's heavy focus on social issues. As Simon drew closer to this style, he was lucky to have the heart of the movement in America headquartered in and around New York City's bohemian Greenwich Village. Gradually Simon started spending more of his free time in the Village, soaking up the atmosphere and admiring the commitment of the musicians. "That was tremendously attractive to me, not to try to have a hit by imitating people who were on the radio," he said. "These musicians in the Village just seemed to be in love with what they were doing. It wasn't all about chart position."

Along with the literature classes at Queens, the singers and songwriters of the Village became Simon's new muses. He didn't respond just to the more challenging nature of the songs but also to a new (for him) and exciting style of guitar playing. Rather than strumming or plucking the strings with plastic picks, the fingerpicking style, popularized by singer-guitarist Merle Travis, required plucking the strings with the fingers. Equally important, the folk songs in the Village clubs, Simon said, "widened the perspective for an audience that was by then of an age able to grasp a message more sophisticated than 'We're so young, but we're in love, and one day we'll be married.' "

One new folk figure stood above them all: Bob Dylan, who had come to New York from Hibbing, Minnesota, in January 1961. To many observers, he was an odd duck, but he generated a force that wouldn't be denied, and the buzz started early. Despite all this stimulus, it wasn't easy for Simon to abandon the doo-wop and rock sounds and embrace a new movement. It was like switching from the Yankees to another team. Paul, at a crossroads, again looked to Dr. Lamont to help give him direction.

When Simon saw her "European Drama" class in the college catalog in the fall of 1962, his final semester at Queens, he signed up immediately. The class proved to be as inspiring as the first one, and Lamont even invited Simon to go with her to see the Romanian writer Eugène Ionesco's play *Rhinoceros*. The ambitious avant-garde drama was set in a post–World War II French village and explored such sociopolitical themes as conformity, morality, and personal freedom. Dr. Lamont was such an admirer of Ionesco that she eventually wrote two books about the man and his art. After the performance, she introduced Simon to Ionesco.

Simon was also inspired by a course called "Music and American Civilization." It was taught by Dr. Joseph Macklow, who took him to Carnegie Hall for a program honoring leading composers of the twentieth century, including Edgard Varèse, a French-born composer who has been hailed as the father of electronic music and has been cited as an influence by such far-ranging figures as John Cage, Pierre Boulez, and Frank Zappa. Macklow took Simon backstage to meet Varèse, who was then seventy-seven. It was a special evening for Simon as a songwriter because he was as fascinated with music as most writers were with words. Listening to Varèse, Simon heard how far music extended beyond the relatively narrow boundaries of contemporary pop and rock—and he would strive throughout his career to push himself as a composer. For most of his career, Simon's songwriting would begin with the music. He would try to find a riff or melody on the guitar or piano that stirred him emotionally. Then he'd try to figure out how to express what he was feeling in words. In that way he was different from most rock writers, whose strengths were in words and themes, not in original music. Still, it was Dylan's words that would soon prove to be the second trigger that spurred Simon's songwriting evolution. He was essentially starting over. By any objective measure, Simon had passion and drive, but he didn't have a vision.

Bob Dylan's second album, *The Freewheelin' Bob Dylan*, released less than three months after Simon's college graduation in February 1963, was packed with Dylan's own songs, including the social commentary of "A Hard Rain's A-Gonna Fall," and an enchanting love song that Simon liked, "Girl from the North Country." Simon found in Dylan's writing a natural way to blend his love of music and everything he had learned in college about writing and the social order.

"Suddenly there was this tremendous relief," he said later. "I was no longer interested in writing a pop hit, which I couldn't do anyway, but finding a new world of music that really appealed to me. Here's Dylan writing about subject matter that is neither teenage nor traditional folk. It wasn't just the thing you heard in so many old folk tunes: 'I stabbed my love in the heart and took her down to the river and drowned her.' He was traveling on his own and writing about what he saw." Simon even loved the cover of *Freewheelin'*. "Bob had this attitude and look. I loved the fact he was walking down the street with this girl by his side. It felt so daring, so new."

Now committed to writing folk songs, Simon didn't have to look far for themes. "He Was My Brother," the first of his folk songs that he sang for friends, spoke of the dangers facing activists who traveled to the South to challenge segregation. Simon was still working at Amy Records when he began writing the song, and it came fairly quickly. He knew it was more ambitious and mature than anything he had written previously, though he didn't kid himself: he also knew "He Was My Brother" was derivative. Instead of mirroring what he heard on the radio, he was now patterning his tunes on what he might hear nightly in Village clubs. It was still a formula, but a step forward.

Simon got onstage at a few open-mic hootenanny nights in the Village, where he again ran into an image problem. He didn't feel welcome in the scene; he felt typecast by some musicians and club regulars as just a kid from Queens, not someone with authentic folk credentials. To come from Queens and try to get a gig at a Village club was much more difficult than if you blew into town from Oklahoma, like Tom Paxton, or the Midwest like Bob Dylan, who made up the story that he'd ridden the rails as a hobo.

Eager for new experiences, Simon had joined the thousands of young people who hitchhiked across the country in the summer of 1962, inspired partially by Jack Kerouac's celebrated 1957 novel *On the Road*. He planned to continue the following summer with a trip to Europe, both to see the sights and, specifically, to check out the music scene, prompted no doubt by the reference in Nat Hentoff's liner notes for *Freewheelin'* to Dylan's having performed briefly in London and Rome.

On the eve of Paul's trip to Europe, Amy Records's Arthur Yale died of a heart attack, and Simon wondered if he shouldn't stick around to make sure he didn't lose his job, but Lou urged him to go. "You can always get a job," he said. "You have time. Why don't you go to Europe? You earned it." With his guitar case in hand, Paul caught a flight the next day to London. Lou had a special reason to encourage his son to pursue his dreams: Lou's heart attacks had made him reconsider his own future. He had long been losing interest in his repetitive club gig and wanted to spend his remaining years doing something he could be passionate about again, which was teaching. He also valued the greater financial security teaching would offer him and his family. Still shaken by his father's bad fortune during the Great Depression, Lou told Bobby Susser he wouldn't be making as much money teaching, but he would have tenure. Eddie Simon also feels his father was bored with the endless club dates and craved intellectual stimulation.

Simon wasn't comfortable in London, and he soon moved on to Paris, which he had heard so much about from Rose Lamont. He fell in love with the romantic currents of the city, and he divided his time between seeing historic sites and busking for spare change at tourist spots. In the spirit of the wandering minstrel, Simon slept, at least for one night, on the concrete embankment of the Pont Neuf, the oldest standing bridge across the River Seine. Mostly he stayed in cheap hotels. While there, he met Dave McCausland, a young Englishman who liked Simon's music and gave him an open invitation to sing at a Sunday-evening folk show he ran in Brentwood, a town outside of London. Simon said he was going to Spain for a few days but would love to perform a set after that. McCausland also arranged for Simon to play another nearby club, the White Swan in Romford.

Returning home, McCausland told some of his Brentwood Folk Club regulars that a wonderful young American folk singer who played an extremely rare, prized Martin dreadnought guitar would be coming to the club. One of those regulars was so interested—especially in that acoustic guitar—that he went to the White Swan show, where Simon sang "He Was My Brother" and at least three songs that had been recorded by Baez: "What Have They Done to the Rain," "The Lily of the West," and "Geordie." The Brentwood clubgoer realized that Simon had heard the songs on one of Baez's live albums because he used the introduction to "What Have They Done" from one of the albums: "the gentlest protest song I know." The club regular, who was enough of a natural historian to keep notes and journals containing his impressions of various performers, and a couple of other fans then took Simon to central London after the White Swan closed in search of some late-night folk clubs. Among the other songs Simon sang that night were "Man of Constant Sorrow," a traditional folk song covered by Bob Dylan on his first LP, and, surprisingly, the Little Willie John hit "Fever." At each stop, the reaction was enthusiastic.

After staying in London that night, Simon showed up the next day at the McCauslands' residence in Brentwood, where he would do a brief set on Sunday at Dave's club. "Paul got along great with my father—with all of us, in fact," recalled Jonty McCausland, Dave's younger brother. "He played a few songs on the guitar and said he hoped to come back to England soon and do some more shows."

Back in New York, Simon didn't get along with Yale's replacement at Amy Records and accepted an offer to become a song plugger at Edward B.

Marks Music Company, one of the world's largest music publishers. The position, which paid $150 a week, required him to make the rounds of record companies and convince them to record E. B. Marks songs. The excitement was dashed when he discovered the company's vast musical catalog was severely dated; not geared at all to the needs of the rock 'n' roll era. "They wanted me to pitch songs like 'The Peanut Vendor,' and nobody was ever going to record them," said Simon. "To make things worse, I wasn't a good salesman."

Feeling guilty about not being able to place the material, Simon gave the company the publishing rights to some of his new songs, including "He Was My Brother" and another folk song, "Carlos Dominguez," a statement about society's lack of compassion that was even more generic than "Brother." Apparently eager to get active in the contemporary market, Marks arranged for the two songs to be released as a single in August 1963 by a tiny label called Tribute. To separate the tracks from Jerry Landis, the record was released under the pseudonym Paul Kane. It disappeared quickly.

During this time, Simon was walking home along Jewel Avenue in Kew Gardens Hills when he ran into, of all people, Art Garfunkel. The old tension melted away, or at least was pushed to the side. Garfunkel had put out some records under the name Artie Garr but was primarily a student at Columbia. Predictably, the conversation got around to music, and Art was impressed when Simon played a few of his new songs: most certainly "He Was My Brother" and possibly "Sparrow." They showcased the new songs at Simon's old fraternity house at Queens College, and they went over well. Still, there was no sense that they were a duo again; they were just old friends sharing a passion.

Simon kept writing songs and allowed Marks to publish two more, "Bleecker Street," a sentimental description of the songwriters' plight on the street at the heart of the Village folk scene, and "The Side of a Hill," a warning of nuclear disaster. In both songs, you could sense Simon struggling to find his own voice and not quite doing it. But he was getting closer. By nature hopeful, Simon was enthralled when President Kennedy made his landmark "Ich bin ein Berliner" speech before 250,000 people in Berlin on June 28 and then again two months later when Dr. Martin Luther King made his inspiring "I Have a Dream" speech on the steps of the Lincoln Memorial in front of another quarter million people.

Yet all that promise of social progress was contrasted, almost daily, with news photos or TV footage of African Americans being denied their rights or even murdered in the South. Those images filled the national media as Simon vowed to find his voice—if indeed he had one. Simon had planned to enroll in Brooklyn Law School that fall, but he decided at the last minute to devote himself to searching for that voice.

PART TWO

The Sound of Silence

CHAPTER FOUR

"The Sound of Silence" didn't come easily in the fall of 1963, even though Simon was working with new purpose and ambition. He tried, over a period of weeks, to create something of his own. While he has sometimes said that song wasn't a conscious reaction to the assassination of President Kennedy, his subconscious was certainly active. Paul played an early version of the song for his father and Eddie in his upstairs bedroom, and he was thrilled when his father responded with, "You wrote this, Paul? It's very good!" Lou Simon was so excited that he brought Paul downstairs to play the song for some musician friends who were at the house with their wives for one of their regular Monday-night get-togethers. They, too, raved. The reaction—especially his father's praise—meant everything to Paul.

Simon wasn't finished with the song when he arrived in England on his Christmas break, but he was so enthusiastic about it that he played what he had for the McCauslands, and Jonty McCausland remembered his dad telling Paul how much he liked the song. "He said it was just the kind of song he loved to hear on the jukebox," said Jonty, who also believed that Simon previewed the song at the Brentwood Folk Club, which was housed above a pub across the street from the town's train station.

Loads of small towns had their own folk clubs in those days, usually informal scenes with maybe fifty to a hundred people at the shows and volunteers pitching in to help keep expenses down. Many of the Brentwood fans would even go to the McCausland house for homemade scones before the show. But Simon was special. "It was like we adopted him and he adopted us," said Jonty's older sister, Lynne. Later, when he was doing shows in other towns, Simon would often return to the McCauslands' well after midnight, around the time Lynne's dad was getting home from work, and they would sit and talk for hours. Eventually, Mr. McCausland began calling Simon his fifth son. When the McCauslands needed $3,500 in 1967 for the deposit on a pub, Paul gave them the money. "It wasn't a loan," Lynne said. "It was a gift."

This second exposure to the British folk scene made a strong impression on Simon. After years of rejection in New York folk circles as the kid from Queens, he was embraced as the kid from America, and it made a world of difference. It also felt good to be known by his own name. "I remember being introduced as Paul Simon from New York, and people actually cheered," Simon said. "We were still close enough to the war that people really liked Americans." In addition, fans in England concentrated on the music. In the States, folk clubs were often in bars, and people would be drinking and making a lot of noise. In England, the clubs tended to be in rooms above the bars, and the audience listened. Paul found it deeply satisfying to play to an audience that was "actually listening to your songs."

Returning to his job at E. B. Marks, Simon dreaded the daily drudgery more than ever. He had been at the company for nearly six months and was looking for a way out, which led him to think about trying again to get a recording contract with a folk label, possibly Vanguard or Elektra. The breakthrough, however, came almost by accident during one of his stops for his job, at the office of Tom Wilson, Dylan's producer at Columbia Records. Simon had met Wilson earlier on his rounds for the publisher, and the two got along well. A six-foot-four Harvard graduate in his early thirties, Wilson hadn't signed Dylan to Columbia or produced his first album (that was John Hammond in both cases), but the producer had a good ear for talent; he championed Dylan when other label staffers ridiculed the young songwriter as "Hammond's folly" after Dylan's debut album sold almost nothing. "I liked Tom a lot," Simon said. "He had a high element of cool. He was a tall, good-looking black guy, Harvard, jazz, well dressed, very calm. He was kind of a musical Obama."

In the meeting that January, Paul, as before, tried to interest Wilson in some of the old-style E. B. Marks songs, but Wilson again passed. Simon, in his eagerness to get a record deal, spontaneously asked Wilson if he would listen to a couple of his own folk songs. Both the number of songs Simon played that day and which actual tunes he played have been in question over the years.

For decades, most published reports of the meeting maintained that Wilson was most excited about "He Was My Brother." He thought it would be perfect for the Pilgrims, a group he was working with that was being pushed as a sort of African American version of Peter, Paul & Mary. "No, no," Paul thought. He wasn't just trying to get Wilson to use one of his songs, he wanted a record contract. The suspicion around the label was Wilson already had a solo folk singer and songwriter in Dylan, but Simon thought he might be open to another vocal group and told Wilson he and a friend had already made records together and would like Wilson to hear their versions of his songs. Fair enough, the producer said, and Simon raced to tell Art the news.

When the pair returned the next day, Wilson was impressed. But he didn't have the power to sign artists, so he needed the duo to make an audition tape to present to the company's executive committee. Paul and Art then went into Columbia Records' historic studio A on Seventh Avenue to record a few tunes. The audition proved promising enough for Wilson to get the green light.

The story about "He Was My Brother" being the key song gained credence over the years because Wilson actually did record it with the Pilgrims, but Simon told a different story in a 2015 interview for an exhibit about him at the Rock & Roll Hall of Fame. In the taped conversation, Simon said that "The Sound of Silence" was the song Wilson favored. On the same subject three years later, he stood by his version. "It's amazing how some stories, however false, have a life of their own," he said. "For instance, people still write that [his first wife] Peggy was a TWA stewardess when I met her, yet she never was a stewardess. Tom might have liked 'He Was My Brother' for the Pilgrims, but he would never have signed us because of that. He was too smart for that. It wasn't that good a song. He signed us because of 'The Sound of Silence.' "

Around the time of the audition, Simon, again impulsively, left E. B. Marks. As part of his job, he had to write a report each week detailing his rounds of the record labels, and this time, for some reason, Simon's boss challenged the report. He charged that it was too good for Simon to have written it. Simon was insulted. "I told him I was an English literature major in college," Simon said, "and 'by the way, fuck you.' " He quit on the spot and later delighted in explaining how his leaving was a big loss for the company because he hadn't turned over his latest song for Marks to publish. Weeks later, Simon would start his own company, Eclectic Music, and publish "The Sound of Silence" himself.

Things were now moving fast with Columbia. The contract, dated February 10, 1964, was standard for a new act, a one-year deal that gave Columbia the right to exercise six additional one-year options, during which the beginning royalty rate was 6 percent of the wholesale price and would escalate to 10 percent. Wilson was especially pleased that Goddard Lieberson, the company's distinguished president, was enthusiastic. "I had a very good relationship with Goddard," Simon said. "He sort of mentored me. He'd pull me in every six months and we'd have lunch in the CBS dining room, and he'd ask me what I was doing. One day, I said, 'I'm thinking of producing some acts,' and he said, 'Don't get started with that. Stay with what you're doing: writing and recording. That's your future.' "

Before going into the studio on the evening of March 10 with Barry Kornfeld on twelve-string acoustic guitar and Bill Lee (father of film director

Spike) on bass, Wilson told Simon and Garfunkel that he wanted to divide the album between six original Simon tunes and six cover songs. His only stipulation regarding the covers was that one be a Dylan song, preferably "The Times They Are A-Changin', " the title track of Dylan's just-released third album. The thinking was that a Dylan song would help promote Dylan's LPs and, with any luck, build a link in the public's mind between Dylan and this new young duo. Among the other cover tunes chosen by Simon and Garfunkel were two socially conscious songs: Ian Campbell's "The Sun Is Burning" and Ed McCurdy's "Last Night I Had the Strangest Dream," an antiwar tune that was popular in the Village clubs and had already been recorded by the Weavers, the hugely influential folk group formed in the late 1940s that included Pete Seeger.

The first Simon song the pair recorded that night was "The Sound of Silence."

Hello darkness, my old friend
I've come to talk with you again
Because a vision softly creeping
Left its seeds while I was sleeping
And the vision that was planted in my brain
Still remains
Within the sound of silence

In restless dreams I walked alone
Narrow streets of cobblestone
'Neath the halo of a streetlamp
I turned my collar to the cold and damp
When my eyes were stabbed by the flash of a neon light
That split the night
And touched the sound of silence

And in the naked light I saw
Ten thousand people maybe more
People talking without speaking

People hearing without listening
People writing songs that voices never share
No one dare
Disturb the sound of silence

"Fools," said I, "you do not know
Silence like a cancer grows
Hear my words that I might teach you
Take my arms that I might reach you"
But my words like silent raindrops fell
And echoed in the wells of silence

And the people bowed and prayed
To the neon god they made
And the sign flashed out its warning
In the words that it was forming
And the sign said, "The words of the prophets
Are written on the subway walls
And tenement halls"
And whispered in the sound of silence.

Years later, Kornfeld didn't remember Simon or Wilson making a big deal of the song, but Simon, with his natural reserve, wasn't one to show outward jubilance. Inside, he was thrilled. "The song seems to me like something that came out of my literature classes," Simon said years later. "It feels like there's Camus in there. When I see the line about the cobblestone streets, I was probably thinking about Manhattan, the Village—not Kew Gardens Hills—just putting myself into that world of singers who were writing about the world around them. Then there's the whole thing in the song about the people who weren't paying attention. It was like I was thinking, 'What's wrong with them? Why can't they hear?'

"Whatever came out, I didn't sit down to write about alienation in America. I'm not saying the song isn't about that, but it wasn't my intention, and that's still true of my writing today. I don't ever set out to write a song about something, though after a while it becomes apparent in the construction of a song that I'm writing about something. Then I have a choice. Do I want to stay with that subject or shut it down?" In the case of "The Sound of Silence," he obviously wanted to stay with the subject.

The only other song the duo recorded that night was "The Times They Are A-Changin'," which wasn't the Dylan song Simon would have picked. Despite his own early step into protest music, he was already moving away from the genre. "I'm not a fan of songs that tell you 'And my point is . . .'" Instead, he would likely have chosen one of Dylan's love songs: perhaps "Don't Think Twice, It's All Right" or "Girl from the North Country." But he didn't make it an issue.

Simon was a happy young man when he walked out of the studio into the cold winter air. Though nothing he had written before "The Sound of Silence" had risen above the level of mediocrity, he now had a song that he felt would stand up against even Dylan. The other important thing that happened during the session was the beginning of the formal relationship between Simon and Garfunkel and a young studio engineer named Roy Halee, who would become such an essential part of the duo's creative process that industry observers would playfully refer to the group as Simon, Garfunkel, and Halee.

Born in the Bronx in the spring of 1934, Halee grew up in a musical family. His father, also named Roy Halee, was the voice of Mighty Mouse in cartoons and later sang with the vocal group featured on record producer–conductor Mitch Miller's hugely successful series of "Mitch Miller and the Gang" sing-along albums. Halee's mother, Rebecca Cauble, appeared in musical comedy on Broadway, once opposite Al Jolson. After getting a job as an audio engineer in the classical division of Columbia Records, Halee moved to the pop division, where he forged a bond with Tom Wilson as part of a new guard that wanted to pull Columbia out of its easy-listening rut. "In those days, the place was so straightlaced that they made Bob Dylan come up in the freight elevator," said Halee. "He was so scrungy-looking in the beginning that they didn't want him to bump into Barbra Streisand or Isaac Stern. When it came to Simon and Artie, no one at Columbia had heard anything like them. Their idea of a folk group was the Brothers Four, who had a hit with 'Greenfields,' but I always thought they were pop-yuck."

Halee was knocked out by Paul and Art. "When I closed my eyes, their vocal blend was very symphonic, yet it was also very catchy, very pop," he said. "As soon as they opened their mouths, I thought, 'Holy hell!' They were singing into one microphone, and it didn't take long for me to realize that's the best way to capture their sound: with one microphone rather than individual microphones, which most people used in those days. As soon as you separated them, something changed. But on one microphone, it was magic."

Seven days later, everyone was back in studio A to record five more songs in an efficient three hours. The tunes were highlighted by three Simon compositions: "He Was My Brother," "Bleecker Street," and "Wednesday Morning, 3 A.M." Where Garfunkel was enthusiastic about most of Simon's songs, he had early reservations about "Bleecker Street," calling it in the liner notes "too much for me at first." He felt the song was "highly intellectual, the symbolism extremely challenging." He was likely thinking the song would be too difficult for a mainstream audience. But he grew quickly to appreciate it, noting, "Admittedly, the song is difficult to understand, but worth the effort." Garfunkel also seemed to have reservations about "Wednesday Morning, 3 A.M.," even though the album was titled after it. The lyrics tell of a young man holding his loved one in his arms one night after he has robbed a liquor store, knowing it is probably his last night of freedom—a dark tale of impending doom that seemed to be little more than a summary of countless film noir plots.

Rather than return for a final session on March 24, Wilson gave Simon and Garfunkel the week off to prepare for their March 30 opening at Gerde's Folk City, the Village's most prestigious club. Simon had played there as a solo artist the previous October, opening for the Irish Rovers, but this would be his first time at Folk City with Art. It's odd that Columbia scheduled this showcase engagement while the album was being recorded rather than hold off until the LP was in stores, but Wilson may have been hoping to build enough early buzz to convince the promotion department to make the album a priority. One of the realities of the record business is that even major labels only have funds to heavily promote the releases they felt the strongest about, which usually meant those by proven hit makers or new acts that were creating momentum through reviews or concerts. If that was Wilson's thinking, it didn't work. Simon and Garfunkel invited friends to the opening show, but even with those boosters, no one described the atmosphere as being anything near electric.

David Geffen, who would go on to become one of the most successful executives in the history of the music business thanks to working with such talents as Joni Mitchell, Nirvana, and the Eagles, was not impressed. "I was new at William Morris [the giant talent agency], and I wanted to see everything in those days," he said. "But when I got to the club, they didn't strike me as all that great. I didn't think 'The Sound of Silence,' for instance, was anything special. Afterward, in the dressing room, Garfunkel told me he was conflicted about the future. He didn't know if he should give his music career a chance or if he should stay at Columbia University. I looked at him, and I said, 'My advice is you should stay in school.'" One person who was excited by the duo's performance was Wally Amos, another William Morris agent who, in 1975, would open his first Famous Amos cookie store. Amos signed them to the agency even though he couldn't get anyone else there interested in them.

On the night after the Folk City opening, Simon and Garfunkel were back in studio A to record the final five songs for the album, including an arrangement of "Benedictus," a sixteenth-century Latin hymn, and Simon's "Sparrow." The latter was a gentler protest song than "Brother," but it feels self-conscious next to the intimacy of "The Sound of Silence." Garfunkel discovered "Benedictus" during a music course at Columbia, and it was a daring effort, especially for a debut album. Those same ambitions, however, were seen by some Simon and Garfunkel critics as pretentious—a charge that was to shadow them during the early stage of their career. They ended the session by recording three covers: "You Can Tell the World," written by folk scene favorites Bob Gibson and Bob (Hamilton) Camp; and two traditional numbers, "Peggy-O," which appeared on Dylan's debut album, and "Go Tell It on the Mountain," a spiritual that had been recorded by such varied artists as Mahalia Jackson and the Kingston Trio.

Simon and Garfunkel were both hopeful, but they knew that a hit album would be a longshot. It was Wilson and Halee who seemed the most excited. "We had been around long enough to know the odds, but we thought these guys were great," Halee said. "If nothing on this album was a hit, there'd be a second album and a third album, and somewhere there would be a hit. With those voices and those songs, we felt it was just a matter of time."

Record companies normally take weeks or even months before releasing an album, but they sometimes put out an advance single in hopes of building interest among disc jockeys and fans. Wilson, however, couldn't convince his superiors at Columbia to release a single—no one saw a potential hit. It was weeks before the album was even given a release date: October 19, 1964. To Simon, it seemed like a lifetime away. Garfunkel had his studies to keep himself busy, but Simon, even though he was now a Columbia Records artist, still felt unwelcome in the Village clubs. On July 10 he returned to England, where he would meet the first love of his life.

Simon no longer thought of himself as a tourist in England. He was there to work, and what better place to be making music in the summer of 1964 than England. After the emergence of the Beatles and the Rolling Stones, the country's music fans—and everyone in England seemed to be caught up by music—were being treated to new bands as fast as the British pop papers could profile them. "I liked the early Beatles, but I really fell in love with them when some of the Lennon-McCartney ballads came out," Simon said. "Everything about them was cool; the way they blended their voices, and they had George Martin in the studio with them. It was an amazing team. I'd listen to their records and go, 'Wow! How did they do that?' Paul had this extraordinary gift of melody and a voice that could go along with it. Songs like 'Here, There and Everywhere,' 'For No One,' and 'Yesterday' are so uniquely him. But it was some of John's songs that probably touched me most, songs like 'Norwegian Wood' and 'In My Life,' where there was this sorrow; this private pain that he revealed." Despite the temptation of jumping aboard that mainline rock 'n' roll train, Simon continued to focus on folk music.

Early in his trip, Simon met Kathy Chitty, who would become his first serious girlfriend and inspire some of his songs. Contrary to repeated reports over the years that they met during Simon's first trip to England in 1963 (Simon recalled simply seeing her taking tickets on the steps of the Brentwood Folk Club at that time), they met formally in April 1964. Simon was performing at the White Swan in Romford when Dave McCausland introduced him to Kathy, a shy eighteen-year-old with long, brown hair. The date was supplied by someone close to Kathy, someone who—with both Kathy's confirmation and permission—wanted to finally set the record straight.

Even if Simon had long forgotten just where they met, he did recall being captivated. Simon had dated a reasonable amount in New York, but nothing serious. Maybe he had been too busy with music, or maybe he just hadn't found the right girl. Instantly, he felt Kathy Chitty was that girl. "It was like love at first sight," he said years later. "I had never felt that. It was just chemistry."

Kathy was born in Romford, a town on the eastern fringe of London, during the closing weeks of World War II. The youngest of three children in a comfortable working-class family, Kathy was trained during high school as a secretary and stenographer, and she was working at a Barclays Bank branch in central London when she met Simon. She had no special career goal except possibly being a secretary in a fashion house. Friends described her as reserved, but not at all a loner. She was, one said, "perfectly sociable, often with her friends at parties or in pubs, but typically sitting in a corner, never in the limelight." They may not have said anything more than hello that first night, Simon remembers, but they spent time together the next night when she and a few other Brentwood folk fans went with him to the Troubadour club in central London, where he sang three songs.

Lynne McCausland said Paul and Kathy were soon seeing so much of each other that everyone around the club considered them a couple. "We were all excited because everyone liked them both," she said. "Kathy was lovely, very gentle, very shy and quiet. Paul also had his quiet and shy side, so they fit each other perfectly."

Simon got deeper into the folk scene, playing at more and more clubs, where he normally earned between $10 to $15 a night, he noted in a logbook he kept that year. To save money, he frequently slept at the club or on the club owner's couch. Of near-equal interest for him was the chance to watch some of the outstanding young British folk guitarists, including Bert Jansch, John Renbourn, and Davy Graham. During the 1960s, Simon was so into guitar playing that he wanted nothing more than to be able to play fast like some of the guitar heroes. "Even more than being tall, I wanted to be able to play fast," he said, "and I probably could have if I had spent enough time practicing. That's what people who do play fast did when they were kids. They spent hours playing, copying other guitarists and memorizing their parts, but, then again, if I had done that, I probably would have been a guitarist instead of a writer. It's the same with Lennon and Dylan: they play well, but it's a kind of rhythm guitar. The only person I know who is an extraordinary musician and a major songwriter is Stevie Wonder."

In England, he could see his playing wasn't up to the standard of Bert or John, which made him compensate by coming up with interesting words for his songs, and that's what helped him attract attention in the clubs there: his words.

Still, Simon was especially eager to meet Martin Carthy, a virtuoso player who was part of a massive wave of guitarists inspired by Lonnie Donegan, a Scottish singer and guitarist who specialized in skiffle, a lively, accessible style of music that to American ears sounded like a blend of good-time folk and country. His recording of "Rock Island Line" became a Top 10 hit in the United States in 1956. Simon had learned about Carthy from Nat Hentoff's liner notes to *Freewheelin'*, which reported that Dylan heard Carthy perform a traditional song called "Lord Franklin" in London and that the song's melody line "found a new, adapted home" in "Bob Dylan's Dream," one of the songs on the album. Hentoff suggested that Dylan must have also heard Carthy's version of another traditional song,

"Scarborough Fair," because one of the lines from that song reappears in his "Girl from the North Country": "Remember me to one who lives there / she once was a true love of mine."

Carthy, who also helped teach Simon the fingerpicking guitar style, apparently never voiced a problem with Dylan's use of the line—he understood the recycling tradition of folk music—but he did have hard feelings when he thought Simon and Garfunkel later recorded his arrangement of "Scarborough Fair" without forwarding him royalties. This situation was resolved years later when Simon learned the royalties he had sent to Carthy's publishing company apparently hadn't been forwarded to the guitarist. He immediately authorized a new payment, which led Carthy to declare that he thought Simon acted "honorably" and to express great respect for him as a performer and writer.

In England, Simon continued to build an audience. Wally Whyton, a singer-guitarist best known in England as a radio-TV performer, heard about Simon even before they shared a bill one night at the Brentwood Folk Club. Still, Whyton, who was in a duo with singer-guitarist Redd Sullivan, was surprised to arrive at the sold-out club and find so much excitement during Simon's set. "It was a phenomenon that I had never seen anywhere," he recalled. "In the days of the Vipers, my group was screamed at, but we were new and frantic. We played hard, fast numbers. But here, Paul was singing 'I Am a Rock,' and girls were screaming, and old ladies were jumping up and down. It was really quite staggering."

As usual, the new songs didn't come fast, but they came steadily. Within fifteen months of finishing the Columbia album, Simon wrote nine songs that he would eventually record with Garfunkel. In July he traveled from London to Paris, accompanied by Redd Sullivan. Simon, who had bought a Sunbeam Alpine sports car, which he eventually took back to the States, spent time busking in the street, but it was as much for fun as for money. It was Bastille Week, and there were celebrations everywhere. Simon was unusually carefree and would even bend over with his guitar and sing playfully when little children came up. His good spirits made it all the more jarring when he got the news that his former Queens College classmate Andrew Goodman had been murdered in Mississippi on June 21. Goodman, who'd taken an acting class with Simon, had gone to the South as part of the Congress of Racial Equality's "Freedom Summer" campaign to help register blacks to vote. Goodman and two colleagues, James Chaney and Michael Schwerner, had spent the day looking into the burning of a Methodist church in Philadelphia, Mississippi, and they were returning to a CORE field office in Meridian when their car was stopped by a deputy sheriff who later turned them over to members of the Ku Klux Klan. They were then taken to another location, where they were shot, and their bodies were buried. The remains were found two months later after an extensive search involving the FBI and four hundred US Navy sailors.

As soon as he heard about Goodman's death, Simon went to the American Express office in Paris to get more information, but he had to go back outside because he was so shaken he was afraid he was going to throw up. In numerous interviews over the years, Simon has said he wrote "He Was My Brother" in tribute to Goodman, and the two events apparently became fixed together in his mind. Even when reporters pointed out in interviews decades later that he had recorded the song before Goodman's death, Simon stood by his story, urging them to double-check their facts. Simon did, however, change the setting of the song after the murder. In the version that appeared on *Wednesday Morning, 3 A.M.*, he warns, "This town's gonna be your buryin' place." In later versions, it became "Mississippi's gonna be your buryin' place."

Soon after Simon returned to London, Art, who was on vacation in Europe, visited him and accompanied him on some club gigs. But they didn't revive Simon and Garfunkel; Simon was still a solo act in England. On their last night in town before returning to America, Simon played a few of his songs, including "The Sound of Silence" and "Leaves That Are Green," at the Flamingo Club. Then he brought Garfunkel onstage to sing "Benedictus" with him. Afterward, Simon was approached by a woman named Judith Piepe, who said she loved his songs and wanted to introduce him to some of her contacts at BBC Radio; maybe they could give him some exposure on the powerful station. Simon thanked her but said he had to get back to New York. The Columbia album was finally coming out, and he finally enrolled in Brooklyn Law School.

Everything was in place for the October 19 album release by the time classes started in September. The name Simon and Garfunkel had been agreed upon, despite some early concerns that it was distracting—the joke was that it sounded like a law firm—or too ethnic. One Columbia staffer suggested the name Catchers in the Rye. Since then, it seems like everyone at the label has taken credit for the decision, but the person whose vote counted most was Goddard Lieberson, and he was strongly in favor of simply Simon and Garfunkel. For the album cover, the Art Department photographed the pair in the subway station at Fifth Avenue and Fifty-Third Street, which made sense for a team from New York, but it was easy to second-guess the decision to have them wear suits, when most of the Village crowd tended to dress more informally—notably Dylan in his jeans. To anyone stumbling across Simon and Garfunkel for the first time, the photo stamped them as awfully square at a time when young music fans were rebelling against convention. Interestingly, another album on the label's crowded fall release schedule was the debut by the other group that Wilson was working with: the Pilgrims. Simon and Garfunkel probably felt lucky when they saw what the Art Department did with that group. On the cover of their album, titled *Just Arrived*, the three members were posed in a small rowboat, dressed in Pilgrim outfits.

When you add the number of times that Garfunkel employed terms such as "poetic personification" or "highly intellectual" or "extremely challenging" or "perceptive psychological characterization" in his liner notes for the LP, it was easy to dismiss these newcomers as awfully pretentious. Though Simon eventually took an active role in deciding on every aspect of his albums, including the cover art, he and Garfunkel relied on the judgment of experienced hands in 1964. They were happy to be on Columbia; they weren't about to lead a rebellion—and they had no hotshot manager to run interference.

Because of its low priority, the Simon and Garfunkel album was pushed back to November on the release schedule to avoid overcrowding October. When finally released, the LP was ignored by *Billboard*, another sign of how little the Columbia promotion staff was pushing it. The trade publications worked so closely with record companies that even the most routine records received at least courtesy reviews if the label pushed hard enough. The Pilgrims' debut, which also featured "He Was My Brother," didn't fare any better. As the New Year approached, Simon and Garfunkel went their separate ways once more. Given the album's scant sales (estimates ran as low as a thousand copies), there wasn't much hope that Columbia would exercise its option with the duo. Garfunkel continued his studies at Columbia University, where he was in graduate school. After just one semester, Simon quit Brooklyn Law School and returned to England. "It wasn't a hard decision," he said. "Law school was a total waste for me. On the other hand, England was magical."

CHAPTER FIVE

Kathy Chitty and the McCauslands weren't the only ones waiting for Simon's return to England in January 1965: there was also Judith Piepe. Born Judith Maria Sternberg in Eastern Europe in 1920, Piepe (she acquired the name through marriage) came to London as a teenager and eventually became a patron saint of sorts for young musicians in the folk scene. She opened the doors of her second-floor flat on Cable Street in the East End to future stars such as Cat Stevens, Sandy Denny, and Al Stewart.

Of all those who passed through the flat, Simon, now twenty-three, became Piepe's favorite, and she served as a one-woman promotional machine, working as hard on his behalf as any manager or agent. She was so devoted to him that there were suspicions she was secretly in love with him. Years later, Simon said he was aware of Judith's feelings, but he called their relationship strictly platonic. In her midforties at the time, Piepe wouldn't take no for an answer at the BBC, all but insisting it was the network's duty to play Simon's music. She believed the songs were deeply spiritual and uplifting, and she called Simon "the songwriter of our time." Even Simon was surprised by her zeal. "She was the first person to believe in me to that extent," he said.

Buckling under Piepe's assault, and to see what all the fuss was about, BBC officials turned one of the network's studios over to Simon to record a few songs. As soon as the session was over, Piepe was on the case, asking her BBC friends when they were going to do a special on Simon's music. "Nobody there knew what to do with it," Piepe said, referring to various departments within the BBC. "The Home Service said it wasn't family entertainment. The Light Programme said it wasn't light enough, and the Third Programme said it wasn't classical enough."

The BBC team finally responded with a spot for Simon's songs on a five-minute daily religious show called *Five to Ten*, which was broadcast on the Light Programme network. As it turned out, the slot was better than it sounded because it was in between two massively popular shows, one of which, *Housewives' Choice*, had about twenty million listeners. The shows, each featuring one Simon song, aired on four consecutive days in March. To no one's surprise, Piepe left nothing to chance, even coming up with her own, sometimes provocative, introductions to the songs. In the second episode, devoted to "A Church Is Burning," Piepe, who had converted from Judaism to Christianity, declared, "A church that isn't worth setting on fire isn't worth calling a church." The head of religious broadcasting was horrified, Piepe said.

To the network's amazement, the response to the songs was enormous. People all over England called the BBC offices asking who this fellow Paul Simon was and where they could buy his albums, all of which prompted the BBC to air four more Simon episodes in May. Sensing an opening, Piepe talked CBS Records in London into making an album with Simon. Tom Wilson flew in from New York to sort out legal details. Reginald Warburton and Stanley West were credited as producers, but what was there to produce? Simon went into Levy's Recording Studio on New Bond Street with an acoustic guitar on Thursday, June 17, and sang into a single microphone. Unlike the Simon and Garfunkel album, these were all Simon songs—no covers and certainly no Dylan. He was back at Levy's on

June 23 and July 5 to finish recording. The whole thing cost less than $150. In between sessions, Paul and Kathy sat on a cobblestone street as photographer David Lowe took a cover shot that echoed the photo on the front of *Freewheelin'*, except that Simon, in his reserved manner, exhibited none of the Dylan swagger. They were shown in shadows. Once again, only the music mattered. In the liner notes, Simon took a shot at Dylan by dabbling in the same kind of free-form expression that Dylan had employed in the liner notes on his latest album, *Another Side of Bob Dylan*.

There had been an underlying strain between Dylan and Simon dating back at least to the night Simon and Garfunkel played Gerde's Folk City. The word around Columbia Records was that Dylan offended Simon with loud talk and laughter during Paul and Art's set, though it appears to have been a misunderstanding. Dylan was there, accompanied by Robert Shelton, the *New York Times* critic who wrote the liner notes for Dylan's first album. In his 1986 biography *No Direction Home: The Life and Music of Bob Dylan*, Shelton wrote that he and Dylan had been doing quite a bit of drinking that night and started giggling over nothing during Simon and Garfunkel's set. "We weren't laughing at the performance, but Simon was furious," Shelton wrote. Years later, Simon disagreed with the assessment. "I wasn't furious," he said. "But I was hurt. Here was someone laughing during my performance—especially someone I admired."

Yet Simon certainly seemed to be taking a shot at Dylan in a song that he recorded on the English solo album that Shelton called a "vicious burlesque" of Dylan, complete with "harmonica playing and shouts for 'Albert' [Albert Grossman, Dylan's manager]." The song, "A Simple Desultory Philippic (Or How I Was Robert McNamara'd into Submission)," was clearly a humorous jab at Dylan's sometimes scattershot rhymes and his mishmashing of cultural images. Simon even barks some of the lyrics a la Dylan, adding to the track's merriment. Years later, Simon said, not totally convincingly, that he was mostly channeling Lenny Bruce. "I was having fun," he said. "I thought it would be funny to use those unusual words, *desultory* and *philippic*, in a song title, and I also wanted to sneak in some Lenny Bruce, who was my favorite comedian. That line, 'How I was Robert McNamara'd into submission,' is pure Lenny."

In additional liner notes for the album, titled *The Paul Simon Song Book*, Piepe raved about each of Simon's songs, which ranged from two that had appeared on *Wednesday Morning, 3 A.M.* ("He Was My Brother" and "The Sound of Silence") to tunes as new as "I Am a Rock" and "Kathy's Song," both of which Simon had written in New York between visits to England. "I Am a Rock" came during a period of depression when he missed Kathy and was discouraged by his stalled career in America. "Kathy's Song," by contrast, was one of his most graceful and open numbers yet, showing Simon at his most vulnerable with lines such as "The only truth I know is you." Kathy first heard it on a tape Simon made of the song in New York. Garfunkel would refer to "Kathy's Song" decades later as his favorite Paul Simon composition. When the solo album and a single ("I Am a Rock") were released in England that summer, neither sold much, which is surprising given all the response to the BBC show. The joke was that maybe Piepe made all those calls to the station herself. On the positive side, the recordings helped build Simon's reputation among folk club operators. Unlike most of the performers bidding for time on the club scene, he actually had an album in stores. After the disappointment of the Columbia album, Simon felt invigorated again.

He enjoyed being back in the studio, and he volunteered to produce an album for Jackson C. Frank, another young American living at Piepe's that summer. Frank was a quiet, sensitive young man from upstate New York who began playing music to lift his spirits while hospitalized in 1954 at age eleven following a furnace explosion at his school that killed fifteen of his classmates and caused burns over 50 percent of his body. With money from a $100,000-plus insurance check he received at twenty-one, Frank headed to England to pursue a career in music. Simon went into Levy's Studio with Frank and helped him cut ten songs, highlighted by a melancholy standout, "Blues Run the Game." The album did not catch on commercially, but the song later found a life of its own and was recorded by various artists, including Simon and Garfunkel. Frank never reached beyond cult status, and his troubled life ended when he died of a heart attack in 1999.

Around the time of the Frank album, Al Stewart, another young singer-songwriter whose own lengthy career would be highlighted in 1976 by the international hit "Year of the Cat," recalled singing "The Sound of Silence" with Simon and Garfunkel one day at Trafalgar Square, one of London's most celebrated public squares. "Paul got out his guitar and wanted to hear what the song would sound like with three-part harmony, so I joined in," he said. "It was Simon, Garfunkel, and Stewart, kinda like an early version of Crosby, Stills, and Nash. Then a policeman came along and told us we had to stop. But Paul wouldn't budge. He told the policeman, 'I'm not doing this for money. It's a free country. I'm just singing. I'm not going to move.' " The standoff lasted several minutes. Garfunkel was bemused by the situation. Finally, Stewart warned Simon that the policeman, getting increasingly angry, was threatening to break his guitar—or maybe, Stewart recalled, break Simon's head—and the message got through.

Meanwhile, out of the blue, the question of Simon and Garfunkel's music was reopened in America. A Columbia Records promotion man notified the head office that a powerhouse 50,000-watt radio station in Boston was playing "The Sound of Silence." Dick Summer was the late-night disc jockey on Boston's WBZ, whose signal was heard in thirty-eight states and parts of Canada, and whose DJs had the freedom to play whatever they wanted. Summer used that freedom to play "Silence." As an English major, he loved the line 'the words of the prophets are written on the subway walls." Soon after he started playing it, college students in the Boston area began requesting that he play it again and again. When other DJs at the station picked up on the song, WBZ became a daily advertisement for "The Sound of Silence." The airplay alone, however, wasn't enough for the Columbia home office to give it a new promotional push. Just because a DJ in one city jumped on a particular record didn't mean that enthusiasm would spread. The record needed a champion at the label to get renewed attention. It soon found one.

While Simon was still in England, Dylan shocked Columbia executives when he told them in late June that he didn't want to work with producer Tom Wilson any longer. Some speculated that it was Dylan's manager,

Albert Grossman, who wanted a producer with a history of hit singles. Others suspected the mercurial Dylan had tired of Wilson and made the decision himself. His ego bruised by Columbia's failure to back him up, Wilson began making plans to leave the label, and he eventually moved to Verve/MGM Records, where he made such adventurous signings as the Mothers of Invention and the Velvet Underground. Before leaving Columbia, though, he wanted to show the company what they were losing. He got an idea during the Columbia Records annual convention, which was held in mid-July in Miami.

At one of the convention parties, Mort Lewis, who managed the folk act the Brothers Four, was sitting in the bar with Wilson when a promotion man told Wilson that a station in Cocoa Beach was getting a ton of requests to play "The Sound of Silence," likely from vacationing college students from New England who had heard the song on Dick Summer's program. "It was like a light went off in his head," Lewis said years later. Wilson wanted to release the track as a single, but with a new arrangement. He loved the twelve-string electric guitar sound on the Byrds' version of Bob Dylan's "Mr. Tambourine Man," which had gone to no. 1 nationally just two weeks earlier. Maybe, he thought, he could add a touch of that newly dubbed "folk-rock" jingle-jangle to the acoustic version of "The Sound of Silence."

It was a crucial moment for Simon and Garfunkel—and the irony is they had nothing to do with it. If Wilson had simply walked away from Columbia in a huff, there is no reason to suspect that anyone else at the label would have made a second version of "The Sound of Silence." Simon and Garfunkel were considered losers. At best, the sales staff might have released the original album track as a single. Without consulting the duo, Wilson went into Columbia's studio A on the afternoon of July 22 with four session musicians, guitarists Al Gorgoni and Vinnie Bell plus bass player Joe Mack and drummer Buddy Saltzman. Tossing out the idea of a twelve-string electric guitar, Wilson went with two electric six-strings, but engineer Halee blended the licks in the final mix in a way that caused them to sound like they came from a twelve-string guitar.

Gorgoni, for one, wasn't pleased with the results. "I liked the original better," he said. "To me, the tempo aspect of the new version was incon-sistent." Simon and Garfunkel, interestingly, were also not fans of the new rendition. "It wasn't my arrangement on the single," Simon said. "To me, it was no different from what the Byrds were doing. It was made to be folk rock, which was a kind of faux genre. It took me years to find my own arrangement, but then it did become one of my favorites." When Wilson stressed that the new version could be a hit, however, the duo went along.

What the producer didn't tell them was that he didn't like the sound on the new single, either. When he got home on the night of the session, he found technical problems in the record. It was hissy. Wilson rushed to the studio the next day to fix it, but he was too late; it was already at the pressing plant. His heart sank—until he heard the record on the radio. For some reason, there was no hiss. It sounded great. The single was shipped to DJs and stores in late September, but the Columbia promotion staff still wasn't fully behind it. Once again, the proof was in the pages of *Billboard* magazine, which ignored the single, just as it had the album. The timing of the record, however, was perfect. Dylan's electrified "Like a Rolling Stone" and Barry McGuire's interpretation of P. F. Sloan's Dylanesque protest song "Eve of Destruction" had been radio blockbusters that fall.

Simon was on the road fairly constantly in England, playing more than sixty dates in four months. In some ways, he was a student again. Just as he had learned the skills of record making during the demo days and had sharpened his intellect at Queens College, he was learning about perform-ing and adjusting to the life of a professional musician. At a folk gather-ing around this time, Simon offered this playful sketch of himself for the event program: "I am Paul Simon. I'm sure of that. It is probably the only thing I am sure of. I was born in Newark, New Jersey, in 1941 and a piece of less relevant information I can't conceive. I started writing at the age of nineteen—perhaps I should say my birthday was 1960. There's noth-ing I did before that year that means a hell of a lot. I write not so much as a means of communicating my thoughts to others, but rather because I might die of internal poisoning if I didn't release the words that spawn in my brain. Oh, man, that does sound dramatic. I'm trying to avoid that. I'm really not in the intense-young-man bag. That's not where I am at all. I just find it easier to sing what I feel than to verbalize it. In recent months, I'm told that several of my songs have been sung at a few of the Folk Clubs. It makes me feel good to know that others [feel about] them in some way, the same as I, and I am grateful. What can I say? Thanks." Looking back at the sketch years later, Simon shook his head at some of the lines. "I really wrote that?" he asked.

Mostly, Simon did one-nighters throughout England as well as occasional dates in Paris and Scandinavia. While the Brentwood club remained a special place for him, Les Cousins became a favorite London hangout. Located in Soho, an entertainment center that included numerous music publishers and clubs, Les Cousins opened in early 1965 and quickly became known for its top folk attractions, especially Jansch, Renbourn, and Carthy. Simon performed there a few times, developing enough of a following to be listed in the honor roll of Cousins artists—along with Joan Baez, Donovan, and others—that ran regularly in the club's ads in music publications.

According to most who knew him in England, Simon was viewed warmly, not simply for his manner but also his openheartedness. "Paul was a very lovable person," Joan Bata said. "He's an extraordinarily sweet-natured man. You never heard Paul be cruel about people. Whatever religion you were, Paul would have said, 'Well, try and be a good one.' "

Bata, a friend of Piepe's who was staying at her flat in London, recalled fondly how Simon often came in at four in the morning with a bag of doughnuts from an all-night bakery, sharing them with everyone while he unwound from the adrenaline after a performance. But not everyone was enamored of him.

In his 2000 biography of Bert Jansch, *Dazzling Stranger*, Colin Harper quotes Pete Frame, who was put off by Simon's attitude, especially by what he felt was an oversized ambition. Frame, the music journalist who made Rock Family Tree charts that traced the career paths of musicians and bands, described Simon as "an arrogant, cocky, privileged little kid."

But Frame didn't deny Simon's talent. "He was an amazing songwriter," he said. Looking back on that period, Simon didn't recall any resentment from the musicians. He found them "tremendously supportive. It was like a family—much different from what I had encountered in the Village."

Part of the problem in London might have been cultural. Unlike the English tendency to be unduly polite in conversation, Simon was forthright. The polarized view of Simon wasn't limited to musicians. "Paul managed to rub some people the wrong way," said one veteran of the British club scene. "He was paradoxical: charming, courteous, shy, arrogant, self-assured, ruthlessly determined. He was eager to learn, to soak things up, open to experiences, yet very opinionated and driven. If you expressed an opinion he disagreed with or information that would be of no use to him, he'd shut down—the eyelids would come down. This led some people to think he was on a mission on behalf of himself, which, of course, he was—you don't get to where he arrived without a powerful and motivated ego ticking away underneath it all. Yet there was always the other, charming side to him. The trouble is that—in the end, you can't help liking him—and that's the very reason some people didn't like him."

Again, some saw in Simon the influence of his father. George Schulman, Simon's cousin, said the description of Paul's attention span—the way he would sometimes walk away in midsentence if he didn't find the conversation interesting—sounded just like Paul's father. "Lou would talk to you for eight hundred hours if it was something that was intellectually stimulating, but he wouldn't devote thirty seconds to small talk," Schulman said. "You'd see him talking to someone, and all of a sudden he was on the other side of the room. And he didn't let anyone push him around. If he didn't like something, he'd say so."

Those words would foreshadow complaints of arrogance or aloofness sometimes made about Simon, especially during the early years of his career, all of which puzzled Simon. "Even Edie [Brickell, his future wife] said to me when we first started going out, 'I heard you weren't so nice.' But I didn't try to pick fights with people. I wasn't impolite. I was having a good time. Maybe people thought I was aloof because I was shy or I was busy working on my music. There are lots of people who don't give a damn if you don't like them, but that's not me. I would have cared if I knew someone didn't like me."

In between engagements, Simon found time to do a few radio or TV appearances, most notably England's popular pop-rock showcase *Ready Steady Go!* The program, which aired live every Friday night, featured the biggest names in pop and rock, from the Beatles to Otis Redding. Simon was delighted to be on such a major stage, though the appearance was a fluke. The only reason a relatively unknown folk musician landed on the July 23 episode was that he had been booked for a much less prestigious folk program, *Heartsong*, but that series was cancelled before his date. Because Simon had already been paid, the production company, which handled both shows, switched him to *Ready Steady Go!* Befitting his status, Simon, who was accompanied to the TV taping by Kathy Chitty and Lynne McCausland, was given the cold shoulder on the set. "When Simon showed up at rehearsal that afternoon, we were sort of snotty toward him because we didn't really want him on the show," director Michael Lindsay-Hogg said years later. "He was folk. He wasn't rock. He didn't fit. Besides, we didn't have time for him. We were overbooked."

Because Simon was a last-minute addition to an already crowded show, Lindsay-Hogg, whose imaginative work on the program served as a blueprint for future music videos, told him he needed to drop a verse from his only number, "I Am a Rock." When the director passed by the makeup area a few minutes later, he found Simon sitting in a chair, leaning on a table, his head in his arms. He seemed beaten down. "You don't understand," Simon told him. " 'I Am a Rock' is a story, and if you cut a verse out of it, you've ruined the story." Lindsay-Hogg, who personally liked the song, apologized, but the verse had to be cut. Simon again felt the sting of being rejected for nothing to do with his talent. First, he was kicked out of the Mystics rock band because of his height, and then he was snubbed in Greenwich Village because he was from unhip Queens, and now he was tossed aside because he was singing folk music, not rock. When asked years later by a British pop journalist to name his worst experience in England, Simon wasted no time in citing *Ready Steady Go!*

Years later, Lindsay-Hogg said he wasn't surprised by Simon's success. "If it hadn't been for rock 'n' roll, which is in his soul, you maybe could see him as a lecturer at a university. And a poet, like MacLeish or Auden. He's driven and intelligent and wishes to be in control of his work as much as possible."

Paul and Kathy saw each other often when he played in and around London. She would take the train to town to visit him at Piepe's flat, where Joan Bata saw an early danger sign in their relationship. "Kathy used to get a bit sulky because she felt that Paul was neglecting her," she said. "He was neglecting her in a way that wasn't deliberately being hurtful. It was just that his mind was totally occupied with something else." That something else, of course, was his music. Paul was almost always working on a song, his guitar either in his lap or by his side. It was, one observer said, almost as if the guitar was part of him.

Quincy Jones, the arranger-producer who may have worked with more acclaimed artists than anyone else in pop music, believes this obsession is another key element in building artistry. "You can have talent, and you can have standards, but you've also got to be obsessive because artistry is no casual matter," he said. "The music has to become your lifeblood so that you don't let anything or anyone stop you from making the best music you can. From the outside, it may look selfish, and it is to a degree. People around them may sometimes feel left out or even ignored, but the artist can't let go. That's the obsession."

Still, there was no question Paul was in love with Kathy, which was why he missed her so deeply during a nine-date tour late that summer in the Liverpool-Manchester area. It was the trip that inspired his second great song, "Homeward Bound." Later, in interviews, Simon would often say the song grew out of the northern England tour, even specifying on occasion the time he sat in a railway station in Widnes, an industrial town southeast of Liverpool. As that story spread, fans headed to Widnes. Welcoming any positive attention—the town was long the butt of jokes because of an awful smell caused by fumes from local chemical plants—townsfolk took pride in and placed a plaque outside the train station to mark the spot where they believed Simon wrote the song. Even though Simon subsequently tried to clarify the situation by saying he thinks he only got the inspiration for "Homeward Bound" in Widnes, the story was hard to kill. After the first two plaques were stolen, a third was set up inside the station, where someone could keep an eye on it.

Geoff Speed ran the Windsor folk club in Widnes, where, on September 13, 1965, Simon sang for maybe an hour—mostly his own songs—which was unusual on the folk club circuit because most performers sang old English ballads. Speed's wife, Pam, was struck by something else. Most performers closed their eyes when they sang, but Simon looked right at the audience. "He made you feel like he was singing just to you," she said. "He was so sincere. Right away, I thought, 'He's got it.' " What surprised the Speeds even more was the attendance. The club's capacity was listed at 150, but more than 200 people somehow squeezed in that night. The Speeds later realized that many of the fans had seen Simon at one of his earlier shows in the area and came to Widnes to see him again.

The final word on "Homeward Bound" belongs to Speed because he was the one who drove Simon to the Widnes train station the day he was supposed to have written the song. "It has always been a sweet story, but there's no way he could have written the song at the station," Speed said. "The thing I remember most about that morning was that we got to the station just as the train pulled in, and Paul had to run to make it. He didn't have time to sit down, much less write a song."

Simon was back in London in plenty of time to celebrate his twenty-fourth birthday and work on "Homeward Bound" while he hoped for word from New York about the "Silence" single—on the unlikely chance it actually caught on. Al Stewart had a room next to Simon's at Piepe's, and he could hear Simon working on his songs through the thin walls. Stewart, four years younger than Simon, was so impressed that he started following Paul around to clubs, even carrying his guitar on occasion, trying to pick up some pointers. "One day I heard Paul searching for the right word," Stewart said. "He'd play 'Sitting in a railway station, got a ticket for my . . .' And then after a long pause, I'd hear, 'destination.' After a while, he came out to the communal area and played it for whoever was around."

I'm sitting in the railway station
Got a ticket for my destination
On a tour of one-night stands
My suitcase and guitar in hand
And every stop is neatly planned
For a poet and a one-man band

Homeward bound
I wish I was
Homeward bound
Home, where my thought's escaping
Home, where my music's playing
Home, where my love lies waiting
Silently for me.

Every day's an endless stream
Of cigarettes and magazines
And each town looks the same to me
The movies and the factories
And every stranger's face I see
Reminds me that I long to be

Homeward bound
I wish I was
Homeward bound
Home, where my thought's escaping
Home, where my music's playing
Home, where my love lies waiting
Silently for me

Tonight I'll sing my songs again
I'll play the game and pretend
But all my words come back to me
In shades of mediocrity
Like emptiness in harmony
I need someone to comfort me

Homeward bound
I wish I was
Homeward bound
Home, where my thought's escaping
Home, where my music's playing
Home, where my love lies waiting
Silently for me
Silently for me

Once again, Simon was longing for comfort.

In New York, Columbia Records's promotion staff was getting encouraging reports from the field about DJ reaction to the reworked "The Sound of Silence." The first breakthrough was when the single entered the Boston airplay chart at no. 21, just eight spots behind the week's hottest new single, the Supremes' "I Hear a Symphony." Still, everyone at Columbia knew the real test was whether "The Sound of Silence" would pop up on charts outside of Boston. As they waited in early November, Simon left London on what would be his last significant tour of 1965: a series of dates in the Netherlands, Denmark, and France. The last he had heard from New York—likely a call or letter from Garfunkel or Belle—was that the single was bubbling under the Hot 100 at no. 111 in *Billboard*. The next two or three weeks would be critical.

In Denmark, Simon took a ferry from Aarhus to Copenhagen the week of November 21 and went straight to his publisher's office to see where "The Sound of Silence" had gone on the latest US chart. As he picked up the new issue of *Cash Box*, a rival to *Billboard*, he was understandably anxious. If "The Sound of Silence" hadn't leaped into the Top 100, it most likely never would. Trying to prolong the suspense, he looked at the bottom of the chart to see what no. 100 was, then slowly looked higher on the list, 95, 90, 85, 80, and his heart began to sink. Just when he was about to give up, he saw it—gloriously!—at 58.

"At that moment," Simon said, "I knew my life was going to change forever."

When he returned to London, Garfunkel was calling from New York. Columbia Records wanted Paul to come home immediately. Rather than simply replace the old version of "The Sound of Silence" on the *Wednesday Morning, 3 A.M.* album, the label brass wanted to record a new album, titled *Sounds of Silence*, and include the new version. That way they could also replace the cover songs with some of the new Simon tunes. A secondary benefit was that the new cover photo would also take them out of their suits.

Suddenly, everything Simon always wanted was waiting in the States. Yet he was torn. He went to see the McCauslands. "He was excited about what was happening in America, but part of him didn't want to leave England; didn't want to leave Kathy," Lynne McCausland said. "He spent a long time talking to my mother about what he should do." This crisis of doubt was puzzling, given his usually strong convictions. To Bobby Susser, however, the conflict wasn't surprising. "Paul is extremely deliberate," he said. "He looks at everything from every angle. He might know deep inside what he wants to do, but he wants to make sure he's not missing something. It's the same in his music. If there are ten options in the studio, he wants to try them all." Ultimately, there was no way Simon was going to pass up the opportunity, but he didn't necessarily think the move would be permanent. He told Kathy he'd go to New York, maybe make some money (he actually mentioned $25,000), and then return to England. With that in mind, on Wednesday, December 8, Simon stepped onto an Air India flight home.

CHAPTER SIX

"The Sound of Silence" was no. 26 in *Billboard* when Simon stepped off the plane in New York, and the Columbia staff had advance word that it would jump another ten places when the new chart came out over the weekend. With that kind of momentum, it was almost certain to go to no. 1. After celebrating with his family, Simon headed the next morning to Columbia's offices, where he and Garfunkel were put on an assembly line. They may have had one of the hottest singles in the country, but the old-timers at the label (and there were lots of old-timers at the label) had seen hit makers come and go. To them, the real stars were mainstream figures like Barbra Streisand, Andy Williams, and Johnny Mathis, all of whom you could count on year after year. Rock 'n' roll and its offspring folk rock were still viewed with suspicion. Even though Dylan had delivered two straight Top 10 albums in 1965, he was still not seen as someone in the Columbia tradition. When Clive Davis took over as head of the label two years later, the old guard was so entrenched that he had to use "dynamite," he often said, to break it up. Roy Halee said he didn't think the people at the label took Simon and Garfunkel seriously: "They had no idea what we were doing in the studio."

That doesn't mean that Columbia didn't recognize there was quick money to be made. After the obligatory pats on the back, the staff gave the duo its marching orders: report to studio A on Monday and knock out the album as fast as possible. The only thing that mattered was that the LPs be in the bins in six weeks. If they didn't have their own songs, they could fill the album with more covers. The label figured it had already lost a couple hundred thousand dollars by not having the album in stores for the start of the lucrative holiday season.

Thankfully, Simon had songs from the British album to draw from, and he used five of them on the new collection, needing only to change the arrangements to fit what was now two voices. In addition, he and Garfunkel recorded two songs Simon had written since *Song Book*, plus "Angi," a Davy Graham instrumental (sometimes spelled "Anji") that Simon learned in England. They also had two tracks that had been recorded earlier, "Somewhere They Can't Find Me," a reworking of "Wednesday Morning, 3 A.M.," and the trippy, minor "We've Got a Groovy Thing Goin'. "

As directed, Simon and Garfunkel went into studio A at seven o'clock on the night of December 13 for their first session with their new staff producer, Bob Johnston, who had also taken over production of Dylan's recordings. A Texan who had recorded a few forgettable rockabilly tunes as an artist after serving in the US Navy, Johnston was an outgoing man with a strong maverick streak. Besides producing *Highway 61 Revisited*, he was already at work on Dylan's landmark *Blonde on Blonde* and later helmed Johnny Cash's signature live "prison" albums, *At Folsom Prison* and *At San Quentin*. But he was known more as an artist's champion than an idea man. While both traits can be valuable, Simon preferred the latter. Simon wanted to be challenged—as long as he respected the challenger.

"It was a terrible disappointment not to have Wilson, who made our first hit," Simon said. "We owe him a lot." Johnston made one valuable contribution by showing Simon the importance of getting great rather than simply adequate studio musicians, even if you had to look beyond

Columbia's regular pool of session players. For the recording dates, which were held in New York, Nashville, and Hollywood, Johnston brought in stellar players such as guitarist Fred Carter Jr., guitarist-bassist Joe South, and harmonica player Charley McCoy from Nashville, as well as guitarist Glen Campbell (before his own recording career took off) and drummer Hal Blaine from Hollywood.

Progress on the first evening session was slow, leaving Johnston with only two recordings, "Angi" and "Leaves That Are Green," a reflection on the uncertainties of life, from *Song Book*. Not jelling with Johnston, Simon and Garfunkel were pleased that Halee was working with them again, and they directed many of their concerns to him. Things were more productive the following night when they recorded all or parts of "Homeward Bound," "Richard Cory," and "I Am a Rock." The latter was brightened considerably in the studio, ending up with more of the folk-rock coloring of the Byrds than the more tentative rendition on *Song Book*. Columbia files show that Simon and Garfunkel also took a stab at Jackson C. Frank's "Blues Run the Game," but it's not clear whether they finished it. In the December 21 and 22 sessions in Hollywood, the pair rounded out the album with "Kathy's Song," "April Come She Will," "A Most Peculiar Man," and "Blessed." The latter was another of Paul's songs from England, one he wrote after stepping inside Soho's St. Anne's Church during a downpour and listening to a bland sermon.

Between those sessions, the duo had plenty to do, including finding a big-time manager, taking a cover photo for the album, and doing a few live shows. Guy Webster, son of Oscar-winning songwriter Paul Francis Webster and a prized young rock photographer in Los Angeles, was hired to take the cover shot, and he chose the outdoors—just the opposite of the subway station of the debut album. He escorted them to a rustic area near the Beverly Hills Hotel, not far, incidentally, from where he had recently taken the cover photo for the US edition of the Rolling Stones' *Big Hits (High Tide and Green Grass)* album. Asked later about the difference between working with these two young musical forces, Webster replied, "Paul and Art weren't stoned."

Not everything that December went as smoothly. Simon and Garfunkel were frustrated when William Morris placed them on generic, multi-act pop-rock shows, which meant they would be limited to two numbers on bills featuring diverse hit makers of the day such as the Four Seasons, the Yardbirds, Lou Christie, and Smokey Robinson and the Miracles. That kind of slot wasn't uncommon for a new act, but Simon, especially, wanted more time onstage and a setting tailored to their style. He felt so strongly about it, Halee recalled, that he even talked about giving up live shows and just making records—something the Beatles would actually do in August of 1966. It was indicative of Simon's growing resistance to compromise.

Hoping to turn things around, Simon asked Goddard Lieberson in late December to recommend an experienced manager. The Columbia president gave Simon two names: Albert Grossman and Mort Lewis. Knowing Grossman already had his hands full with Dylan, Simon asked Lieberson, "What was the second name again?" Lieberson recommended Lewis highly, explaining that he was an industry favorite who had worked with jazz stars Stan Kenton and Dave Brubeck before signing the Brothers Four, who had scored a Top 10 single in 1960 with the folk song "Greenfields." Though the group never repeated that success, Lewis used his connections in college booking offices and his negotiating skills to keep the Brothers Four supplied with a steady flow of campus and TV appearances. Beyond his talents as a manager, Lewis, who was forty-two at the time, was fun to be around: he had a comic's instincts and could weave wonderful yarns. As it turned out, Lewis had been following the progress of "The Sound of Silence" ever since being with Wilson in Miami. "I wasn't accustomed to hearing something so thought provoking," Lewis said. "My only concern initially was that Paul's words might be over people's heads, so I was pleased to see the record going up the charts. I asked Paul and Artie to come over to the apartment that evening."

If Lieberson's endorsement wasn't enough to make Simon and Garfunkel want to work with Lewis, the duo was on board as soon as they saw an autographed copy of the new Lenny Bruce album next to the phonograph player in Lewis's apartment. Mort actually knew one of their heroes! After a half hour of hearing Bruce stories and meeting Lewis's wife, Peggy, Simon turned to the business at hand. "We need help," he said. Most of all, he said, they needed someone to help them get good concert bookings. As the pair kept talking, Lewis also sensed they were overwhelmed with all the decisions they were suddenly being asked to make. Lewis liked them. "There was a certain humbleness about both of them," he said. "They were very up front about needing help." Mort took them to dinner at a deli across the street, and he sketched out a contract on a paper napkin. It was a standard deal for a beginning act: Lewis would receive 15 percent of revenue from live shows and 10 percent of the money from recordings.

Peggy Lewis, whose maiden name was Harper, grew up in a poor family at the foot of Tennessee's Smoky Mountains, about ten miles from the tiny town of Newport. She may well have stayed there, like so many young people in Appalachia, except that a high school home economics teacher encouraged her to apply to Berea College, a private college just south of Lexington, Kentucky, that offered free tuition to qualified students. Peggy, who was deeply attractive, had just enough daring and aspiration to follow up and was accepted. Rather than return to Newport each summer, Peggy, now hungry for more of the outside world, took summer jobs in places as far away as what was then called Mount McKinley National Park in Alaska. During the summer before her senior year, she went to Atlantic City, New Jersey, where she happened to meet John Paine of the Brothers Four, who gave her a phone number in case she ever got to New York City.

Tired of college, Peggy and a girlfriend headed to New York City that fall and called the number, which belonged to the group's manager, Lewis. He took the girls under his wing. "Mort was kind of a father figure," Peggy said later. "He was fifteen years older, and he had a big heart. He wasn't going to let us starve to death. He got us a place to stay and helped us get a job." The relationship deepened in time, and the couple was married on November 15, 1961. They both later acknowledged they weren't compatible. Lewis was always looking forward to going out to clubs or having friends over for the evening, while Peggy was more quiet and retiring. She preferred nothing better than a simple night at home. Her personality was much closer to Paul's, and the two enjoyed talking on those nights when he'd stop by the apartment to see Lewis.

Eventually millions of Simon fans would see his 1983 song "Train in the Distance" as an admission that Simon had stolen his manager's wife:

She was as beautiful as southern skies the night he met her
She was married to someone
He was doggedly determined that he would get her
He was old, he was young

Asked later about the narrative, Simon replied, "Songs are not memoirs. You've always got to be careful when you try to read lyrics as a series of facts. In a single song, I'll often mix facts and imagination. Some lines are absolutely true, but others can come from anywhere, including what you've seen or even just heard. As a songwriter, you are looking for truthful emotions, but that's not always the same as telling what actually happened to you. That's why you can be unhappy and write a happy song or be in a happy state and write a sad song." In fact, "Train in the Distance" was part memoir and part imagination. Memoir: Peggy was beautiful, from the South, and married to someone else. In addition, Simon was young, Lewis was older. Imagination: the suggestion that Simon took Peggy away from his manager. In fact, their relationship didn't become serious until after the couple's divorce in 1967.

Before signing, Simon, who had learned the importance of lawyers from his father and his years of demo work, contacted Harold Orenstein, one of the city's premier music attorneys, to look over the proposed contract. When he and Garfunkel met with Lewis in Orenstein's office, everything went well. However, Lewis thought they were finished when Orenstein, very casually, turned to him and asked how much money he thought the duo would be making in six months. "I thought it was just small talk, but I wanted to give him a reasonable answer, so I thought about the Brothers Four," Lewis said. "They usually did a couple of shows a week and got paid about three thousand dollars a show. Because I thought Simon and

Garfunkel were going to be a much bigger act, I told Harold, 'They'll be making ten thousand dollars a week in no time.' "

Noticing that Simon was frowning, Orenstein asked Lewis to step out of the room briefly. The manager was confused. Was Simon expecting more money? After a couple of minutes, Lewis returned to hear Orenstein declare that everything was fine with the terms, but he wanted to put in one small clause in the pact: if Simon and Garfunkel weren't making $10,000 a week within six months, they wanted the right to terminate the contract. Lewis was surprised by the request, but he felt his estimate was a reasonable one, and he wanted to work with these guys. "No problem," he said.

Despite the excitement, Paul and Art found it hard to relate to their sudden success. Their world didn't seem all that different. Both were still living at home, riding the subway into Manhattan, and dreaming about getting beautiful girlfriends. Simon remembers a night in January 1966 when he and Garfunkel were listening to the radio in a parked car on 141st Street in Queens. He recalled, "The disc jockey introduced 'The Sound of Silence' as the number one record in America, and Artie looked at me and said, 'Wow. I bet those guys are having a great time.' " In truth, Simon said, "We didn't know what to do. It hadn't really hit us yet. We were trying to adjust to everything." To Bobby Susser, the reaction was an example of how Simon would always look at things from every side. "It was part of his makeup," Bobby said. "He'd go, 'Our record is number one, so I should be happy, but what if it wasn't number one? Should I be unhappy? What does it mean? It's the same record. I'm the same guy.' "

Mort Lewis's first step after the meeting was to phone Nat Lefkowitz, veteran head of the East Coast office of the William Morris talent agency, to ask why the company wasn't getting Simon and Garfunkel any bookings. He wasn't pleased by Lefkowitz's stock answer: "Just because an act is on the charts doesn't mean the world is going to pay to see them live." Lewis then went on the offensive. He told Lefkowitz he was going to try booking them himself—and insisted that William Morris waive its commission on any dates he secured. Lefkowitz agreed.

Back in his office, Lewis began thumbing through his Rolodex. He has gotten high praise over the years for recognizing that colleges, rather than theaters or clubs, were the ideal venue for Simon and Garfunkel, and that's partially true. The main reason he started calling college reps, however, was that the circuit was his specialty. It's where he had been booking acts since his days with Kenton and Brubeck. "Hi, this is Mort Lewis, remember me?" he'd say. "I've got a new act, Simon and Garfunkel. They have a new record out." That was as far as he got most of the time. Despite the success of the single, the duo still wasn't well known among college talent buyers. Plus, the schools usually booked months in advance, so they had no immediate openings.

Lewis kept dialing, probably fifty calls in all, before he got a nibble. The rep at Brown University in Providence, Rhode Island, knew the record, and the college had an opening on a Friday night at the end of January. Lewis would have accepted $1,000 for a date, but he negotiated his way up to $2,500. The manager then secured contracts for shows that same weekend, for $2,000 each, at Rensselaer Polytechnic Institute in Troy, New York, and Oneonta State Teachers College, near Utica, New York. At the RPI performance, Simon and Garfunkel would be the opening act, but they would have a full forty-five-minute set.

Then things got even better. When the headliner at RPI didn't show, college officials asked Lewis if his act, which had gone over great with the students, would fill in for the missing musicians. Lewis said a second show would be fine, but only if his act got paid the $4,000 that the top act would have received—in addition to the $2,000 the guys had already earned. The result was that Simon and Garfunkel were paid $10,500 for their first weekend of shows with Lewis.

"After the concert, I drove Paul and Artie back to the city in my Lincoln," Lewis said. "During the ride, Paul, who is sitting next to me up front, tells me, 'Remember when we asked you to leave the room in Harold's office? It was because you said we'd be making ten thousand dollars in no time. I was so disappointed when I heard that because, up to that moment, I thought you were a terrific guy. But after you said we'd make that much,

I decided you were a bullshitter. I wanted a way out in case you were. But you were right. I can't believe it.' "

Soon Lewis's contacts across the country were eager for Simon and Garfunkel. The early fees ran from a minimum of $1,000 to $4,500 a night, and Lewis still felt no obligation to share the money with William Morris. He passed along the commission savings to the guys. Having lived almost a decade with the "one-hit wonder" tag, Simon and Garfunkel were especially delighted when Columbia promised them that "Homeward Bound" and "I Am a Rock" would also be Top 10 singles. The label had tested both records with top DJs around the country, and the response was phenomenal.

"The thing that struck me was how relieved Paul was," Lewis said. "Because he wrote the songs, he always felt responsible for what happened to the records. He didn't see it so much as people responding to Simon and Garfunkel as responding to the songs—and they were his songs." Simon was doubly pleased that "Homeward Bound" was generating the most interest and would be released first, because he preferred it over "I Am a Rock." Surprisingly, Columbia didn't put "Homeward Bound" on the *Sounds of Silence* album. The staff was so certain it would be a hit that they wanted to save it as a sales lure for the third Simon and Garfunkel album, which they wanted to release during the following Christmas season. It was a gamble, but the staff was convinced that the demand would be there.

Released in mid-January, less than six weeks after Simon's return home, *Sounds of Silence* began a two-and-a-half-year run on the charts, eventually certified by the Recording Industry Association of America as selling more than three million copies in the United States. There was so much excitement over the duo that enough fans bought the *Wednesday Morning, 3 A.M.* album for it to also be certified by sales of more than one million. *Billboard* was enthusiastic about "Homeward Bound," declaring the song had more commercial potential than the new singles by Barbra Streisand and the Byrds. Even the old-timers at Columbia were starting to take this duo seriously.

Few publications in the early months of 1966 devoted space to rock 'n' roll. *Rolling Stone* magazine, which would become the print voice of rock music, didn't begin publishing until the fall of 1967, and few daily newspapers had full-time rock critics until the early 1970s. The earliest substantial review Simon and Garfunkel received was in *Crawdaddy*, which would become the first US rock magazine to gain national respect. In its first issue, printed in a Brooklyn basement two weeks after *Sounds of Silence* was released, Paul Williams, its seventeen-year-old editor, hailed the collection as "easily the best American album" since Dylan's *Bringing It All Back Home.*

Williams, a freshman at Swarthmore College, near Philadelphia, lauded the duo's vocal harmony, but he directed most of the perceptive 1,200-word review to Simon's songs: "They are universal without being impersonal. Simon writes about everyone, but he writes, as one must, from what he sees and feels. And what comes out is in this album. It's not quite rock 'n' roll, nearly but never folk. So what do you call it? Call it poetry . . . call it music. And call it good." One of the five hundred mimeographed copies of *Crawdaddy* found its way into Simon's hands, and he phoned Williams to thank him.

With a few days off before he and Garfunkel would start formal touring, Simon invited Kathy to New York for a two-week visit. The trip gave them a chance to see what their life might be like together amid the demands upon him in America—far different from the mostly calm, comforting surroundings during their time together in Britain. In addition, Simon was eager to introduce Kathy, who was raised Roman Catholic, to his family. "Kathy was adorable, and she stayed at my house," Simon's mother said. During the stay, Simon said to Belle, "She's very good to me, Mom, and she's an incredibly sweet girl. Would you be unhappy if I married out of our religion?" His mom replied, "Yes, I would be unhappy if you married out of our religion. Would I stop talking to you? No."

Years later, Simon said he asked his mother more out of curiosity than any sense of seeking permission. He felt no obligation to marry within the Jewish faith. Was he seriously thinking about marriage? Yes, he said. At the end of the two weeks, however, there was no decision about the future. Kathy returned to England, and Simon prepared for his new life in rock 'n' roll.

The lure of the road was as much a wonder of rock 'n' roll as the fabled sex and, eventually, drugs. On February 19, Simon got another taste of his old Elvis fantasies when he and Garfunkel performed at the University of Massachusetts, the start of their first real touring cycle. It wasn't just the cheering of the fans at the concert he enjoyed, it was the whole experience: looking forward to the show, riding to the university in Lewis's shiny Lincoln, walking into the venue, sitting in the dressing room, feeling the anticipation out in the hall, meeting with fans after the performance, the four-hour drive home, and then getting up the next morning and doing it all over again, this time at Penn State University.

Because Garfunkel was still in graduate school and because Lewis had a fear of flying, Lewis tried to limit touring to weekends, usually at colleges within driving distance. But they had to fly to some engagements, which, along with comfortable hotels and room service, added to the glamour of the new life. When performing at, say, Florida State University or Marquette University in Milwaukee, they'd land in what was usually a new city for them, and Lewis would rent a fancy car to drive them to the gigs. "We loved it," Simon said later. "Here we were, best friends, sharing the same room. We'd stay at a Holiday Inn someplace, and you'd put a quarter in this little box, and the bed would start vibrating. Then we'd rush off to the pool. Everything was fun in those days."

Plus, as Goddard Lieberson had promised, their manager was a constant source of entertainment. "Mort was great," Simon said. "He was a big guy, six foot two or three, and friendly with everybody in the business, whether it was the record company or the venues. He taught us how to be professional, and he kept us informed about how much money we were making. We had total faith in him. He always had us laughing, but he also had a temper—but even that was funny. He'd get disgusted at us from time to time because we were always late. He'd always be at the airport gate early, and we were always late. One time he got so fed up and said, 'Aw, fuck you. I'm going home.' After that, we made it a point to get to the airport three hours early, but we got caught up getting a newspaper or having coffee once, and we missed the flight. Fortunately, there was another flight two hours later, but we missed that one, too. So we charted a plane and made it to the show just in time at a college somewhere in the Midwest."

On their first formal tour, Simon and Garfunkel headlined twenty-eighty concerts, earning them together $71,418 in performance paychecks. There was also the occasional TV show, including singing "Homeward Bound" on *Hullabaloo*, a youth-oriented pop music program on ABC. The highlight of this period was the pair's first hometown show: May 1 at Columbia University's McMillan Theater, a small (688 seats) but lovely room devoted to the arts. In the audience that night was Robert Shelton, the *New York Times* critic, who focused on Simon's songwriting in his review. "Most of the songs," he wrote, "touched on subjects ordinarily of little concern to pop singers: loss of communication, show business loneliness, illusions, suicide, a factory hand's anger and envy, subways and dignity . . . In most instances, Mr. Simon's songs are well crafted, communicative, and melodically alive. The poetry strikes responsive nerves of emotion. The performances gathered increasing forces of involvement and drama to do the material justice." Beneath the good times and cheer, Lewis noticed moments of rivalry between the two, most of which he put to insecurity. "I think they both went through periods where they envied the other's place in the team," he said. "Paul often thought the audience saw Artie as the star because he was the featured singer, and some people probably thought Artie even wrote the songs. Meanwhile, Artie knew Paul wrote the songs and thus controlled the future of the pair. I don't think he ever got over what happened with Tom & Jerry." Years later, Garfunkel confirmed that thought by saying, "I never forget, and I never forgive."

In England, Simon and Garfunkel's music was finally introduced to the charts in a big way in the spring of 1966, much to the delight of those who had believed in him so early. "Homeward Bound" reached no. 9 on the singles chart, and *Sounds* climbed to no. 12 on the album chart. In addition, two other groups turned to Simon for material. The Seekers, a folk-flavored pop group from Australia best known for its later hit recording "Georgy Girl," made the Top 15 with their rendition of a song Simon wrote but never recorded, "Someday, One Day." The association with the Seekers also led to another song, the lively but lightweight "Red Rubber Ball," which Simon cowrote with the group's guitarist Bruce Woodley. Though the Seekers recorded the song, Simon didn't think enough of the tune to tackle it. The Cyrkle, an American pop group guided by Beatles manager Brian Epstein, released it in May as a single on Columbia and ended up with a Top 10 US hit.

Around the same time, the Bachelors, a decidedly unhip pop group whose last single was "Hello, Dolly," recorded a glossy version of "The Sound of Silence" that broke into the Top 10 in England. Simon wasn't pleased. While he voiced no complaint about the Seekers' record, he told the British press that he was no fan of the Bachelors' single. The reaction revealed how Simon was becoming conscious of his reputation as a songwriter. He wasn't happy to be associated with just a hit; he wanted the cover versions to reflect the original character of the songs. But he was also unhappy about the recording because the Bachelors' success meant there was little chance Simon and Garfunkel's version of the song could be a hit in England. "What really upset me was they, in essence, stole our hit," Simon said.

Despite the accelerating success, Simon continued to feel melancholy or, at least, unsettled. While Art's place in the graduate school program at Columbia helped anchor him, Simon missed the comforts of his life in England and Queens. He had been so busy that he asked someone at Columbia Records to find an apartment for him, which turned out to be at 200 East End Avenue on the affluent Upper East Side of Manhattan. Simon felt isolated in the apartment, which was doors from Gracie Mansion, the official residence of New York City mayors. He thought about moving to the hipper Village, but he kept putting it off. There was so much else to deal with. "I didn't know what to do with myself," he said of the period. "I had never even lived in Manhattan. I'd been washed away from the friends I had before the success. The success was pushing me into money and places I wasn't prepared to deal with. I didn't know who to be friends with or where to live or where to go."

The *San Francisco Chronicle*'s Ralph J. Gleason was primarily a jazz writer, but he was widely admired within the music business for recognizing top talent in various genres, from country to rock. Gleason saw Simon and Garfunkel's performance on May 28, 1966, at the Berkeley Community Theater and was deeply impressed. After the show, Lewis asked Gleason, an old friend who had lots of tapes of Lenny Bruce's stand-up act, if he could bring Simon and Garfunkel to his house in Berkeley the next day to listen to some of them. Gleason was more than happy to get to know these two gifted musicians. When they arrived, he introduced them to Denise Kaufman, a young singer-songwriter who was a big Simon and Garfunkel fan and who would soon form the Ace of Cups, one of the first all-women groups of instrumentalists.

"We spent the whole afternoon listening to the tapes, and at the end of the day I offered to show Paul around town," she said. "Since neither of us had a car, he said we could call a taxi, but I said, 'Let's just hitchhike,' and that's what we did. I really liked him. I saw quickly that he was adventurous, and there were no airs about him, not at all." On their rounds of North Beach clubs, they stopped at Coffee and Confusion, a coffeehouse where Denise had performed a few times. When someone asked her to do a couple of numbers, she instead talked Simon into stepping onstage. "At first, people in the room didn't pay a lot of attention," she said. "He borrowed someone's guitar and opened with a couple of new songs, so people were just talking through them until he started singing 'The Sound of Silence,' and people were just amazed. That's when they knew he was Paul Simon."

Simon and Kaufman stayed at a friend's apartment that night, and in the morning, she took him to Haight-Ashbury, the heart of the counterculture movement in town. Simon then invited her to go with him to Southern California, where he and Art played three nights at Melodyland, a 3,200-seat theater-in-the-round near Disneyland, and she accepted—over the strong protest of a young Berkeley college student who was in love with her. When the student later started a music magazine, he vowed to never write anything good about Simon, she said. The incident wouldn't even be a footnote in Simon's story, except that the student's name was Jann Wenner.

One thing Kaufman remembered years later about meeting Simon was his concept of songwriting. "He said some writers looked at life as if it were this huge garden, and they tried to capture the big picture," she said. "But he liked to focus on this one flower and try to learn as much as he could about that one flower."

Though Simon didn't appear on the cover of *Rolling Stone* during the Simon and Garfunkel years, in 2018 Wenner denied that it had anything to do with his relationship with Kaufman. "I never said I wouldn't write about Paul Simon," he said. The reason Simon and Garfunkel never had a cover in the 1960s, he said, is that their music was outside the magazine's early raw and rebellious focus. "Simon and Garfunkel's sound was too soft," he added. "But when music opened up in the 1970s, we were quick to put Paul on the cover," along with such artists as Elton John and James Taylor.

It was soon after the Berkeley concert that Simon and Garfunkel began work in the studio on their next album, and they were still leaning heavily on songs Simon had written in England. The first thing they recorded, on June 10, was "Patterns," a song from *Song Book* that was given an aggressive sonic coloring. It was an early sign of Simon's desire to move beyond the pair's acoustic folk trademark. Two days later, they recorded "Cloudy," a lilting tale of youthful questioning and wonder written with the Seekers' Bruce Woodley, who received half the royalties for the song but no writing credit on the album because Simon felt Woodley's contribution was minuscule.

Bob Johnston was again the formal producer, but Roy Halee said it was clear in the studio that Simon was emerging as his own producer. "Paul came in prepared, really ready to go," the engineer said. "He'd play the songs first for Artie and me, and ask our opinions, and he really wanted our feedback. Art would often be critical, which was fine. Paul loved to look at things from all directions. This is also where we began to experiment with sounds, which is when he would look to me for suggestions."

After a weekend break, recording resumed in mid-June, focusing on "A Simple Desultory Philippic," the Dylan spoof. The only previously unrecorded song they had at this point was "A Poem on the Underground Wall," which described a lonely man's desperate desire to be heard. Based on a scene Simon observed at a London tube stop, the song's narrative suggests Simon's early interest in prose, including periodic stabs at a novel. The session produced "The Big Bright Green Pleasure Machine," which was a jab at the grandiose claims of massive ad campaigns promising to solve all your problems. While all those songs ended up on the record, the three most important tracks were still to come: "The Dangling Conversation," "Scarborough Fair/Canticle," and "7 O'Clock News/Silent Night."

"The Dangling Conversation," which he labored over for months, took up the entire session of June 21. In the heart of the song, Simon spoke about the breakdown of a relationship. The key verse:

> And you read your Emily Dickinson
> And I my Robert Frost
> And we note our places with bookmarkers
> That measure what we've lost
> Like a poem poorly written
> We are verses out of rhythm
> Couplets out of rhyme
> In syncopated time
> And the dangling conversation
> And the superficial sighs
> Are the borders of our lives

Simon later criticized the song on the same grounds as he did "I Am a Rock"—"adolescent"—but he liked it at the time, and Johnston, always out to please his artist, lobbied for it to be the single after "I Am a Rock," which had peaked at no. 3 in mid-June. "Rock," incidentally, was one of two Simon songs in the Top 10 that same week. The other one was the Crykle's version of "Red Rubber Ball." That twin success contributed greatly to Columbia selling more singles during the week ending June 17 than any other week up to that time in the company's long history.

A month after the session, Mort Lewis watched proudly as Simon and Garfunkel performed at the Columbia Records convention—just one year after the night Tom Wilson got the idea to redo "The Sound of Silence." The once-wary label employees called the duo back for two encores. Leading the applause was Clive Davis, the thirty-four-year-old general counsel who was being groomed by Lieberson to replace him as president. "Simon and Garfunkel meant a lot to me because they represented the direction I thought Columbia needed to move," Davis said later. "They were young, extremely bright, and immensely talented. I figured they would be one of our special acts for years. Beyond the music, I enjoyed being around them. We had a lot of things in common. We were Jewish, we all loved baseball, and we were from Queens. I innately felt a commonality that I didn't necessarily feel for artists in general." The following week in New York, Simon and Garfunkel recorded a track that combined "Scarborough Fair," the English folk ballad Simon had learned from Martin Carthy, with "Canticle," a redesign of the antiwar ballad "The Side of a Hill" from *Song Book*.

Before going back on the road, they performed a hometown concert on August 6, this time opening for the Mamas & the Papas at Forest Hills Stadium in Queens. It was a strong bill, combining two of the freshest acts in contemporary pop. Like Simon, John Phillips, the creative force behind the Mamas & the Papas, was essentially a singer-songwriter with folk leanings. And as with Simon and Garfunkel, Phillips's quartet wrapped its songs in wonderfully seductive melodies and tasteful, somewhat sophisticated arrangements. The songs, however, lacked the literary weight of Simon's compositions.

Two weeks later, Simon and Garfunkel recorded "7 O'Clock News/ Silent Night," a conceptual piece that once again addressed the gap between the country's ideals and such disheartening news as continuing civil rights setbacks, the escalation of the Vietnam War, and the senseless drug overdose of a personal hero (Lenny Bruce, to whom the album was dedicated). "I was driving home, and I just started singing 'Silent Night,' and the news was on, and I started playing around with the volume, and the piece came together," Simon explained. On the track, Simon and Garfunkel sang the Christmas carol "Silent Night" while an announcer read the mock newscast. As the track continued, the solemn news report gradually drowned out the hopes contained in "Silent Night."

In an August 28 *New York Times* article titled "A Law Firm They're Not," Robert Shelton profiled the pair. Despite his closeness to Dylan, Shelton couldn't have been more complimentary, all but saying "amen" when Simon told him, "Pop music is catching up with film as the leading medium in which to make some comment about the world for a large audience, just as films have caught up with literature." But he also said he was trying to add to his musical arsenal by learning how to play the Indian sitar, and he expressed awe over the singing of a female world music vocal choir from Bulgaria. To underscore his point, Simon mentioned that he hoped to write a novel or perhaps something for the stage. "You see, the new pop music can incorporate all these influences and more." One thing about Shelton's profile, however, must have raised a lot of eyebrows in the Brill Building: in tracing the duo's history, there was no mention of Tom & Jerry or Simon's years in the shallow teen-pop trenches. It's a part of their history that Simon and Garfunkel never brought up. When Shelton later heard of that missing piece, he was not happy.

Around this time, Ralph Gleason agreed to write the liner notes for the new album. In his two-thousand-word essay, Gleason, who later co-founded *Rolling Stone* magazine with Jann Wenner, not only praised Simon and Garfunkel but also defended the new rock generation, which was still frowned upon by most people over thirty. "The New Youth of the Rock Generation has done something in American popular song that has begged to be done for generations," he wrote boldly. "It has taken the creation of the lyrics and music out of the hands of hacks and given it over to poets."

In New York, recording for the album wrapped up the first week in September with "A Hazy Shade of Winter," yet another song written in England, and "The 59th Street Bridge Song (Feelin' Groovy)." It felt strange to Simon to be writing such a carefree song, but that's the way he felt one morning crossing the Queensboro Bridge (commonly called the 59th Street Bridge) and Simon liked the tune. "Feelin' Groovy" was the obvious title, but it seemed too common. Simon thought "The 59th Street Bridge Song" offered more character and appeal. Either way, the recording was too short, at just under two minutes, to be released as a single.

While he and Garfunkel resumed touring on weekends (they netted just over $75,000 for twenty-one shows in October and November), a review in *Billboard* summarized the industry excitement over the album, again stressing Simon's songwriting skills. Even that enthusiasm didn't prepare those at the label for the way the album, *Parsley, Sage, Rosemary and Thyme* (a line in "Scarborough Fair"), entered the chart in late November at a robust no. 28. The album climbed to no. 4 and was eventually certified by the RIAA as selling three million copies, ultimately giving Simon and Garfunkel a total of seven million sales for their first three LPs.

Meanwhile, Simon proved right about "The 59th Street Bridge Song" having hit potential. Just after the new album was released, Harpers Bizarre, a vocal group in California, recorded an expanded version of the song, featuring an a cappella choral section and a woodwind quartet. Simon was so impressed by the record, a Top 10 hit in the spring of 1967, that he looked up its producer, Lenny Waronker, during one of his trips to Los Angeles. Years later, Simon and Waronker would work on an album together.

Less than a year after he had been taking in less than $50 a night in England, Simon's earnings, thanks to royalties and concert fees, topped $300,000 in 1966. The only major career disappointment at the end of 1966 was the failure of "The Dangling Conversation" to make the Top 20 despite all the promotional money Columbia had put behind it. Even the relatively minor follow-up single, "A Hazy Shade of Winter," proved more popular.

Simon came away from the episode vowing to focus more on albums than singles, and the decision was a good reading of what was happening in the music business. Almost overnight, the LP replaced the single as the format of choice for young record buyers. Fans were becoming so passionate about their favorites that they wanted entire albums. This cultural shift was perfect for serious artists, giving them the freedom to experiment without worrying about whether the record would fit the narrow boundaries of Top 40 radio. Why a three-minute single? Why not a six- or ten-minute track if the material warranted it? The broader canvas also encouraged musicians to think about concepts. This resulted in a lot of self-indulgence in the 1960s and beyond, but some of the albums greatly lifted the horizons of rock. The Beach Boys had moved in that direction with *Pet Sounds* in 1966, and the Beatles would soon raise the bar even more with *Sgt. Pepper's Lonely Hearts Club Band.*

"When *Sgt. Pepper's* came out," Simon said, "it was another time when I thought, 'I can't believe that these guys are always ahead of us!' Still, it was liberating—the awareness of what you could do in the studio with the new technology and the time to do what you wanted to do rather than rush out singles. I started thinking about a concept album myself, and I knew that would take time." When Columbia started talking about how it would be ideal to have another album by the fall of 1967, he said no.

Eighteen months is an eternity in pop music, where commercial tastes can change overnight, but that's how long it would be before Simon and Garfunkel released their next album. And indeed, tastes underwent a radical shift during that time—one that would threaten Simon and Garfunkel's place in the pop consciousness. To prevent the duo from disappearing from radio airwaves, Simon and Garfunkel went into studio A in January 1967 with Halee for their final studio session with Bob Johnston, who would soon take over Columbia's country operation in Nashville. In fact, the separation had already begun. For the first time, the Columbia Records session log read Johnston and Simon and Garfunkel as coproducers. The song, "At the Zoo," felt like a reaction to the resistance "The Dangling Conversation" encountered. The seriousness and alienation gave way to a joyful lilt that was a precursor to the galloping rhythm of "Mrs. Robinson," only a year away. As much as anything they had done, "At the Zoo" made it clear that Simon worked as hard on his music as his words. There is as much playfulness and wit in the melody as there is in the lyrics.

Simon had been frustrated over the group's "serious" image. He and Art even joked about it, coming up with such sarcastic album titles as Simon and Garfunkel: *So Young Yet So Full of Pain.* They followed up the session by recording their sold-out January 22 concert at New York's 2,700-seat Philharmonic Hall. The concert was a generous overview of the duo's career, from "He Was My Brother" through "Homeward Bound" and "For Emily, Whenever I May Find Her." Robert Shelton checked in with another rave in the *New York Times*, underscoring Simon's concentration on music as much as lyrics: "On the musical side, nothing but praise can be offered for their glove-in-hand vocal blend, the gently playful or angry interplay of their voices and guitar, the rhythmic flexibility, and the overall polish. So here is another aspect of the new music—artistry, depth, communication, and musical expertise—all assimilated for an adulatory public. Simon and Garfunkel have arrived, and it's fair to say they will be playing a strong musical-literary role for a long time to come."

CHAPTER SEVEN

Mort Lewis sensed that Simon and Garfunkel were about to take a significant step forward when he got a phone call in early 1967 from director Mike Nichols, who wanted the pair to contribute music to his next film. Nichols was coming off the Oscar-winning smash *Who's Afraid of Virginia Woolf?*, starring Elizabeth Taylor and Richard Burton. For all its success, the duo was still viewed as part of the youth market. Nichols could be a door to the wider cultural mainstream. The proposed film, based on Charles Webb's 1963 novella *The Graduate*—a look at a young man's coming of age during a time of rapidly shifting values—was to star Dustin Hoffman, in what would be his breakthrough role as the young Benjamin Braddock, and Anne Bancroft as Mrs. Robinson, the married woman and family friend who seduces him.

Simon didn't care much for Webb's book, but he was flattered by the offer. He and Garfunkel were both fans of Nichols's smart, penetrating humor from his prefilm days as a member of a comedy duo with Elaine

May. In truth, Nichols hadn't known much at all about Simon and Garfunkel. When he contacted Lewis, he didn't even know that Simon wrote the music; he thought they were cowriters. It was the director's brother, Robert, who introduced him to *Sounds of Silence* and *Parsley, Sage, Rosemary and Thyme* while he was in the early stages of production on the movie. Nichols, however, quickly fell under the spell of the songs, which reflected some of the sociocultural views of the film. He started getting up early to listen to the music before heading to the Paramount lot in Hollywood. On occasion, he even played various songs to actors on the set to help them understand what he intended in a particular scene. William Daniels, who played the father of Hoffman's character, said that hearing "The Sound of Silence" made him realize *The Graduate* wasn't solely a comedy. Eventually Nichols asked Simon to write a couple of songs for the film, and Simon agreed. He was paid $25,000.

At the same time, Simon and Garfunkel's high standing in the pop world was underscored when the organizers of a three-day, summer pop-rock festival in Northern California reached across the country to enlist the duo's participation. The event, scheduled for the weekend of June 16–18 at the Monterey County Fairgrounds, was originally designed as a for-profit venture with the Mamas & the Papas, Simon and Garfunkel, and the Beach Boys as headliners. But John Phillips and Simon, among others, changed the focus to a free event aimed at demonstrating that rock 'n' roll had evolved into a legitimate art form. Proceeds would go to charity.

Popularly known as the Monterey Pop Festival, the event would become a landmark in rock history, a precursor of the Woodstock Music and Art Festival of 1969, thanks to a bill that included such revolutionary newcomers who would redefine the rock 'n' roll experience: Jimi Hendrix, the Grateful Dead, the Who, Jefferson Airplane, and Big Brother and the Holding Company, which featured a raspy-voiced blues singer named Janis Joplin. Simon not only helped choose the acts, festival cofounder Lou Adler said, but also came up with the idea of giving $50,000 of the festival proceeds to set up classes for young musicians in Harlem.

One of the acts Simon suggested for the festival was a twenty-year-old folk singer from England who went by her first name, Beverley. Born Beverley Kutner, she and Cat Stevens were the first two artists signed by Deram Records, but she wasn't known in America. Simon had met her in 1965 at Les Cousins, and the two became involved a few months later in what Beverley described in her 2011 memoir as a "romance and a really good friendship." The brief relationship was not enough to dislodge Simon's love of Kathy. The affair with Beverley, however, apparently resumed briefly when she came to the States early in 1967 to accompany him on tour. She was in the studio when they recorded "Fakin' It" a few days before the festival. She can be heard on the record saying a line that referred to folk singer Donovan, whose last name was Leitch, "Good morning, Mr. Leitch, have you had a busy day?"

Though life was increasingly hectic—Simon and Garfunkel performed nearly a hundred concerts and appeared on at least three national TV shows during the year—Simon rarely went a day without thinking about songs for the next album. While pleased with the *Parsley* LP, he wanted to step up his game. That musical ambition was a mixed blessing for Clive Davis. While the new label chief had faith in Simon's artistry, he worried about his ability to produce albums in a timely manner, which was important to growing the company. Davis was especially concerned about Simon and Art's desire to produce their recordings. But he wanted to be supportive, so he agreed to let them take over after Bob Johnston headed to Nashville. As weeks went by, however, he gave them gentle pep talks, stressing the importance of getting another album in the stores as soon as possible.

When Simon and Garfunkel got together in the studio in May, Simon was talking openly about a concept for the album, though the storyline wasn't defined. He was just trying to assemble good songs and see where they led. That first session was devoted to "Punky's Dilemma," a song Simon later submitted to Mike Nichols for *The Graduate*. It was a comic, absurdist reflection on what struck Simon as the alienation that someone, like the Dustin Hoffman character, might have gone through growing up in Southern California. Things didn't go well at the session and they returned to the studio on May 9 for additional work. After a few college dates, they went back into the studio to work on the song, but things continued to go slowly.

Hoping for a breakthrough, Davis assigned a young staff producer, John Simon (no relation), to see if he could help speed things along. The move could have backfired, but John was a good choice—a songwriter himself who was musically sophisticated. Before moving over to Columbia's pop division, he had worked in its classical division, which helped sharpen his feel for arrangements and orchestral shading. Their first session together was in early June when Simon and Garfunkel started recording "Fakin' It" and "Overs," a melancholy ballad about the breakup of a marriage that Simon would also offer to Nichols. Like every single since "I Am a Rock," "Fakin' It" was a hit, but a modest one.

During this period, Mort Lewis's marriage fell apart. On June 8 Peggy filed for divorce in New York City and headed the following week to Juarez, Mexico, where decrees could be granted quickly, which, in her case, turned out to be June 16, the opening day of the Monterey Pop Festival. After getting the grant, she went to Monterey, where Beverley described Peggy as "edgy" and "uncomfortable" when she saw her and Paul together. Beverley, whose relationship with Simon ended shortly after Monterey and who would eventually marry British musician John Martyn, wasn't the first one in the Simon and Garfunkel camp to suspect that Paul and Peggy were having an affair, but, in fact, they were still just friends. Peggy would spend most of the summer in Ireland, where she became involved with an Irish singer.

The official capacity of the Monterey County Fairgrounds' open-air seating area was only 7,500, but another 1,500 or so fans squeezed in for some of the weekend's performances, and more than 100,000 people gathered on the adjoining property to be part of the counterculture experience. In all, including television rights, the festival grossed around $500,000. For anyone who hadn't spent time around Haight-Ashbury, the weekend offered an unforgettable showcase of colorful psychedelic fashion, drugs, and free spirits. Besides music, the festival featured hundreds of craftsmen offering tie-dyed T-shirts, incense, posters, and hash pipes.

Simon and Garfunkel closed Friday's opening-day program with an acoustic set featuring "Homeward Bound" and "At the Zoo," but it was largely lost amid the fireworks to come. Even their modest turtlenecks seemed out of place next to the majestic attire of the audience and the other performers. In fact, most of the opening-day acts, which also included the Association, Lou Rawls, Johnny Rivers, and Beverley, would be ignored in accounts of the festival. The weekend's energy picked up dramatically on Saturday with performances by the electrifying Joplin and the soulful urgency of Otis Redding. On Sunday, the Who took the stage in all the British quartet's guitar-smashing glory, the Grateful Dead cast its cosmic, acid-rock spell, and then Jimi Hendrix did things with a guitar, including setting it on fire, that few in the audience or even backstage had ever imagined.

The Mamas & the Papas closed the festival on Sunday night only to find that, for all practical purposes, the weekend had ended with Hendrix's set. The quartet's glossy cheer, as nice as it was, simply couldn't compete. The Mamas & the Papas and Simon and Garfunkel may have been the two acts who did the most to make the festival possible, but nobody was talking—or writing—about them in the days immediately afterward. The festival's importance went beyond what happened onstage. In many ways, the weekend ignited rock journalism. Young rock fans were stepping forth, eager to take over for Gleason at the *Chronicle* and Shelton at the *Times*, and write about the music from their fiercely partisan points of view. Lou Adler recalled requests for more than a thousand press passes. The first issue of *Rolling Stone* was only five months away.

To this new generation of writers, the rock 'n' roll clock started, in many ways, at Monterey. Though the Beatles, Dylan, the Stones, and select others would be grandfathered into the new musical order, Simon and Garfunkel and the Mamas & the Papas were seen by many young writers as tied to the music's past. In a lengthy essay for *Newsweek*, Michael Lydon, a staff reporter who soon joined Jann Wenner at *Rolling Stone*, touched on what was going on when he declared, "Simon and Garfunkel finished off the [opening] night, and what can one say about them? 'Homeward Bound' brought back memories of the time when a sweet folk rock seemed to be the new direction, but though the song sounded nice enough, they seemed sadly left behind."

Part of the challenge for Simon and Garfunkel was image. To much of this new, progressive wing of pop music, Simon and Garfunkel came across as elitist New Yorkers. Mitch Schneider, a music publicist whose clients have included David Bowie and Tom Petty, called Simon's artistry "incomparable," but he felt Simon was often viewed as "privileged" and "aloof" in contrast to the underdog, working-class struggles of rockers such as Bruce Springsteen and Neil Young. He also wasn't a "badass" like Dylan or a left-field bohemian like Tom Waits.

Simon addressed this point in a 1984 *Playboy* interview. "It's a profession where it's almost required to have that pose," he said. "Unsophisticated, working class, nonintellectual. Aside from Lennon and Dylan, who made a point of their working-class backgrounds—which turned out not to be true, anyway—the idea that rock could be an art form that people with a brain might work at was always treated with derision. And that still exists. It turns out that there are a lot of smart guys in this profession, but they don't express that side."

After Monterey, Simon and Garfunkel's critical and commercial standing from earlier in the year was in question. To an emerging group of critics, Simon and Garfunkel simply didn't come down forcefully enough on the side of rock 'n' roll's youth culture. One of the duo's biggest "sins" was that much of its music could appeal to both young people *and* their parents. Ellen Willis, an influential young critic who looked at music through a strong cultural and sociopolitical lens, hit Simon hard. "I consider his soft sound a cop-out," she wrote in her *New Yorker* column. "And I hate most of his lyrics; his alienation, like the word itself, is an old-fashioned, sentimental, West Side–liberal bore."

Years later, Quincy Jones would look back at the Monterey backlash as yet another significant moment in Simon's creative evolution. "Whenever there is a radical shift in music, there is an accompanying test of artistry," he said. "If you are part of the old guard, you can either try to join the herd or you can simply remain on your own path. The true artists stay on their path because that's their passion. You can't be a great artist and follow the crowd. When I saw what Paul did *after* that festival, I knew he was a genuine artist."

Simon was aware a revolution was going on in rock, but he took it in stride. He was too busy making new music, including the songs for Mike Nichols, to worry about changing musical tastes. "When Artie and I came out of Monterey, we felt the whole world was changing, it was all going to be hippies, and we were going to be out," Simon reflected years later. "But you know what? Six months later, it wasn't all hippies, and we weren't forgotten. Actually, we were bigger than ever because of *The Graduate*."

Mike Nichols and film editor Sam O'Steen used three old Simon and Garfunkel songs—"The Sound of Silence," "Scarborough Fair," and "April Come She Will"—as placeholders in the film until Simon delivered the two new songs to them. But neither "Punky's Dilemma" nor "Overs" felt right to Nichols. That's when Garfunkel mentioned they had been working on a song called "Mrs. Roosevelt." All Simon had was the melody and the "deet-de-deet" chorus, which included the evocative line "Jesus loves you more than you will know." Nichols loved it, simply changing the name to Mrs. Robinson and, without waiting for more lyrics, weaving the number into an exhilarating seven-minute sequence of the film. In the final cut, Nichols also kept the three earlier songs that he had used as placeholders.

With the movie music settled, Simon took some time off in New York, where he tried to get perspective on his life. "I was so wrapped up with what was going on in my career that I felt I was ignoring everything else," he said. "I wanted to slow down and take a step back."

During this time, Simon, whose drug use was generally limited to pot, decided to take one of the purple LSD tablets that he'd been given in Monterey by Owsley Stanley III, the Grateful Dead's soundman, who manufactured his own acid. Simon had heard of some of the hallucinogenic drug's side effects and didn't want to take acid in front of other people, which is why he waited until he was home alone. That decision, he learned, was a big mistake. "It's very important with psychedelics to take them in a very friendly, safe environment and with friends," he said. "It is not a good idea to take it alone, but I didn't know that at the time. All of a sudden I felt I was up on the ceiling, looking at myself on the bed. I felt panicky and thought it would help if I took a bath, so I walked into the bathroom, telling myself not to look in the mirror. So what do I do? I look in the mirror, and I see my head had turned into a skull. I get into the shower, and I start seeing these big bugs in the tub."

This went on all night. In the morning, he called Mort Lewis and told him to hurry over. By the time the manager arrived, however, the sun had come up, and it looked beautiful outside. Simon was suddenly so serene that he wanted to go into Central Park and record the sounds of birds and children playing, so he called Columbia and told them to send over an engineer with a tape recorder. "I thought I was making great art," Simon wisecracked years later. "But it didn't amount to anything."

Simon experimented with other drugs in the 1960s and later, but he said he didn't have an addiction problem. "There were times in the sixties and seventies when that stuff was ubiquitous," he said. "But I found most of the drugs, especially cocaine, were a waste of time. Cocaine made you want to party all night, and then you were exhausted and couldn't breathe the next day. Pot could make you kind of dreamy and imaginative, but cocaine just made you want to run around. It wasn't contemplative. I don't think I ever wrote anything on cocaine. It was also bad for your voice."

While on break, he flew to London to see if he and Kathy could figure out a way to make their lives compatible. On the way, he visited Peggy in Ireland, but it was strictly a social visit. "It certainly wasn't any attempt to lure me back to the States," Peggy said years later. If anything, she added, she was more enamored of Simon than he was with her in those days. In London, he and Kathy acknowledged what had been apparent to them both for some time: their lives had simply drifted apart. As much as anything, Kathy was intimidated by Simon's new world. She was too insecure, friends said. It was a sad, reluctant parting on both sides. "There was no big drama in our breakup," Simon said years later. "I don't remember ever having an argument with Kathy."

Returning to New York, Simon threw himself back into his work. By the end of spring, Simon and Garfunkel were in the studio to record "Overs," another song for their next album, *Bookends*, before heading west again for a series of summer shows. Simon was feeling the strain of the new album. He was spending virtually all his time on his music, which contributed to his loneliness and isolation. Worried that Simon was becoming too stressed, Mort Lewis urged him to take time off and relax, but Simon continued to pursue songs for the next album. He did, however, make one personal move: he turned again to Kathy, inviting her to the United States for a few days, which included a July 28 concert at the 17,500-seat Hollywood Bowl. But there was no turning back. The parting in London was confirmed.

While in Los Angeles, Simon spoke with Pete Johnson of the *Los Angeles Times*, the first of two interviews around that time in which he outlined his plans for the new album and acknowledged that he was feeling the pressures of songwriting. "I have worked out a statement, a theme, and a construction for the album," he said. "One side will have songs in sequence like the chapters in a book. The other will have three hit singles and songs from *The Graduate*." Then, out of the blue, he added that *Bookends* might be the team's last album. "I wonder if I'm creating something that's valid," he said. "Art worries whether he is creating anything."

Simon was equally candid in an interview a few days later with James Stevenson, who was doing a profile for the *New Yorker*. "Writing is often an excruciating process," he said. "I've been working on one song for three months now. In the past, I could go faster, but I wouldn't accept those songs now. Now I say, 'No, it's got to be framed right.' Every time I pick up the guitar, I start on the song. When I go to sleep, I spend half an hour thinking about it. Songs get stagnant, and they turn on me. Lines that were good you begin to discard."

Simon then switched themes. He suddenly seemed a little less sure of himself. "I used to think I was much sharper than everyone else—very aware, perceptive, seeing things," he said. "Then, recently, I realized it wasn't true. Everyone's perceptive. Everyone is sensitive, and they all know what pain is. I have compassion for that. There's a gentleness and understanding in young people today, and there's only one choice: the human race must come to the aid of the human race." Some of the remarks may have been an outgrowth of his experience with the flower children of Monterey, but they also reflected something else that had been causing him occasional anxiety ever since the success of "The Sound of Silence."

He was realizing that it's as hard to protect artistry as it is to achieve it. All he had to do was look around at the self-destruction of his peers to understand that he had to safeguard himself against everything from drugs to fame. To do so, he needed toughness, discipline, dedication, and constant reassessment. "I think I found out relatively quickly that fame is bogus," he said years later. "It comes and goes arbitrarily. I could see that fame wasn't necessarily attached to something significant. People are interested in you just because you are the person who wrote 'The Sound of Silence' or 'Blowin' in the Wind' or whatever. If those songs had been flops, people wouldn't care about you at all—but the songs would have been the same. There's an old story, although maybe I'm paraphrasing it, about Einstein and Charlie Chaplin on a train, and there are hordes of people coming to see Einstein, and Einstein says to Chaplin, 'What does it all mean?' and Chaplin says, 'Nothing. It means nothing.' And that's what I feel about fame and attention. You want people to care about your music, but you don't want them to interrupt your life."

Simon felt that his fame and wealth (he was now a millionaire) also took a toll on his own family, especially his father. "That's the hardest part," he said. "All of a sudden, in my midtwenties, I was the richest person in the family and the one with the most power. If someone had a problem or got sick, it was like, 'Just call Paul, and Paul will solve the problems or find the right doctor.' When my father retired, I gave him the money to move out of his house and get a new place, a better place. My mother had no problem with it, but I think my father may have been confused; maybe he even felt usurped. He was an unusually smart guy, maybe the smartest guy I've ever known, but I was famous, and that put something between us that wasn't necessary. He did say at one point, 'I'm not going to compete with you because I know I'm going to lose.' "

Progress on the new album continued to be slow. It was now a full year since the final session for *Parsley, Sage*. Eventually Columbia executives were so concerned that they ordered an attorney to send Simon and Garfunkel a letter saying they had violated their contract by not delivering the album sooner, but Paul and Art ignored it. They took the label's urgings so lightly that they brought a small tape recorder with them to their next meeting with Clive Davis to tape his latest plea to hurry, so they could later have fun playing it for Halee and others in the studio.

Simon's slowness as a writer wasn't the only reason the albums took so long. In an unpublished memoir, producer John Simon described the kind of studio experimentation that caused the recording delays. "I met with them, and they outlined their ideas for an overdub on 'Save the Life of My Child,' a song they had already recorded," he wrote. "They wanted violins, but softer and lower, so I suggested muted violas. Then they had some brass punctuation in mind and some percussion as well. They sang a few lines for me, and I wrote out an arrangement." On the night of the session, he continued, a dozen viola players showed up, and Simon and Garfunkel were intrigued by the sound of them warming up. They told John Simon to forget the arrangements and record the players warming up.

The producer and the musicians tried for hours to reproduce the random tuning that the duo liked, and never were able to get it right. All this time, numerous other musicians—brass players and percussionists—had to wait outside, which didn't bother them at all because they were being paid overtime. But John Simon was struck by the "extravagance" of Simon and Garfunkel. Checking around, he subsequently learned that Columbia was paying for the sessions, not, as was typical, the artists. Simon had insisted on it in their contract.

A few nights later, the producer went into the studio to do more work on the song and saw his first synthesizer. Roy Halee had arranged for Robert Moog, the inventor of the musical instrument, to bring one of his large creations to the session after he and Paul saw one being demonstrated at Monterey. The keyboard, which looked a lot like a telephone operator's switchboard, would eventually become hugely popular, especially in disco and electronic music, but at this stage, it was largely unknown. Simon was so intrigued when Moog arrived that, in Halee's words, "He was like a kid in a candy store." Meanwhile, Simon and Garfunkel spent several more nights working on the song; then, in early October, they turned their attention back to the elusive "Punky's Dilemma." Even though Nichols had passed on it, Simon and Garfunkel still wanted it on *Bookends*.

As the pressure for the album mounted, Simon began depending more and more on Peggy. "I was lonely, and I wanted a relationship, which in those days to me sort of meant you were married and had a house in the country," Simon said. "So what do I do? I found a house in the country, and you can imagine the rest." Simon bought a house in New Hope, Pennsylvania, a small, lovely town in Bucks County, on the west bank of the Delaware River, about seventy-five miles southwest of New York City. Mort Lewis described the house as more modest than mansionesque, but surrounded by lots of serene acreage to provide privacy. Eddie Simon remembers it as a "very cool house and beautiful land—old stone maybe a hundred years old or more." It felt safe and secure.

PART THREE

Bridge Over Troubled Water

CHAPTER EIGHT

The Graduate would be ranked as one of the ten best American movies of all time in an American Film Institute poll in 1998, but its box office prospects in 1967 were considered shaky. When producer Joseph E. Levine previewed the film for industry colleagues in December, the reaction wasn't good. To make things worse, leading critics largely dismissed the movie. Ultimately, the film proved to be a litmus test of which side of the generation gap you were on. Older viewers, in large part, felt their values were being ridiculed; younger ones saw their values championed. And it was young people who flocked to theaters when the movie opened just before Christmas—and that enthusiasm didn't let up. With a budget of just $3 million, *The Graduate* went on to take in $104.9 million in the United States alone, making it the top-grossing film released that year. It was also nominated for seven Academy Awards and won one: Nichols, for Best Director. Though "Mrs. Robinson" wasn't nominated for Best Song, an AFI poll in 2004 named it no. 6 on the list of best songs ever in a movie, trailing only "Over the Rainbow," "As Time Goes By," "Singin' in the Rain," "Moon River," and "White Christmas."

Clive Davis then added to the triumph. Despite being told by an aide that there was not enough Simon and Garfunkel music in the film for a soundtrack album, Davis decided to check out the film himself. Rather than wait for the studio to set up a private screening, he simply walked down the street to a theater where the movie was playing. From the opening moments, he understood the emotional pull the film was having on young audiences—that is, record buyers. Davis's aide was right: there wasn't enough Simon and Garfunkel music to fill an LP, but there was plenty of Dave Grusin's score to supplement the duo's music for a thirty-six-minute collection. Davis knew most people bought soundtrack albums as souvenirs of the film, and this album would be perfect. As he walked back to his office, he thought sales of five hundred thousand copies would not be out of the question. Paul and Art were against the idea. They didn't want their fans to think *The Graduate* was their new album, and they didn't want to push back the release of *Bookends* to make room for it. Simon also wanted to be sure all of the label's attention was focused on *Bookends*.

To ease their concerns, Davis said he'd put a photo from the film on the cover of *The Graduate* to make clear it was a soundtrack album, and he stressed the LP wouldn't delay the release of *Bookends*. In fact, he told them, the soundtrack would help build an audience for their studio album. He all but guaranteed them that both records would reach the Top 10. The arguments worked, and the soundtrack was rushed to stores. True to Davis's word, the catchy cover shot was a scene in which Bancroft is seducing young Hoffman, but the label didn't shy away from using the Simon and Garfunkel angle with retailers and radio programmers. "Two of the biggest stars of *The Graduate* aren't even seen," proclaimed a full-page ad in the February 24 issue of *Billboard*, promoting both the soundtrack LP and the release of "Scarborough Fair" as a single.

Lewis was so caught up in the early box office reports for the film that he wanted to celebrate with three weekend shows, January 26–28, in three of the nation's most prestigious venues, Convention Hall in Philadelphia, Carnegie Hall in New York, and Symphony Hall in Boston. The dates were part of a move to broaden Simon and Garfunkel's appeal beyond the collegiate market. Lewis also booked them as guests on the January 3 episode of the adult-oriented *Kraft Music Hall* variety show on NBC. In keeping with its adult audience, the episode was hosted by comedian-pianist Victor Borge.

As tickets for the three shows went on sale city by city, Mort waited nervously for tallies from the promoters to see if his artists had indeed attained a new level of popularity. The first call came from Lou Robin, who handled the concert in Philadelphia. It was an instant sellout. Lewis recalled, "All of a sudden I'm thinking, 'Holy Christ.' " Still, that was just one city. The real test was Carnegie Hall. Lewis was furious when he picked up the *New York Times* on the Sunday before tickets went on sale to see that promoter Ron Delsener had bought only a tiny one-inch, one-column ad. Lewis couldn't reach Delsener on Sunday, but he was on the phone early Monday and screamed, "You idiot! What's the matter with you? A one-column, one-inch ad?" Lewis went on and on about how they've got to sell all three thousand tickets, or it'll embarrass Paul and Art in their hometown. Delsener listened to Lewis's tirade and then coolly informed him that there were only fifty or so seats left, and the phone was still ringing off the hook at the Carnegie Hall box office. He wanted permission to add a second show. "A second show? Holy Christ!" Lewis said. It, too, sold immediately. Boston was also sold out.

To celebrate, Lewis chartered a plane to fly them to and from Boston for the final show. Simon was in, but Garfunkel wanted to hitchhike. That made everybody else nervous because something could happen, and he might not get to the show on time. But Garfunkel insisted. On the day of the concert, Lewis recalled, Garfunkel headed for the highway, where a young, Boston-bound couple in a VW gave him a ride. Garfunkel was sitting in the backseat when he noticed the husband, who was driving, staring at him in the rearview mirror. Finally, the driver said, "You look like that singer in Simon and, you know . . . Simon and the other guy."

Garfunkel replied, "That's me. Art Garfunkel." The driver countered, "Don't kid me, there's no way *Art Garfunkel* would be hitchhiking." Garfunkel spent the rest of the trip trying to convince the couple that he really was the pop star, but the driver wouldn't even look at his driver's license. When the couple let him off on the outskirts of Boston, Garfunkel gave it one final try: "Give me your name, and I'll leave a couple of comps for you at the box office." As he drove away, the husband snapped, "Why don't you grow up!" Garfunkel managed to get to Symphony Hall just in time for the five o'clock sound check, but Simon didn't enjoy that kind of suspense. Anyone backstage that day could have seen this wasn't the way Paul wanted to work. Simon's concern was renewed a few weeks later when Garfunkel, after working on "Mrs. Robinson" all night in the studio, missed the flight from New York to London, where the duo was to perform a sold-out concert at Royal Albert Hall that night. Mort Lewis and Simon were already in London when they got the news. Because it was too late for Garfunkel to catch another flight, Lewis had to cancel the show at the last minute, causing a furor. So that he could blame the cancellation on illness, Lewis told Garfunkel to check into a New York hospital. While there, Lewis said, Garfunkel accidentally hit his head on a table and hurt his eye, which required medical attention.

The soundtrack entered the *Billboard* Top 200 chart at no. 114 in the issue dated March 16 and then leaped to no. 4 the following week. The stampede for Simon and Garfunkel product also caused two earlier albums, *Parsley, Sage* and *Sounds of Silence*, to rebound strongly on the chart. Two weeks later, things got even hotter. *The Graduate* reached no. 1, where it would remain for nine weeks. Topping Clive Davis's own early estimate, *The Graduate* passed the two million sales mark, and there was so much interest in the forthcoming *Bookends* album that advance orders from retailers were huge. Columbia took out another full-page ad in the trades to share the news. Simon and Garfunkel were now cultural superstars. The impact of their "sensitive" music on young people around the world was so strong that church and school counselors in various countries used the duo's songs as a way to get young people to open up. "When we were in seminary in Dublin," said Father Jarlath "Jay" Cunnane, a Roman Catholic priest, "we had religious education practice in local high schools, and no class was complete without playing some popular record—mostly Simon and Garfunkel—and then discussing the message."

Simon finished writing the songs that would be the heart of *Bookends* in January. He and Garfunkel then went into a studio in Hollywood, where they and Halee were again on their own because John Simon had left Columbia to become a freelance producer. By then, the album's concept was in place: a group of songs on side one would address aging. In Hollywood, Simon opened the session with "America," a story of a young couple on a bus trip, searching for the heart and spirit of the country during a time of rapidly shifting values. In the song, there is a sense of anticipation and hope, a suggestion of an underlying goodness and honor in the country that was still divided over many of the same issues that had inspired "The Sound of Silence."

In "America," the narrator's companion is a young woman named Kathy, which, understandably, led fans to assume that he and Kathy Chitty had taken a trip together during her visit in 1966, but there was no Simon-Kathy bus trip, Simon said. The images in the song were based on his own travels, all the way back to the summer he had hitched to California and through to the scores of cities, big and small, he had visited while touring. Interestingly, the song is one of the rare pop songs that has no rhymes. It's all straight prose. Nobel Prize–winning poet Derek Walcott called it one of his favorite Simon songs. He particularly liked the line "and the moon rose over an open field" for its "Zen-like elegance."

"It's the story of people setting off to find out who they are and where they are going," Simon said. "The line about marrying our fortunes together was a joke, of course, because the couple had nothing. The 'real estate in my bag' was grass. We bought some cigarettes, which is true, because I smoked then. Some people thought there was no such thing as Mrs. Wagner's pies, but they were little packaged apple pies, like Hostess made, and distributed regionally." These touches contributed to a certain innocence that has helped the song resonate with future generations, much like "The Boxer" and "The Sound of Silence." Simon also gives Garfunkel credit for coming up with the high vocal arrangement that gives such power and yearning to the song's ending lines.

On the second night of the session, Simon and Garfunkel recorded the extended version of "Mrs. Robinson," a noteworthy step in Simon's slowly evolving creative process. Until then, he had largely written straight-forward narratives and framed the lyrics with evocative but familiar folk-accented shading. In "Mrs. Robinson," the music itself was bolder and more aggressive, competing fiercely for attention with the lyrics. Equally important, his lyrics were more economical. In just two dozen or so words, Simon offered images that touched poignantly on cultural attitudes. This was commentary without the harsh insistence of traditional protest music. In taking this approach, he was trusting the listener to fill in the blanks. All this was the result of Simon's deliberate pace; he'd spend days or even weeks searching for the right word or musical accent. Music requires in-spiration, but it also demands the obsession Quincy Jones spoke about.

In "Mrs. Robinson," Simon first tells us about the Bancroft character's loss of faith.

> *And here's to you, Mrs. Robinson*
> *Jesus loves you more than you will know, wo wo wo*

Then he matched the line with a reflection on the country's loss of inno-cence.

> *Where have you gone, Joe DiMaggio?*
> *A nation turns its lonely eyes to you.*

Later Simon heard that the Yankees' Hall of Fame center fielder had been offended by the reference to him in "Mrs. Robinson" and had even con-sidered a lawsuit. But, to Simon's relief, Joe was charming when they hap-pened to meet in an Italian restaurant in New York, though he did bring up the song. "What I don't understand," he told Simon, "is why you ask where I've gone. I just did a Mr. Coffee commercial. I'm a spokesman for the Bowery Savings Bank. I haven't gone anywhere." Simon, in turn, told the baseball great that he hadn't meant the lines literally; he was speaking of him as an American hero and suggesting that real heroes were in short supply. What Simon didn't say was that one reason he used DiMaggio rather than his beloved Mickey Mantle was because *DiMaggio* had the right number of syllables. Throughout his career, Simon stressed that he had an advantage in the studio over other songwriters because of all the experience he had gained during the "demo" years. The "Mrs. Robinson" session showed what he meant. The music and words interacted in ways that would become one of his most distinctive traits.

While in Hollywood, Garfunkel visited a senior citizen complex and taped comments, often philosophical, by various residents. He and Simon wove some of the remarks (along with further reflections taped in New York) into a nonmusical track entitled "Voices of Old People," which gave the album a warm, intimate edge. (Simon and Garfunkel later chuckled when fans shouted out for the "song" in concert.) *Bookends* was then wrapped up in New York with the recording of "Old Friends." A rare reflection on aging by young pop rockers, the song pushed the barrier of the Beatles' "When I'm Sixty-Four" one decade further with the line "How terribly strange to be seventy."

Clive Davis was ecstatic. He felt the songs showed that Simon was no longer just a writer of hit songs but a writer of enormous depth. Davis was confident his prediction would hold and *Bookends* would be a Top 10 album. But he also had an idea for *Bookends* that angered Simon. As part of a variable-pricing sales strategy of charging a premium for special— that is, superstar—albums, Davis tacked $1 onto the retail price, thus charging $5.79. Fortunately for Simon and Garfunkel, their contract was up for renewal amid all this success, and Davis upped their royalty rate generously.

Tragically, on the day after the April 3 release of *Bookends*, Dr. Martin Luther King Jr. was assassinated in Memphis, where he was supporting striking sanitation workers. Some observers have tried to make the case over the years that one reason *Bookends* was such a hit was that its wistful tales offered comfort and hope to the nation in another shattered moment. More likely, *The Graduate* film and album had created such an enormous interest in the duo's music that it would have been a hit under any circumstances.

The Graduate was still no. 1 when *Bookends* entered the *Billboard* pop chart in the issue dated April 27, and it remained no. 1 until *Bookends* replaced it in the top spot on May 25. Between the two albums, Simon and Garfunkel held the no. 1 LP in the country for sixteen weeks. For two weeks during that span, the duo had three albums in the Top 6, only the third time that feat had been accomplished. (The others were the Beatles and Herb Alpert & the Tijuana Brass.)

Mainstream reviews for *Bookends* mostly offered high praise, but there was dissent from the rock press. In *Rolling Stone*, Arthur Schmidt wrote, "It is nice enough, and I admit to liking it, but it exudes a sense of process, and it is slick, and nothing too much happens. It is, also, and this is certainly not a fault *per se*, not rock and roll, whatever that is. For instance, 'Overs,' the weakest cut on the LP, would lend itself well to a Streisand styling." Yet there was no denying the power and appeal of "Mrs. Robinson." Wrote Schmidt, "In 'Mrs. Robinson' . . . Simon has composed perhaps the best song of the movie genre. It follows the plot, but it explains it in imagery outside of the strict confines of that plot. It is also a wonderful song about America, even a rock and roll song, and it is rather poignant." The charge that Simon and Garfunkel were no longer rock 'n' roll might have stung the sensitive Simon except for one thing: he no longer thought of himself in terms of folk music or rock 'n' roll.

The *New York Times Magazine* ran a flattering profile in October that pointed out the duo's "madrigal-like harmony appealed to both [Leonard] Bernstein and the Beatles—and their message seems to have transcended the generation gap." For the feature, Josh Greenfield traveled to a Simon vacation rental in Stockbridge, Massachusetts, and to Simon's and Art's respective apartments in Manhattan. The vacation estate belonged to a former ambassador, which is why a mantel was covered with autographed photos of high-ranking governmental officials, including some presidents. Simon joked to the reporter that he was going to add a photo of Lenny Bruce to the group before heading home to New York. Garfunkel lived in a multistory apartment on the Upper East Side that had many stylish features—"a study in textures, an exercise in design, dramatically multi-leveled and multicolored"—and was clearly the apartment of "an architecture student with an unlimited budget." Simon's two-room apartment, some twenty blocks farther up on the East Side, was in a high-rise building that overlooked the East River. Aside from rose-orange carpet and a large wooden carousel horse that had been converted into a rocker, Greenfield found the unit "nondescript, antiseptically modern."

Simon tried his best to sidestep de rigueur celebrity lifestyle questions, but he came alive when the subject switched to his craft. Unlike artists who feel uncomfortable talking about the meaning of songs or the songwriting process, Simon proved unusually open and thoughtful. "Once I start on a project," he told Greenfield, "I never let up. I pace about the living room. I look over the river. I play some licks on the guitar. Or else—I'll just go off to the Cloisters and sit there and think. I always work on the music first because I like to think that I'm stronger in words, they come easier. But I'm not a poet. I've tried poetry, but it has nothing to do with my songs. And I resent all the press-agentry. The lyrics of pop songs are so banal that if you show a spark of intelligence, they call you a poet . . . The people who call you a poet are people who never read poetry."

As he had told Pete Johnson of the *Los Angeles Times* a few months earlier, Simon said he could see an end to making music. "Right now, it's all kicks, and one day it'll stop being kicks, and we'll stop," he said. "Anyway, in pop music if you have five years, that's extraordinary. And we've had three already . . . Man, I don't know about the future. Maybe I'll even get married—if that romantic notion doesn't get knocked over."

What he didn't say was that his relationship with Garfunkel was increasingly shaky. On April 15—the same week that Columbia ran the full-page ad announcing the release of *Bookends*—Garfunkel sent Simon a long, deeply emotional and profoundly sad letter outlining his frustration over their relationship. In the handwritten note, Garfunkel traced his emotional pain all the way back to the time Simon made the solo record for Sid Prosen at Big Records ten years earlier. In a way, it is remarkable that Paul and Art kept their differences private for so long.

When Mike Nichols phoned Mort Lewis about his next movie, Lewis assumed the director was looking for more music. He was surprised when Nichols told him he wanted the pair as actors, not musicians, for *Catch-22*, which would be based on Joseph Heller's best-selling 1961 novel about the madness of war. Paul and Art admired the book, which was set in World

War II, and were delighted that Nichols wanted them to be in it. They were told the filming, chiefly in Mexico, would start in January 1969 and take only two or three months. Nichols cast Garfunkel in the role of Edward Nately, the nineteen-year-old son of a wealthy Long Island family. The director eyed a much smaller role of another serviceman for Simon, but the character was cut from the script before filming began. Though that move was later pointed to as having widened the breach between Simon and Garfunkel, Simon said his disappointment was only momentary. He had plenty of music to work on, including an autobiographical song that felt especially promising. In fact, he said, Nichols asked Simon's permission to go ahead with only Garfunkel. "Mike called me one night and said they needed to drop my part because the script was too long, and then he added, 'So I guess that means Artie will be out, too,' " Simon said. "But I said, 'Oh, no. You don't have to take him out. I'm fine with it.' "

At the same time, Art, who continued to fret about what he perceived as his junior status in the team, saw *Catch-22* as an opportunity to boost his position. "For Art Garfunkel to be a little bit of a movie actor in addition to my role in Simon and Garfunkel is very nice for the identity of the group," he said in a 1990 interview with music writer Paul Zollo. "After all, Paul plays the guitar onstage; Arthur just has his hands. Paul writes all the songs. So it beefs up my side of the group. It's almost as if George Harrison suddenly did an acting role to balance out the McCartney-Lennon contribution . . . I thought I was going to help give my side of the group a little more interest, and I'd be bringing it back to the duo after we had our rest from each other, and we'd go on and make more albums." Garfunkel also confirmed in the same interview the tensions between him and Simon at the start of *Catch-22*. "We were not getting along particularly well, and there were lots of conflicts that were unpleasant conflicts," he said. "I remember thinking, 'When this record's over, I want to rest from Paul Simon.' And I would swear that he was feeling the same thing."

Simon's confidence was soaring in the closing months of 1968. He and Garfunkel were stronger than ever on the concert trail, where, in just three months, the pair's net for thirty-three shows was nearly $425,000. Above all, "Mrs. Robinson" and the *Bookends* songs reinforced Simon's assurance as a writer, emboldening him to look more deeply inside himself for material. It was, he said, like sitting on top of the world. The most immediate result was "The Boxer," which again showed Simon's disinterest in doing the expected. The song, which he wrote largely on the back of an airline air sickness bag, continued neither the musical zest of "Mrs. Robinson" nor the conceptual unity of *Bookends.* It was a deeply personal account of his early anxiety as a budding songwriter. The story wasn't addressing just Simon's struggles in the music business but also his triumphs, and the latter left him open to the same ridicule often directed at such chest-beating, self-congratulatory declarations as Frank Sinatra's "My Way," the lyrics of which were written by Paul Anka in 1968.

Equally dangerous from an image standpoint, Simon was returning to the Dylan-inspired folk style that he had largely abandoned partly because he wanted to avoid the Dylan comparisons from critics. "I never hid the fact I admired Dylan and even tried to be like him when I wrote 'The Sound of Silence,' but I knew pretty quickly that I had to move on because I wasn't as original in that style as Bob," he said. "What he represents is the rebel poet, the darkness, the idiosyncrasies of all that. It's an archetypal American thing. I couldn't be Dylan any more than I could be Elvis. In writing 'The Boxer,' I wasn't imagining what Bob was thinking any more than I was in 'The Sound of Silence.' I was looking inside and thinking about my own journey."

The opening verses of "The Boxer" outline Simon's background in a way that anyone familiar with his history can trace, from Queens and the Brill Building to the demo studios to, even, the railway station in Widnes. But it's not necessary to know Simon's history to appreciate his storytelling. About the lyrics, he said, "I read a lot, and I'll come across something and think, 'That's a good line. I should remember that.' Some of the lines in 'The Boxer' come from the Bible . . . lines like 'workingman's wages' and 'seeking out the poorer quarters.' I could have easily been in a hotel room somewhere when I saw them."

When talking about the song over the years, Simon has wrestled with its theme. "Looking back, I don't recall thinking I went through years of struggle," he said. "I was never poor, and I had a family that loved me. But I have to say singing 'his anger and his shame' still makes me feel uncomfortable, so there must have been some anger and shame. I think some of the feelings in the song started when I was a kid; it wasn't a traumatic injury you can point to, but there was something." That "something," of course, surely included the matters of his size, his hair, the failure and occasional humiliation of the Jerry Landis years, being snubbed by the Village folk crowd, and, later, having to fight to gain respect in the rock community. The song had a liberating effect on Simon.

As in many of his best songs from then on, Simon demonstrated in "The Boxer" that once he finds a strong, personal theme, he becomes so intense in his writing that he breaks through any blocks and connects with what may have been repressed feelings. In the end, the song was about survival. "I had to end the song with resilience because that's me," he said. "I couldn't have written Janis Ian's 'At Seventeen' "—an expression of emotional despair—"because I was resilient."

I am just a poor boy
Though my story's seldom told
I have squandered my resistance
For a pocketful of mumbles
Such are promises
All lies and jest
Still, a man hears what he wants to hear
And disregards the rest

When I left my home and my family
I was no more than a boy
In the company of strangers
In the quiet of the railway station
Running scared
Laying low, seeking out the poorer quarters
Where the ragged people go

Looking for the places only they would know
Lie-la-lie . . .

Asking only workman's wages
I come looking for a job
But I get no offers
Just a come-on from the whores on Seventh Avenue
I do declare there were times when I was so lonesome
I took some comfort there
Lie-la-lie . . .

Then I'm laying out my winter clothes
And wishing I was gone
Going home
Where the New York City winters aren't bleeding me
Leading me
Going home

Then, the key verse about struggle and eventual triumph:

In the clearing stands a boxer
And a fighter by his trade
And he carries the reminders
Of every glove that laid him down
Or cut him till he cried out
In his anger and his shame
"I am leaving, I am leaving"
But the fighter still remains
Lie-la-lie . . .

Soon after the song was finished, Simon played "The Boxer," as was his custom, for several friends. He studied their reactions the same way a comedian might try out a joke as part of his personal quality control system. "When Paul sang it for me, I got chills," Roy Halee said. "And then I thought about the challenge we all faced. What can we do in the studio to bring out all the emotion and character? We spent a lot of time trying to get it right, but each step was a thrill."

Hoping to record "The Boxer" before Garfunkel left for Mexico, Simon asked Mort Lewis to suspend touring as much as possible in the final weeks of the year. Indicative of his intensity, Simon reserved Columbia's Nashville recording studio for twenty-seven days, though he eventually returned to New York after just seven. Charlie McCoy, the Nashville harmonica player, continued to marvel at Simon's vision in the studio, noting that the songwriter "knew just what he wanted the musicians to play, and he was invariably right."

The sessions were so epic for Simon that he had no trouble recalling them in fine detail fifty years later. "The recording started in Nashville with Fred Carter and me playing the opening guitar part," he said. "The first line is a lick he wrote while his guitar was in a special tuning. Ever since, guitarists get their fingers all twisted up trying to play that part, and they can't, because they don't know the tuning. The two of us played, sitting about three feet apart and completely locked into it. We did it over and over until we got the take you hear on the record. It's live on the record; no edits. Roy and Artie were in the control room, and they were really happy with the way the guitars meshed together—Fred was playing a Martin and I was playing a Guild—and that our guitar part got us off to a great start. Then we added bass and drums in New York with Joe Osborn and Hal Blaine. The drum part that everyone remembers happened when Roy put Hal's snare drum in an elevator shaft to make sure it would sound explosive."

Blaine, the Los Angeles drummer who played on hundreds of hits by artists such as producer Phil Spector, the Byrds, and even Simon and Garfunkel, was brought in to create, in his words, a massive "cannonball-like" explosion to add a dramatic counterpoint to the lilting sing-along quality of the song's "Lie-la-lie" chorus. "Roy was brilliant," Blaine said. "He didn't use any electronic equipment to measure the sound from place to place; he'd just walk around clapping his hands until he found the sound he wanted. We were in a huge studio, two stories high, and there was a ramp along one wall that led up to an elevator shaft that was used to move equipment in and out of the room.

"I set up two huge tom-toms and put on a headset so I could hear when the music got to the 'Lie-la-lie' part, where I hit the drums as hard as I could. There was this massive explosion in the room, which is what you hear on the record. It was amazing, but the thing I remember most about the session is when the elevator door opened just as I came down on the drums, and this elderly security guard looks out and he hears this *pow*! It nearly scared him to death. He jumped back into the elevator, closed the door, and took off. We never saw him again, but I think about his face every time I hear 'The Boxer.' "

Next came the vocals, which were also recorded in the Columbia studio, and then the horn parts, done in a small cathedral up by Columbia University. "Again, that was Roy's decision," Simon said. "He wanted to get the natural echo sound that occurs there. Then we went back to the Columbia studios to record the strings. But we didn't just record the strings while the musicians were playing along with a track of the song; we also had the musicians play the same part without listening to what we had already recorded, which is called a 'wild track.' Roy then put pieces of the wild track alongside the other string part during the fade to create that memorable ending."

By then, Simon, Garfunkel, and Halee had spent nearly a hundred hours on the track, and they still weren't through. "We went back to Nashville to record this beautiful instrumental section that blended a high-C trumpet and a pedal steel guitar," Simon said. "It was a beautiful part that Artie wrote, maybe the piece of writing that Artie is most proud of."

During this intensive process, Halee realized that he needed more than the standard eight-track recording machine, which had recently come into use, so he is believed to be the first person who came up with the idea of connecting two eight-track machines to create a sixteen-track machine. The goal was to have more options during the mixing process. For years, record makers used monaural tape, which meant they could record whatever was happening in the studio on only one track—the voice, the orchestra, everything. If anyone made a mistake, they had to redo the entire take again. Then someone invented a way to record two tracks, or channels, which created stereo—allowing you to record, say, the vocal on one track and the band on a second. If the singer made a mistake, they'd just have to rerecord that part. This led to four tracks and, ultimately, eight tracks, which allowed you to record eight singers and/or musicians separately. But it still wasn't enough for Halee. He wanted the freedom of sixteen tracks. (Decades later, Simon would end up working with 128 tracks.)

It was this kind of dedication that would eventually lead some to accuse Simon of being a perfectionist or a control freak, but he wasn't intimidated. "My response is I'm looking for something in the studio and I'm not hearing it. I want to hear on the record what I'm hearing in my head. It's like the ear goes to the irritant. I'll think 'No, that's not right' or 'That's not the way I want it to sound.' But I never think this must be perfect. I'm open to other people's ideas. Over the years, I've been in awe of what Roy and others bring to the music."

At this point in their career, no one was pressuring them to hurry up, one of the benefits of having sold millions of albums. In the end, Halee would call "The Boxer" the best record Simon and Garfunkel ever made. And the song would get even better. During some concerts over the years, Simon sang another verse, one that wasn't on the record:

> Now the years are rolling by me
> They are rocking easily
> I am older than I once was
> And younger than I'll be
> But that's not unusual
> No, it isn't strange
> After changes upon changes
> We are more or less the same
> After changes we are
> More or less the same

Eddie Simon also loved "The Boxer," and he again thought about how so much of his brother's resilience and determination came from his father— a determination Eddie saw during his father's early days as a teacher in the 1960s. "The thesis of my dad's doctorate was that if you broke words into elements called phonemes rather than syllables, the new word divisions would be helpful when working with students who had a hard time reading," Eddie said. "He thought these separations would be easier for the brain to pick up. Because there were no word processors at the time, my dad bought an electric typewriter that had the ability to do half spaces, and he typed up hundreds of mimeograph pages to show words segmented into phonemes—and it took him hundreds of hours because he couldn't really type; he had to hunt and peck with the keys.

"When my folks went away for the weekend on vacation, these papers, for some reason, were left in the backseat of the family car. One of my friends borrowed the car, and the pages were gone when he returned it. There were no copies, so what does my father do when he gets home? I come downstairs the next morning around seven, and Dad's on the back porch. He didn't waste any time wondering what happened or complaining. He simply started typing all those pages again."

When Art arrived on the set of *Catch-22*, which was built in the desert near the Mexican port of Guaymas, it was soon apparent that the filming was going to take longer than two or three months. In a colorful piece for the *New York Times*, Nora Ephron described the scene in Guaymas as being close to the manic chaos found in the pages of Heller's novel. She listed a litany of cast and crew complaints, from the food in the mess hall, to the hotel accommodations, to the difficulty in making long-distance calls. The best quote was from comedian Bob Newhart, cast as a squadron leader who tried to avoid contact with his men. "We make bets on who's going to go insane or who's already gone insane," he said. "In fact, maybe we've all gone insane and we're all together and we don't know it and we'll go home and my wife will call Paramount and say, 'Listen my husband is insane.' We have no norm here. We have no way of judging."

In New York, Simon was not pleased at the news. He was ready to record. At least Garfunkel got time off to attend the Grammy Awards ceremony that month in New York. They had picked up three joint nominations together—Best Record; Best Contemporary Pop Vocal by a Group or a Duo, both for "Mrs. Robinson"; and Best Album, *Bookends*. In addition, Simon was nominated for Best Song, "Mrs. Robinson," while he and Dave Grusin were cited for Best Original Musical Score, *The Graduate*. Though a rock single had never won the Grammys' Best Record Award, a breakthrough was expected, but voters faced a difficult choice: "Mrs. Robinson" was competing against the Beatles' "Hey Jude" on a list of nominees that also included Glen Campbell's classy country-pop hit "Wichita Lineman." The longshots were Jeannie C. Riley's country novelty "Harper Valley P.T.A." and Bobby Goldsboro's syrupy ballad "Honey."

At the March 12 awards ceremony, Simon and Garfunkel's chances didn't look good when *Bookends* lost in the Best Album category to Campbell's *By the Time I Get to Phoenix*, and "Mrs. Robinson" lost to another country-tinged entry, Bobby Russell's "Little Green Apples," in the Best Song balloting. Simon and Garfunkel picked up honors in secondary categories: the duo was honored for Best Contemporary Pop Vocal ("Mrs. Robinson"), and Simon and Grusin for Best Original Film Score (*The Graduate*).

What about Best Record? Simon and Garfunkel had to wait two more months to find out. To build suspense for NBC's Grammy Awards special that would air on May 12, Grammy officials didn't announce the Record of the Year winner at the initial awards ceremony. In the days after the event, NBC taped performances and acceptance speeches by each of the Best Record nominees for use on the special. Rather than simply sing into the camera, Simon and Garfunkel suggested something novel: show them running playfully around the bases at an empty Yankee Stadium (a tip of the hat to Joe DiMaggio) while their recording of "Mrs. Robinson" played in the background.

At the telecast, "Mrs. Robinson" was named the winner in the most prestigious Grammy category. True to his tendency to downplay his achievements, Simon was as surprised as anyone. "I thought I couldn't possibly win—not because I had any idea whether 'Hey Jude' was better than 'Mrs. Robinson,' but I thought, 'You can't beat the Beatles,' " he said years later. "It felt like the story that night was 'Hey Jude' loses the Grammy, not 'Mrs. Robinson' wins the Grammy. But that was me. It was years before I saw myself on that level."

After the ceremony, Simon had to continue to wait for Garfunkel, who had resumed work on *Catch-22*. There was, however, another bit of good news. "The Boxer," which had been released as a single in March, was a hit. It was especially pleasing that two of the artists who had influenced him, Bob Dylan and Joan Baez, both eventually recorded the song.

Garfunkel knew Simon was seething about having to wait all this time for him to finish the album. He even second-guessed himself for not confronting Nichols when filming fell months behind schedule. "Mike held me in Mexico for, like, four and a half, five months," he said. "And I should have really said to him, 'You don't need me this long. I've got to work in New York. You know? Call Paul Simon. Call Roy. What am I doing down here?' I should have said that. But I was many miles away. And you don't realize what you're missing when you're out there."

Simon was already well into crafting another song that he had a special feeling about. Michael Tannen, Paul's lawyer at the time, said Simon was so excited that he wanted to sing it for Michael and his wife, Mary, at Michael's twenty-ninth birthday party on April 3, even though Simon had such a bad cold he could only get through half the song. Tannen recalled Simon telling him, "I think I've written my 'Yesterday.' "

CHAPTER NINE

"Bridge Over Troubled Water" began one night in early 1969 as Simon sat in his East End Avenue apartment hour after hour, strumming on his guitar and listening to a gospel album by the Swan Silvertones. His rule continued to be: never set out to write a song by picking a theme; let the music itself lead the way. Once again, it was not misleading to think of his subconscious as his cowriter. In fact, Simon sometimes spoke about an "imaginary friend" who accompanied him and often whispered things in his ear—things, he suggested, he might not have consciously noticed but that provided interesting lines or images.

Simon had been interested in gospel music ever since hearing Sonny Til and the Orioles' recording of "Crying in the Chapel" as a teenager. "I loved the emotion of the singers and the songs, and there was something mysterious just about the word *chapel* because I didn't know, at twelve or thirteen, what a chapel was or looked like. It probably would have been different if they had sung, 'Cryin' in the Synagogue.' " Now he was drawn to one track on the Silvertones' album: "Oh Mary Don't You Weep," a spiritual from pre–Civil War days. At one point, the group's lead singer, the Reverend Claude Jeter, injected a line common in church parlance: "I'll be a bridge over deep water, if you trust in my name." The line doesn't stand out in the clamor of the record. You have to be paying attention to even catch it. Simon was paying attention.

Out of the blue, he wrote his own melody, which felt gentle, caring, and undeniably beautiful. Then he started writing the words that became the first two verses:

When you're weary, feeling small
When tears are in your eyes
I will dry them all
I'm on your side
When times get rough
And friends just can't be found
Like a bridge over troubled water
I will lay me down
Like a bridge over troubled water
I will lay me down

When you're down and out
When you're on the street
When evening falls so hard
I will comfort you
I'll take your part
When darkness comes
And pain is all around
Like a bridge over troubled water
I will lay me down
Like a bridge over troubled water
I will lay me down

"It was just like that," Simon said. "The essence of the song took maybe twenty minutes; the first two verses were done in two hours. And the melody was something like fifteen notes, which is long. I thought, 'This is better than I usually write.' It just seemed to flow through me. In a way, you don't feel you can really even call it your own, but then again, it's nobody else's. I didn't know where it came from, but I knew it was exceptional. It's as if there's this chemical feeling, the creating of something that is so exceptional it's addictive. It's one of the things that keeps you writing your whole life—you're trying to get to that place again."

Eventually, Simon would be so intrigued by the way a song seemed to "flow" through him—something that happened only occasionally—that he asked a neuroscientist friend about what was going on in the brain to give him that sensation. He was told that the brain chemical serotonin is secreted and produces a feeling of well-being. At the same time, dopamine flows in the brain, and that is associated with feelings of awe and even spiritual bliss. Finally, there is adrenaline, which gives you this remarkable burst of energy, allowing you to work until four in the morning without even realizing it.

"Those three elements combine and produce flow," Simon said, "but the thing that is mysterious about it is that if you gave an artist those three chemicals, it wouldn't necessarily produce flow. There's also no answer to the question of whether a song preexists in your brain or whether it's somewhere out there in the universe, waiting to be born. That's all part of the mystery of creativity."

Though the song's theme fits nicely into Simon's tendency to empathize, the opening lines contain a strong element of memoir. "I like the first lines of a song to be truthful, and those were," he said. "I was feeling weary because of the problems with Artie and other things. I was also feeling small. But then the song goes away from memoir. It comes from my imagination." Regarding the song's open arms, he said, "I've always been able to feel what it's like to be on the outside even though I've kind of been at the center of things in my own life. On the other hand, I'm in a minority, and I'm unusually small for someone who is at the center of attention. I'm essentially a selfish guy. I always did for the most part what I wanted, but with something inside saying, 'Don't step on people.' I know everything could be reversed in an instant." Simon even remembers feeling sorry for the pitcher the time he stole home. "I knew him vaguely," he said, "and I worried afterward about how he must have felt."

Simon was still going over the song a few days later when he took a break to fulfill a childhood dream. Michael Burke, president of the New York Yankees, invited him to throw the ceremonial first pitch at the team's home opener. Burke was a fan of Simon and Garfunkel and thought Simon would be a natural after hearing "Mrs. Robinson." Simon tossed the ball to catcher Jake Gibbs, who walked it back to Simon as "Mrs. Robinson" played over the PA system. Simon's brother, Eddie, was with him that day and recalled years later the joy he felt. "Every once in a while, Paul does something ridiculously amazing," he said. "This was one of those times. I mean, how many people have brothers who do that?"

Soon after, Simon played an early version of "Bridge" for Halee. "Paul came into the control room with his guitar and these two verses, and I thought, 'Wow,' " Halee said. "I just wish I had a tape of that now. You've got to remember this was right on the heels of 'The Boxer.' Two absolutely brilliant songs—back to back." Those two songs helped Simon and Halee keep up their spirits during a time when both felt abandoned by Garfunkel.

"Artie had walked away from our album so he could be a goddamn movie star," Halee continued. "I felt betrayed. I think Paul was angry at first, but then I think there was also a sense of sadness. It showed in some of the songs he was writing." Halee was referring to two songs Simon wrote with Garfunkel in mind: "The Only Living Boy in New York" and "So Long, Frank Lloyd Wright." The first is a wistful, largely affectionate number that begins, "Tom, get your plane right on time," a reference to both the old Tom & Jerry days and Art's move into movies. "I thought of it as a kind of 'Good luck' message to Art," Simon said. "I was saying, 'Go do it,' a kind of a 'Hey Jude' type of song."

In "Frank Lloyd Wright," Simon alludes to Garfunkel's dream of being an architect and all the nights of rehearsal as teens when they would "harmonize till dawn." But it ends with a long fade of Garfunkel singing "So long . . . so long . . . so long." Hard-core fans noticed another voice buried deep in the mix at the end of the track, saying, "So long already, Artie."

Many assumed that it was Simon speaking; maybe even sending Garfunkel a message that the partnership was ending. In fact, it was Halee's voice, and he was just making a joke about how long the segment was running.

Art was touched by "Living Boy," noting, "[It] has a very tender thing about it. There's something really musical and from the heart about that song. It's indescribably sweet. The attitude of the lyric." He was less enthusiastic about "Frank Lloyd Wright." "It is another kind of song," he said. "The chords don't have that emotionalism. It's more about cleverness."

Simon and Garfunkel finally got together again in early June 1969 in the studio in Hollywood, where Halee was now living and three of the chief session players were based: drummer Hal Blaine, bassist Joe Osborn, and keyboardist Larry Knechtel. The duo was so glad to be working on the album that the hard feelings took a backseat momentarily. The atmosphere in the studio was urgent because Columbia, as usual, wanted the album for the holiday season, and all they had in the can were "The Boxer" and its flip side, "Baby Driver." Knowing they might be in Los Angeles for a few months, Garfunkel rented a three-bedroom house at 1567 Blue Jay Way, a street in the Laurel Canyon neighborhood that in the late 1960s and early 1970s was a haven for musicians, including Joni Mitchell, James Taylor, and Carole King. It was the same house where George Harrison had been inspired to write "Blue Jay Way" for the Beatles. It had a pool and offered gorgeous views of the city.

The summer vacation feeling led to playful evenings, notably the night Eddie, who frequently traveled with his brother during those days, started pounding out such a lively rhythm on a piano bench that the others—including Paul, Peggy, Art, and a couple of friends—joined in, using whatever pieces of wood or silverware they could find. The sound they produced was so intriguing that they taped it on a Sony recorder and took the tape into the studio, where they added to the dynamics by dropping a handful of drumsticks on the parquet floor and even threw in a few notes on a xylophone. Halee turned the spontaneous recording into a catchy three-minute loop, and Simon came up with what would be the opening lines of the song "Cecelia": "Cecilia, you're breakin' my heart / you're shaking my confidence daily."

"The whole thing was a piece of fluff, but magical fluff," Simon said. Simon and Garfunkel recorded two other songs in Hollywood: "Why Don't You Write Me," a lighthearted nod to Jamaican ska and reggae music, and a whimsical, brassy ball of energy originally titled "Mr. Engineer" but later changed to "Keep the Customer Satisfied."

Simon also decided it was finally time to record his version of an instrumental he had heard in Paris just days before flying home in 1965. At the celebrated Théâtre de l'Est Parisien, the bill included Los Incas, a group of South American musicians who employed pan flutes, keyboard, guitar, and other instruments in playing Andean folk music. He was especially struck by one song, "El Condor Pasa," which he was told was a traditional folk song that had been given a new arrangement by the Incas' Jorge Milchberg. Now Simon wrote lyrics to the original melody in a vaguely philosophical folk style that made the music and words feel like they had been passed down in Andean villages for generations. The song began,

I'd rather be a hammer than a nail,
Yes, I would
If I could
I surely would

Instead of getting US musicians to duplicate the sound of the Incas' record or hiring the group to rerecord their version, Simon had the novel idea of simply licensing the original recording from Philips Records and adding his vocal to the track, which became "El Condor Pasa (If I Could)."

Throughout this period, the song on everyone's mind in Hollywood was "Bridge." By the time they began recording it in mid-August, it was clear that Simon and Garfunkel once again weren't going to deliver the album in time for the holiday season. They had taken on too much. Besides the LP, they were committed that fall to an NBC special and a ten-city tour.

Because of the landmark nature of the song and the duo's reputation for taking a lot of time in the studio, the recording of "Bridge" has become another urban legend—maybe, some suggested, even longer than the hundred hours attributed to "The Boxer." In truth, Simon says, the instrumental track was done in five days in Los Angeles, and Garfunkel's vocal was done later over two days in New York during a break from the brief tour. It was, however, certainly an intense seven days. From the start, Simon imagined Garfunkel singing lead, though Art wasn't particularly receptive. "He felt it was his best song," Garfunkel said. "I felt it was something less than his best song, but a great song." Once Art relented, Larry Knechtel was given the task of adapting the song for piano, and it wasn't easy. Simon wanted a gospel feel, but "not too gospelly." Working on the changes for most of two days, Knechtel went through dozens of takes before Simon felt it was right.

Knechtel's adaptation so extended the song that Garfunkel and Halee began to feel a third verse was needed. Simon and Garfunkel then pictured something that would give the song a dramatic lift, like the one they admired in some of producer Phil Spector's recordings with the Righteous Brothers, where a song, such as "You've Lost That Lovin' Feelin', " would move along simply until near the end, when Spector injected a sudden, massive touch of instrumental drama. Simon took on the challenge and wrote a new verse on the spot. That morning Peggy, two years older than Simon, was upset when she noticed a couple of gray hairs in the mirror. Simon flashed back on the incident and came up with lines that were meant as a good-natured piece of reassurance. In less than ten minutes, he had the third verse:

Sail on, silver girl
Sail on by
Your time has come to shine
All your dreams are on their way
See how they shine
If you need a friend
I'm sailing right behind
Like a bridge over troubled water
I will ease your mind

Like a bridge over troubled water
I will ease your mind

The additional verse worked well, giving the song a teasingly mysterious image similar to what Jimmy Webb had done the year before with "MacArthur Park," a hit for the Irish actor-singer Richard Harris. There was as much head-scratching over "Sail on, silver girl" as there was over Webb's reference to the cake left out in the rain. (For years, a popular theory among listeners was that "silver girl" refered to a heroin addict's needle.) With that verse added, the recording of the song went quickly—until they got to the strings.

Halee gave a demo of the song to Ernie Freeman, a veteran arranger who had worked with scores of recording artists, including Frank Sinatra. But when Freeman returned the next day with string arrangements written out for each of the musicians, Simon lost all confidence in him when he saw the title Freeman had written on the music sheets, "Like a Pitcher of Water." "I was pissed off," Simon said. "It looked like he didn't listen to the demo long enough to get the right title. I hated the arrangement so much that I walked out of the studio. I was abrasive at times in the studio, but that's my job: to protect the music. It doesn't matter what anybody thinks of me. I'm not going to let anything bad happen to a piece of work. It's like your child." As he did so often, Halee found a way to make the arrangement work so that they didn't have to bring back the musicians for another try, though Simon always looked at the string part as a bit too syrupy.

On the final day of recording in Los Angeles, Simon sang "Song for the Asking," a sweet reflection on the joys of sharing thoughts and emotions through music. Placed at the end of the album, it felt like a personal message to fans from Simon, which may be why he sang it himself.

The closing lines:

Ask me and I will play
All the love that I hold inside

Simon and Garfunkel went from the session to a brief US tour that would end on November 28 at Carnegie Hall. For the first time, they brought along a band—the three Hollywood session players and guitarist Fred Carter Jr.—to duplicate the increasingly colorful sounds they were creating in the studio. Some fans complained that the instruments were an intrusion, but the band gave the music increased energy and range. It was a modest step toward the more varied and ambitious sounds Simon would later explore on his own. Halee joined them on several tour stops to record the shows, the highlights of which were released in an album forty years later.

When it was time to record Garfunkel's vocal for "Bridge" in New York, he told Simon that he didn't want him in the studio. Halee worried that the request might fuel the tension between Simon and Garfunkel, but Simon understood. He knew it was important for Art to be relaxed so he could focus on the song. Simon loved the result. On "Bridge," Garfunkel delivered one of the great vocal performances of the modern pop era; a truly inspired mix of classic pop and soulful gospel.

The network television special wasn't as successful.

Given CBS's success with *The Glen Campbell Goodtime Hour* and *The Smothers Brothers Comedy Hour* in 1968–69, NBC and ABC were aggressively looking for contemporary musical variety shows of their own. After canvassing the field, NBC set its sights on Simon and Garfunkel. Here was a duo whose music and image were comfortable enough for older viewers and edgy and hip enough to appeal to the younger viewers that advertisers coveted. Rather than a weekly series, the network proposed Simon and Garfunkel have their own prime-time special sponsored by AT&T.

Simon and Garfunkel insisted on the same creative control they had on their recordings. They wanted to produce the special, and they wanted to select the director. Somewhat surprisingly, the network gave in on both points. Doing the TV show on top of the album was crazy in a way, but Simon said years later that it was just the bravado of youth. "When you're twenty-seven years old, there's virtually nothing you can't do—or at least nothing you think you can't do," he said. "There's this endless energy. We would often stay in the studio recording until six in the morning. We'd play all night. So why not a TV special? 'Sure,' we said, 'we can do that.' "

To help them, Simon and Garfunkel turned to Charles Grodin, a thirty-four-year-old actor and comedian whom Garfunkel had met while filming *Catch-22*. Grodin encouraged them to sidestep the normal concert documentary, which is what the network expected, in favor of a program that showed how the pair's music reflected the sociocultural issues of the day, including poverty, civil rights abuse, farmworkers in California, and the war in Vietnam. In the program's most dramatic sequence, "Bridge Over Troubled Water" was played while viewers saw endearing scenes of the Kennedy brothers and Dr. Martin Luther King Jr., followed immediately by images of funeral trains and mourners. Though the duo had performed the song on some stops during the tour, this would be the first time most Americans heard it because the album wouldn't be released until early in 1970.

Network and advertising executives gasped when they saw the final product. Grodin said an agency representative asked if Simon and Garfunkel were open to changes, such as lowering the volume when Coretta Scott King talked about poverty and hunger being violent acts against children. When Grodin asked how much lower, he was told, "Inaudible." AT&T dropped its sponsorship, and NBC washed its hands of the special, but CBS stepped in, and the show was scheduled for nine o'clock on Sunday, November 30.

Back in the recording studio in mid-November, Simon and Garfunkel were so drained they couldn't agree on a song to fill out what they had planned to be a twelve-track album. Simon wanted to use his "Cuba Si, Nixon No," a lighthearted bit of commentary wrapped in a Chuck Berry rhythm, but Garfunkel refused to sing it. Simon admitted later it wasn't much of a song. Garfunkel proposed a Johann Sebastian Bach chorale piece for the twelfth selection, but Simon wasn't interested. Emotionally fatigued, they decided to go with just eleven songs, one of which was a live version of "Bye Bye Love" from the tour.

It was during this period that Simon learned from Grodin that Art, despite the tensions caused by *Catch-22*, had agreed to make another film with

Mike Nichols, this one a comedy-drama titled *Carnal Knowledge* and written by satirist Jules Feiffer. Furious, Simon confronted his partner. "I asked why he didn't tell me, and he said he was afraid I would stop working on 'Bridge Over Troubled Water,' " Simon said. "In other words, he hid it from me. He knew how I'd feel, but he did it anyway. Mike told Artie he was going to be a big movie star, and Artie couldn't say no. He later told me he didn't see why it was such a big deal to me; he would make the movie for six months, and I could write the songs for the next album. Then, he thought, we could get together in the studio again and record them.

"I thought, 'Fuck you, I'm not going to do that.' And the truth is, I think if Artie had become a big movie star, he would have left. Instead of just being the guy who sang Paul Simon songs, he could be Art Garfunkel, a big star all by himself. And this made me think about how I could still be the guy who wrote songs and sing them. I didn't need Artie. Peggy encouraged me. She thought it was time for me to leave and do what I wanted."

Simon and Garfunkel was almost over, but they still had the album to finish.

From the moment they recorded "Cecilia," Simon believed it should be the single to accompany the January 1970 release of the album, which would be titled *Bridge Over Troubled Water*. As much as he loved the title song, he feared it was too long at nearly five minutes and too heavy a ballad to pick up the massive radio airplay that is the stepping stone to hit singles. "Cecilia," on the other hand, seemed perfect: under three minutes and supremely infectious. That thinking changed in late November when Paul and Art first played the album for Clive Davis in Columbia's Manhattan studio. "As soon as I heard 'Bridge,' I could feel the adrenaline building inside," Davis said. "I felt 'Cecelia' would be a hit, but 'Bridge' was something more. It was a landmark record."

There was no way Simon was going to disagree after he saw the impact of the song during the Carnegie Hall concerts on November 28 and 29, and the CBS special the following night. The applause in the intimate Carnegie Hall on that first night was chilling. Yet in his *New York Times* review, critic John S. Wilson savaged the song: "In its mawkish, undiluted sentimentality, it was reminiscent of the songs of faith that were once great favorites on the lesser concert circuits." But he couldn't deny the audience's fervor, describing the crowd's "enthusiastic cheering" as "astonishing."

The response that night was bittersweet for Simon. Since it was only Garfunkel singing on the song, Simon remained in the wings, leaving only Garfunkel and pianist Knechtel in the spotlight. As the massive applause began, Garfunkel bowed, thanked the audience, and introduced Knechtel, but he didn't acknowledge Simon; he didn't call for him to come out onstage or even announce that Simon had written the song. Simon was crestfallen—excluded from a special moment in his hometown. "That's my song," he said to himself. "And I'm not even out there."

There was more heartbreak that weekend. Ratings for the TV special were awful. "During the first commercial, which came just after Robert Kennedy's funeral train, one million people turned over to a Peggy Fleming figure skating special," Grodin said. "The show was just too honest for a lot of people." Even so, Simon looked back on the special with pride. "We got a lot of hate mail after the show aired . . . a lot of that 'America, love it or leave it' stuff," Simon said years later. "But I'm proud of the show. It represented what we honestly believed about the country, and we didn't back down. The craziest point was when the network representatives complained about the funeral trains during the 'Bridge Over Troubled Water' segment. They said, 'You can't use that because they are all Democrats,' and we said, 'No, they were all assassinated.' "

Simon was comforted, however, by one thing. He knew he had written a classic.

For the rock generation, the 1960s was a decade of great promise and deep disillusionment; a time of Camelot and the Vietnam War. The emotional toll was heavy—and much of the most memorable music reflected the volatility of a world that appeared all the more out of control because it was often seen through a drug-infused haze. The start of the new decade offered hopes of a second chance, and some of the most inspiring songs of 1970 resonated with comfort and reassurance. The Beatles stepped forward the first week in March with "Let It Be," which promised sanctuary in times of darkness and doubt. James Taylor entered the charts six months later with "Fire and Rain," a reflection on the turbulence caused in Taylor's personal life by the suicide of a friend and his own heroin addiction. George Harrison followed in December with "My Sweet Lord," a humble statement of spiritual quest.

Even in that distinguished company, "Bridge Over Troubled Water" stood out. The single was not only released first (the final week of January), but also it remained the most celebrated of those recordings a half century later. The song topped pop charts around the world, including six weeks at no. 1 in the States. It has been recorded by such towering artists as Elvis Presley, Aretha Franklin, Stevie Wonder, and Johnny Cash. Next to Art's, Simon's favorite vocal interpretation was Aretha's. On the heels of "Mrs. Robinson" and "The Boxer," the song triggered enormous added respect for Simon in the mainstream music community, especially the seasoned pros who composed the bulk of Grammy voters and who had been slow to embrace rock 'n' roll. To many of them, "Bridge" was an inspiring link to the supreme craftsmanship of the Great American Songbook tradition.

The album was even a greater triumph commercially, spending ten weeks at no. 1 and eventually selling eight million copies. In the midst of this success, however, Simon continued to wrestle with many of the same anxieties that had contributed to him writing the song. When Loraine Alterman interviewed him for *Rolling Stone*, she did not see in him any sign of someone celebrating his mushrooming superstardom. "Paul arrived wearing a blue loden coat with the hood turned up," Alterman wrote. "Beneath it he had on black trousers and a black shirt. He does not crave attention." In the same interview, Simon said he was thinking of moving into the woods, possibly in New England, because the farmhouse in Bucks County wasn't secluded enough. And, he confided, he was so troubled that he was going to analysis three days a week.

For all the tensions with Garfunkel, Simon knew there could be a void when they went their separate ways. Art had been one of his best friends for most of his life, and Simon, so focused on his music, wasn't quick to make new friends. He found himself depending more and more on Peggy for companionship and unwavering support in his desire to leave Simon and Garfunkel. "I'd say, 'I'm gonna leave,' and she'd say, 'Yeah, you should,' " Simon said later. "She'd say, 'What do you have to be afraid of? You're the one who writes all the songs.' "

With Alterman, he did speak vaguely about a future without Art. "It may sound strange, but time is running out," he told her. "You go on to do things because once you get to a certain point, you've got to ride your energy while you have it. As long as you have energy and curiosity and drive, you use it . . . [but] there are so many things I want to learn."

Alterman knew that he was teaching a songwriting class that spring at New York University—one limited only to songwriters he felt had promise—and she asked him about it. Simon had long thought about teaching a course, and what better subject than songwriting? "You can't teach someone how to write a song," he replied, no doubt welcoming the chance to get away from the subject of Simon and Garfunkel. "But I am dealing with people who already write songs, so what I can do mainly is tell them what I've learned and go into the studio and [talk about] what problems will arise in the studio when you go in to cut the song. It sort of prepares you a little bit for going in there. Otherwise you just come in, and you're lost. You're just in the record company's hands, and you're lost."

Maggie and Terre Roche, two young sisters who would later form the Roches trio with another sister, Suzzy, attended the class, hoping to impress Simon enough for him to take them under his wing. Decades later, Terre still spoke about the contrast between Simon's warm, down-to-earth nature when he wasn't talking about music and his frankness when he was. Knowing they lived in New Jersey, Simon gave them a ride after the first class to the George Washington Bridge, where they could take a bus home. But when they worked up enough courage to ask him if he thought they were any good as singers and songwriters, he told them, in effect, they had enough of a gift to maybe win some talent shows in their hometown, but they needed to get a lot better if they wanted a professional career. "It was such a powerful experience, that ride," Terre said years later. "On the one

1. Simon's parents, Lou and Belle, around the time of their marriage in 1938.

2. Simon (*left*) and his son Adrian when they were each around eighteen months old.

3. Young Paul delights in accompanying his father as Lou walks his sister, Rose-lynd, down the aisle.

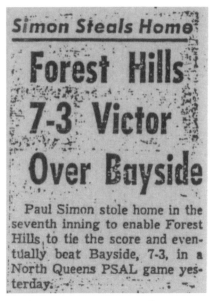

Forest Hills 7-3 Victor Over Bayside

Paul Simon stole home in the seventh inning to enable Forest Hills to tie the score and eventually beat Bayside, 7-3, in a North Queens PSAL game yesterday.

5. This 1958 newspaper clipping reports Simon's greatest baseball feat: stealing home for his Forest Hills High School team.

4. Long before he thought about writing a song, Simon's chief passion was baseball—not only playing games in local schoolyards but also listening to New York Yankee games on the radio.

6. Lou Simon's years as a bandleader and upright bass player—he played Thursday afternoons for years at Manhattan's celebrated Roseland Ballroom—greatly influenced his son's high standards and drive as a songwriter and his deep respect for musicians.

7. Simon was surely thinking of his first great rock 'n' roll hero, Elvis Presley, as he posed with a guitar during a break from his summer camp chores in 1957.

8. As Tom & Jerry, Paul Simon and Art Garfunkel had their first hit in 1957 with "Hey, Schoolgirl," a tune influenced by the rockabilly zest of the Everly Brothers' "Wake Up Little Susie."

9. The "Hey, Schoolgirl" single. It reached no. 49 on the US sales chart, but a misunderstanding led Simon and Garfunkel to end their partnership for five years.

10. Simon found some of his earliest encouragement in folk clubs in England in 1964 and '65. He was no longer put down, as he had been in New York's Greenwich Village folk circles, as the kid from Queens but embraced as the kid from America.

11. The cover of Simon's 1965 solo album, *The Paul Simon Song Book*, features Simon and his first love, Kathy Chitty. She would inspire several of his early songs, including "Homeward Bound" and "Kathy's Song."

12. Simon and Garfunkel in the Columbia Records studio in Manhattan during a recording session for their debut album in March of 1964.

Meeting fans backstage during : Parsley, Sage, Rosemary and yme tour in 1967.

14. A rare photo of Simon and Garfunkel's camera-shy but persuasive and fun-loving manager, Mort Lewis, who stopped by the dressing room on the 1967 tour.

15. Belle, on vocals, and Lou, on bass, join their sons (Paul on guitar and Eddie on keyboards) at a party in 1971 to celebrate Lou's PhD in linguistics from New York University.

16. Simon and his first wife, Peggy Harper, with the family dog at their home in New Hope, Pennsylvania. Lonely and depressed, Simon had hoped marriage would bring him the same comfort and joy he saw in his parents' relationship, but it didn't.

17. Paul and his brother, Eddie—shown here in a recording studio control booth in the early 1970s—have been close from childhood, when they played basketball with a rolled-up pair of socks in their bedroom, to adulthood, when Eddie comanaged his brother's career.

18. Disappointed that fans often missed the humor in his lyrics, Simon made sure no one missed his lighter side on the Thanksgiving episode of *Saturday Night Live* in 1976 by dressing up in a turkey suit.

19. Simon's relationship with actress Carrie Fisher stretched across a decade but couldn't overcome a series of irreconcilable issues. She thought right away that Edie Brickell would be perfect for Paul—someone who could give him the comfort and family he wanted.

20. During a trip with *Saturday Night Live* mastermind Lorne Michaels from Crowley, Louisiana, where Simon recorded a track for the *Graceland* album, to Memphis, Tennessee, to check out the music scene there, Simon was given a speeding ticket in Mississippi.

hand, he was doing us a favor, but on the other hand, he was very critical. He was like a surgeon." Ultimately, Simon was impressed enough by the sisters to have them sing on one of his solo albums and sign them to his publishing company.

Simon felt he couldn't be more forthcoming about his future with Garfunkel during the *Rolling Stone* interview because he and Art still had a few remaining tour dates in April and May in Europe, a two-day stand at the Forest Hills Stadium on July 17–18, and then the Grammy Awards ceremony, where *Bridge* was considered an early favorite for Best Album. He didn't want the distraction of people talking about the breakup, and he found the sentimentality surrounding farewell events embarrassing, especially for artists under thirty. One other thing that Simon didn't tell Alterman was that he and Peggy were engaged.

To keep Peggy company, Simon invited his mother to London when he and Garfunkel performed on April 25 at Royal Albert Hall, one of the world's great concert buildings. Before the show, Belle and Peggy talked about Paul's disappointment over feeling left out after "Bridge" at Carnegie Hall. Maybe, they hoped, Garfunkel would introduce him this time. It didn't happen. "Paul waits in the wings," Belle said. "Art got great applause . . . He was very good, and the song was so great, so Art stood there, taking bow after bow, and he finally went up to the pianist [Knechtel] and introduced him, and that was it! I'm sitting next to Peggy, and she's like, 'Why doesn't he bring Paul out? Why doesn't he bring the author out onstage?' I'm saying the same thing. Paul's got something big, a real terrific song, and [Art] doesn't even have the nerve to give him the credit: 'I sang it, it was me you loved, but here's the guy who wrote it.' Never did."

Four weeks later on May 24, Paul and Peggy were married in a civil ceremony in New Hope attended only by Lou, Belle, and Eddie. They then hosted a couple dozen guests, including Garfunkel, the Tannens, Mort Lewis, Roy Halee, and Bobby Susser, at an outdoor reception on their property. In line with his penchant for privacy, Simon didn't make a public announcement, whereas most pop stars would have milked the event for publicity—even inviting a select magazine or two to the ceremony. "I don't think there is any deep, dark reason for why I prefer privacy," Simon said later. "It's just part of my nature. I'm not shy. I'm comfortable around people, but I was never too keen on people looking in on what I was doing and reporting about me. To me, it takes another personality, something even beyond extrovert, to invite people to document your life and look at you and your life in the camera."

To some guests that day, the wedding felt both sudden and inevitable. In the broadest sense, Peggy represented for Simon a piece of the comfort he himself was longing for in "Bridge." If fame hadn't brought him peace of mind, Simon thought marriage and an eventual family might, especially the warm, nurturing family life that he had treasured as a boy. At the same time, people around Simon had concerns. One of the reception guests said he could understand why Simon married Peggy. She was pretty, and she was on his side. But the guest could also see even then why the marriage probably wouldn't last. Simon needed her at that moment, but he was really married to his music, which would be a major challenge for Peggy.

Rather than feel Simon had "taken" Peggy from him, Mort Lewis said he was "relieved" by the divorce and held no animosity toward Simon when the pair started dating. He said he and Simon even had a heart-to-heart conversation agreeing not to let the matter disrupt their business ties.

The day after the wedding, Paul and Peggy headed off on a seven-hundred-mile trip in his two-seat Mercedes convertible to the Smoky Mountain Music Festival in Gatlinburg, Tennessee. Paul thought Peggy would enjoy going back to her southern roots, but, in retrospect, she saw it chiefly as a sign that Simon's world—even on his honeymoon—would revolve around music. It wasn't a happy prospect for her, but she figured they'd adjust.

Two months later, Peggy was in the audience as Simon and Garfunkel stepped onstage at their hometown venue, the Forest Hills Stadium, for the first of what would be their final two concerts as a dedicated team; every time they'd sing together onstage from then on, it would be for a benefit, television appearance, or a one-off reunion tour. By all accounts, the evening was lovely, and there wasn't an inkling of a pending breakup in the *Billboard* review: "Take a full moon in the sky, a balmy summer breeze, a flying Frisbee and a glowing sparkler; add two young guns, one in dungarees, one with a guitar and a baseball cap. Put them onstage before 14,400 people, and you have a sight to remember. If the two guys are named Simon and Garfunkel, that is, and the stage is the Forest Hills Tennis Club."

Lewis wasn't fooled. Watching Paul and Art walk to the parking lot after the second night's concert, then pause, shake hands, and go their separate ways, he sensed it was over. In subsequent years, he often asked himself if he should have stepped in and tried to talk Simon out of walking away from the team. And he always came to the same conclusion: no. Lewis respected Simon too much to intervene. "I knew he wanted to be on his own," he said. "He needed to grow." Besides, the affable manager had been around the music business for a long time. He had seen all sorts of great jazz outfits break up over the years. Hell, even the Beatles had broken up a few months earlier. Life goes on.

True to his private nature, Simon didn't announce his decision publicly the way Paul McCartney had after leaving the Beatles. He didn't even tell Garfunkel about it. One possibility is that he was trying to hedge his bets in case he didn't find his solo career as rewarding as he expected, but Simon rejected that notion. "Making an announcement isn't something that I ever thought of," he recalled. "I wasn't into that kind of thing. I remember when I first met Derek Taylor and found out he was the Beatles' press secretary. I thought to myself, 'Why would you even want a press secretary?' With Artie, there was no reason to talk about it. When he agreed to make *Carnal Knowledge*, something was broken between us. There was no way I was going to change my mind, and I certainly didn't want to get into a fight about it. I just wanted to move on. We were finished."

Simon continued to see Garfunkel socially during the summer. He not only invited Art to the wedding but also accompanied him to a screening of *Catch-22* shortly before the Forest Hills dates. There was so little public suspicion of a breakup that no one sensed anything strange three weeks after those final shows when Simon appeared at nearby Shea Stadium without Art. It was the Summer Festival for Peace all-day concert designed to raise money for antiwar candidates in the fall 1970 midterm elections.

Soon after, Simon finally informed Clive Davis of his decision. "I wanted Clive to hear about my plans before word got out on the street," he said. "We met in his office, and he was very cordial. He said he was looking forward to our next album and, in the course of the meeting, asked when we were planning to record it, and I said, 'We're not.' "

Davis was deeply concerned. Years later, he said, "Ever since we had the problem over pricing on *Bookends*, I had tried to build a relationship with Paul. During the making of *Bridge*, we went out to lunch from time to time, and he told me about the issues he was having with Art. But I had no idea he was thinking of leaving Simon and Garfunkel, and I told him frankly during our meeting in the office that I thought it was a major mistake. I told him how much I respected him as an artist, but I also pointed out how few musicians from best-selling groups were able to do even remotely as well on their own."

Now it was Simon who was let down. "I had gone to see Clive hoping that he would understand and be supportive," Simon said. "But he was just thinking commercially. He warned me that leaving Simon and Garfunkel would be the biggest mistake of my life, and I didn't necessarily disagree with him. I knew I'd probably never be as big as Simon and Garfunkel again, but that wasn't the point. I wasn't thinking of sales. I wanted to do what was best for my music. I was hoping for a long career and making enough good records that someday people would look back at Simon and Garfunkel and say, 'Oh, this is what you did in the beginning.' "

Fans and pop historians would spend decades trying to figure out just what went wrong, but clues were scattered all around. The breakup has been blamed variously on raging egos, grating personality differences, and Garfunkel's decision to pursue a film career. In retrospect, each of these factors contributed to Simon's decision, but they weren't, even collectively, ultimately responsible for it. As both Quincy Jones and critic-turned-manager Jon Landau pointed out, Simon was too talented and ambitious a songwriter and record maker to limit himself to writing songs for Art Garfunkel to sing. The relationship was too restrictive. Simon wanted the freedom to move beyond the mostly soothing folk strains that lifted Simon and Garfunkel to superstar status in rock. He heard a whole new world of music in his head, and he wanted to pursue it.

"There are a lot of factors that comprise great artistry, including passion, musical curiosity, and fearlessness," said Quincy Jones, who would follow Simon's career for more than fifty years. "And the first rule of being an artist is you've got to protect all three. If Paul hadn't left Garfunkel, a piece of that artistry could have died. He did what he had to do."

There was one more bit of Simon and Garfunkel business at the start of the 1970s. With still no announcement of a break, they walked onstage at the thirteenth annual Grammy Awards ceremony the evening of March 16, 1971, at the Hollywood Palladium in Los Angeles. Thanks to the *Bridge Over Troubled Water* album, the duo entered the night with more nominations (seven) than anyone previously in Grammy history, but the competition was strong. James Taylor and the Beatles were also up for Best Record and Best Song ("Fire and Rain" and "Let It Be," respectively).

It proved to be no contest. In the nationally telecast program, Simon became the first artist ever to sweep the three most prestigious Grammy categories: Best Album, Best Record, and Best Song. He shared the first two with Garfunkel, but the song honor was his own. Together the pair was also given Grammys for Best Contemporary Group Vocal and Best Arrangement Accompanying Vocals (shared with Jimmie Haskell, Ernie Freeman, and Larry Knechtel). In addition, Simon won for Best Contemporary Song ("Bridge" again), and Roy Halee was honored for Best Engineered Recording. At the end of the evening, Simon and Garfunkel stood at the pinnacle of American pop music. To anyone watching them accepting their awards, Paul and Art's future together looked unlimited. But it was an illusion.

CHAPTER TEN

Simon went through long periods of insecurity after deciding to leave Garfunkel. He was so unsettled, especially after the meeting with Clive Davis, that he thought everyone at the label, including Roy Halee, had lost faith in him. In his mind, they all believed Garfunkel would be the bigger star. When Simon asked the producer to work with him on his first solo album in the fall of 1970, he was relieved to hear him say yes. Informed decades later about Simon's anxiety, Davis was surprised. "When he first told me about leaving Simon and Garfunkel, I spent a long time talking about how much I believed in him as an artist," he said. "I felt he had already joined Dylan and Lennon-McCartney as the premier songwriters of his generation. In fact, I felt his talent went beyond his generation. He also fit in with the greats before him, the Cole Porters and Irving Berlins, as someone who combines an incredible feel for melody with a literate lyric sense that is second to none. I told him I would look forward to his records regardless, but I thought he should know what he was giving up commercially."

Halee, too, said he always saw Simon's future as brighter than Garfunkel's, but he understood why Simon felt everyone was down on him. The feeling around the record company, Halee said, was that it was over for them both. "The pressure on him was enormous when he worked on that first solo album."

Before starting the album that fall, Simon served as a judge at the Fifth International Popular Song Festival competition in Rio de Janeiro, Brazil. "I like other kinds of music," he said. "The amazing thing is that this country is so provincial. Americans know American music. You go to France. They know a lot of kinds of music. You go to Japan, and they know a lot of indigenous music. But Americans almost never get into other sounds." The relative lack of interest in world music among most American rock musicians in the early 1970s was in part because the "foreign" strains didn't seem commercial. But Simon wanted to explore any sounds that might inspire him to writer better songs.

Soon after the festival, he headed for San Francisco, where Halee ran a new Columbia studio to serve the label's Bay Area acts. "After all the production on *Bookends* and *Bridge*, Paul wanted to keep things as simple as possible," Halee said. "It was like he was starting over, and he wanted to concentrate on his songs and his guitar. At the same time, he was eager to experiment. This was his chance to break free." Simon worked with top musicians during the sessions, including Donald "Duck" Dunn, who was the bassist with Booker T. and the MG's, Memphis's ultrasoulful quartet. But nothing felt right, and he headed back to New York and Peggy. They were now living in a brownstone apartment building on Ninety-Fourth Street. During that time, they went to dinner one night at Say Eng Look, a restaurant in Chinatown, and Simon noticed an item on the menu that intrigued him: Mother and Child Reunion. It was a chicken-and-egg dish, and he thought it would make a great title for a song, though he had no idea what the song would be about.

Besides concentrating on his own music, Simon kept track of a handful of songwriters. Since his early admiration of Dylan and Lennon-McCartney, he had also grown fond of Randy Newman. "He's really the only writer who can make me laugh out loud, at least consistently," he said. "His writing is very compositional, and when he gets emotional, it's particularly emotional because he's so intelligent and cynical. He's also got his own sense of Americana that I love." Other favorites included Brian Wilson. "I didn't pay a lot of attention to Brian for a while because the Beach Boys' subject matter was so West Coast," he said. "But then he got into this really touching music with songs like 'In My Room,' and 'Good Vibrations' was amazing. The melodies are so beautiful, almost perfect. I began to realize he was one of the most gifted writers of our generation."

In the early 1970s, Simon was also looking beyond rock to a wide range of writers, including Antonio Carlos Jobim, whose Grammy-winning 1964 album with Stan Getz, *Getz/Gilberto*, was an inspired mix of jazz and bossa nova, and heralded Broadway composer-lyricist Stephen Sondheim. "Sondheim was so intellectually sharp," Simon said. "He is a very, very clear and efficient storyteller." Simon singled out Richard Rodgers as a favorite melody writer in the musical theater. Rodgers, who teamed over the years with lyricists Lornez Hart and Oscar Hammerstein II, wrote the music for numbers such as "My Funny Valentine" and "People Will Say We're in Love." Simon also had a fondness for Hoagy Carmichael, Johnny Mercer, and George and Ira Gershwin.

The split from Garfunkel may have liberated Simon artistically, but it did nothing to speed up his writing. When he began work on his first solo album, the shelf was bare. So, guitar in hand, he began searching for ideas, day after day, week after week, in 1970 and early 1971. He blamed the dry spell initially on writer's block and wrestled with the anxiety that each batch of songs might be his last. "I'm neurotically driven," he said. "What happens is, I finish one thing and start to take a vacation. I lay off for a while, and then I get panicky. I say to myself, 'Oh my God, I'm not doing anything. I can't write anymore. It's over.' Then I tell myself, 'Don't be silly. This is exactly what happens every time you finish an album.' " And, sure enough, the ideas slowly started coming, none more persistently than the Jamaican ska sound that he had attempted without success on "Why Don't You Write Me" on the *Bridge* album.

Young Jamaicans heard R&B records by artists such as Fats Domino and Smiley Lewis on radio stations broadcasting from New Orleans and other southern cities in the 1950s. When they began making their own music, they combined those R&B touches with a wide array of Caribbean styles, including mento and the closely aligned calypso. Simon heard an early US touch of ska in a piano part in "Florence," a 1957 single by the Brooklyn doo-wop group the Paragons. The Beatles also played with ska in the quirky, uplifting "Ob-La-Di, Ob-La-Da" in 1968, but the music was still very much a fringe sound in the United States when Simon fell under the spell of Jimmy Cliff's 1969 antiwar song "Vietnam."

Cliff, who would later star in the classic, music-packed Jamaican gangster film *The Harder They Come*, wrote "Vietnam" about a mother who learned by telegram that her son was killed in battle. Rather than turn the story into stark protest, Cliff wrapped the theme with a light, almost danceable ribbon. At the end, the mother was waiting for her son's body to be shipped home. Simon asked himself how he would deal with the loss of someone else close to him, and his father's heart attacks always made that possibility a threat. In the mysterious ways that creativity works, "Vietnam" and the morbid thoughts it provided began to intersect with the Chinese dish.

"Paul just fell in love with ska," Halee said. "But he didn't want to try having American musicians duplicate the sound again. He insisted on going to Jamaica and working with actual ska musicians, which was a revolutionary concept." Not knowing the scene in Jamaica, Simon phoned Leslie Kong, the Jamaican producer of the "Vietnam" recording, who was delighted to have someone of Simon's reputation interested in his country's music. If Simon had a hit, he figured, it could open a door for such artists as Cliff and Bob Marley. Kong urged Simon to come to Jamaica. When Simon and Halee got to Kingston, they found an all-star group of musicians waiting for them, including several who had played with Cliff and Toots and the Maytals—among them guitarist Hux Brown, drummer Winston Grennan, and percussionist Denzil Laing. When Simon first met with the musicians, he said, enthusiastically, "Let's play some ska," only to be surprised when they answered they didn't play ska. "Well, what do you play?" he asked. They replied, "Reggae." "Okay," he continued, "let's play reggae."

Because of the poverty in Kingston, the trip had its uncomfortable moments. Paul and Roy were embarrassed when they were picked up in a fancy Mercedes and driven through the poorest section of town on the way to the studio, causing them to lean forward in their seats so they were out of sight. The studio also turned out to be so cramped that equipment was stored in shoeboxes, and an assortment of animals, including goats and chickens, wandered the grounds outside. But the music was spectacular. During several all-day sessions, Simon played lines on a guitar to give the musicians a feel for what he wanted, and then encouraged them to add lively reggae touches of their own. Gradually Simon shaped the track, which offered hopeful, even spiritual tones. There were still no words, so Simon simply sang various sounds phonetically to give the track a sense of structure. Afterward, Simon and Halee returned to New York, where they added Larry Knechtel's piano and female backing voices, including that of Cissy Houston, Whitney's mother.

The challenge now was writing lyrics, tailoring individual words to the precise twists and curves of the instrumental track. In the process, the songwriting took the abstract approach of "Mrs. Robinson" to an ambitious new level. The result produced a sense of mystery that made "Mother and Child Reunion" a crowd favorite that retained its freshness for decades. Whatever the song's precise story, it offered a better day. The opening line said it all:

No, I would not give you false hope
On this strange and mournful day
But the mother and child reunion
Is only a motion away

Simon was delighted with the song, and it helped ease the anxiety that had been hanging over him. He was encouraged further when he began work on another song that would also prove to be a concert favorite, "Me and Julio Down by the Schoolyard." The title evoked all sorts of playful and provocative elements, and the song enabled him to employ some of the Latin music touches he had loved ever since the hours with his father at Roseland Ballroom, where his father's band alternated with a Latin group.

In piecing together a story, Simon went even deeper into free-association wordplay:

The mama pajama rolled out of bed
And she ran to the police station
When the papa found out, he began to shout
And he started the investigation

It's against the law
It was against the law
What the mama saw
It was against the law

The mama looked down and spit on the ground
Every time my name gets mentioned
The papa said, "Oy, if I get that boy
I'm gonna stick him in the house of detention."

Well, I'm on my way
I don't know where I'm going
I'm on my way
I'm taking my time
But I don't know where
Goodbye to Rosie, the queen of Corona
See you, me, and Julio
Down by the schoolyard
See you, me, and Julio
Down by the schoolyard

In a couple of days they come and
Take me away
But the press let the story leak
And when the radical priest
Come to get me released
We was all on the cover of Newsweek

And I'm on my way
I don't know where I'm going
I'm on my way
I'm taking my time
But I don't know where
Goodbye to Rosie, the queen of Corona
See you, me, and Julio
Down by the schoolyard
See you, me, and Julio
Down by the schoolyard
See you, me, and Julio
Down by the schoolyard

Decades later, fans were still asking themselves just what was going on in the song. What was against the law? Who was Rosie? How did they get involved with the radical priest? The mystery added to the appeal of the song, the foundation of which also showcased much of what Simon loved about music, including warmth, wit, commentary, and a hint of mystery. He was pulling images from everywhere. The "radical priest" referred to brothers Daniel and Philip Berrigan, the antiwar Jesuit priests who were on the cover of *Time* magazine in the summer of 1971, but Simon changed it to *Newsweek* because it rhymed with "let the story leak." He threw in some phrases just because he liked the sounds of them or enjoyed the challenge of fitting them into a pop song: phrases such as "the house of detention" and "Rosie, the queen of Corona."

But Simon was also thinking of special moments in his life. When

Bobby Susser listened to the song, he heard a salute to the days at the Kew Gardens Hills school playground—and, oh yes, he believed that Julio was a reference to him. "It is part Bobby and the old school yard, but there's also someone else in there," Simon said. "It's also about my friend Carlos Ortiz and a playground in a Latin neighborhood on Seventy-Ninth Street where kids were always playing basketball. I didn't hang out there. I was grown up by then, but I would often pass by and see the good time they were having. Plus, I thought it would be cool to use the name Julio in a song. That's probably the happiest song I ever wrote."

"Duncan," another new song that would also remain part of Simon's concert playbook for decades, was a return to the storytelling, troubadour tradition of "The Boxer." But the song's theme was lighter, addressing the unforgettable bliss of a first taste of young, free-spirited sex. On the record, Simon also playfully saluted the Andean folk strains of Los Incas first heard on "El Condor Pasa (If I Could)." "Duncan" was as much of a breakthrough for Simon as "Mother" and "Julio." While he had offered touches of humor in the old songs, he had never done so with such ease and command.

> *Couple in the next room*
> *Bound to win a prize*
> *They've been going at it all night long*
> *Well, I'm trying to get some sleep*
> *But these motel walls are cheap*
> *Lincoln Duncan is my name*
> *And here's my song, here's my song*
>
> *My father was a fisherman*
> *My mama was the fisherman's friend*
> *And I was born in the boredom*
> *And the chowder*
> *So when I reached my prime*
> *I left my home in the Maritimes*

Headed down the turnpike for
New England, sweet New England

Holes in my confidence
Holes in the knees of my jeans
I was left without a penny in my pocket
Oo-we, I was destituted
As a kid could be
And I wished I wore a ring
So I could hock, I'd like to hock it

A young girl in a parking lot
Was preaching to a crowd
Singing sacred songs and reading
From the Bible
Well, I told her I was lost
And she told me all about the Pentecost
And I seen that girl as the road
To my survival

Just later on the very same night
I crept to her tent with a flashlight
And my long years of innocence ended
Well, she took me to the woods
Saying here comes something and it feels so good
And just like a dog I was befriended
I was befriended

Oh, oh, what a night
Oh, what a garden of delight
Even now that sweet memory lingers
I was playing my guitar
Lying underneath the stars

Just thanking the Lord
For my fingers
For my fingers

"One of the things about 'Duncan' is it has a false beginning," Simon said. "I'm talking about the couple in the next room, but they have nothing to do with the rest of the song. Normally, you might go back and change it, but I thought it was interesting. It's like that Preston Sturges film *The Great McGinty*, where it opens with these two guys in a fight in a bar, and it spills out into the street just when the main character in the film walks by. In both cases, it's just a way of entering into the story, and beginnings are always important."

Despite aiming for less lush production values, Simon and Halee ended up spending at least ten months on the album, setting up shop in studios ranging around the world. In Paris, he hooked up with jazz-inclined violinist Stephane Grappelli on the instrumental "Hobo's Blues." In Los Angeles, he reached out to Stefan Grossman for some bottleneck guitar licks on "Paranoia Blues." Elsewhere, he worked with some old friends—Charlie McCoy on harmonica and Hal Blaine on drums—and welcomed newcomers into the fold, including jazz bassist Ron Carter and Brazilian-born percussionist Airto Moreira on "Julio."

By the time he was finished in October 1971, Simon had formally severed ties with folk rock and unveiled a cosmopolitan mix of pop, jazz, and world music uniquely his own—songs as universally embracing as "Mother and Child Reunion" or as exquisitely personal as "Peace Like a River." Instead of the youthful attitude and dreams that had made Simon a star, the themes reflected adult anxieties, doubts, and adjusted aspirations. At thirty, he was now quicker to ask questions than to judge. All this placed Simon in a relatively rare place in pop. While Paul McCartney and Elton John excelled in a genre that combined the vitality of rock with the accessibility of pop, only Stevie Wonder, among major sellers, demonstrated as much consistent musical sophistication and ambition as Simon. Both men were complete artists—accomplished songwriters and consummate record makers. Simon reveled in his new freedom. "I am really happy to be by myself now and not have to share decisions," he said when the album was finished. "Now I do things almost entirely to my taste. That's not to say I don't listen to other opinions, but my new record is probably the most accurate one I've made, in the sense that it sounds the way I want it to sound."

Two of the most influential of the new breed of rock critics championed the solo album, titled simply *Paul Simon*, more enthusiastically than they had the Simon and Garfunkel recordings. In a full-page *Rolling Stone* review, Jon Landau, who would later manage Bruce Springsteen, declared, "Simon's first solo album is also his least distracted, most personal and painful piece of work thus far—this from a lyricist who has never shied away from pain as subject or theme. On *Parsley, Sage, Rosemary and Thyme*, Simon offered 'For Emily, Whenever I May Find Her,' the fantasy image of a perfect love that could save him from emptiness and despair. At the end [of the new album], we are offered 'Congratulations,' an eloquent, direct, simple song which says, 'I'm hungry for learning / Won't you answer me please / Can a man and a woman / Live together in peace?' "

Robert Christgau, a pugnacious stylist who would reign for decades as the self-proclaimed "dean" of American rock critics, wrote in his Consumer Guide column, "I've been saying nasty things about Simon since 1967, but this is the only thing in the universe to make me positively happy in the first two weeks of February 1972. I hope Art Garfunkel is gone for good—he always seemed so vestigial—but it's obvious now that two-part harmony crippled Simon's naturally agile singing and composing. And the words! A+."

Clive Davis, who had recently been elevated to the position of chairman of the CBS Records group, shared that enthusiasm. "Simon showed on the album that he could write terrific, infectious songs for himself as well as for Simon and Garfunkel," he said. "No question 'Mother and Child Reunion' and 'Me and Julio' were going to be big records. But I also had to be a practical record man, and there was no way the new album was going to be comparable in the marketplace to a Simon and Garfunkel album."

In the end, the LP *Paul Simon* did respectably. It sold more than a million copies and produced the expected two smash singles, "Mother and

Child Reunion" and "Me and Julio," and one more modest hit, "Duncan." For industry pros fixated on the *Bridge* figures, however, the sales were a disappointment, and that stigma likely contributed to Grammy voters passing over *Paul Simon* when filling out their nomination ballots. It didn't help Columbia's marketing plans when Simon refused to tour because he was nervous about his drawing power, and he didn't have enough new songs to fill out a set list. The only exception to not doing live shows in 1972 was joining Joni Mitchell and James Taylor at a fund-raising concert for Senator George McGovern's campaign for the Democratic presidential nomination. At the April 28 event at the Cleveland Arena, Simon sang three tunes from the new album—"Mother and Child," "Me and Julio," and "Congratulations"—in an eight-song set otherwise featuring signature songs from the Simon and Garfunkel days. Simon did not view McGovern, a strong opponent of the Vietnam War, with the adulation he felt for John F. Kennedy or Robert F. Kennedy, but he believed the South Dakota native was a good, honest man and, above all, that he would be the strongest alternative to Richard M. Nixon's reelection.

"I think it's impressive that people are willing to put aside the cynicism that has been nurtured for six or seven years and come out for a candidate again," he told Jon Landau in an interview in the summer of 1972 for Simon's first *Rolling Stone* cover. "A lot of people felt after 1968, 'I'm not gonna get duped into this system again, this crap.' And yet now they're doing it again. I'm not going that idealization route again for these people. Politicians as a group have dirtied their names to the point where they have to *earn* our respect again . . . But I'm not indifferent. When Nixon was elected, I cried. I actually cried. I remember putting on the TV set in the morning, and I saw he was coming down to make his acceptance speech. Tears started rolling down my eyes."

The Cleveland concert was the second in a series of three organized by actor Warren Beatty; the first, on April 15, in Los Angeles had featured Barbra Streisand, Carole King, James Taylor, and Quincy Jones; and the third, in New York's Madison Square Garden on June 14, offered a coup: the first reteaming of Simon and Garfunkel. The *New York Times*'s music critic, Don Heckman, noted differences in the former partners during their Garden set, which included "Mrs. Robinson," "The Boxer," a medley of "Cecelia," "Mother and Child Reunion," and "Bye Bye Love," and, of course, "Bridge Over Troubled Water." Pointing out that Garfunkel strained to "hold up his part on the higher vocal lines," Heckman said, "it was good to hear and see the burgeoning solo gifts of Paul Simon. His old songs are classics, and his new ones—with or without Garfunkel—are every bit as good."

But those remarks didn't dampen the enthusiasm of millions of Simon and Garfunkel fans, and Columbia was eager to give those fans what they wanted. The same week as the New York concert, the label released *Simon and Garfunkel's Greatest Hits*, and it was a forceful reminder of the duo's popularity. The album remained on the chart for more than two years, versus just twenty-six weeks for Simon's solo album, and would eventually pass *Bridge Over Troubled Water* (fourteen million copies to eight million) as the duo's biggest-selling album in America.

In the months after *Paul Simon*, Simon returned to a favorite genre; gospel music. In that mode, he was one of 2,500 people who attended a nine o'clock morning gospel concert on July 9, 1972, at Manhattan's Radio City Music Hall. Anthony (Tony) Heilbut, the author of the book *The Gospel Sound: Good News and Bad Times* and the guiding force behind the concert, put together a crowded bill that included Marion Williams, Jessy Dixon and the Dixon Singers, and the Dixie Hummingbirds—all marquee names in the field. Two weeks later, Heilbut was surprised when he got a phone call from Simon, whom he knew vaguely because his brother, Wilfred, had attended Queens College with him. When they subsequently met at Heilbut's apartment, Simon was especially eager to learn more about the Jessy Dixon Singers, who struck him as precisely the youthful gospel group he needed as vocal accompanists in the studio and possibly on tour. Heilbut, however, felt the Dixie Hummingbirds would be a better fit, and he played him several Hummingbird recordings to press his point. Simon followed his advice and brought the Hummingbirds into the studio to sing on two tracks on his second solo album.

"What has impressed me over the years is that Paul isn't one of those pop artists who's only interested in something because it's trendy," Heilbut said. "Gospel wasn't particularly hot when he went to the concert that morning. He just loved it, and he never lost the love. He also had a deep interest in the musicians themselves. When I introduced him later that year to Claude Jeter"—whose vocal aside had inspired "Bridge Over Troubled Water"—"Paul didn't just thank him for his inspiration, he wrote him a check to show his appreciation—and I can tell you Jeter needed the money. After Paul left, Claude was so grateful that he cried."

CHAPTER ELEVEN

The last thing Simon expected when he headed back to the studio to begin work on his second solo album in the fall of 1972 was another Art Garfunkel roadblock. Simon knew Halee was producing Garfunkel's first solo LP, but they had started the album early in the year, so he couldn't believe it when Halee said it still wasn't finished. How long could it take? Garfunkel didn't write, so all he had to do was gather some songs—which Halee helped him do—and then record them. Simon had even sung and played guitar on one session, a painful experience because he aggravated an earlier injury to his left index finger, which made playing guitar difficult for years.

The problem was Garfunkel's decision about three-fourths of the way through the album to take a break and "go off walking in Russia or somewhere," Halee said. Roy didn't resent the walking trips—which Garfunkel found invigorating—only the timing. "Right while I'm waiting, Paul calls and wants to start his album," Halee said. "I was caught in the middle. If I had known Art's album would take so long, I would never have agreed to do it. Paul was the one I wanted to work with. But now that I had started the album, I felt obligated. It didn't seem right for me to just walk away."

Given Simon's respect for Halee, it's easy to imagine him telling Halee that he'd wait until he completed the album—if he had been working with any other artist. But Garfunkel was a red flag. Simon told Halee he had to choose. Roy felt trapped, and he couldn't just abandon Garfunkel. When Simon said he was moving on, Halee was crushed. He later called it the biggest mistake he ever made. It'd be nine years before he worked again with Simon. To make matters worse for Halee, he had already recorded one song with Simon for the new album, and he loved it.

Simon was in great spirits during the "Tenderness" session that Halee loved. The recording was a week after Peggy gave birth to their son, Harper James Simon, on September 7, 1972, in New York City. For Simon, the birth was one step closer to the family life he hoped would bring him the joy of his own upbringing. It's ironic, then, that "Tenderness" was a ballad about a strained relationship. The song's opening lines:

> *What can I do?*
> *What can I do?*
> *Much of what you say is true*
> *I know you care for me*
> *But there's no tenderness*
> *Beneath your honesty*

The song's arrangement was a mix of gospel, jazz, and modernized doo-wop. Once again, Simon chose his musicians with care, supplementing New York session players with the Dixie Hummingbirds, whose southern roots went back nearly fifty years, and Allen Toussaint, the writer-producer-arranger who was the dean of New Orleans R&B and was later inducted into the Rock & Roll Hall of Fame. He was also a Simon fan: "When I heard 'Bridge Over Troubled Water,' I used to tell people, 'That song had two writers: Paul Simon and God.' It was so perfect, so profound."

Meeting Simon in the studio, Toussaint, like so many musicians before him, was struck by his workmanlike manner. "Paul didn't waste time on small talk," the arranger said. "He was very serious and very self-assured, but he was also very respectful of all the musicians." After Simon played him an early version of "Tenderness," Toussaint was momentarily lost for words. "I thought the track sounded pretty complete, almost to the point that I didn't know why I was even there," he said. "I finally told Paul I thought it was great the way it was, but he said he'd like a horn part in there, so I did my best to write something that stayed out of the way of what he had."

Needing a new producer for the rest of the album, Simon, partially on Halee's recommendation, turned to Phil Ramone, who, like Halee, was a respected engineer turned producer. Ramone, who would coproduce four numbers on the album, had even filled in for Halee as engineer on "Me and Julio" and helped engineer "Tenderness." A South Africa native who was raised in Brooklyn, Ramone, seven years older than Simon, had a reputation for being able to work equally well in various musical styles, from pop and rock, to jazz and beyond. He won a Grammy in 1965—one of an eventual fourteen Grammys—for his contributions as engineer on *Getz/Gilberto*, which was also awarded a Grammy as Album of the Year. "Phil brought a real sound to the records, a real distinctive sound," Simon said. "He also introduced me to a wider group of musicians. He was great at finding the right person for the right song."

During the summer of 1972, Simon had listened to a lot of southern gospel and R&B, and one song stood out: the Staple Singers' "I'll Take You There," which also featured a winning touch of Jamaican-flavored music. The single had topped the nation's R&B chart for four weeks that spring and even made it to no. 1 on the pop chart for one week. Simon finally did exactly what he had done with the Jimmy Cliff album. He looked at the label credits and then called Al Bell, who was listed as writer-producer. Bell was co-owner of Memphis's Stax Records, once the home of such soul greats as Otis Redding and Booker T. and the MG's. Simon told Bell that he wanted to record with the musicians who had given "I'll Take You There" such superb shading. He had assumed the musicians were African American and based in Memphis. As it turned out, the musicians worked in a studio some 150 miles away in the Muscle Shoals area of northwest

Alabama. Known as the Muscle Shoals Rhythm Section, they had played on countless R&B hits, including Aretha Franklin's "Respect" and Percy Sledge's "When a Man Loves a Woman."

When Simon arrived at the Muscle Shoals Sound Studio, he figured the young white guys sitting around the studio console were employees or visitors. But they were, in fact, the band: Barry Beckett (keyboards), Roger Hawkins (drums), Jimmy Johnson (electric guitar), David Hood (bass), and Pete Carr (acoustic guitar). The musicians were, in turn, surprised when Simon told them he might need the studio for a few days to do a single track, "Take Me to the Mardi Gras." They prided themselves in finishing even the most challenging track in an hour. Despite no history with reggae, they picked up on the sound when Bell played them a Jamaican instrumental, "Liquidator," by the Harry J. All Stars, just moments before the session. And sure enough, the Rhythm Section finished the joyful, reggae-gumbo hybrid in what was fast even by their standards: a half hour.

"Paul was flabbergasted that it took us so little time to get the groove and the attitude of the song," Beckett said. "Attitude is something that Paul really concentrates on. He goes for attitude, then groove, and then color, and we caught all those ingredients very fast—and all at once." Beckett learned about Simon's focus on attitude when Simon walked over to him early in the session with a suggestion. "Barry," he said, "by every indication, the gentleman in the song is going to get to go to the Mardi Gras. He wants to go, so he's going to go. Nowhere in the song does it say he might not go. Is it possible to get that feel?"

Simon, who played acoustic guitar on the song, was so pleased with the result that he rewarded the band with a coproducer credit on the track, as well as the same credit on four other tracks. But he still wasn't finished with the record. Later he and Ramone added horns by New Orleans's historic Onward Brass Band and a falsetto backing vocal by the Reverend Claude T. Jeter. Again, Simon was not leaving anything to chance: he brought in the best people, no matter how small the part. With time left over at the studio, he challenged the hotshot rhythm section with another tune, this one having no overt ties to gospel, R&B, or reggae. The song was "Kodachrome," which was the brand name for one of Eastman Kodak's color films. The musicians came through with a track so dynamic that Simon again listed them as coproducer.

"When I first wrote that melody, I started singing the words 'going home,'" Simon said. "But my instincts as a songwriter told me you couldn't sing a song called 'Going Home.' Everybody in the world has written a song called 'Going Home.'" This is the point in artistry where discipline and standards come into play, as Quincy Jones stressed when talking about the song. "When you come up with words that fit," the producer said, "like Paul did in this case with 'going home,' it's tempting to simply use them. They feel like they are in perfect harmony with the music. But you've got to be strong enough to set them aside and keep working to find something else. It sometimes takes weeks of extra work, but you can't compromise just because it's easy."

In this case, Simon played the melody over and over, searching for another, fresher image. "I started thinking of words that sounded like 'going home' and I finally came up with 'Kodachrome.' That sounded interesting," he said. "So I began thinking of what Kodachrome means to me, and I was on my way." For Simon, Kodachrome photos evoked many of the same images as "going home," including childhood, high school, and how time colors many of those memories. "The thing about Kodachrome is that when you get those slides, they look better than in real life," he said. "Their color is richer than real life. The greens are greener. A color photo is like a hype. What I'm saying in the song is that I know it's a hype, but I don't care. I'll take it. I feel that's the way we all are. We're pretty willing to take a hype even if we know it's a hype."

Simon was so energized by the Muscle Shoals musicians that he and Ramone returned to the studio for three days in March, during which they recorded four more tracks, three of which shared a warm, optimistic sheen. They included the gospel-driven call-and-response celebration of "Loves Me Like a Rock," which again featured the Dixie Hummingbirds, and the carefree, reggae-coated "Was a Sunny Day" with Maggie and Terre Roche on backing vocals. For his help in deepening his understanding of gospel, Simon dedicated the album to Tony Heilbut. The third song was "St. Judy's Comet," a lullaby for Harper. For those fans of the song who have long been intrigued by the title, there is no record of an actual comet named St. Judy's. Simon got the title from the name Robert St. Judy, the drummer in Clifton Chenier's zydeco band. He liked the sound of the name, and he wanted to salute the drummer.

In the end, the album's two most important songs were both tender reflections: one spoke to the country's political malaise in an era of national despair—the time of Richard M. Nixon, Vietnam, and Watergate—and the other addressed matters of the heart. "Something So Right," which Simon recorded in his first session with Phil Ramone as coproducer, was the final version of a song drawn from his relationship with Peggy that Simon had been sketching out for months; he performed an earlier treatment, then titled "Let Me Live in Your City," on Dick Cavett's TV show that previous July. By the time he recorded "Something So Right," the lyrics were among his most vulnerable.

You've got the cool water
When the fever runs high
You've got the look of lovelight
In your eyes
And I was in crazy motion
'Til you calmed me down
It took a little time
But you calmed me down

When something goes wrong
I'm the first to admit it
I'm the first to admit it
But the last one to know
When something goes right
Oh, it's likely to lose me
It's apt to confuse me
It's such an unusual sight
Oh, I can't get used to something so right
Something so right

They've got a wall in China
It's a thousand miles long
To keep out the foreigners
They made it strong
I've got a wall around me
That you can't even see
It took a little time
To get to me

When something goes wrong
I'm the first to admit it
I'm the first to admit it
But the last one to know
When something goes right
Oh, it's likely to lose me
It's apt to confuse me
It's such an unusual sight
Oh, I can't get used to something so right
Something so right

Some people never say the words
"I love you"
It's not their style
To be so bold
Some people never say those words
"I love you"
But like a child, they're longing to be told

When something goes wrong
I'm the first to admit it
I'm the first to admit it
But the last one to know
When something goes right
Oh, it's likely to lose me

It's apt to confuse me
It's such an unusual sight
Oh, I can't get used to something so right
Something so right

There are conflicting currents running through "Something So Right" that help make it a memorable love song. It simultaneously offers gratitude and confesses a lingering inability to commit. In the end, there is no resolution, simply an acknowledgment of the delicate balance in a relationship. For the string arrangement, Simon turned to Quincy Jones. "Something So Right" conveys the elegance and maturity of Cole Porter and the best writers of the Great American Songbook era.

The other song on the new album that would be regarded as one of Simon's most memorable was "American Tune," a rare case of him not writing the music. The music was based on a melody line from a seventeenth-century German tune: a chorale from Bach's *St. Matthew Passion*. Simon knew the melody already, but Garfunkel urged him to write words to it. The melody frames the lyrics memorably. About the song, Simon said years later, "I always think of that as my Nixon sore-loser song. I was writing about what I felt was the end of sixties beliefs—that idealism—in the lines 'I don't know a soul who's not been battered. I don't know a dream that's not been shattered.' I'm sure I was aware of the irony of being so over the top to call a song 'America'—as if you could wrap up the country in a song—so to call the new song a 'tune' rather than a 'song' has the opposite effect. It's kind of the equivalent in poetry of doggerel, as if you just tossed it off, but the song was much more serious than that."

Many's the time I've been mistaken
And many times confused
Yes, and I've often felt forsaken
And certainly misused
Oh, but I'm all right, I'm all right
I'm just weary to my bones
Still, you don't expect to be

Bright and bon vivant
So far away from home, so far away from home

I don't know a soul who's not been battered
I don't have a friend who feels at ease
I don't know a dream that's not been shattered
Or driven to its knees
Oh, but it's all right, it's all right
For we've lived so well so long
Still, when I think of the road
We're traveling on
I wonder what's gone wrong
I can't help it, I wonder what's gone wrong

And I dreamed I was dying
I dreamed that my soul rose unexpectedly
And looking back down at me
Smiled reassuringly
And I dreamed I was flying
And high above, my eyes could clearly see
The Statue of Liberty
Sailing away to sea
And I dreamed I was flying

Oh, we come on the ship they call the Mayflower
We come on the ship that sailed the moon
We come in the age's most uncertain hours
And sing an American tune
Oh, and it's all right
It's all right, it's all right
You can't be forever blessed
Still, tomorrow's going to be another working day
And I'm trying to get some rest
That's all I'm trying to get some rest

Simon titled the album *There Goes Rhymin' Simon*—which came to Peggy in a dream—and called it a "joy to make." Clive Davis, too, was delighted, but he again disagreed with Simon's choice of the first single: in this case, "American Tune." The label chief thought the song was wonderful but lacked the overall appeal of "Kodachrome." Once again, Simon accepted Clive's advice. In *Rolling Stone*, Stephen Holden declared that the collection showed "once and for all, that Simon is now the consummate master of the contemporary narrative—one of a very few practicing songwriters able to impart wisdom as much by implication as direct statement. Here, even more than in the first album, Simon successfully communicates the deepest kinds of love without ever becoming rhetorical or overly sentimental. The chief factor in his remarkable growth since Simon and Garfunkel days has been the development of a gently wry humor that is objective, even fatalistic, though never bitter."

The next step was touring, and Simon was ready, knowing he now had enough new songs to carry a two-hour concert. To join him on his first solo tour, which began in May 1973, he brought along the Jessy Dixon Singers and Urubamba, a spinoff of Los Incas. Despite occasional shouts for Garfunkel, the early dates went smoothly, and the audience response was warm, both when Simon played songs from the new album and when he offered new arrangements of the earlier ones, including dramatic lead vocal interchanges with Dixon and the Singers on "Bridge Over Troubled Water" and "The Sound of Silence." On "Bridge," the pop-gospel nature of the original version was replaced by a down-home gospel fervor, including an inspired call-and-response vocal exchange.

By the time the tour reached Los Angeles two weeks later, Simon was relaxed enough to talk about this new time in his life. "The reason I wanted to do this tour now was that I wanted to be visibly on the scene. I didn't want to appear to be retired or anything like that. I felt that the second album was good, that it was probably going to make an impact, and I wanted to say, 'Look, I really care. I'm not just sending down albums from some mountaintop to you.' " He was also realistic about his solo place in the music world. "I wanted to see how people would react to me," he said. "I think the vast majority of people don't know who I am. If you say, 'Paul Simon of Simon and Garfunkel,' then the identification comes through. So, for me, I have to show my face a little so people will have some idea of who I am."

At the same time, he spoke about the transitions he went through as a writer. "What happens is that you begin writing autobiographical songs, usually about what it's like to be scufflin', what it's like to try and not succeed, what the world looks like for somebody who is sensitive but not accepted," he said. "Then, suddenly, you are accepted, and your mental state is not in harmony with your actual physical state. For a while you are still writing songs, then you have to say, 'Now I am accepted.' So your first instinct is to write songs about what has happened to you. But you find it not so interesting to write, 'Well, I made it, and I'm living in a big house now.' That's not as interesting as the other way. That's when a songwriter comes to one of his first crises. Instead of saying, 'This is what is happening in my life,' you have to say something else. You have to look a little deeper. If you make it into that, you are into another area of richness."

In the midst of these good times, Simon's professional world was jolted. On May 29, 1973, Clive Davis was forced out as head of the CBS Records group in an ugly episode during which the label charged him with misusing almost $94,000 in corporate funds for such things as a bar mitzvah for his oldest son. The widespread feeling in the record industry was that the firing was CBS's attempt to distance itself from a pending federal investigation of payola in the record industry. The fear was that the probe could result in the Federal Communications Commission's lifting of CBS's radio and television licenses. The charges against Davis were ultimately discredited, and he went on to have a legendary career in the industry, building two labels, Arista and J, both virtually from scratch, and launching the careers of stars such as Whitney Houston, Barry Manilow, Patti Smith, and Alicia Keys. As it turned out, the CBS radio and television properties were never in danger; the federal probe didn't result in any major indictment. Davis's firing, however, proved costly in one way: Simon's contract was coming to an end, and there was considerable fear at Columbia that Simon, in Davis's absence, might not re-sign with the label.

———

"Kodachrome" and "Loves Me Like a Rock," released as singles in May and July, respectively, both reached no. 2. All this radio exposure helped *There Goes Rhymin' Simon* to be certified platinum (one million copies sold). When "American Tune" was finally released as a single in December, the Columbia sales staff was shocked that it reached only the middle of the sales chart, though *Rolling Stone* named it the Song of the Year.

There was so much respect by now for Simon that *Time* magazine planned to do a cover story on him for the July 7, 1973, issue, but the subject was switched at the last minute. The man who wrote "American Tune" lost the cover to one of Watergate's key figures, John Dean, the former White House counsel who had, on June 25, begun his testimony before the Senate Watergate Committee. In August Simon and Garfunkel came together again at Columbia Records's annual convention, this time in San Francisco, where Garfunkel performed four songs to salute the release of his first solo album, *Angel Clare*. The LP—a ballad-heavy collection of songs by writers such as Jimmy Webb and Randy Newman—qualified for a gold record (a half million sales), but Stephen Holden, writing in *Rolling Stone*, declared, "Garfunkel employs too uniform an approach to too wide a range of material. He wants to make everything pretty, and he invariably succeeds, though in doing so, he sometimes obscures the character of the material."

Instead of the talk about how Simon's first album suffered a huge drop in sales from the Simon and Garfunkel days, *Rhymin' Simon* caused the record industry and media to focus on the excellence of the music. Equally noteworthy, Simon wasn't constantly being compared with Simon and Garfunkel. With two albums, Simon had largely achieved the goal he outlined when leaving the duo: that people would eventually look back on those years as merely the first stage of his career. Where Simon wrote at least six great, lasting songs during his seven years with Garfunkel, he had already passed that figure in the four years since the split, and he was still only thirty-two.

PART FOUR

Still Crazy After All These Years

CHAPTER TWELVE

In the months after the release of *Rhymin' Simon*, you couldn't tell the state of Simon's private life by his public success. While his music was all over the radio, he was still grappling with many of the old issues of fame, loneliness, writer's block, and now, above all, his marriage. His relationship with Peggy had been brightened immensely by the arrival of Harper, but the distance between them gradually widened. Peggy compensated by devoting herself to home and Harper. Simon, as usual, found solace in his music. Peggy didn't know what to make of Paul's increasing time away from the apartment, especially the long nights. She understood his obsession with music, but she had also been around show business long enough to know that infidelity was common. She didn't ask him about it.

Without any evidence that he was unfaithful, she still found herself wondering when Simon would come home late and take long showers as if he were trying to wash away the shame.

Asked years later about those nights, Simon said no, he spent all that time in the shower trying to wash away the *sadness*.

During a particularly long shower one evening, Simon was so unhappy that he broke into tears. How, after all his success, could he feel so bad? Suddenly, a phrase came to him that would summarize his feelings. Ironically, the phrase, born in sorrow, would be the title of a song embraced by millions as an upbeat expression of survival: "Still Crazy After All These Years."

The break with Peggy came within days of the January 13 announcement that *Rhymin' Simon* was nominated for a Grammy in the Best Album category. They had planned to drive to their place in New Hope, but first Simon wanted to check out his chief competition for the Grammy, Stevie Wonder's socially conscious *Innervisions*. He had been listening to Wonder's album only a few minutes before Peggy asked him to come on, but he was too caught up in the music to join her. After a few more minutes, she yelled again for him to hurry. Suddenly his sadness turned to anger. He asked himself, "Can't she see this is important to me? Can't I even listen to my music anymore?" When Peggy called out a third time, the marriage was over. Simon walked out of the townhouse and headed to the Stanhope Hotel, across the street from the Metropolitan Museum of Art on Manhattan's Upper East Side. He chose the hotel because it was close to the apartment, so he could see Harper daily.

"I was shocked," Peggy said years later, sitting in the living room of her house in one of Nashville's toniest neighborhoods. "It's not that I thought we had this fairy-tale relationship. We had drifted apart. In some ways, we were living in different worlds. Even so, I had no idea he wanted out of the marriage. There was no scene or shouting match, simply acceptance. I couldn't believe that he wanted to marry me in the first place. I liked him a lot. I was even obsessed about him in some ways. But I didn't think I was worthy. He was already rich and famous, and I didn't have much going for me except for my looks, and I try to be a good person. I kept asking myself, 'Why does he want to marry me? Aren't I the lucky girl?' "

In return, Simon placed much of the blame for the failed marriage on himself.

"Ultimately, I wasn't ready for marriage," he said. "The marriage didn't solve the loneliness. I knew right away I had made a mistake. I didn't know how to be a good companion. I wasn't a very mature person. I didn't understand that you had to work at problems. I wanted the marriage to solve my problems." To Mort Lewis, the success of *Rhymin' Simon* may have contributed to the breakup. "I think it showed Paul that he could stand on his own," he said. "Paul didn't need Peggy to tell him he'd be okay anymore. From then on, I believe he knew music would always be his real bridge—the thing he could always count on."

Still, the transition to single life was difficult, partially because of Simon's tendency during those years to be so hard on himself. Looking back in 1984 at some of his nagging, negative feelings, Simon said, "Most people look at me and wonder, 'How could that guy be depressed?' And I now feel that people were seeing a more accurate picture of me than I was. I eventually realized, 'Jesus, all I've been looking at is this thin slice of pie that has got the bad news in it. And I'm disregarding the rest of the picture.' There's something in me—in a lot of people—that says, 'Gee, if I admit that things are actually going well, maybe they'll stop.' Or 'If I admit I'm happy, maybe I won't be able to write.' I think the psyche comes up with all kinds of contrivances to protect what it thinks is vulnerable. And sometimes those contrivances are that you stay in a state of unhappiness. Or victimization. It's almost saying, 'Hey, don't get mad at me for being so successful and doing so well, because look at how unhappy I am.' "

Asked what it was he saw as bad news, Simon replied, "Being short. Not having a voice that you want. Not looking the way you want to look. Having a bad relationship. Some of that is real. And if you start to roll it together, that's what you focus on. I was unable to absorb the bounty that was in my life. Even when people would say a simple statement that I used to hear countless times—'Hey, man, I love your music'—you'd think that I'd begin to feel something good about my music, right? But that's a big statement I would ignore. Totally ignore it."

On the matter of size, Simon said in 2017 that he's been sensitive about it all the way back to the Tom & Jerry days. "I remember during a photo session at Big Records, something happened, and Artie said, 'No matter what happens, I'll always be taller than you.' Did that hurt? I guess it hurt enough for me to remember sixty years later. But even during Simon and Garfunkel, I realized that people thought Artie wrote the songs, and I finally asked someone, 'Why do you think he wrote the songs?' and they said, 'Because he looks like he wrote songs.' Or, in other words, 'You don't.'

"It came up all the time. There is a prejudice against small men, and that has been a problem at times because I happen to be a sort of alpha-male-ish-type guy. It becomes a competitive thing. There's this attitude that 'I'm taller, so I could beat you up, or I should be in charge.' Eventually, somewhere in my thirties or forties, probably, I told myself, 'Listen, man, if you're going to make a big issue out of what you don't have, you're taking your actual gifts for granted.' So I said, 'That's the hand I've been dealt. That's the way I'm going to play it.' "

He even put together a humorous game to drive home the point. "I'd pretend God would come to me and say, 'If you could be six foot two with a mop of hair, would you pay a million dollars?' I said, 'Absolutely.' Then God said, 'Would you pay five million?' and, again, I said, 'Absolutely.' Then the question changed: 'If you could be six foot two with a mop of hair, would you give away ten of your songs?' and that's when I said, 'No.' That was too much. The songs are really a part of you. Not all of you, but kind of the best part of you. It's not the vain part of me or the pissed-off part of me, it's the generous part."

On March 2, 1974, at the Grammy ceremony at the Hollywood Palladium in Los Angeles, Simon lost in the Best Album category to *Innervisions*, but he still felt validated. Three of his last four albums had been nominated for the record industry's top award. To capitalize on the publicity surrounding the awards, Columbia released *Paul Simon: Live Rhymin'*, a somewhat disjointed LP drawn from Simon's solo concert swing. It included eleven of his songs, five of which were from the solo albums. Though certified gold, it stalled at no. 33. Its chief virtue was in reminding pop fans how far Simon had moved from the delicate strains of Simon and Garfunkel's earliest recordings.

———

Free from the distress that had formed around his marriage, Simon tried to spend as much time as possible with Harper. His son was the only thing he really cared about in the divorce settlement, said Michael Tannen, Simon's friend and attorney. "Paul was so relieved that he could still be with his son. He just adored Harper." Long before the divorce papers were final, Simon told Peggy he'd buy an apartment for her and Harper. There was no thought of anyone remaining in the townhouse. Who would want to live with such bad memories? "I started looking on the West Side, as I had always lived on the East Side, and the agent showed me this lovely place in the Dakota," Peggy said, referring to one of the city's most prestigious residential buildings. Located at the northwest corner of Seventy-Second Street and Central Park West, the exclusive cooperative has been home over the years to celebrities such as John Lennon and Yoko Ono, Lauren Bacall, and Leonard Bernstein. Peggy didn't know the history of the Dakota, but she fell in love with apartment number 57, which had been home to a ninety-year-old man for his whole life, and everything was intact. She called it "gorgeous."

Against all odds, a rival bidder emerged. Would you believe: Art Garfunkel? Paul and Peggy met with Art and his first wife, Linda Grossman, an architect, to try to talk them into backing away, but the couples ended up bidding against each other for the apartment, which was in the low $100,000 range. Paul and Peggy won with a bid that she recalled was about $2,000 or $3,000 higher. Before buying himself an apartment nearby on Central Park West to be close to Harper, Simon remained at the Stanhope.

Hoping to break through the gloom, Simon was eager for new friends and adventures. He found the latter in May 1974 when John Lennon invited him and Garfunkel to take part in a "covers" album that John was producing for Harry Nilsson, a singer and songwriter who sang Fred Neil's "Everybody's Talkin' " in the film *Midnight Cowboy*. Long a fan of Nilsson's music, Lennon had become drinking buddies with him in 1973 while John was in Los Angeles during his separation from Yoko Ono. It was a time often described as his drunken "lost weekend." Over the course of weeks in Los Angeles, such friends as Paul McCartney, Stevie Wonder, and Ringo

Starr stopped by to visit or play on tunes such as the Bill Haley hit "Rock Around the Clock" and Bob Dylan's "Subterranean Homesick Blues."

Simon and Garfunkel got involved when the sessions moved to New York. Nothing went right the night they worked on the record. They hadn't sung together in so long they had trouble rounding out their harmony parts and ended up yelling at each other angrily. By far, though, the larger problem was John's drunkenness. When Simon started playing acoustic guitar on "Rock Island Line" before John signaled, Lennon told him to stop. Each time Simon started to play again, John reached over and muted Paul's guitar strings with his hand, recalled Jimmy Iovine, who was an assistant engineer at the session and would later become one of the music world's most powerful figures as cofounder of Interscope Records and then as a top executive with Apple Music. Simon finally had enough. He snapped back, "John, I play guitar, too."

May Pang, who stayed with John during the Los Angeles period with Yoko Ono's blessing, said Lennon was irritated "by Simon's behavior, realizing, perhaps, that Paul Simon, unlike almost everyone else who entered John's orbit, had a powerful sense of himself and could actually refuse to be treated badly." When the album, titled *Pussy Cats*, was released that summer, "Rock Island Line" was not included. Simon dismissed the evening as "useless self-indulgence."

More productively, Simon took music classes—something he had begun soon after leaving Simon and Garfunkel. During one of his many bouts of writer's block, a musician friend told him he needed to expand his musical arsenal beyond the few chords he was using. He began by studying classical guitar and had recently begun taking lessons from jazz-based composer-bassist Chuck Israels and vocal coach David Sorin Collyer, who helped him with breathing and projection. Simon showed his appreciation by dedicating his next album to both men. Simon also spent at least an hour most days exercising at the local YMCA, where he enjoyed talking to actor Elliott Gould and playwright Israel Horovitz, whose son Adam would later be a member of the hip-hop trio the Beastie Boys.

Simon was so open to new ideas in 1974 that he took a surprise career sidestep. After turning down many film score offers following *The Graduate*, he agreed to write music for the new film by Warren Beatty, whom he knew from the McGovern benefit concerts. The movie, *Shampoo*, was a satirical look at America's social, sexual, and political values in the late 1960s. Simon's chief contribution was a moody, melancholy instrumental titled "Night Game," which effectively shadows the Beatty character's attempt to deal with his aimless drift. Simon's involvement led to him think seriously about making a movie himself—possibly, both as writer and actor, like Beatty. The experience also made Simon take notice of a young actress who made her film debut in the role of a teenage sex kitten: Carrie Fisher.

His music was singled out for praise in numerous reviews, but Simon was disappointed that Beatty didn't use one of his new songs over the end credits. Simon thought one song was perfect for the film's disconsolate tone; it was the one whose title came to him during one of those long showers in the apartment when he was engulfed by sadness: "Still Crazy After All These Years."

I met my old lover
On the street last night
She seemed so glad to see me
I just smiled
And we talked about some old times
And we drank ourselves some beers
Still crazy after all these years
Still crazy after all these years

I'm not the kind of man
Who tends to socialize
I seem to lean on old familiar ways
And I ain't no fool for love songs
That whisper in my ears
Still crazy after all these years
Still crazy after all these years

Four in the morning
Crapped out
Yawning
Longing my life away
I'll never worry
Why should I?
It's all gonna fade

Now I sit by my window
And I watch the cars
I fear I'll do some damage
One fine day
But I would not be convicted
By a jury of my peers
Still crazy after all these years
Oh, still crazy
Still crazy
Still crazy after all these years

When Eddie Simon heard the song, he was touched by its open, unguarded nature. In it, he imagined his brother saying, "Look, I'm working every day. I'm trying to do the right thing and get through the best way I know how. I've been famous and not famous, bad-mouthed and broken up inside. I've traveled. I've seen a shrink. I've been in love and gotten married, and that bottomed out, too. But you know something? After all that work, after all that pain and trouble, all these years—I'm still crazy."

Years later, Paul recalled the emotions that went into the song. "I made two solo albums, and both were successful," he said. "The second one was a very happy album. But now I'm in this marriage, and I feel trapped. I step into the shower one day, and boom, this line comes into my head. It was just a comment on my condition. Why is my life so depressing? After all the success, I'm back here: still crazy after all these years. I didn't think right away, 'Oh, that's a good title' or 'That would be a good song.' I was just disappointed in myself. It was later at the hotel that it became a song.

I would sit for hours with my guitar, just looking out the window, which is where that line comes from—*Now I sit by my window / And I watch the cars.* That's all I could do was sit there. I was so sad I couldn't even get up and go. There's also the line *I'm not the kind of man / Who tends to socialize.* Years later, Edie [Brickell] said she didn't know why I wrote that line, because I do like to socialize, and that's true. But she's speaking about a much different time and a much different me.

"Well, I came up with a guitar part and a melody and I inserted the still crazy line, and it fit perfectly. That's how the song was finally born. I immediately think this is another song that will sound better on piano than guitar, which is nice, since my albums tend to be guitar-centric. By making a couple of piano pieces, the texture changes and allows me to write in a flat key. Mostly I use sharp keys, which are all great for guitar. On the piano, it's more flat keys, which are easier on the ear. That's something I learned from my father. When I'm planning a set, sometimes I'll say to the band, 'Let's play a song we normally play in A in A-flat or B-flat tonight.' That makes a big difference for the audience.

"Most albums are sequenced by tempo to avoid having too many ballads in a row. But to me, you don't always need to rely on change of tempo; just a change in the key will accomplish what you want. I started doing that consciously around the time of *Rhymn' Simon.*"

Far from the joviality on *Rhymin' Simon*, Paul knew that this song required a different musical frame, something moodier and jazzier. Because of his success with the Muscle Shoals Rhythm Section, he and producer Phil Ramone turned again to the Alabama outfit when they began recording the song on December 19, 1974. This time, however, things weren't wrapped up in half an hour. Keyboardist Barry Beckett called the first day of the session the most frustrating of his career, because Simon kept asking him to play in a different key as he tried various modulations to find the one that best fit the bridge that begins with the line *Four in the morning / Crapped out / Yawning.* Simon finally decided on a modulation that he had never used, one that went up a whole step and was tied to a major seventh in the melody. Once he found it, the recording went relatively quickly. Ramone, relying on his background in jazz, was responsible for Simon's using jazz saxophonist Michael Brecker to add a bittersweet accent and jazz keyboardist Bob James to write the string and woodwind arrangements.

Before finishing the album, which would be titled *Still Crazy After All These Years*, Simon wanted to record a final track in Muscle Shoals—a song that caused a buzz around Columbia Records because it reunited Simon and Garfunkel. Ramone told label executives that the duo was simply doing one number, "My Little Town," for Art's next album, but the execs couldn't help but hope that if the track was a hit, they could talk the pair into doing a whole new album together.

Ever since their break, Simon had kept an eye on what his old friend was doing in the studio, and he didn't like a lot of what he had heard. He thought the music on *Angel Clare* was too soft. He believed Art's next album should have something edgy and unexpected, and he ended up writing a song for the collection. "I knew Artie was doing a new album, so I played him some things I had written," he said. "He really liked the melody of 'My Little Town.' I hadn't even written the lyrics yet, but he said he'd like to do the song. So I said, 'Fine, it's yours.' In writing the words, the only thing I had in mind was for it to be nasty. It's not the story of our little town, Kew Gardens Hills. I just went off on my own."

When he sang the song for Art, his old partner wasn't sure what to think about lines such as these:

> *After it rains*
> *There's a rainbow*
> *And all the colors are black*
> *Nothing but the dead and dying*
> *Back in my little town*

Finally, Garfunkel started singing harmony and suggested they record it together. The idea caught Simon by surprise. If Garfunkel had suggested making a record together even twelve months before, Simon would likely have turned him down. But times had changed. "It wasn't until *Rhymin'*

Simon that I began to get my own identity," he said. "After that, I began to feel I could do a record with Art without people saying they're getting back together for good. It seemed okay now. Besides, 'My Little Town' sounded really good."

Though Simon gave Garfunkel the song for his next album, *Breakaway*, Garfunkel generously suggested that Simon use it on his own new album as well. Both LPs would be released around the same time that fall. Simon thought the recording session went well, but Garfunkel felt the old tension resurface. Despite all the hopes at Columbia Records and among fans, the chances of another joint Simon and Garfunkel album appeared to be zero.

With Ramone's help, Simon assembled a spectacular musical cast for the New York sessions for "Still Crazy," which began in mid-February 1975 and continued on and off into September. The players not only continued to work closely with Simon for years but also became so in demand that they played on countless sessions for other artists: Tony Levin on bass, Steve Gadd on drums, Hugh McCracken on guitar, and Richard Tee on keyboards. Several of the songs for the new album were inspired by Simon's failed marriage, leading one critic to call the collection "sad" because it spoke about how things could only get worse.

One upbeat spot on the record was "50 Ways to Leave Your Lover," whose snappy rhymes grew out of a good-natured rhyming exercise Simon had with Harper. Steve Gadd's light, almost martial snare–bass drum pattern on "50 Ways" ranks with Hal Blaine's explosiveness on "The Boxer" as two of the most distinctive moments of drumming in Simon's catalog. Simon first recorded "Gone at Last" as a Latin-tinged number with Bette Midler, but then redid it in a bluesy style with Phoebe Snow, one of pop's brightest new stars. More to the thematic heart of the album were the deeply emotional "I Do It for Your Love" and "You're Kind." Backed by a lush melody, "I Do It for Your Love" ends with a verse that pointed to his ill-fated marriage, alluding even to their vastly different New York and Tennessee backgrounds:

The sting of reason
The splash of tears
The Northern and the Southern hemispheres

For Simon, "I Do It for Your Love" came from the same deeply rooted sadness as "Still Crazy." He has described it as a very truthful and emotional song. "You're Kind" was an engaging musical stew, combining a touch of the R&B precision of Lloyd Price's "Stagger Lee" and the wry commentary of Randy Newman. The song looked casually at the often fragile nature of relationships:

I like to sleep with the window open
And you keep the window closed
So goodbye
Goodbye
Goodbye

Another dark track was "Night Game," with words added to the instrumental passages used in the movie *Shampoo*. Paul turned to his beloved baseball for some grim imagery of a pitcher who drops dead on the mound with the score tied and two men down in the bottom of the eighth.

Simon's vocals on the album reflected a greater maturity and range, which has generally been attributed to the lessons he took. But Simon disagreed. "I learned some things about singing, such as how to warm up your voice and how to hold your breath to get a little bit more resonance," he explained. "But, essentially, it didn't change my voice at all. I wasn't interested in trying to achieve sound qualities they try to get out of people who sing on Broadway or anything. The real growth comes from experience and learning what kinds of songs suit your voice. For instance, I can sing a certain type of rock 'n' roll, but I can't sing gospel. So I wrote 'Loves Me Like a Rock' in a way that fit my voice."

Generally, Simon feels his voice works best on soft tunes, and he is especially fond of singers who specialize in gentle songs: Mel Tormé among prerock singers and Sam Cooke among early R&B stylists. "I like them because that's naturally where I am," he said. "Eventually your voice becomes the person you are. I didn't overuse it. I didn't do too many shows or sing that hard." With the album finished in the summer of 1975, Simon's mood had brightened considerably, thanks to the music, his time with Harper, and a wide range of new friends, none more important than a young TV executive from Canada who would become his best friend since his Kew Gardens Hills days.

CHAPTER THIRTEEN

Lorne Michaels had so much in common with Simon that it's not surprising they became instant friends in the spring of 1975. They were roughly the same age (at thirty-one, Michaels was three years younger), both Jewish (Lorne's birth name was Lorne David Lipowitz), had relatives with a toe in show business (Lorne's grandparents ran a movie theater in Toronto), were English majors in college (Lorne at the University of Toronto), performed in high school variety shows (Lorne did comedy sketches), and dreamed of being in show business. They were also both smart, competitive, and loved a good joke. In fact, comedy may have been the key. "Lorne allowed me to be comedic," Simon said. "It's one of the things that made the friendship so solid. Comedy was more of a bond than music."

One of Michaels's earliest memories of Simon was the night they had dinner at a Korean restaurant in Manhattan, and Simon showed him some baseball cards he'd bought for Harper. When Michaels said he used to play a game where he and other kids tossed cards five or ten feet to see who could get them closest to a wall, Simon challenged him to a game. Which is how they ended up on Fifty-Fifth Street at one in the morning throwing baseball cards against a wall. Because Paul had prided himself on his ability to beat any kid in the neighborhood at tossing cards, he was impressed when Michaels proved to be a good match. It was one more thing to like about his new friend.

At the time, Simon was far more successful than Michaels, whose background in US television consisted chiefly of being a writer on such Los Angeles–based TV programs as *Rowan & Martin's Laugh-In* and *The Beautiful Phyllis Diller Show*. His top credential was being part of the writing team that won two Emmys for its work on Lily Tomlin specials. In addition, Michaels had costarred on *The Hart and Lorne Terrific Hour*, a TV variety show in Canada that, in retrospect, seemed like a warm-up for the eventual *Saturday Night Live*. The Canadian forerunner featured comedy bits, including satirical news reports, and showcased musical guests such as Cat Stevens and James Taylor. Its cast even included a promising young comedian named Dan Aykroyd.

Michaels, however, was about to take a big career step that spring, one that would place him among the most powerful and admired figures in television for decades. His work had caught the eye of Dick Ebersol, the twenty-seven-year-old boy wonder who in 1974 was named director of weekend late-night programming for NBC. When the network decided to drop Saturday-night reruns of *The Tonight Show* in 1975 because of low ratings, Ebersol was asked to design an eleven thirty replacement, and one of his ideas was a live variety show that he brainstormed with Michaels. NBC president Herb Schlosser embraced the idea, and Michaels was hired as executive producer. Moving to New York, Michaels began putting together a show that loosely combined *Hart and Lorne* and England's free-spirited *Monty Python's Flying Circus*. He had enough ideas in place by June 20 to write a detailed memo to Ebersol containing some of the show's eventual features, including rotating guest hosts. Among the possibilities he cited: Bette Midler, Richard Pryor, and his new friend Paul Simon.

Michaels had been introduced to Simon soon after his arrival in New York by Edie Baskin, a photographer who was working on the program and was dating Simon at the time. "I was already a huge fan of Paul's," Michaels said. "The moment you heard his music, you knew he was an original voice. The thing that impressed me was you felt he was speaking directly to you in the songs. During my last couple of years in Los Angeles, the two albums I listened to all the time were [Dylan's] *Blood on the Tracks* and *Rhymin' Simon.*"

Early on, Baskin invited Michaels to visit Simon's beachfront house in Bridgehampton, Long Island. "Paul and I stayed up most of the night just talking about all kinds of things," Michaels said. "That's when our relationship started building. It was a wonderful summer. We were both excited about what we were doing. I'd go to sessions for the *Still Crazy* album, and Paul would come to our production meetings. He got along with the people on the show because he shared their sense of humor." The friendship helped Paul emerge from his lingering depression. "You could see him blossom during that summer," Bobby Susser said. "Lorne introduced him to new people, people outside of music, where there was no sense of competition. He was enjoying life again. He felt good about himself again. He reminded me of the kid I knew who loved playing baseball."

When Michaels asked Simon to host the second episode of his new show, which would air on October 18, Paul agreed immediately, partially because the appearance would be good promotion for the new album, which was being released the following week. He also liked the idea of performing on what promised to be a hip comedy show; he hoped it would reveal a different side of him than was offered by his serious, Judge Cardozo image. Simon also wanted to help his friend.

Without Clive Davis to help pick the first single from the upcoming album, Simon conferred with Bob Sherwood, Columbia's national singles promotion director, who recommended "My Little Town" because the label's research team reported DJs around the country were hugely enthusiastic about it. And why not? It was the first new Simon and Garfunkel single in five years. Simon was wary of releasing "My Little Town" as a single because it could lead to more pressure for him to get back together with

Garfunkel, but he set aside his reservations—he liked the song. Columbia's marketing plan was to release Simon's "Gone at Last" and Garfunkel's "I Only Have Eyes for You" as singles in August to build early interest in the albums, and then follow with "My Little Town" a week before the LPs reached stores in late October. To the label's delight, Garfunkel also agreed to go on *Saturday Night* (the program's name until it was changed to *Saturday Night Live* in 1977) to sing their joint single, even though it was probably hard to be a guest rather than a cohost with his old partner.

Long before the program settled on its celebrated format of a couple of musical breaks amid the otherwise nonstop comedy, music and comedy were equal partners. On the opening show, October 11, the emphasis was on comedy, led by guest host George Carlin; highlights included Andy Kaufman doing his classic Mighty Mouse lip-synch skit and Chevy Chase introducing the satirical "Weekend Update" segment that would become one of the show's signature features. Michaels saved Simon for the second show. "It's always been a strategy of mine to try to make the second show 'hotter' than the first because you want the ratings and the word-of-mouth to go up, and I thought Paul could do that. But I also didn't want to put a friend in the first show," Michaels said. "I didn't know if it would be a disaster or not. I felt I had the ingredients, but not necessarily the recipe."

To maximize Simon's impact, Michaels designed the opening shot so that the first thing the viewers saw was Simon sitting on a stool in a sport coat and jeans, singing "Still Crazy After All These Years." There was no introduction or graphics indicating the name of the show. It was only after the song that Chevy Chase, in the role of a stagehand, stumbled and fell while carrying some equipment behind Simon. Hitting the ground, he looked up eagerly and declared, "It's Saturday Night!" Turning to comedy for a scene shot earlier in a gym, Simon engaged six-foot-eight NBA all-star Connie Hawkins in a game of one-on-one basketball. With "Me and Julio Down by the Schoolyard" playing in the background, hoops announcer Marv Albert called the action as Simon tried to dribble around Hawkins and under his legs. The segment was Simon's idea.

For most viewers, the highlight of the evening was when Simon brought out Garfunkel to reprise "The Boxer" and "Scarborough Fair" before singing "My Little Town," and the old friends seemed to enjoy being back together. They smiled a lot, and when Art reached out at one point to put his hand on Paul's shoulder, Paul responded by gently reaching back to him. Coupled with the single, fans surely thought a reunion album or tour was possible. There were a few other bits, including a short film by comedian Albert Brooks, but the ninety-minute show seemed like a Paul Simon special—some might say a Paul Simon infomercial.

Reviewing the broadcast for the *New York Times*, TV critic John J. O'Connor made fun of the blatantly promotional nature of Simon's and Garfunkel's appearances. His opening sentence: "Purely by business chance, it seems, the television reunion of Simon and Garfunkel on Saturday night neatly coincided with the release of separate recording albums by Paul Simon and Art Garfunkel." That said, O'Connor felt the music was "nice," though he didn't like much else of what he saw in the show or in the second half of the opening-week episode. (He admitted he had missed the first half because he'd gotten stuck in traffic.) "Even an offbeat showcase," he wrote, "needs quality, an ingredient conspicuously absent from the dreadfully uneven comedy effort of the new series." Those words in such an influential publication could have been the show's death knell, but Simon's appearance started enough buzz to buy Michaels time, and he used it well. In turn, the *Saturday Night* exposure served as a strong push for both the "My Little Town" single, which went to no. 9, and the two albums: *Still Crazy* became Simon's first no. 1 solo album, and *Breakaway* reached no. 7. Surprisingly, however, *Breakaway* was eventually certified platinum by the RIAA, while *Still Crazy* earned only a gold certificate.

To promote his album, Simon went on a brief US and European tour that ended in London in late December. He was backed by a strong musical cast built around the New York session team of McCracken, Levin, Gadd, and Tee, as well as the Jessy Dixon Singers. Even Garfunkel showed up as a special guest on a few dates. Reviews were overwhelmingly positive for the album and tour, but *New York Times* critic John Rockwell had scathing words for Simon in his account of the November 27 show at Avery Fisher Hall, the prestigious concert facility at Lincoln Center. "The songs Mr. Simon writes owe their obvious debts to the early-1960s folk movement, and particularly to its polished, commercially packaged side that shared much with the tradition of American cabaret and show tunes," he wrote. "At their best, they are sensitive or gently clever. But Mr. Simon never seems to be risking as much as the rawer sort of folk and folk-rock singer epitomized by Bob Dylan, although that may be an illusion based more on style than what the two men actually attempt."

Equally harsh, Rockwell added, "As a vocalist, Mr. Simon is nothing special—a modest, husky low tenor incapable of much expressive variance. Too often in the songs best known in their Simon and Garfunkel incarnations he is reduced to the awkward position of singing inferior cover versions." The comparison to Dylan and folk music in 1975 seemed curiously out of date, considering that Simon had largely moved away from the folk style after "The Boxer" six years earlier.

On the other side of the critical ledger, Ken Emerson, whose taste leaned more toward pop, raved about *Still Crazy* in a *New York Times* review that scoffed at the continuing calls for a Simon and Garfunkel reunion album or tour. "Simon and Garfunkel have each released a new solo album that . . . draw[s] upon elements of the music they once made together, but the results are so dramatically different that it seems inconceivable that Simon and Garfunkel could ever rejoin forces on a permanent basis," he wrote. "For Simon's new album, quite possibly his best, is an eloquent expression of adult despair, while Garfunkel's is an exercise in juvenile sentimentality."

All this debate only reinforced Simon's rule of not reading most reviews of his work—not only to avoid being hurt emotionally but also to not be seduced into changing his style. "Whether someone is saying you're a genius or whether they're saying you're not, it's just somebody's opinion," he said. "I might have avoided reading reviews when I was young because I was insecure. Later on, I may have avoided them because I was the opposite, like I was thinking, 'Who gives a damn what they say?' But over time, you want to cut out the distraction. When you are writing a song or making a record, you're the only judge that matters. You can listen to people you trust for their thoughts, but it's still your decision. The less clutter you allow into the process, the better off you are."

In the end, the music establishment sided with Emerson. When Grammy nominations were announced on January 13, 1976, Simon was again in the running for Best Album, Best Male Pop Vocal, and (with Garfunkel) for Best Vocal by a Group, Duo, or Chorus ("My Little Town"). To add to the good news, "50 Ways to Leave Your Lover" was on its way to being Simon's first no. 1 single since "Bridge Over Troubled Water." At the awards ceremony on February 28, Simon won in both of his nominated solo categories. In accepting the Best Album Grammy, he playfully thanked Stevie Wonder for not having released an album that year. Wonder had won Best Album in both 1974 and 1975, and he would return in 1977 to win a third. It was a good-natured comment, but the choice of *Still Crazy After All These Years* was a popular and deserved one.

Meanwhile, Simon's relationship with Garfunkel had taken another hit. It was hard enough on Garfunkel to read Emerson's *New York Times* review, but the words that hurt the most were Simon's in a *Newsweek* interview with Maureen Orth just before Christmas 1975. Orth said that Simon was "adamant" he would continue with a solo career. "I can't go back and do anything with Artie," Simon said. "That's prison. I'm not meant to be a partner." The word *prison* stung. In a handwritten letter to Simon dated simply "early December," Garfunkel accused his ex-partner of being insensitive and using him for his own selfish career purposes. It was one in a stream of emotional letters Garfunkel sent Simon over the years.

Ultimately, the most revealing thing about the *Newsweek* piece was the way it laid out Simon's plans. "Pop music is in a terrible state right now," he said. "The staple of American popular music is all three- or four-chord, country or rock oriented now. There's nothing that goes back to the richest, most original form of American popular music— Broadway and Tin Pan Alley—in which sophisticated lyrics are matched by sophisticated melodies." Simon, in effect, laid down a straightforward manifesto for his post–"Bridge Over Troubled Water" career. If rock critics weren't going to notice his ambitious new direction, he would spell it out. Simon also told Orth that he was growing tired of contemporary pop, and there was no way his next album would be comprised of ten random pop songs. More likely, the album would be based on songs for a film or a Broadway musical.

Garfunkel wasn't the only one troubled by Simon's remarks. Some of the execs at Columbia didn't like the idea of their golden boy moving away from mainstream pop. But the concern might soon be moot. Simon owed Columbia only one more album before his contract was over, and there was no guarantee he would re-sign with his longtime label. He felt increasingly uncomfortable in the absence of Clive Davis.

Five years after nervously walking away from Simon and Garfunkel, Simon was feeling good about a lot of things, including his personal life, chiefly the time spent with Harper and the exhilaration of being around Michaels and the television gang. For anyone eligible, the *SNL* set was the best social club in town. The network included Jann Wenner and his wife, Jane, which made things awkward. In his 2017 biography of Wenner, Joe Hagan wrote that the *Rolling Stone* cofounder accused Simon of trying to steal his wife. Jane and Paul both downplayed the seriousness of their relationship. About Simon, Wenner said in the book, "Paul and I have always had a very prickly relationship. He's very, very full of himself, but he's a certifiable genius." In a 2018 interview, Wenner said he considers Simon a friend, pointing out that he was invited to Simon's seventieth birthday party. About his artistry, he added, "He's in the very top rank of songwriters. I'd put him alongside Dylan and Lennon-McCartney."

Gradually Simon encountered people from all of the arts: books, painting, theater, and movies. He found talking with them more stimulating than sitting around with other musicians. He was delighted when Woody Allen offered him a small part as a smarmy record producer in his upcoming film *Annie Hall.* Allen was a director on his way to becoming even more of a voice of alienation and self-questioning than Simon's early songs.

Allen was such an admirer of Simon's work that he wouldn't think of writing lines for someone who knew the music business far better than he did. He asked Simon to come up with some words of his own; his only request was to include the word *mellow* somewhere in his comments. *Annie Hall* marked an important transition for Allen, a Bronx native who was six years older than Simon. After a series of broadly humorous movies, Allen wanted to make a more serious (though still funny) film about relationships. His character, Alvy Singer, was a comic with many of the neurotic tendencies that would be associated with Allen in subsequent years. He falls in love with Annie Hall (Diane Keaton), whose appealing sweetness and openness appear to be his exact opposite. In his role as record producer Tony Lacey, Simon tries to steal Annie from Alvy by promising to help further her goal of becoming a singer. Filming started on May 19, 1976, in New York. The brief association made Simon think even more about making his own movie. Where many actors complain about the long delays between shots on the set, he felt comfortable with the pace, given all the hours he had spent in recording studios.

He also came away from the film with a new girlfriend. Though she had only a cameo as a rock critic, Shelley Duvall, a Texas native in her midtwenties, had already appeared in such notable films as director Robert Altman's stylish western *McCabe & Mrs. Miller* and his recent satirical look at American social values, *Nashville*. Duvall would go on to star opposite Jack Nicholson in Stanley Kubrick's *The Shining*, a classic tale of psychological terror. When Simon learned that Duvall was planning to spend the weekend with a girlfriend at a house near his on Long Island, he offered her a ride. They ended up talking most of the night, and Shelley soon moved into Simon's new Central Park West apartment. It was his first serious relationship since his marriage. Shelley was fun, full of life, and adoring. She was also a link to the intriguing new world of film.

The idea of a Broadway musical, which he'd mentioned in the *Newsweek* interview, was fleeting, but Simon had been thinking about a rock 'n' roll movie all the way back to Elvis's early films. Despite his dismissing Presley's Hollywood years as mostly a terrible waste, he was confident he could avoid the same mistakes. He would do a serious film. The music film he most admired was the reggae-gangster masterpiece *The Harder*

They Come, which brought Jimmy Cliff attention in the United States. That 1972 movie wasn't just a celebrity vehicle, like Elvis's films, but a work with music that was as inspired as the story. Simon even had a rough concept in mind about the difficulty faced by pop figures of the 1960s as they adjusted to the changing tastes and times. "It touches on the problem of prolonged adolescence," he said. "Somewhere in your early thirties, you start noticing that the garment of your youth is becoming frayed. What do you do then? It's a crucial time. Some people make it through: Dylan, McCartney, the Stones. But a lot of others don't."

Despite his outsized confidence at the time, Simon wasn't naïve enough to think he could do the film by himself. His initial plan was to work with an established screenwriter on the script, but none of the writers on his short list were available. So he started sketching the story himself in the summer of 1976, figuring he could bring in another writer later. As the script unfolded over several months, Simon chronicled the story of a fictional folk singer-songwriter, Jonah Levin, who had achieved attention with an antiwar protest song, "Soft Parachutes," but was adrift in the 1970s, trying to find his way in a new, slicker musical climate—a struggle all the more difficult because he faced an unsympathetic record company president. In addition, Levin was going through the strain of a broken marriage and trying to spend as much time as possible with his young son. Obviously Simon was mixing his own experiences and observations in much the same way that he drew upon both resources in his songwriting.

The process wasn't easy. As he went through endless rewrites, he got advice and encouragement from filmmaker friends, including Mike Nichols and Herb Gardner, the latter of whom received an Oscar nomination for his 1965 adaptation of his Broadway play *A Thousand Clowns*. In an April 1977 interview in the *Village Voice*, Duvall even said that Nichols had agreed to direct a musical screenplay being written by Simon about a young songwriter and that the couple would costar in it, but Simon didn't recall the conversation.

All the while, Simon's relationship with Lorne Michaels continued to grow, and he agreed to return to *Saturday Night* to host the show again on November 11, 1976. George Harrison was Simon's musical guest, and he sang "Here Comes the Sun" and "Homeward Bound" with Paul, who was so comfortable that he agreed to walk onstage in a Thanksgiving turkey suit to sing "Still Crazy After All These Years." Simon also held his own in a skit during which he was interviewed by Dan Aykroyd, who gave an exaggerated impression of the verbose, self-absorbed real-life talk-show host Tom Snyder. During the skit, Aykroyd kept confusing Simon with the playwright Neil Simon. The episode was such a hit that Michaels started talking to Simon about doing his own network special. Despite the head-aches associated with the Simon and Garfunkel special in 1969, Simon was all for it. He knew he would be safe with Michaels.

The following summer, Simon paused to absorb the August 16 death at age forty-two of his first pop hero, Elvis Presley. It was another reminder to him of the dangers of stardom. "What struck me was how great Elvis was and how he let it all slip away with those movies and things," Simon said years later. "He had such great taste, and something big distracted him. To me, it was the fame thing again—the danger of not making the music your top priority. For my generation, Elvis started out as an incred-ible inspiration, but he turned into a role model you didn't want to follow."

After more work on his script, Simon headed to Los Angeles with Shel-ley in January 1978 to attend the Los Angeles Film Critics Association's annual awards ceremony. During the evening, Shelley was honored as Best Actress for her performance in Robert Altman's eloquent and mysterious *3 Women*, and Simon accepted the Best Screenplay award for *Annie Hall* on behalf of Woody Allen and Marshall Brickman. At a party afterward, Duvall introduced Simon to Carrie Fisher—who was at the ceremony be-cause the movie in which she costarred, *Star Wars*, was honored for Best Film—and Shelley couldn't help but notice an attraction. The teenager who'd first caught Simon's eye in *Shampoo* was now twenty-one, and her personality was so electric that she glowed. What he didn't know was that Fisher had a crush on him. Two years earlier, she had even sung "Bridge Over Troubled Water" to great applause during her mother Debbie Reyn-olds's cabaret act.

CHAPTER FOURTEEN

Mental toughness can be as crucial as raw talent in determining the quality and longevity of an artist's work. Simon's resolve in the studio was tested from the start, but his biggest fight came after Clive Davis's ouster from the CBS Records group. His replacement, Irwin Segelstein, was cordial enough but didn't have his predecessor's feel for music or understanding of the artistic temperament. In fairness, the former CBS-TV executive was switched to the corporation's music division to help calm the waters in the suddenly embattled label. In an official history of the label, he was even described as a placeholder.

The real conflict began in early 1975, when Segelstein's post was given to a bolder, some would say ruthless figure: Walter Yetnikoff. The Brooklyn native had been a lawyer in the same New York firm as Davis before joining CBS's legal team in 1962, but he possessed little of Clive's gracious manner or ear for a hit. He did, however, have one enormously effective trait: he knew how to get results by putting the fear of God into employees and anyone who stood in the label's way. During his fifteen-year run as head of the CBS Records group, Yetnikoff made billions for the company by energizing its promotional resources behind artists such as Michael Jackson, Bruce Springsteen, and Billy Joel. Most dramatically, in the 1980s he forced MTV, the powerful new music video cable channel, to abandon its largely white-rock-only playlist by threatening to withhold all CBS videos from the channel if it didn't play videos from Jackson's *Thriller* album. Despite this success, Yetnikoff would be remembered as the embodiment of greed and excess in the music business—sometimes driven to reckless extremes by his own freely admitted cocaine and alcohol abuse. Like most executives, Yetnikoff had a favorites list, and Paul Simon wasn't on it.

"I never liked the way Paul left Art," Yetnikoff declared in his 2004 memoir, *Howling at the Moon*. "I thought he lacked loyalty. . . . As a person, Paul struck me as pretentious and self-important." Yetnikoff's opinion of Simon dropped even more when he visited Paul backstage after one of Simon's concerts. "His entourage treated him like little Lord Byron, hanging on his every word," he wrote. "When I walked in, he was stretched out on a couch, smoking a joint, pontificating about the nature of poetics." There was some sympathy around Columbia for Yetnikoff's position. Even those close to Simon believed that the success of *Still Crazy* and all that time with the *SNL* gang gave him an inflated opinion of himself.

Yetnikoff soon got caught up in a battle with Mo Ostin, the head of Warner Bros. Records, which was overtaking CBS as the dominant sales force in the US record industry. Based in Los Angeles, Ostin was the opposite of his New York rival in almost every important way. Warm and supportive rather than crude and intimidating, Ostin had genial relationships with artists and other industry executives. None of which mattered to Yetnikoff as much as the fact that Warner Communications was paying Ostin and its other executives far more than CBS was paying him and his team.

As Warners's fortunes soared, Yetnikoff declared war on what he enjoyed referring to as the Bugs Bunny Company. He vowed to do everything in his power to beat it down, even if it meant stealing top Warners artists. To underscore his determination, Yetnikoff ordered banners for the company convention that read, "Fuck Warner. Fuck the Bunny" to ridicule his rival. The campaign was viewed mostly with amusement until the closing weeks of 1976, when Yetnikoff lured away one of Warner's most prized artists, James Taylor, with an offer that reportedly included a $2.5 million signing bonus and a guarantee of $1 million an album. The raid led to speculation among industry pros about how Warner Bros. would retaliate, but Ostin professed to ignoring CBS, which probably riled Yetnikoff all the more. "It was a big, big loss, but I never set out to 'get back' at Columbia," Ostin said in reference to James Taylor. "I just kept concentrating on doing what we did at the label. That was our answer to Columbia. Our market share just kept growing."

Ostin, however, made no secret of his interest in signing Simon. It's telling how different Ostin's view of Simon was—even before they worked together—than Yetnikoff's. Mo and Simon met during the 1960s, and Ostin was impressed at how "cerebral and passionate" he was about music and how open he was to other people's ideas. Mo had even pursued Simon early in his solo career, but Simon's attorney, Michael Tannen, said he doubted Paul would leave his longtime musical home.

While Simon continued to work on his film script in the summer of 1977, the conflict between him and Yetnikoff grew more intense over the terms of a new contract. Whatever his personal feelings about Simon, Yetnikoff knew he was a valuable property whose drive would propel him for years to come. But that didn't lead the CBS president to tone down his bluster.

Apart from the contract talk, Simon worked with the label on *Greatest Hits, Etc.*, a best-of Simon package that Columbia wanted to release over the holiday season. He recorded two new songs for the album—"Slip Slidin' Away" and "Stranded in a Limousine"—in early September in New York. "Slip Slidin' Away," an especially appealing work about the uncertainty of relationships, had been written during the *Still Crazy* sessions. Unlike the jazzy undercurrents of that album, however, Simon wanted a more bouncy, upbeat arrangement, which led him to bring in the Oak Ridge Boys, a country-gospel group that would soon become hugely successful in Nashville. Released as a single in October, "Slip Slidin' Away" was a hit, peaking at no. 5. But the frisky "Stranded in a Limousine," which was released during the height of the contract fight, didn't make the chart at all, and Simon believed Columbia deliberately buried the record to warn him of what would happen without the label's backing.

Released in November, *Greatest Hits, Etc.* topped the one million sales mark within a matter of weeks, which served as a perfect setup for the December 8 NBC special Simon was working on with Lorne and, once again, director Charles Grodin. Coincidentally, the NBC executive whose approval Michaels needed for the special was Irwin Segelstein, the man who had replaced Davis at Columbia. When Michaels brought up the special, Segelstein was understandably wary. He had been at CBS when the Simon and Garfunkel special bombed. But Michaels argued that times had changed and that he would personally oversee the show.

In the end, the Simon special was as far from the traditional pop music variety show as the 1969 special, only without the politics. The concept involved a spoof of the usual bland, mostly uneventful TV music specials. Simon, as himself, was followed around on the show by a hapless producer, played by Grodin, who kept assuring him that everything was going well despite obvious signs to the contrary. When Simon walked onstage to find a nearly empty hall, for instance, Grodin explained it was all a booking foul-up. Nothing to worry about, Grodin continued. He'd edit in shots of an audience so no one would know Simon was singing to an empty house. The inserts proved to be wildly inappropriate, ranging from shots of uproarious rockers at a stadium concert to a gathering of passive senior citizens. The end result was sharp and funny.

Elsewhere in the special, Grodin forced Paul and Art (whose hurt over the *Newsweek* article had apparently eased enough for him to again accept a supporting role) to endlessly rehearse the most routine introductory remarks. Despite the special's inventive touches, reviews were mixed, and ratings were again dismal, finishing no. 57 among the week's sixty-nine prime-time broadcasts. Ultimately, Simon's and Michaels's work was rewarded, along with the rest of their writing team, with an Emmy for best writing in a comedy-variety or music special.

———————

Tired of the battle with Yetnikoff, Simon instructed his attorneys in January 1978 to file suit in London to stop CBS from manufacturing and distributing the old *Song Book* album, confirming for industry insiders the long-rumored rift between him and the label. Mo Ostin immediately phoned Tannen and made Simon the biggest offer Warner Bros. had made to that point: $13 million, which included a $3 million guarantee for four albums and a $1 million signing bonus. Tannen called back a few days later to say Simon was vacationing in Hawaii and would love to have dinner with Mo and his wife, Evelyn, in Los Angeles on his way back to New York. "I was hoping for good news at the dinner, but Paul made it very clear that he wasn't going to sign with us," Ostin said years later. "He said, 'I really like you, and I think you have a wonderful company, which is why I wanted to tell you my decision face-to-face rather than on the phone. I live in New York. I'm a New Yorker to the bone. Goddard signed me. I respect him enormously. I just can't leave Columbia.' " Mo figured his dream was over.

Back in New York, however, Simon accused Yetnikoff of reneging on a previously agreed contract provision that would give Simon the right to release one album that would have his songs but where he might not be the performer—such as a soundtrack or Broadway cast album. Tannen tried to patch things up with Yetnikoff during a flight to Los Angeles, but Tannen said Yetnikoff became enraged and pulled the Columbia offer from the table. By the time Tannen got to his hotel that night, he feared he had blown Simon's deal. Anxiously, he phoned Ostin at home to say that his client might be willing to sign with Warner Bros. after all. Delighted, Ostin outlined a deal in less than an hour the next morning in his office. The pact was signed February 15, 1978. Though Simon mentioned his film plans to Ostin, the contract was tied strictly to studio recordings; Paul was still free to turn to any studio for the film. Upon hearing the news, Yetnikoff reportedly threatened lawsuits to hold up Simon's recording for Warner Bros., pointing out that Simon still owed Columbia one more album.

Final albums in a contract are often a source of conflict because artists are tempted to hold back their best material in case they decide to go to another label. Understandably, Yetnikoff thought Simon was holding back when Tannen told him Paul planned to make his next album a collection of Elizabethan sonnets set to music. Yetnikoff said, in effect, no one will buy it. As the argument continued, it turned nasty. At one point, a frustrated Yetnikoff called Simon a "teeny, tiny little squirt." The fighting went on for months.

Paul Wasserman, a leading publicist who represented Simon in the 1970s and 1980s as well as worked with the Rolling Stones, Bob Dylan, Linda Ronstadt, and U2, was aware of the heated exchanges, and he admired Simon for standing up against the assault. "I've seen lots of artists completely collapse under that kind of hostile behavior," he said. "It breaks down their confidence, and they begin to lose perspective on their own music. They start turning musical decisions over to the executives. But Paul got stronger and more determined the longer it went with Yetnikoff."

Meanwhile, Simon's two-year relationship with Shelley ended in May 1978, just before she headed to London to begin work on *The Shining*. Duvall said in 1980 there was no special reason for the split. "Just like in one of his songs ['You're Kind']," she said, "he liked to sleep with the window open, and I liked it closed. Your basic incompatibility." A year later, however, she acknowledged the role of another woman—the one she had introduced him to in Los Angeles—Carrie Fisher. But she didn't seem to resent the younger star. "If Carrie hadn't come along, somebody else would have," she said. "This may sound surprising, but Paul and I are better friends than we were lovers. I still speak to him all the time."

Simon's interest in Carrie started before the Duvall relationship ended. In April he and Carrie had met for the second time—where else?—on the *Saturday Night Live* set, which was only natural because Carrie represented the live-life-to-the-fullest excesses of several of the show's stars. If Kathy and Peggy had been shy and largely anti–show business, Carrie—far more than Duvall—was a creature of show business. She jokingly called herself a product of Hollywood inbreeding; specifically, the 1955 marriage of Debbie Reynolds and Eddie Fisher.

Reynolds's wholesome image and widescreen smile established her as America's young sweetheart in the 1950s through such showcase films as

Singin' in the Rain and *Tammy and the Bachelor*, and her competitiveness led her to be one of the country's true showbiz troupers for decades. Eddie Fisher was a young, best-selling pop crooner in the 1950s until the rise of Elvis Presley and rock 'n' roll left his recording career dead in the water. The marriage, meanwhile, turned into a massive Hollywood scandal in 1959 when Fisher left America's sweetheart and two-year-old Carrie and her younger brother, Todd, to marry the world's most beautiful actress, Elizabeth Taylor, who in turn left him in 1964 for husband number five, Richard Burton. The public never forgave Fisher for walking out on his family. He spent the rest of his life in the shadows of show business. All this left its mark on Carrie, her father believed. Fisher even quoted her as saying, "My father was extremely unavailable. And that has affected how I relate to men. I don't trust them."

Yet she was drawn to Simon. "As a teen, I *loved* this man's lyrics," she said. "They were one of the reasons I fell in love with words. I apprenticed myself to the best in him and bickered with the worst. And to top it off, we were the same size. I used to say to him, 'Don't stand next to me at the party—people will think we're salt and pepper shakers.' " Who wouldn't fall in love with someone as funny as that? Besides, Carrie was becoming what has been a fantasy for many rock stars: a starlet. Elvis dated Natalie Wood and Ann-Margret during his early days in Hollywood. Thanks to her role as Princess Leia in *Star Wars*, Carrie was being hailed as Hollywood's next big star.

She and Simon spent time together in the weeks after their meeting, but it was mostly casual. Simon dated others during that time, and Carrie was wary of entering a serious relationship. "I was twenty-one," she said. "I felt like a kid around Paul and Lorne," who were thirty-six and thirty-three, respectively. "I didn't know if I could fit in with them. When Paul asked me to join him and Lorne and some friends on vacation in Greece that August, [screenwriter] Buck Henry told me, 'Don't go. You'll end up in a relationship.' I said, 'No I won't,' but, of course, I did. We should have gotten married in Greece, for all practical purposes." Carrie and Paul would be together, on and off, for the next decade, but it was far from the calm, reassuring relationship that Simon sought. It wouldn't help that Carrie's mother was not a fan. Debbie Reynolds looked upon Paul Simon as Eddie Fisher redux.

While the argument over the final Columbia album dragged on, Simon kept working on the film, and he was feeling good enough about it by the fall to ask Tannen to seek a studio deal. His timing couldn't have been better. Hollywood was fascinated by pop music and its young stars. Bette Midler, Neil Diamond, Elton John, Rod Stewart, and David Bowie either had films in the works or were being courted by studios. They were following in a trail that also included Barbra Streisand, Bob Dylan, Mick Jagger, and Diana Ross. On October 2 Simon and Tannen flew to Los Angeles to outline their plans for Warner Bros. and Twentieth Century-Fox executives. Both studios submitted offers, but Simon chose Warner Bros. to put the album and film under the same corporate umbrella.

There was one remaining roadblock: the stalemate over the final Columbia album. Just before Christmas, Simon's lawyers filed suit in New York State Supreme Court to end his obligations to CBS so that he could formally start recording for his new label. The suit maintained it was unreasonable to make Simon deliver a final album to CBS because the label was out to "destroy Simon's career and reputation" and would, thus, "bury" the new LP. The court ruled two months later that Simon was free to record for Warner Bros. as long as he paid $1.5 million to CBS in lieu of the final album. Suddenly Simon's world was bright again: he had Carrie; a great friend in Michaels (they eventually bought adjacent apartments on Central Park West); a second Grammy for Best Album; a new, supportive record label; and a film contract.

Because Simon came to Hollywood with a reputation as a pop star with a need for control, skepticism was high around town. To many old-timers, here was another hotshot with no film experience trying to tell everyone what to do. Almost as soon as word leaked about the movie, there were whispers about the studio resisting Simon's desire to star in it. There were even reports that Warner Bros. wanted a proven actor in the film so badly that executives tried to get Mo Ostin to intervene, but both Simon and Ostin denied it. In fact, Simon said, the studio's interest in the film was based on him starring in it. He said he was the one with reservations about acting.

Simon spoke to some actors, including Richard Dreyfuss, but soon realized he needed to portray the lead character, Jonah Levin, because he wanted the same voice on the album and in the film. He certainly didn't want anyone having to lip-synch. "I didn't want to do a film about music that I couldn't believe in," he said. "That's the biggest problem I found with other [rock-related] films. They seemed false. Take *A Star Is Born*. It didn't seem like a rock film to me. They had a story, and they just grafted it onto a rock backdrop, and not in the most accurate way. You don't really believe Barbra Streisand is a rock star. You always know it's really Barbra Streisand." Simon took the authenticity issue so far that he wanted his own musicians—Gadd, Levin, Tee, and guitarist Eric Gale—to portray Jonah's band in the film, which was eventually titled *One-Trick Pony*.

To prepare for his role, Simon took acting lessons from Mira Rostova, a Method school proponent whose most famous pupil had been Montgomery Clift. She was recommended by the ever-present Charles Grodin. That left the issue of director. Most of the big names Simon approached were worried that their vision would be overshadowed by Simon's. His eventual choice was recommended by the studio, Robert M. Young, who had just directed a widely praised 1977 prison drama, *Short Eyes*.

In the middle of all this struggle, Carrie, who had been filming *The Empire Strikes Back* in England, flew back to America to celebrate their first anniversary as a couple. But the relationship was soon in what would prove to be one of its many down periods. "For all the good times, there were problems that took me a long time to understand, problems that led to a lot of breakups, but we would then get back together," Carrie said years later. "For one thing, he could be very critical, which struck me as odd because he was usually this sensitive, caring person. Then I learned where it came from when I met his father. The first thing Lou said to me—before hello—was 'Your father couldn't carry a rhythm. He had no rhythm.' "

Carrie also thought she and Paul had different tolerance levels when it came to conflict. "On one hand, I came from such an eccentric, show-business background that I was quite used to conflict and maybe even expected it—watching my mother's [three] marriages collapse. I had no idea why they stayed together or what drove them apart," she said. "But Paul wanted peace and comfort, which is what he needed to write, and writing a good song is everything to Paul. He loved his work more than money or fame. Whenever there was a big problem, I'd go off on a job or something, and Paul interpreted that as the job being more important to me than he was. He wanted someone by his side. He didn't like being alone. He wanted companionship. At one point, I even tried to be this intellectual geisha. I took cooking classes and massage lessons." But the breakups continued.

After finishing *The Empire Strikes Back*, Carrie joined her *Saturday Night Live* buddies John Belushi and Dan Aykroyd in the cast of *The Blues Brothers*, which began shooting in Chicago in the summer of 1979. She played Belushi's angry ex-girlfriend, but she adored him in real life. In many ways, they were kindred spirits, always looking for something more out of life. In *Wired*, his 1984 biography of Belushi, Bob Woodward wrote, "John seemed always somewhat dissatisfied, as if he were protesting, 'This can't be it. This can't be all of it. This isn't enough. There has to be more, something else.' Fisher felt it, too." But, it turned out, she was closest to Aykroyd, and the relationship evolved quickly to the point that he proposed on the set. "We had rings and got blood tests, the whole shot," she said. But then she backed out because she realized she still wanted Paul. For Simon, there was little time to digest the news. Once on the film project, Paul focused on it with the same intensity he brought to his music.

On September 23, Simon sang "The Sound of Silence" and "The Boxer" at the closing night in the series of five "No Nukes" benefit concerts at Madison Square Garden, which were designed to promote a nuclear-free policy in America. He was then off to Cleveland to start filming *One-Trick Pony*. The band performed in front of the cameras at the Agora Ballroom, a celebrated venue known for showcasing many of rock's finest newcomers over the years, including Bruce Springsteen and U2. Jonah Levin's musicians, of course, weren't rock newcomers. In the film, they portray fading veterans who open for some up-and-coming new-wave hotshots, the real-life B-52's. After shooting additional life-on-the-road scenes, the production moved to New York, where the core of the footage was completed by mid-February 1980. But postproduction took several more months. Word of mouth around the Warner Bros. lot (and therefore all of Hollywood) was not good and—sure enough—studio executives were not impressed when they saw a rough cut that summer. Tannen believed the studio didn't use its promotion muscle on the film, thus killing its box office prospects. One of the executives was reportedly so down on the film that four years later, when he was again displeased by one of the studio's ventures into pop—this time, it was Prince's *Purple Rain*—he stood up in the screening room and shouted at Mo Ostin, "Well, Mo, looks like you've given me another one of your rock fuckups." As it turned out, however, *Purple Rain* went on to gross nearly $80 million worldwide.

While Simon waited for the film to open, he and Carrie attended the May 17 world premiere of *The Empire Strikes Back* at the Kennedy Center in Washington, DC, and a second premiere in London. They were accompanied on both trips by Garfunkel, who was now dating Carrie's best friend, Penny Marshall, costar of the popular TV sitcom *Laverne & Shirley*. The verdict on *One-Trick Pony* followed that fall. *Variety* and numerous other trade publications gave it decent reviews, but, generally, the film took a drubbing. David Ansen in *Newsweek* called it a "vanity production" with "a fatal lack of pulse." A widespread complaint was that the film simply wasn't believable; ironically, it lacked the one thing Simon most wanted, which was authenticity.

In hopes of building an audience for the soundtrack album and film, Simon took his band on the road for short tours of the United States and Europe, but it didn't help. When the film was released in October, moviegoers yawned big-time. With a budget of nearly $7.5 million, *One-Trick Pony* grossed a pitiful $843,000 domestically, giving Warner Bros. little reason to even release it in England. In postmortems, fingers were pointed at the script, Simon's acting, Young's direction, and the lack of chemistry between Simon and Blair Brown, who played his estranged wife. Simon took full responsibility. "Once I did *Still Crazy*, I thought about what ambitious thing I could do next, and I was arrogant enough to think I could do a movie, even though I wasn't prepared to make a movie," he said. "I ended up making a series of bad decisions, and the movie was such a flop that I kind of withdrew and licked my wounds and asked myself what the hell happened here."

Simon's frustration was compounded when the soundtrack became his first album to fall short of the Top 5 in the United States. The LP had a standout single, "Late in the Evening," which shared much of the Latin music undercurrent and youthful nostalgia of "Me and Julio" without feeling like a copy. It got enough radio airplay to reach the US Top 10 and surely would have gone higher if the film had been better received.

Simon felt he had let down Ostin and his team. The label head kept telling him not to worry about it; Warner Bros. was a big company, and it could cover the losses. No one could guarantee a hit. But Simon wouldn't accept that, Ostin recalled. He promised Mo that he'd one day pay back the money the label lost on the album. Mo appreciated the gesture, but he figured Simon would get over it. No other artist had ever even brought up the subject of paying back the company. The guilt over the album's poor sales was one in a series of issues that caused Simon to go into the deepest depression since his struggles with fame and insecurity in the early 1970s. He said, "I didn't feel anything I did had any worth." Still, he carried on publicly. On February 25, 1981, he hosted the Grammy Awards at Radio City Music Hall. The four top honors—Album, Record, Song, and New Artist—were swept by Christopher Cross, a nondescript singer-songwriter from Texas. But Simon was able to cheer victories by some of his cohorts, including Phil Ramone (Producer of the Year), Bob James (Pop Instrumental Performance), and Quincy Jones (Instrumental Arrangement).

During the telecast, Simon was assigned a young man from England named Nick Laird-Clowes to be his personal assistant. When Simon learned that Laird-Clowes, who turned out to be a Simon fan, was a singer-songwriter with an album that had been reviewed favorably in

Rolling Stone, he invited him to bring the album with him to the apartment the next day. While Simon was listening to the LP, titled *Too Late at 20*, some friends stopped by, and they started gushing over the music: "incredible," "wonderful." When the album ended, one guest asked Simon if he didn't agree. In his usual unguarded appraisal, Simon said, "No, I don't think so. It has some good things, but it's not there." Laird-Clowes's heart sank.

If the story ended there, it would be another tale of Simon's reputation for sometimes being overly blunt, but the rest of the story offers a revealing look at Simon's generosity in reaching out to artists if he senses they will be responsive. Actually, Simon was impressed enough with Laird-Clowes's music to ask the young Englishman to keep in touch—and that's exactly what the musician did. "Several months later, I went to see Paul at his office in the Brill Building, and he started playing the piano," the songwriter said. "After a few seconds, he asked me what key he was playing in, and I had no idea. I guessed, 'Is it G?' and he said, 'No, it's D.' " He then picked up a legal pad and spent several minutes writing down various chords and other musical notations. He told me to go learn them before I came back. I think he was trying to see how dedicated I was to songwriting. Before I left, he showed me the lyrics to the song that became 'Hearts and Bones,' which he had been working on for a year. He said, 'If you want to become better than anyone else, you've got to work harder than anyone else.' "

When Laird-Clowes saw Simon next, he had learned everything Paul had written on the page. Simon was pleased, and they spent considerable time discussing songwriting. Later Laird-Clowes formed a new band, the Dream Academy, which Ostin signed to Warner Bros. Thanks to a gentle, nostalgic tune called "Life in a Northern Town," the band had a major hit in England in 1985. The song eventually became a success around the world, and the young songwriter went on to a long career in music, including composing for soundtracks and documentaries.

"The amazing thing is that Paul did all this while he was going through problems with his own career," Laird-Clowes said. "I remember he came to London after Dream Academy had a hit, and he was still extremely depressed, but he still had his sense of humor. He said to me, 'The way things are going, I'll end up singing backing vocals on someone's album. People will see my name in the liner notes and go, 'Oh, so that's what he's doing now.' But the thing I'll never forget was how pleased he was for me and my group. We eventually went on *Saturday Night Live*, and Paul was in the audience. Before the show, he pulled my chain: 'Don't make me look bad.' It was amazing. He was so gracious."

Unable to shake his latest bout of writer's block in the spring of 1981, Simon, on a friend's recommendation, contacted Dr. Rod Gorney, a Los Angeles psychiatrist whose father, Jay Gorney, was a noted songwriter who cowrote the Depression-era hit "Brother, Can You Spare a Dime?"; encouraged by their phone conversation, Simon flew across the country and went directly to the psychiatrist's house.

"I'm here," he told the psychiatrist, "because, given all the facts of my life—given the fact that I'm young, and I'm in good health, and I'm famous; that I have talent, I have money—given all these facts, I want to know why I'm unhappy. I can't write anymore. I have a serious writer's block, and this is the first time I can't seem to overcome it." Simon also talked about his troubles with Carrie, including their constant breakups. Faced with a problem that made them uncomfortable, they were inclined to say, "Hey, I don't need this." They were, Simon said, spoiled because they were both used to being the center of attention. At the end of the visit, Gorney told Simon that he felt further sessions would be useful. He also pointed to a guitar in his living room and urged Simon to take it to his hotel and try to express his feelings in a song.

Simon was so drained that night he didn't even open the guitar case. Besides, he told Gorney when they got back together the next day, it takes him months to write a song. Gorney said he understood, but again suggested that Simon try to write a song. Back in the hotel that second evening, Simon did start writing. He came up with part of the melody and some early words for a song, "Allergies," that eventually included these lines:

I go to a famous physician
I sleep in a local hotel
From what I can see of the people like me
We get better
But we never get well

Gradually, Simon recalled, the conversations with Gorney turned more philosophical. "My problem," Simon told him, "is that I really don't see what difference it makes if I write or don't write." The psychiatrist got him to admit that a song like "Bridge Over Troubled Water" made a difference in people's lives, and he encouraged Simon to write more songs that made a difference. Simon returned to New York. He finished "Allergies" and began working on other songs for a new album; mostly personal songs about relationships. The talks with Gorney didn't erase all of Simon's troubles, by any means, but they helped him reconnect with his songwriting. As Carrie said, "When Paul had problems, he would often go into his music. Music was a very good friend to him."

He played "Allergies" for Carrie in New York, and she was touched. "As soon as I heard the words—'My heart is allergic to the women I love, it's changing the shape of my face'—I knew the song was about me," she said. "But I didn't take it personally. I was honored."

Simon was still trying to regain his balance a few months later when he got a call from his old manager, Mort Lewis. The city of New York wanted Paul to do a concert in Central Park in the summer or fall of 1981.

CHAPTER FIFTEEN

When Lewis was contacted by Ron Delsener about Simon doing a free show in Central Park, he assumed that the city's premier concert promoter was talking about Simon and Garfunkel. Almost weekly since the breakup, the manager had been getting inquiries about putting the team back together. It was several minutes into the conversation before he realized Delsener was talking about just Paul. The idea for the concert came from Gordon J. Davis, the city's commissioner of parks and recreation. A huge Simon fan, he asked Delsener for help in making his dream come true. The promoter phoned Lewis, assuming he still managed Simon, but Lewis's only involvement was passing along the message. Simon had largely managed himself since the early 1970s.

To his surprise a few days later, Lewis heard that the free Simon concert in the park had turned into a free Simon and Garfunkel concert. The date was set for the evening of Saturday, September 19. "My guess is Paul would never have agreed to do the concert if Davis wanted Simon and

Garfunkel," Lewis said. "Paul had spent so much time turning down all the offers, but he was the one who brought Art into the Central Park picture. He knew Barbra Streisand had drawn hundreds of thousands of people in Central Park, and he didn't know if he could draw that big a crowd by himself."

As Lewis suspected, the move was prompted by anxiety. "I got pulled back by fear," Simon said. "I was still licking my wounds from *One-Trick Pony*. My confidence wasn't high. When I spoke to Delsener, I thought doing the park concert was a good idea, but then I got to thinking about it. My first idea was to bring Artie onstage for three or four numbers, just like I had done on a few of the solo shows. But then I thought you couldn't have Simon and Garfunkel opening for me, and I didn't want to open for Simon and Garfunkel. I kept going back and forth until I got to the point where I figured it would be better as a Simon and Garfunkel reunion." Garfunkel jumped at the chance, though it soon became apparent that Simon was still running things, and disagreements began almost immediately, Roy Halee said.

The chief issue, according to Simon, was that Garfunkel wanted to go back to the acoustic days when it was just the two of them onstage, while Simon wanted something grander, something that incorporated more of the sense of his new music. Just when things looked like they might break down, David Geffen stepped in. A friend of both, Geffen was hoping to acquire the rights to any live album for his new Geffen Records label. He told Garfunkel flatly, "Whatever Paul tells you to do, do it."

Lorne Michaels, whom Simon brought in early on, enlisted members of his *Saturday Night Live* staff to design a stage backdrop of the city—a water tank and skyscrapers—while Halee and Phil Ramone handled the sound. Because the city had no budget for all this, Simon spent around $750,000 on the production. During three weeks of rehearsal in an empty theater in Manhattan, Simon enlisted eleven session musicians, including his old standby Richard Tee on keyboards and a five-piece brass section, while he and jazz composer-arranger David Matthews redesigned various arrangements.

As soon as executives at Warner Bros. and Columbia (still Art's label) learned of the free concert, they began pushing for a live album, eventually agreeing that Warner Bros. would get US and Canadian distribution rights, while Columbia would receive overseas rights. Ultimately, Columbia passed its rights to Geffen, whose label was distributed overseas by Columbia. Fans started hoping for a tour and maybe even a long-awaited reunion album. Lewis began getting offers from around the world for a Simon and Garfunkel tour, but he didn't mention them to Simon because he didn't want to add to the pressure on him. Indeed, Ostin, who flew in from Los Angeles for the concert, found Simon to be extremely nervous, but then Mo realized that Simon, like most artists, was always worried.

Concertgoers, many of them carrying chairs or blankets, began showing up at dawn, hoping for choice spots near the stage as workmen scurried around under threatening skies to get things in shape. By early afternoon, Halee saw tens of thousands of fans already stretched out on the park's Great Lawn. "That's when I knew we were doing something magical," he said.

By show time, the crowd filled the concert area. As Carrie watched from the wings, Simon and Garfunkel walked onstage and shook hands at the microphone. Neither had any idea of the size of the crowd in the twilight. It just looked enormous as the band began playing the opening strains of "Mrs. Robinson." It was the perfect opening number because it brought the audience back to the days of Simon and Garfunkel, but not all the way back to the folk days. With the point established, Simon, wearing a dark suit with a white T-shirt, and Garfunkel, in a white dress shirt, black vest, and jeans, continued with "Homeward Bound," causing another burst of excitement in the crowd. Afterward, Simon welcomed the audience: "Well, it's great to do a neighborhood concert."

During one of his solo turns, Paul sang a new, unreleased song, "The Late Great Johnny Ace," which is about death and innocence in rock. The title refers to an R&B singer who at age twenty-four died of an accidental, self-inflicted gunshot to the head on Christmas Day 1954 (the rumor was that Ace was playing Russian roulette), while one verse refers to John Lennon, who was shot to death in 1980 by a fan in front of the Dakota, just a few hundred yards from where the concert was held. Seconds after Simon mentioned Lennon in the song, a young man leaped onstage and headed toward him, saying, "Paul, I have to talk to you," before a security guard led him away. From a distance, it was a frightening moment, though Simon said the fan didn't look like he wanted to harm him. He and Garfunkel then closed the formal set with "The Boxer" and then returned for the encore, which ended with "The Sound of Silence." After several minutes of applause, they returned to the stage again to play "Late in the Evening."

Probably the only people at the show who didn't understand the significance of the evening were Simon and Garfunkel themselves. In the moments after the concert, Simon, who tends to underplay his emotions when assessing a performance, thought to himself, "It was okay." Garfunkel, he said, whispered to him, "Disaster." It wasn't until Simon got back to his apartment on Central Park West and watched the news accounts of the concert on TV with Carrie that the impact of the event finally sank in. The crowd estimate was a half million.

"I felt like a witness to what was happening more than a musician most of the day because I wasn't still connected musically to a lot of the old songs to really get into it on a musical level," he said. "But then I began to think about the music and what it represented to people in a new light. The music was good-hearted, warm, caressing. We've been living in just brutalizing times, and anytime you come across any public figure or figures that represent the opposite, they become very important."

Years later, the rock star Jack White picked up on the same theme. "The thing I love about Paul's music," he said, "is its universality." When he, one of ten children in Detroit, went on a picnic with his family years ago, he said, everyone was asked to sing a favorite song, and everyone picked a Paul Simon song. "I was amazed, but I can understand why—his music is so inescapably human."

Concert offers poured in from around the world—and not for the eighteen-thousand-seat arenas that Simon and Garfunkel had played at their height in the 1960s, but stadiums with capacities of forty thousand to seventy-five thousand, sometimes multiple nights. There were also plans to air the

Central Park concert on the Home Box Office cable channel and to release the live album. Simon and Garfunkel were bigger than ever. Even Simon's rocky relationship with Carrie seemed smooth. *People* magazine had adopted them as a "sweetheart couple," reminiscent of the role Carrie's parents occupied in the 1950s. Along with other celebrity-driven publications, *People* took advantage of every public outing to run a photo of the pair, whether they were visiting Count Basie backstage at the Savoy, a new club in Times Square, or taking in a Broadway show.

Not all was upbeat. The Central Park concert differences reminded Simon of the frustrations of making music with Garfunkel, and the run-ins continued during lengthy postproduction on the live album. Unhappy with his vocals at the concert, Garfunkel insisted on rerecording all of them in the studio, which left Halee with the painstaking task of having to match each of Garfunkel's notes with Simon's vocals from the concert to make them sound as if they came from the same microphone. Halee described the process as "torturous."

One other thing stood in the way of a reunion album. After writing about mostly fictional characters in *One-Trick Pony*, Simon was looking forward to writing again about his own experiences. He began writing the songs before the Central Park concert, and they were so personal, he told Carrie, that he couldn't imagine adding Art's voice to his own.

Still, the demand for a tour and reunion album continued. Response to the *Concert in Central Park* LP, released alongside the February 21 HBO special, was a sign of the fans' continued devotion to the duo. The double album spent two years on the US chart, selling more than two million copies, matching *The Graduate*. Overseas, the live album reached the Top 10 in more than a dozen countries, including England, Japan, and the Netherlands.

Finally, Simon agreed to the tour; he could deal with the reunion album issue later. Billed as the Summer Evening tour, the shows started in May with five shows in Japan, and then switched to Europe for concerts from Madrid to Berlin, Stockholm to Paris (two shows, drawing a total of 130,000), Zurich to London. Outdoor shows were problematical because the harmonies tended to drift away at times, but stadiums were the only practical option given the huge demand for tickets. For all his earlier complaints, Garfunkel even seemed on board with moving forward, telling a journalist that he was more receptive to singing Paul's up-tempo songs and to singing in front of a band. With concert offers continuing to arrive, a second leg was added the following spring for Australia and New Zealand. The shows would reach the United States in mid-July 1983 and continue through late May, finally ending in Tel Aviv, Israel, on September 26.

Night after night of hearing the thunderous applause led Simon to gradually accept the inevitable. He and Garfunkel began talking casually about a reunion album. "We just sort of got swept away," Simon said. "There was a lot of pressure. I don't mean record company pressure because that's pretty insignificant. I don't even mean money pressure. But there seemed all this other pressure. People kept asking, 'Well, are you going to make an album together?' or 'God, it would be great if you made an album together.' And I felt that Art wanted to be involved very much. I also realized that by including him on it, I probably would improve the overall quality; certainly would improve the sales. I also knew we'd end up in some terrific fights over points I really didn't want to fight about. And that's exactly what happened."

Whenever Simon was free from touring, he resumed writing. As time went by, he decided to go into the studio with a new producer: Lenny Waronker, who had overseen the 1967 hit "The 59th Street Bridge Song (Feelin' Groovy)" for one-hit wonder Harpers Bizarre. Waronker, who was born the same month as Simon in 1941, had an easygoing manner but was known to be straightforward with his views in the studio. At Warner Bros., he had worked with a tasteful group of artists, including Randy Newman. While in Southern California for shows in Los Angeles and San Diego, Simon met with Waronker in Burbank to go over some of the new songs. In keeping with the idea of a Simon and Garfunkel album, Waronker invited Garfunkel to drop by too, and he sensed tension immediately, but he was impressed by Garfunkel's seriousness once Simon started playing "Allergies."

"Art was very attentive," Waronker said. "There was no more fooling around. He liked the song and immediately started sketching out some musical notes, showing how his voice could be added to the arrangement. We all agreed he'd come back the next day and record something. At that point, I was really hopeful this was going to work out." The optimism didn't last. The following day, Waronker found Simon at the microphone before Garfunkel arrived, singing background parts himself—in effect, usurping Garfunkel's role. Waronker tried to downplay it when Garfunkel arrived, and things did cool off. When Garfunkel finally stepped up to the microphone and sang his background part, Waronker thought it was gorgeous and said so. But Garfunkel, graciously, tried to redirect the praise to Simon. Waronker thought they were making progress, but he could tell by the look in Simon's eye that he didn't agree. They decided that Simon would keep working on songs, and everyone would get back together in a few weeks.

Before returning to New York, Simon followed up on his promise to help offset Warner Bros.'s losses on *One-Trick Pony*. According to Mo Ostin, Simon told him, "I want you to take any money you lost on that album out of my royalties for the Central Park album."

"I again told him he didn't need to do that, but he insisted," Ostin recalled. "The result was he paid us back a million dollars, maybe even a million and a half. It was extraordinary." The Warners "rebate" wasn't Simon's only act of generosity in connection with the Central Park event. A few days later, he handed an equally surprised Mort Lewis a check for $100,000 for his help in arranging the concert. "I couldn't believe it," Lewis recalled. "I said, 'Paul, you don't have to do this. All I did was pass along a phone call.' Then he put his hand on my shoulder and said, 'Mort, you'll always be Simon and Garfunkel's manager. This is your commission.' " He could afford both checks. He was, by now, one of the wealthiest figures in pop music.

Before Simon and Garfunkel reconvened in the studio, Lenny Waronker was promoted to president of Warner Bros. Records, a popular choice because he was the first "music man" in years to run a major label—a position normally given to attorneys, artist managers, or promotion men.

He would still report to Ostin, who assumed wider duties as board chairman, but he could no longer produce albums. The reins on the tentative Simon and Garfunkel album went to Waronker's longtime cohort Russ Titelman, who had already been assisting on the project. Titelman, a Los Angeles native who was three years younger than Simon, would go on to win Grammys for his production work with Eric Clapton and Steve Winwood. Simon also brought in Halee and moved the recording sessions to New York to be closer to Carrie and his core musicians.

The plan was to complete the basic tracks for the album that would be titled *Hearts and Bones* by early 1983 and then bring Garfunkel in to add his vocals. As soon as Halee heard the personal nature of some of the new songs, he couldn't imagine them ever ending up on a Simon and Garfunkel album. "I was surprised he was even considering it," he said. "I kept thinking, 'How is this going to work?' I knew everyone at Warners wanted a Simon and Garfunkel album. Mo wanted it. Waronker wanted it. Russ wanted it, and I knew the fans did, too. But these were such personal songs. The whole time we were recording the basic tracks, there was this giant elephant up ahead: Artie's vocals. The tension was quite heavy."

Just before Christmas 1982, Simon recorded a version of what would be one of the album's strongest pieces, "René and Georgette Magritte with Their Dog After the War." In the gentle song, he drew a parallel between an old couple's enduring love and the innocence and joy of doo-wop. He got the title from a photograph he happened to see in a book at Joan Baez's house when he played the annual Bread & Roses Festival of Music charity concert in Berkeley, California, in 1981. The nod to Magritte's surrealist paintings by juxtaposing the doo-wop groups came to him later while driving. Simon had these two interesting images—the Magrittes and the Moonglows and other groups—and he wanted to put them together. Magritte was a surrealistic painter, and Simon wanted it to be a surrealistic song. Unlike most of his songs, he started singing the words before picking out the music on guitar or piano. At first, he worried the theme was too esoteric, but he couldn't set aside the song. The lyrics began:

René and Georgette Magritte
With their dog after the war
Returned to their hotel suite
And they unlocked the door

Easily losing their evening clothes
They dance by the light of the moon
To the Penguins
The Moonglows
The Orioles
And the Five Satins
The deep, forbidden music
They'd been longing for
René and Georgette Magritte
With their dog after the war

Simon felt equally strongly about the song "Train in the Distance," the reflection on Tennessee-bred Peggy and life's recuperative powers. One of Fisher's favorite memories with Simon was the night he played "Train" for her. "It was obvious the song was about Peggy," Carrie said. "As soon as it started, he came over and gave me a hug. He was afraid I might be hurt. It was so sweet."

A third highlight in the new album for Simon was "Hearts and Bones," a love song about Carrie built around a vacation trip in New Mexico. They had been together—off and on—for five years now, and Simon captured both the magnetic attraction and underlying uncertainty of the relationship.

One and one-half wandering Jews
Free to wander wherever they choose
Are traveling together
In the Sangre de Cristo
The Blood of Christ Mountains

Of New Mexico
On the last leg of a journey
They started a long time ago
The arc of a love affair
Rainbows in the high desert air
Mountain passes slipping into stones
Hearts and bones
Hearts and bones
Hearts and bones

Thinking back to the season before
Looking back through the cracks in the door
Two people were married
The act was outrageous
The bride was contagious
She burned like a bride
These events may have had some effect
On the man with the girl by his side
The arc of a love affair
His hands rolling down her hair
Love like lightning, shaking till it moans
Hearts and bones
Hearts and bones
Hearts and bones

And whoa, whoa, whoa
She said, "Why?
Why don't we drive through the night?
We'll wake up down in
Mexico"
Oh, I
I don't know nothin' about, nothin' about no
Mexico

"And tell me why
Why won't you love me
For who I am
Where I am?"

He said, "Cause that's not the way the world is, baby
This is how I love you, baby
This is how I love you, baby"

One and one-half wandering Jews
Returned to their natural coasts
To resume old acquaintances
And step out occasionally
And speculate who had been damaged the most
Easy time will determine if these consolations
Will be their reward
The arc of a love affair
Waiting to be restored
You take two bodies and you twirl them into one
Their hearts and their bones
And they won't come undone
Hearts and bones
Hearts and bones
Hearts and bones

Except for a three-week tour of Australia and New Zealand in February 1983, Simon continued to write and record in New York until the start of the US leg of the stadium tour the following July in Akron, Ohio. As soon as Simon finished his vocals, Garfunkel started adding some of his own touches. But it didn't get far. The tussles with Art in the studio wore him down. Simon felt it was like the nightmare of *Bridge Over Troubled Water* all over again. Gradually he went from not wanting Garfunkel's voice on particular songs to not wanting his voice on the album at all. He didn't look forward to disappointing all those fans, or Mo, or Art, but he would rather live with that than years of regret.

"We had grown apart," Simon said. "We didn't think the same musically. We'd had eleven years of making our own records, where you didn't have to agree on it. You just did what you wanted. If you were collaborating with someone who was contributing in the same direction that you were going, then it was a good collaboration. But if you were pulling at each other, it was torturous, and that's what that was. Artie would write a harmony that he really liked, and I would say, 'I don't like that harmony,' and he'd say, 'Well, that's the harmony,' and I'd say, 'No, you can't just write the wrong harmony to my song.' "

Finally, Paul said, "We're at an impasse. We shouldn't be making a record together if we disagree about what's the right and what's the wrong harmony." Garfunkel, in turn, thought the music was wonderful. But ultimately, it wasn't his decision.

Not knowing the seriousness of the disagreement, Warner Bros. Records had been dropping hints for months that a Simon and Garfunkel album was on the way. A tentative release date was set for mid-August, which was wholly unrealistic and was pushed back to late October 1983. On the eve of the US stadium tour, however, Simon's anxiety about the album surfaced in an interview with the *Los Angeles Times*. "I was writing a group of songs that seemed very special to me," he said candidly. "I didn't want it to be a Simon and Garfunkel album because I felt it was my piece of work. It didn't have to do with Arthur. I think, in a certain way, he improves my records. He makes the sound of them more agreeable to many, many people. But I don't care. It's an odd situation. I essentially see myself as a writer, and I don't want to obscure the writing. I think my voice is a good vehicle for my writing even with its flaws."

Talk like this caused understandable nervousness at the record company. "They were always looking for reassurance," Roy Halee said. "They were always asking, 'This is still a Simon and Garfunkel album, isn't it?' When we played some tracks for some executives, they would hear a voice in the background and they'd go, 'Is that Artie's voice?' "

In the end, the person Simon felt most obligation to regarding the reunion album was Ostin, not Garfunkel. When he was secure in his decision, Simon asked Mo and Lenny to meet with him in New York during a break in the tour to discuss the album.

"He unloaded on us," Ostin recalled of the meeting. "He was very, very emotional as he told us what he had been going through. He was telling us about how personal these songs were and how he wanted to keep them personal on the record, but he also knew how much a Simon and Garfunkel album meant to us. Suddenly, it hit me. Paul was asking our permission. He wanted *Hearts and Bones* to be a solo album. I had never had an artist do that before, and I was touched. Of course, we wanted the Simon and Garfunkel album. Waronker, in fact, really liked that version. But in the end, you have to give the artist the freedom to do what he wants. So we gave Paul our permission. I had faith in him, and I wanted him to be comfortable with us. This was just one album. I knew there were lots of others ahead."

With that decision made, Simon's attention went to his relationship with Carrie. Despite his feeling that dating someone in show business might be an advantage, it wasn't. When Simon confided to Eddie Fisher about having trouble with his daughter, Fisher replied, "Who told you to fall in love with an actress?" But there were deeper problems between the couple. By 1983, Carrie was having serious drug issues and had been diagnosed as suffering from bipolar disorder. "I was told [about the disorder] for the first time when I was twenty-four," she said in a *People* magazine interview about *Return of the Jedi*, the third in the Star Wars series. "It was kind of when I was doing [the movie] *Under the Rainbow.* By then, I was supercrazy. I mean, my behavior was really . . . it wasn't just the drugs. I was really nuts then. I think I was taken from that set in an ambulance." In the interview, she also revealed that she and Paul had broken up again. She was living alone in a log cabin in the Hollywood Hills.

Asked to comment for the story, Simon reflected on Carrie's challenge of living up to the *Star Wars* phenomenon. "Anybody as bright as her in the biggest movie of all time at nineteen knew it wouldn't be long before she faced the question of who she was. But she drove herself to learn. She's gutsy and a real fighter." About the latest breakup, Simon added, "There is no animosity. We still care very much for each other. There is nobody else like Carrie. She's got one of the fastest, funniest minds I've ever known. She is absolutely unique." Privately, Simon told friends that, as much as he cared about Carrie, he didn't know if he could deal with the strain of her addiction, her desire to live in Hollywood, or the increasingly public nature of their relationship.

It was a classic case of can't live with each other, can't live without each other. Soon after the *People* article, the pair came together again. Carrie even brought up marriage, but Simon, ever cautious, wasn't sure. He had gone into his first marriage with doubts, and they proved correct. He wanted time to think. The Yankees happened to be in town, and Paul went to a doubleheader against the Toronto Blue Jays on August 8. He was in luck: the Yankees won both games, 8–3 and 11–3. Before leaving Yankee Stadium, Simon decided life with Fisher would be worth the gamble. They agreed that night to get married, and they wanted to do it before Simon and Garfunkel went on tour the following week. They picked Tuesday, August 16, and chose a traditional Jewish ceremony, which pleased Simon's mother. The guest list included Simon's closest ties to Kew Gardens Hills— his parents, Eddie, and Bobby—as well as his son, Harper; both of Carrie's parents; Art and Penny Marshall; Lorne; *Star Wars* creator George Lucas; Charles Grodin; and Randy Newman.

In the rush, there was one final piece of business. Simon had to tell Garfunkel that *Hearts and Bones* wasn't going to be a reunion album. He broke the news in a phone call that exemplified the pair's unusual ability to separate their friendship from their business dealings. In the call, he told Garfunkel he was dropping his vocals from the album, and then told him he was marrying Carrie and invited him to the ceremony. At the wedding, Eddie Fisher gave away the bride and Simon's attendants were Lorne and Eddie. Penny was bridesmaid. The party lasted late into the night, with Billy Joel entertaining on piano.

Simon and Garfunkel's next concert was in Houston, but it was cancelled because of Hurricane Alicia. On Saturday, Carrie came onstage at the Oakland Alameda County Coliseum to thank the thirty-two thousand fans for "joining us on our honeymoon." Afterward, Simon flew to Vancouver, British Columbia, for another concert, while Fisher returned to Los Angeles, where she played Thumbelina in a series of fairy tales (*Faerie Tale Theatre*) hosted and created for Showtime by, of all people, Shelley Duvall. After the final tour stop in Boulder, Colorado, on August 30, Simon returned to New York to wrap up production on the album with Halee. Near the end of the project, Russ Titelman left to work on the second solo album by Fleetwood Mac's Christine McVie. He would still be listed as coproducer.

Then it was back on the road—with Carrie—for two shows in late September at the Ramat Gan Stadium in Israel. It was an emotional ending to the long tour, and Arlen Roth, a guitarist in the band, noticed that Garfunkel seemed glum before a show. When he asked what was wrong, Garfunkel told him, "Well, how would you feel if you just found out you'd been erased from an entire album?" At the same time, a Warner Bros. spokesperson was announcing in New York that *Hearts and Bones* had been redesigned as a Simon solo effort.

In October Paul and Carrie finally got a chance for a formal honeymoon. They took a cruise along the Nile, accompanied by Lorne Michaels and Penny Marshall, and then visited Kenya. The couple then returned home and waited for the release of the album. Critics applauded. Writing in the *New York Times*, Stephen Holden dismissed the absence of Garfunkel. "Listening to it, one wonders what Mr. Garfunkel might have contributed beyond the commercial value of his name . . . For *Hearts and Bones* is pop music of the most personal and introspective sort. None of its songs requires the kind of inspirational folk-pop belting that made Mr. Garfunkel the right voice for 'Bridge Over Troubled Water.' " He added, "The most ambitious songwriting on *Hearts and Bones* has a visionary beauty and eloquence that go beyond anything Mr. Simon has done before."

As strong as the key songs were, the Warners sales staff worried about a potential backlash from fans who had looked forward to a Simon and Garfunkel album. In its enthusiastic November 5 review of the album, *Billboard* addressed that exact point, expressing hope that the music would be enough to lure those fans who had been looking forward to a reunion album. This challenge Warner Bros. faced was compounded by the lack of an obvious hit single on the LP. The label finally released "Allergies," which few would claim was a prized Simon recording. Radio programmers— perhaps also feeling let down after waiting so long for a Simon and Garfunkel package—largely passed. The single reached only no. 44. Without radio exposure, the album didn't have a chance; it was the first Simon LP not to be certified gold. Industry estimates placed its sales at barely four hundred thousand. "To me, that record was a masterpiece, though it took many years before most people got around to realizing how incredible it was," Ostin said in 2015. "Paul was so shaken when the album didn't do better, especially coming after *One-Trick Pony*, that it made him question his ability to continue as a successful recording artist."

Glancing through *Billboard*'s first issue of 1984, Simon found more sobering news. In a cover story, leading radio programmers from around the country went on and on about how their listeners wanted new voices in music. Simon recalled, "They mentioned a lot of new-wave acts and there was this one guy who said, 'We're not going to play Paul Simon anymore.' And I thought, 'Well, okay, they're not going to play me anymore. So now what?' "

PART FIVE

Graceland

CHAPTER SIXTEEN

The first half of 1984 was bleak. Simon spent part of the time reflecting on what went wrong with *Hearts and Bones*, still believing in the songs but feeling that he was so distracted by the tour, the Garfunkel reunion album issue, and his relationship with Carrie that he didn't do a good job of recording them. Careerwise, he realized that many of the factors contributing to the weak sales were out of his control—namely the powerful new role of music videos in the hit-making process and the corresponding emphasis in the industry on younger artists. Nothing symbolized this convergence more than the unprecedented success of Michael Jackson's *Thriller*, which spent thirty-seven weeks at no. 1 on the US album chart in 1983. As the weeks dragged by, Simon became increasingly discouraged over his future as a recording artist. He was now forty-two, ancient next to Michael Jackson, Prince, and Madonna—three MTV favorites.

The biggest blow was that his marriage, after less than a year, had fallen apart, which shook Simon's confidence far more. As was typical, Paul kept mostly quiet on the divorce, but Carrie did address it in two memoirs, usually cloaked in protective humor and generally taking the blame. "Poor Paul," she wrote in 2008's *Wishful Drinking*, her first memoir. "He had to put up with a lot with me. I think, ultimately, I fell under the heading of: Good anecdote, Bad reality. I was really good for material, but when it came to day-to-day living, I was more than he could take."

For Simon's part, he again tried to turn to his bridge—music—for comfort, but the losses were too much. He felt numb some days, able to think of nothing better to do than sit in his car and idly watch workmen build a house that he had planned for Carrie and himself in Montauk, a beach community on the eastern tip of Long Island—where Simon's parents had taken him and Eddie on childhood summer vacations. At the construction site, Paul would often smoke a joint (which he had picked up again after an eleven-year break) and listen to tapes, choosing them pretty much at random—until he noticed one day that he had been playing a particular tape of South African music over and over.

That tape eventually led him to Johannesburg, where, surprisingly, he welcomed the low expectations surrounding him in the industry. "Part of me actually thought, 'Great, no one is going to be looking over my shoulder saying, "What's the next single going to be?" or "What the hell are you going to Africa for?" ' Suddenly, no one's saying anything about me, and I'm just going by my instincts. I'm not clever enough to say, 'I was defeated. I must come back from this to show everybody. I must go back to my previous state of being on top, and I'm going to do that by going to South Africa.' I was just excited by this music."

Simon got the tape from Heidi Berg, a singer-songwriter and guitarist he'd met through Lorne Michaels. She was a member of the house band for *The New Show*, Michaels's attempt to come up with a prime-time version of *Saturday Night Live*. He had quit SNL in 1980, unhappy, in part, over the network's refusal to give him greater autonomy. "Paul liked a couple of my songs and started talking about going into the studio and making a record," Berg said years later. "We'd meet at his office in the Brill Building every couple of weeks, and he'd listen to my songs and tell me about the importance of finding a distinctive sound to create a special position for me in the music world. He also encouraged me to bring in recordings I liked in hopes of finding that position." One of the tapes Berg brought him was *Gumboots: Accordion Jive Hits, Volume II*, a cassette that a friend in South Africa had sent her. Her family was from Norway, and she grew up listening to music from Europe, and the accordion was a big part of that. That's the sound she loved on the tape.

In his excitement, Simon phoned Ostin, who had become as much a friend as a record executive, to say he wanted to play something for him, but Mo was stuck in Los Angeles on business and suggested that Paul get together with Lenny Waronker, who happened to be in New York. "I was a little nervous because of all Paul had gone through in recent months, but I was relieved as soon as I heard the new music," Waronker said. "As time went on, I realized he had figured out a way in *Graceland* to do something that is incredibly artful and incredibly commercial. He was making a smart dance record. I called Mo and said, 'This is going to be great.' "

Halee never doubted Simon's ability to bounce back from his post–*Hearts and Bones* depression. "What I realized during the Simon and Garfunkel days was Paul was the most competitive person I've ever known," he said. "I knew he'd give me a call someday, and we'd be heading back into the studio. And sure enough, he played the South African tape for me in New York, and it was sensational. I knew he was back."

On the same subject, Randy Newman, another of America's greatest songwriters, said, "Paul wants to be better than anyone else—better than Bob Dylan or Stevie Wonder or whoever you want to name—and so do I. Competitiveness is the nature of what we do. I was playing Wiffle ball with him once, and I was catching and he was batting, and he kept saying to himself, 'I've gotta hit it, I've gotta hit it.' He could have been kidding, but it felt serious. He really cared about that stupid Wiffle ball game."

Simon had loved challenges ever since the school yard. "It's important not to let the chance of failure stop you," he said. "Everybody makes mistakes, just as every career has ups and downs. If you don't give yourself the opportunity to do something extraordinary, the chances are you won't. It's like being at the plate when the game's on the line with two outs in the bottom of the ninth. That's when I want to be at the plate."

After meeting with Waronker, Simon asked Ostin if he knew anyone in South Africa who could help him track down the musicians on the tape. Mo put him in touch with record producer Hilton Rosenthal, who worked with Juluka, an integrated South African group that was signed to Warner Bros. and had, in fact, already played in the States. When Rosenthal traced the instrumental track to a group called the Boyoyo Boys, Simon asked if he could license a copy of the original studio tape so that he could add a vocal to the top of it as he had done with "El Condor Pasa." No way, Rosenthal informed him. The original recording wouldn't be up to acceptable technical standards. As an alternative, he offered to bring the Boyoyo Boys into a state-of-the-art, twenty-four-track studio in Johannesburg, where Simon could rerecord the song with them. Rosenthal also sent Paul some albums that introduced him to a wide range of South African musical styles in case he wanted to work with any other musicians while he was there. Months of depression started to fade.

When Simon met Heidi Berg again backstage at a concert on August 19 in Saratoga Springs, New York, he shared the exciting news—well, exciting to everybody but Berg. She was shocked to hear he was going to South Africa. "I loaned him the tape because I wanted to make a record," Berg said. "I didn't loan him the tape so he would make a record." Simon thanked her prominently in the album credits, but Berg was bitter, implying he took her idea. When asked in 2016 if she had ever thought of going to South Africa to record the kind of music that was on the tape, however, she said no. She was interested only in the accordion part.

In South Africa, meanwhile, Rosenthal, a white South African, turned to Koloi Lebona, a black producer, to help assemble the musicians Simon had selected. A target date of February 1985 was set for the sessions. Around that time, Lenny Waronker contacted Roger Steffens, an expert in Jamaican and South African music, in hopes of finding other stimulating South African music for Simon, and Steffens sent Paul numerous cassettes, from Nigeria's King Sunny Ade to, crucially, South Africa's Ladysmith Black Mambazo.

Before heading to South Africa, Simon joined nearly fifty pop stars, including Michael Jackson, Bob Dylan, and Bruce Springsteen, on the night of January 28, 1985, at A&M Recording Studios in Hollywood to add their voices to "We Are the World," a record designed to raise money for African famine relief. At the session, Simon told Harry Belafonte, who also sang on the record and was famous for his social activism, of his plans and asked about the cultural implications. Simon was fully behind a boycott against Western musicians performing in Sun City, a supposedly independent tribal "homeland" built in Bophuthatswana, ninety miles from Johannesburg, as a way to enable white South Africans, chiefly, to see Western performers who wouldn't be comfortable playing Johannesburg. Frank Sinatra and Liza Minnelli had played there (and Elton John and Queen would do so later), but Simon and Garfunkel turned down an offer. However, Simon wasn't sure how the United Nations cultural and academic boycott applied, if at all, to Western musicians going to South Africa to record with South African musicians.

"I thought it was an excellent idea," Belafonte said, "but I also suggested that he contact people directly involved with the boycott issue [including the African National Congress] to explain the reasons for his trip." Simon appreciated Belafonte's thoughts, but he didn't like the idea of artists having to obtain permission to simply make music, and he didn't follow through on the recommendation. He had already been told by Hilton Rosenthal that the musicians were eager to record with him, and that was all the approval he felt he needed—though he got further assurance from Quincy Jones, who added simply, "Just be sure everybody gets paid and that everybody likes you." (Simon paid the musicians triple US scale.)

What Simon didn't know was that the reaction among South African musicians wasn't unanimous. Rosenthal ran into resistance as soon as he began talking to black musicians about recording with Simon. Representatives of the group the Soul Brothers told Rosenthal they had been advised by members of the antiapartheid movement not to participate, and they passed. Koloi Lebona, the South African record producer, also weighed the boycott issue. "It was definitely a risk," he said, but he saw Simon's visit as an opportunity. "Until then, South African music was regarded as third world music. I thought if our music gets a chance to be part of mainstream music, surely there can't be any harm. So when Paul Simon came, I deliberately withheld some of the risks involved. I thought, 'What the heck? This is a chance in a million. We must do this.' "

When Simon and Halee got to Johannesburg, they were delighted to find that Ovation Studios was, indeed, state of the art. The game plan wasn't to come up with finished songs but to work on instrumental sketches that Simon would later turn into songs in New York. "I was very conscious of not wanting to repeat the mistake of *Hearts and Bones,*" Simon said. "I didn't want to end up liking the songs but not the tracks. So I decided to make sure I had a track that I liked, *then* I could focus on the song. If I didn't like the way the song turned out, I could just throw it out and start over, which actually happened during the making of the album."

Not all the South African musicians recognized the name Paul Simon. "I listened mostly to township music," said Bakithi Kumalo, a young fretless bass player so gifted and adaptable that Simon made him a permanent part of his touring band. "So when Koloi called, I said, 'Who is Paul Simon?' Then Koloi started singing 'Mother and Child Reunion,' and I recognized it right away. 'Oh,' I thought, 'so that's Paul Simon.' But then I asked myself why someone as famous as Paul Simon would want to record with me. I was only playing music part-time. My regular job was working as a mechanic in a car garage. But there's no way I could let the opportunity pass."

Initially, Halee felt the musicians were stiff—so accustomed to life under apartheid that they were reserved, even meek, and very careful to address white visitors as "sir." The sessions also had to end promptly at five o'clock to allow the musicians to be bussed back to their township as required by law. But as they became more focused on the music over the next couple of days, the mood loosened. "Everyone started having fun," Halee recalled. "Simon was so caught up in the music that he would stay in the studio from noon to past midnight, long after the musicians had left, to work on bits and pieces of music from the day's session."

Simon found early allies when the group Tau Ea Matsekha introduced him to Forere Motloheloa, a veteran accordionist who didn't speak English but who made an invaluable contribution to the album. Kumalo said it took the musicians time to adjust to Simon's direct approach in the studio. "We were used to just playing what we wanted to in the studio, but Paul had his own ideas," he said. "We'd start playing something, and he'd tell us to change this or try this or stop that. But eventually everything came together, and we were like this big family. At the same time, I kinda wondered what we were doing. I mean, I continued to ask myself, 'Who is going to want to hear this township music in America?' "

The sessions demonstrated Simon's musical approach—the playing at once informal, experimental, and spontaneous. "We were able to get a really great sound on the accordion, but [Forere's] performance was all over the place," Simon said of the track that became "The Boy in the Bubble," one of the album's defining numbers. "I would say, 'Could you change the chord over here or change the root in the chord, because I want to make a chorus here,' and Bakithi would translate. I'd give Forere a signal, and he'd just start to play, and then everybody would fall in behind him. When I wanted them to stop, I would signal them. At the end of the session, I remember saying, 'Did you like it? Are you happy?' Through Bakithi, the accordionist said, 'If you're happy, I'm happy.' "

Things worked so well that Simon kept working with various musicians, hoping something else might emerge—and he was rewarded with the underpinnings of the song "Graceland." Nothing caught his ear during that one session except the drumming by Vusi Khumalo, which reminded Simon of the "traveling" rhythm in American country music, especially the freedom and energy in the Sun Records singles by Elvis Presley and Johnny Cash. He told Halee to take the accordion and bass elements off the track and just keep the drumming part so he could come back to it later. A couple of days later, Simon met Chikapa "Ray" Phiri, the guitarist with the group Stimela, one of South Africa's top bands, and Paul saw right away that Ray had high musical sophistication. Simon began to use Phiri, Kumalo, and drummer Isaac Mtshali as his core rhythm section. The way the musicians worked, Halee said, was to start most days just improvising, waiting for Simon to direct them. If Paul heard something he liked, he'd ask them to build around that passage. It was during that give and take when Simon heard Phiri play a lick that became the defining pulse of "You Can Call Me Al."

In his hotel room at night, Simon kept thinking about one South African sound that he hadn't been able to connect with in Johannesburg yet: the uplifting vocal harmony of Ladysmith Black Mambazo, the eleven-member (sometimes more, sometimes less) male choir recommended by Steffens. The music captured the soulfulness and vitality of the South African experience, and indeed, the sound was built upon traditional Zulu vocal elements that had been embraced for years by the country's mineworkers. Ladysmith had considerable success in South Africa in the 1960s—the first black South African group to earn a gold album for twenty-five thousand sales—but it was still largely unknown outside of its native land when Simon arrived in the country. Simon was so engrossed by the group's singing that he listened to Ladysmith tapes over and over at night, sometimes falling asleep to them. But the music was self-contained, and he wondered if there was any room for him. Uncharacteristically, he was too intimidated to approach Ladysmith about taking part in the sessions, but someone at the studio, probably Rosenthal or Lebona, picked up on Simon's enthusiasm and invited Ladysmith leader Joseph Shabalala to come, as a guest, to one of the final sessions.

The rapport was instant. Shabalala was warm and gracious, and Simon was charmed when the singer gave him a bagful of Ladysmith tapes. Finally, Paul worked up enough courage to ask if it would be okay if he would write a song for Ladysmith when he got back to the States and send Shabalala a tape of it. The offer came with no strings attached: Shabalala could change it any way he wanted, or he could throw it away. Of course, Shabalala told him, "Please send a song," and the two men embraced. It was, Shabalala said later, the first time he had ever hugged a white man.

For all the excitement of the Johannesburg sessions, Simon returned to New York in the early weeks of 1985 with just the tentative tracks for what would turn out to be six songs: "Graceland," "The Boy in the Bubble," "You Can Call Me Al," "I Know What I Know," "Gumboots," and "Crazy Love, Vol. II." Most of the work was still to come. "The task was enormous," said Halee. "There were no songs, no arrangements. We were looking at months of editing, editing, editing—taking things from here on a track, putting them there, take this out, and recopying things. Paul had to turn the tracks into songs, and then he had to put words to each one."

Simon also had to come up with ideas for four or five more songs to round out the album, which is why he was at a Louisiana Cajun music showcase on April 20 at New York's Carnegie Recital Hall. Knowing that accordions were a feature of Cajun music, he thought the instrument might be a way to link that sound to the South African tracks. At the concert, Simon ran into Dickie Landry, a saxophonist, photographer, and painter from Louisiana's musically rich Cajun territory, and they started talking about the evening's bill. When Simon mentioned he was not excited by the music, Landry—an ambassador of all Louisiana musical styles—suggested that Paul check out zydeco, another Cajun style that also relied on the accordion but was more rhythmically driven than Cajun music. Simon and Halee found themselves a few weeks later spending three days in Master-Trak recording studio in Crowley, Louisiana, working with three groups, but most productively with Good Rockin' Dopsie and the Twisters, an outfit featuring accordionist Alton Jay Rubin, who went by the stage name Dopsie (pronounced *Doopsee*).

Like most zydeco musicians, Dopsie, who was nine years older than Simon, had been playing the accordion so long he couldn't remember a time when it wasn't in his hands. One of his trademarks was holding the instrument upside down; it's how he happened to originally pick it up as a child and never saw a need to change. In the studio, Simon jammed with the musicians the way he had done in South Africa. "The funkiest studio of all the *Graceland* recordings was the one in Crowley," he said. "It was in the back of a record store. The place reminded me of when I first started to do demos as a teenager."

Along with the music, Simon fell in love with the region, and he returned to the area, about 135 miles west of New Orleans, several times, occasionally with Michaels. He enjoyed the art, the bayous, the Spanish moss on the trees, even the heat. At one point, Lorne joined him in Crowley, and they enjoyed Mulate's, a Cajun restaurant in Breaux Bridge that bills itself the Crawfish Capital of the World. Normally the quiet observer,

Simon was so relaxed in the Lafayette-area clubs that he asked the band in one club if he could sit in with them, Landry said. The musicians had no idea who Simon was, but they welcomed him onstage.

Of all the songs that would end up on the new album, Simon felt "Graceland" was the best example of world music, and he recalls its evolution with the same detail as his account of the making of "The Boxer."

"It began with a track that featured a drum part by Vusi Khumalo that sounded a lot like a country rockabilly shuffle, which is something that I've loved since I was a kid," Simon said. "On the second day of recording in Johannesburg, I met Ray Phiri and played the drum track for him, and he starts to play something that has a sort of rockabilly feel, even though Ray doesn't know Sun Records or rockabilly. He does, however, know American country music, at least vaguely. And it sounded good with the drums. He's going from an E to an A, and suddenly he's in a groove. He plays a C-sharp minor, which surprised me because South African music doesn't usually have minor chords. I asked him why he played the relative minor chord, and he said because he had listened to my records, and I used it all the time. So I realize Ray is taking information from American country music and my music and integrating it with South African music. That's why I say the track is a mixture of the two musical worlds; not something that was an intellectual decision, but an organic experience."

During the months that followed, Simon worked on the music he recorded in Africa at home in Montauk. He spent hours in his bedroom listening to the track that was the foundation for "Graceland" and going over the phrase "I'm going to Graceland, Graceland." His first thought was, "That doesn't work. I'm not writing a song about Elvis Presley in an album of South African music. But the line stuck with me, and after a couple of months, I decide I ought to go to Graceland, since I'd never been there. So, after recording the zydeco track that became 'That Was Your Mother' in Crowley, Louisiana, I rent a car and drive to Memphis. While I'm driving through Mississippi, I'm suddenly singing the line *The Mississippi*

Delta / Was shining like a bottleneck guitar / I am following the river / Down the highway / Through the cradle of the Civil War / I'm going to Graceland / Graceland / In Memphis, Tennessee.

"I loved it immediately. For one thing, I love to use the words *Memphis, Tennessee* in a song. It goes all the way back to first hearing Chuck Berry sing it [in the song "Memphis"] in the 1950s. The line about the 'poor boys and pilgrims with families' came up because I never called anyone at Graceland in advance to get a guided tour or anything. I just bought my ticket and sat in the waiting room with everyone else until the bus came and we all went up to Elvis's house.

"Now I'm back in Montauk and I start writing about the journey, and I come up with a story about a traveling companion who is nine years old, who is the child of my first wife. That's Harper, though he wasn't really on the trip with me. It was just storytelling. But I still don't know where the song is going. But when I get to *I've reason to believe / We'll both be received / In Graceland*, I think, 'That's interesting, the spiritual connotation of it.' The word *Graceland* becomes a metaphor for the album.

"The next line—*She comes back to tell me she's gone*—is half-funny, but it's also heartbreaking, about how hard it is to break up—and it's as if she's telling me something I don't know, as if I didn't know my own empty bed. Now, the song is starting to take shape. This is a search for something, and there's been a breakup. That was me and Carrie. And then we got to the lines about *Losing love is like a window in your heart / Everybody sees you're blown apart.*

"When that came out, I thought someone had punched me in the heart. I lost my breath. I just sat down. At the same time, that part of my brain that is the songwriter thinks, 'That's good.' I thought that was the end of the song. There was nothing more to say. But then, as I was walking past the Museum of Natural History in Manhattan, the line *There's a girl in New York City / Who calls herself the human trampoline* came to me. She really has no place in the song, but it's interesting, and the line deserves a place in the song. What does it mean, bouncing into Graceland? Then I think maybe we are all bouncing into Graceland.

"Eventually I understood that the song is about why we are traveling to Graceland—to find out how to get healed—and that's why I named the album *Graceland*. It seemed to be about finding something you could call a state of grace—the healing of a deep wound. And that's what was going on in South Africa. There was a deep wound, and then an attempt at a healing process."

Things were moving quickly now. Simon also put together his three key musicians from South Africa with a few New York session players to build upon the music from Johannesburg; specifically the tracks that became the dance-happy "You Can Call Me Al" and the tender "Under African Skies." Phiri was so helpful in the process that Simon gave him coarranger credit and royalties on both numbers. As individual tracks took shape, Simon played them for a few musicians and friends, including Philip Glass, the influential American avant-garde composer whose work stretched from classical music to pop rock and jazz.

"Paul just phoned me up one day, I think it was around 1981, and he said he'd love to talk about music," said Glass. "I was flattered because I had known his music ever since 'The Sound of Silence' and 'The Boxer,' and I admired the way he kept growing as a writer. I understood fully when he went on his own after Simon and Garfunkel. He was like a plant who had outgrown the pot. He had to let his talent grow. I invited him to my place, and the first thing he wanted to talk about was his musical education—or lack of it. He said he couldn't read music, which almost made me laugh. I said, 'Paul, you've written some of the greatest songs in contemporary American music. Why do you think you need to read music?' "

The pair kept in touch, and Simon would often seek Glass's advice on a new song, which is what happened with the early *Graceland* material. "I went over to his apartment with my wife, and he played a song, and, as he often does, he started singing the words over the music. I thought it was amazing. I said, 'Paul, this is a real breakthrough. It's going to be a masterpiece!' "

As Simon continued to work on the album tracks, he realized that he was rethinking his whole approach to songwriting, especially lyrics, and it meant a lot to him that Glass noticed. Glass also asked him to participate on an album for which Glass would write music to lyrics contributed by contemporary pop songwriters, including David Byrne of Talking Heads and Laurie Anderson. Paul passed along some lyrics he had been working on recently that didn't seem to work for the South African project. Glass loved the lyrics and set about putting them to music for the 1986 album *Songs from Liquid Days.*

In light of the success of the Louisiana trip, Lenny Waronker thought it might also be fruitful for Simon to go into the studio with Los Lobos, a promising young Latino-based band Warner Bros. was promoting. Los Lobos's first full-length album for a major label, *How Will the Wolf Survive?*, was voted the third-best LP of 1984 in a poll of the nation's leading pop critics, trailing only Bruce Springsteen's *Born in the U.S.A.* and Prince's *Purple Rain.* The band's work combined flavorful Mexican roots music with stylish touches of social consciousness. Its sound was even built around the accordion.

Simon trusted Waronker's instincts, so he went into Amigo Studios in North Hollywood in June to see if he could find something for the album. The arrangement was for Los Lobos to be paid double scale for the sessions, according to Warner Bros. files. But there were trouble signs early. The band was used to making its own records, and the members found Simon and Roy Halee off-putting. Steve Berlin, the group's saxophonist, said, "We'd find an idea that we'd chase around for an hour, only to have Paul say, 'Nah—that's not working. Do something else.' " Frustrated, Los Lobos went to Waronker, hoping to get out of the rest of the three-day commitment, but the Warner executive urged them to give it a little more time. Eventually, Berlin said, David Hidalgo started playing something on guitar that caught Simon's ear. They went over the passage a few more times, and the session ended.

Simon described it differently.

"When we got to the studio, I said, 'I'm looking for a generic up-tempo song,' " he recalled. "They said they wanted to play a ballad; I said, 'No, I'm not looking for a ballad. I want something up-tempo.' I could feel a little tension, so I said if they didn't want to do it, they could leave, and I'd still be a fan. I wasn't trying to force them to do anything. I already had my guitar part for the verses of the song. Later, they start playing this guitar line that I liked. It was perfect for the chorus, and we ended the session. I later got together with David and [guitarist] Cesar Rosas for some more work on the track, and I felt things went well."

With the album's foundation in place, Simon started working in earnest on the songs in New York, trying again to describe in words whatever emotions the music stirred in him. It was pure exploration. "When I first [heard South African music], it all seemed familiar to me," he said. "[The music] had a feeling that was something like fifties rock 'n' roll. But the guitar lines were different from American lines. That was something I didn't notice until I was writing back at home . . . I realized that the guitar part was playing a different symmetry than I had assumed, and the bass was doing something that was more important, and maybe I should follow that. That was the big jump: I really began to listen harder to rhythm. South African music is extraordinary in its vocal sounds and its three-chord harmonies. It's all in major keys for the most part, while West African is more polyrhythmic and has different harmonies. I began to think about what effect that would have on the lyrics, on the storytelling. That was the great gift that I received from making the trip to South Africa. It was like I had taken a master class working with really great musicians like Ray and Bakithi. I began to raise the bar in my own writing."

Simon credited Phiri, specifically, with opening musical doors. "Ray is South African, but [his family] comes from Mali, so he plays with a certain fluidity and kind of bluesiness," he explained. "On the track that became 'Graceland,' he's playing figures that are South African; then he played a relative minor because he knew that I use it quite often in my music—something that would have not been in a typical South African song—and I began writing an absurdist lyric that would never appear in a South African song: the part about a girl who calls herself 'the human trampoline.' It's a very New York lyric."

In working with the instrumental tracks, Simon found himself stretching in other ways. "Another new thing was working with a lot of syllables: 'falling, flying / Or tumbling in turmoil I say / Oh, so this is what she means / She means we're bouncing into Graceland.' That was also something I hadn't done before: taking an important word from the chorus and putting it into the verse. Usually the chorus has its own repeated phrase or word which you never hear in the verse. I understood then that you could go a lot of different places beyond the typical song structure as long as you had a sense of symmetry going on without feeling chaotic."

For the album, Simon kept a legal-sized notebook of lyrics, and the first entry, marked July 3, 1985, was "The Boy in the Bubble." Contrary to the popular concept of lyrics coming to a writer in flashes of inspiration, these words—many of which would be reworked or discarded—would stretch over eight pages, the final one dated September 22.

The original opening lines:

This is the dream
That urged me awake
Of moonlight slapping (sliding)
On a midnight lake.

They fit the track's grooves, but they didn't lead to a story Simon wanted to tell. The only line from the entire first page that would end up in the song was: "It's every generation throws a hero up the charts." In the first and subsequent pages, Simon moved back and forth between contrasting images with the suddenness and twists of the music itself. Gradually the images began to interact in ways that spoke about the modern age with imagination and commentary: contrasts between countries and cultures, the privileged and the oppressed, joyful times and terrorism, liberating scientific advances and those that dehumanized, significant trends and trivial ones.

Simon also benefited during the long incubation of "Bubble" from the feedback of musicians and friends, especially Lenny Waronker and Russ Titelman. "A lot of artists get attached to something, and they won't listen to anyone else's opinion," said Waronker. "But the great thing about Paul is that he is so open to ideas. One of the first things I heard from the album was 'Boy in the Bubble.' I loved it, but it didn't sound finished. I felt it needed background voices, but Paul wasn't convinced. He spoke to Russ, who told him the same thing. So Paul calls back six hours later, and he plays Russ and me a new version, and it was sensational."

At one crucial point, Simon realized that he had discarded some of his best ideas before starting the notebooks—the lyrics he had passed on to Philip Glass. Was it fair to ask Glass, who had already built music around the lyrics, to give them back? Probably not, but Simon's need ruled the day. He called Glass, promising to give him new lyrics in return. Glass wasn't thrilled, but he understood, and he graciously returned them, which included one of the song's most memorable phrases: the "days of miracle and wonder."

In its final form, "The Boy in the Bubble" stands as one of the album's grandest creations:

It was a slow day
And the sun was beating
On the soldiers by the side of the road
There was a bright light
A shattering of shop windows
The bomb in the baby carriage
Was wired to the radio

These are the days of miracle and wonder
This is the long-distance call
The way the camera follows us in slo-mo
The way we look to us all
The way we look to a distant constellation
That's dying in a corner of the sky
These are the days of miracle and wonder
And don't cry, baby, don't cry
Don't cry

It was a dry wind
And it swept across the desert
And it curled into the circle of birth
And the dead sand was
Falling on the children
The mothers and the fathers
And the automatic earth

These are the days of miracle and wonder
This is the long-distance call
The way the camera follows us in slo-mo
The way we look to us all
The way we look to a distant constellation
That's dying in the corner of the sky
These are the days of miracle and wonder
And don't cry, baby, don't cry
Don't cry

It's a turnaround jump shot
It's everybody jump start
It's every generation throws a hero up the pop charts
Medicine is magical and magical is art
Think of the Boy in the Bubble
And the baby with the baboon heart
And I believe
These are the days of lasers in the jungle
Lasers in the jungle somewhere
Staccato signals of constant information
A loose affiliation of millionaires
And billionaires, and baby

These are the days of miracle and wonder
This is the long-distance call

The way the camera follows us in slo-mo
The way we look to us all, oh yeah
The way we look to a distant constellation
That's dying in a corner of the sky
These are the days of miracle and wonder
And don't cry, baby, don't cry
Don't cry, don't cry

"The Boy in the Bubble" was a look at a rapidly changing social order; a collection of images and events that would be as timely in the twenty-first century as when they were written: from the terrorism of a bomb in a baby carriage to the flood of information on the internet. The song was all the more effective because of the disarming use of everyday images such as a basketball jump shot. "I put in those touches a lot," Simon said. "If I use an image or idea that is somewhat complex for a song, I'll follow it with a cliché or something that is very easy to digest, so you'll have a little more time to chew on the unusual line and you won't lose your place in the song."

Simon played the song for Carrie, who was back with him, at least off and on, within months of the divorce. "Paul was so thrilled with the song that he played the instrumental track for me in his car and sang the words in my ear," she said. "It was so brilliant. I was so happy for him."

Where "Bubble" gave the new album a firm social relevance, the song "Graceland" proved to be as deeply personal an expression of salvation and hope as "The Boxer" or "American Tune." Once the song started taking shape, it came much quicker than "The Boy in the Bubble," requiring only half as many pages of revisions. One minor change—the description of a guitar in the opening verse—was a reminder of Simon's devotion to detail. Most songwriters (and listeners) would have been fine with Simon's first image on a page marked July 15: "The Mississippi Delta was shining like a bottleneck guitar." But he changed it four days later to the marginally better "open-tuned guitar." Eventually he wrote down "National guitar," which gave the line a more distinctive and evocative edge, especially for anyone familiar with the distinctive, ultraresonant, all-metal silver instrument. Even the name, National, helped underscore the song's scope and sense of community and purpose.

> *The Mississippi Delta*
> *Was shining like a National guitar*
> *I am following the river*
> *Down the highway*
> *Through the cradle of the Civil War*
>
> *I'm going to Graceland*
> *Graceland*
> *In Memphis, Tennessee*
> *I'm going to Graceland*
> *Poor boys and pilgrims with families*
> *And we are going to Graceland*
> *My traveling companion is nine years old*
> *He is the child of my first marriage*
> *But I've reason to believe*
> *We both will be received*
> *In Graceland*
>
> *She comes back to tell me she's gone*
> *As if I didn't know that*
> *As if I didn't know my own bed*
> *As if I'd never notice*
> *The way she brushed her hair from her forehead*
> *And she said, "Losing love*
> *Is like a window in your heart*
> *Everybody sees you're blown apart*
> *Everybody feels the wind blow"*
>
> *I'm going to Graceland*
> *Memphis, Tennessee*
> *I'm going to Graceland*

Poor boys and pilgrims with families
And we are going to Graceland
And my traveling companions
Are ghosts and empty sockets
I'm looking at ghosts and empties
But I've reason to believe
We all will be received
In Graceland

There is a girl in New York City
Who calls herself the human trampoline
And sometimes when I'm falling, flying
Or tumbling in turmoil I say,
"Whoa, so this is what she means"
She means we're bouncing into Graceland
And I see losing love
Is like a window in your heart
Everybody sees you're blown apart
Everybody feels the wind blow

In Graceland, in Graceland
I'm going to Graceland
For reasons I cannot explain
There's some part of me wants to see Graceland
And I may be obliged to defend
Every love, every ending
Or maybe there's no obligations now
Maybe I've a reason to believe
We all will be received
In Graceland

Whoa, in Graceland, in Graceland
In Graceland,
I'm going to Graceland

—————

Ever since returning from Johannesburg, Paul had frequently thought about writing an a cappella song for Ladysmith, but it wasn't until he had finished "Graceland" and "The Boy in the Bubble" late that summer that he sat down at the piano and made a demo tape of the song that would become "Homeless." Taking an image he had earlier considered for the opening of "The Boy in the Bubble," Simon sang simply, "Homeless, homeless / Moonlight sleeping on a midnight lake." He sent Joseph Shabalala the demo along with a note that reiterated his earlier invitation to change the song any way he wanted. Shabalala replied almost immediately, saying he liked the song and had some ideas. Eager to follow up, Simon arranged for Joseph and the group to join him in London in early October to record at Abbey Road Studios, home most famously of the Beatles. Simon didn't want to return to Johannesburg; he couldn't tolerate any more of the harsh apartheid regime.

On October 9, they tried to mix Simon's lyrics with words Shabalala had written in Zulu, but the collaboration lacked spark. Back in their hotel, Shabalala and the Ladysmith singers felt they had let down their new friend. Working until midnight, Shabalala revised his part of the song, employing lyrics that better reflected Simon's "Homeless" theme. The Zulu words, Joseph said, "told of people living in caves on the side of a mountain, cold and hungry, using their fists as pillows." When they returned to the studio the next day, the music came together, two songs, in essence, sewn together. The whole thing took less than two hours—a sprint by Simon's standards. It was everything Paul had been hoping for all these months.

Years later, Shabalala still spoke about the time in the studio with Simon with affection. "I like Paul Simon," he said. "He's a musician. I am sure he is not like other producers who don't know how to sing. You see, Paul Simon chooses what he likes, and he tells you, 'This is good because of this and this,' and he expects you to talk with him and tell him what is right and what is wrong." On the song, Simon and Shabalala were listed as cowriters. Their relationship would become so close that Simon would produce Ladysmith's first Warner Bros. album, *Shaka Zulu*, a 1987 collection that won a Grammy for Best Traditional Folk Recording.

Simon's album, now titled *Graceland*, was far enough along in the fall of 1985 for Warner Bros. to put it on its late-spring release list, which was all Lorne Michaels, in his first year back in charge of *SNL*, needed to book Simon for the May 10 program. Trusting Simon's enthusiasm, he named Paul cohost of the show (with actress Catherine Oxenberg, who played Amanda on the 1980s prime-time soap *Dynasty*) and designated Ladysmith as the evening's musical guest. Simon and Halee spent the rest of the year getting the collection ready. It now included ten songs and ran just under thirty-eight minutes, short by contemporary standards, but acceptable.

CHAPTER SEVENTEEN

Early in 1986, Simon was finally ready to preview *Graceland* for the Warner Bros. Records staff. Later, after the album had become an international success, the story around the label was that the sales and promotion execs went wild when they heard the music. Roy Halee laughed at that narrative. "I remember it as if it were yesterday because the reaction was so uniform," he said. "You've got to remember, Warners was hot with Prince and Madonna at the time, and Paul was coming off two disappointments. A lot of people in the room were probably wondering why they were wasting their time with another Paul Simon album. As the music started, I could see people looking at each other going, 'What the hell is all this African stuff?' They wanted a hit single, something that would go on the radio right away. There was a lot of shuffling in the room and people looking at their watches." One exception was Lenny Waronker. "He just sat there listening intently, but when it was over, he got up and said, 'This is wonderful. This is great. This is exciting.' The same with Mo. Suddenly—and it is so typical of how people at record companies react when the bosses get enthusiastic—people who had been scratching their heads through the whole record started going over to Paul and patting him on the back."

The exuberance led Warner Bros. to take *Graceland* off the spring release schedule to give the company more time to put together an ambitious sales and promotional campaign. The delay could easily have caused Lorne to cancel Paul's May appearance, but he was so caught up in the music and this new singing group that he kept Paul and Ladysmith in the *SNL* slot. On the show, Simon sang three songs, including "Homeless" with Ladysmith, and the pairing was a knockout musically and visually. "Everyone was in kind of awe," Michaels said. "It wasn't like anything that was on the show before. You could feel the excitement in the studio." The performance caused so much buzz among viewers that radio stations started getting requests. All Warners could do was tell program directors they would have to wait until the fall to get a copy. After writing him off two years earlier, radio again was looking forward to Paul Simon.

Simon took advantage of Ladysmith's trip to New York to record a song he felt was ideal for them, the high-spirited "Diamonds on the Soles of Her Shoes." As they did with "Homeless," Shabalala wrote separate parts and shared songwriting credit. At the start of the track, Ladysmith, singing in Zulu, proclaimed loosely the independence of women in the modern age, while Simon chronicled in English a love affair between a poor boy and a girl so rich she had diamonds on her shoes. The nearly six-minute track pushed the album's length to forty-three minutes.

By now, two other albums had focused, in quite different ways, on the music and/or culture of South Africa. "Sun City," released in the fall of 1985, was the title track of an LP put together by Steven Van Zandt—a key member of Bruce Sprinsteen's E Street Band—and record producer Arthur Baker as a consciousness-raising campaign to strengthen the cultural boycott being violated by Western artists who accepted huge amounts of money to play Sun City. The engagements were then used by the South African government as propaganda to paint a positive picture about life for all races. The all-star cast, appearing under the group name Artists United Against Apartheid, featured stars such as Springsteen, Bob Dylan, Bono,

Bonnie Raitt, and Miles Davis. The single from the album was named Best Single of the Year in a *Village Voice* poll of US music critics.

Simon had been invited to sing on the record but declined because he objected to how the song denounced specific pop artists who had played Sun City, including Linda Ronstadt, who said she didn't know about the cultural boycott in 1983 when she accepted an offer to play there. As it turned out, Van Zandt said the names had already been dropped from the song and Simon was sent an early version by mistake. Regardless, the two parties never got together. Van Zandt was also outspoken in his opposition to Simon recording with South African musicians. He felt it violated the spirit of the boycott. It was a charge that would escalate dramatically once the album was released.

The second album, *The Indestructible Beat of Soweto*, was a compilation from Earthworks/Shanachie Records in early 1986 that contained tracks recorded in the early 1980s by South African artists, including Ladysmith. Where "Sun City" fell into the pop-rock tradition of protest music, *Soweto* was inescapably world music, thus foreign in every sense to US pop sensibilities. Despite enormous critical praise in America, the LP didn't crack the Top 200. This resistance to world music among Top 40 radio programmers likely contributed to Simon and Warners selecting "You Can Call Me Al" as the first single from *Graceland*. While the song had world music shading, it could—unlike the title track or "The Boy in the Bubble"—pass for straightforward pop rock. In fact, Lenny Waronker, after first hearing it, said, "This is great. It's a *pop* record."

The title came from a night in the early 1970s when Paul and Peggy threw a party for some musicians and friends at their apartment on Ninety-Fourth Street. One of those they invited was Stanley Silverman, a composer and conductor, and he brought along Pierre Boulez, who had just been named musical director of the New York Philharmonic. At the door, Silverman introduced Paul and Peggy to Boulez. When they left, Paul said goodbye to Boulez at the door, and he responded, "Thank you, Al, and please give my best to Betty." The couple went around for months calling each other Betty and Al. In the song, the story turns into the good-natured "I can call you Betty / and Betty, when you call me / You can call me Al."

Underneath the fun, however, the song speaks of a man in an apparent midlife crisis over an emptiness in his life who is looking for redemption or purpose. He eventually is driven to shout "Amen!" and "Hallelujah!" when he sees "angels in the architecture." The tune would prove to be a spectacularly effective concert number.

As soon as "Al" was picked as the single, Warner Bros. made a promotional video built around Simon's performance of the song during his May appearance on *Saturday Night Live*, but Simon found it too conventional and asked Lorne and *SNL* filmmaker Gary Weis for some ideas. Michaels played the song for Chevy Chase, who suggested that he lip-synch to Simon's vocal. Simon came up with the idea of lugging various large instruments around the room while Chase "sang." In a single afternoon, they produced one of the most memorable pop videos of the decade. Paul and Chevy walk into a room, sit in adjacent chairs, and shake hands as if equal members of a duo. Just as Paul starts to sing "Al," however, the comedian takes over and gleefully begins lip-synching the words. With nothing else to do, a crestfallen Paul walks out of the room, only to return with a conga drum almost as tall as he is. Finally, Chevy and Paul pick up a trumpet and saxophone, respectively, and execute a series of playful Motown-like steps to match the song's cheerful rhythm. The video also pokes fun at Simon's height. Chase was six-foot-four.

As the September release of the single approached, Simon, anxious to make sure his motives in going to South Africa were understood, hired the crisis management firm of Howard J. Rubinstein, whose clients over the years have included media mogul Rupert Murdoch, the Museum of Modern Art, and the New York Yankees. Dan Klores, a young account executive there whose specialty was political strategy, was more interested in jazz and classical music than in pop in the mid-1980s, but he was impressed by Simon's seriousness, and he loved the music on *Graceland*. He became a valuable advisor to Simon for years.

As soon as Simon explained what went into making the album, Klores anticipated there could be a backlash, especially in the African American community, so he invited several black leaders and opinion makers into the studio, a few at a time, to listen to the album. Simon also used the sessions to talk about why he went to South Africa. "He was very open, speaking from the heart, and he made a good impression," Klores said. "I was touched by Paul's sensitivity; how very much he takes it to heart when he is criticized or misunderstood. At times, I've seen him retreat so he can disguise his feelings with a sort of 'I don't give a fuck' indifference, but underneath, he takes it very much to heart."

Despite the flurry of radio enthusiasm for Simon's performance with Ladysmith on *Saturday Night Live* earlier in the year, the promotion staff at Warner Bros. knew that getting airplay for *Graceland* would be tough when "You Can Call Me Al" was released in late July. Reports from the label's regional radio promotion team were not encouraging. It was like stepping into the batter's box with two strikes: the first was the anti–world music bias at Top 40 radio, and the second was Simon being viewed as passé. Their fears were realized when "Al" entered the national pop chart the week of August 9 at an underwhelming no. 83. Things got worse over the next three weeks, as it climbed only to no. 65. By contrast, the single was a Top 10 hit in numerous countries around the world where world music wasn't such a radio handicap. Dickie Landry, the Louisiana musician, was in frequent contact with Simon during this period, and he found him extremely nervous about how the public would react. "I didn't want to jinx it or anything," he said, "but I kept telling Paul how great the album was."

Then the "You Can Call Me Al" video came to the rescue. MTV loved the playfulness of Paul's and Chevy's interaction, and the cable channel added the video to its playlist the first week in September. The sales impact was strong—not on the single but on the album. Just like in the Simon and Garfunkel days, fans wanted the entire collection. While "Al" stalled at no. 44 the week of September 13, *Graceland* entered the album chart at no. 94 and, thanks largely to the MTV exposure, jumped seventy-four places over the next four weeks to no. 17. The single, too, rebounded. By the end of the year, *Graceland* was well on its way to becoming Simon's first million-selling album since *There Goes Rhymin' Simon*. The momentum was also helped by Simon's return visit with Ladysmith Black Mambazo to *Saturday Night Live* on November 22, where they performed "Diamonds on the Soles of Her Shoes" with great flair. Simon also sang "The Boy in the Bubble" and "The Late Great Johnny Ace." His relationship with Garfunkel had healed enough for his old partner to appear on the show in a humorous, nonmusical skit.

The album also benefited from rave reviews. Robert Christgau's *Village Voice* critique began, "Opposed though I am to universalist humanism, this is a pretty damn universal record. Within the democratic bounds of pop accessibility, its biculturalism is striking, engaging, unprecedented—sprightly yet spunky, fresh yet friendly, so strange, so sweet, so willful, so radically incongruous and plainly beautiful. A." In the *Voice*'s year-end poll of US pop critics, *Graceland* was voted the best album of 1986. The album was also responsible for Simon's being named International Artist of the Year in England's equivalent of the Grammys, the BRIT Awards. Many observers spoke of how Simon kept reinventing himself, but it wasn't in the shifting persona adopted by, say, David Bowie, who shook up his fans by moving from one carefully plotted role to another: from Ziggy Stardust, the alien space rocker, to the Thin White Duke, the blue-eyed soul singer. Simon's changes were organic, dictated largely by his constant pursuit of new musical expression. But there were still trouble spots ahead.

After *Graceland* became a hit, Rockin' Dopsie, the zydeco musician, demanded cowriting credit and related royalties on "That Was Your Mother," the track cut in Lafayette. He claimed he had written the music for the song. Simon's lawyers hired a Cajun music scholar to look into the claim and found it invalid. The matter was dropped.

The second complaint over songwriting credit was more tangled. When the members of Los Lobos heard the final version of the song they had worked on, "All Around the World or The Myth of Fingerprints," they were surprised to see "Words and music by Paul Simon." Knowing that a few of the South African musicians had received cowriting credits on the album, Los Lobos had assumed they would as well, because, they said, the music they played during the sessions came from a song the quintet had been working on.

Los Lobos' complaint could have been reinforced if the band had had an earlier tape of the music they played at the Simon session, but they didn't. The quintet turned to Waronker, hoping he could help settle the dispute, but he said it was Simon's creative decision, and Simon's judgment was that Los Lobos didn't deserve cowriting credit. "For a song, you've got to have words and a melody, and it wasn't there," he said.

There was an exchange of letters between law firms that apparently ended with one from Simon's attorney in November of 1987 declaring, "This is to confirm our telephone conversation of November 7th in which you stated that your client, Los Lobos, does not intend to make any legal claims to the authorship of the composition 'All Around the World,' which appears on Paul Simon's *Graceland* album, nor any further financial remuneration for their work in connection with that composition." Los Lobos was not happy, however. In interviews nearly three decades later, Steve Berlin still complained about the lack of credit.

Simon was troubled by the Los Lobos issue (and earlier grumbling from members of the Muscle Shoals Rhythm Section about wanting more credit and royalties) because he prided himself on his relationship with his fellow musicians. Over the years, he had not only tried to treat the musicians well but paid them handsomely, because he had such great respect for the role they played—another tendency he picked up from his father. Beyond salaries, he spent probably a million dollars to help musicians in various ways, from medical bills to helping send their children to school, his future comanager Jeff Kramer said. "This isn't something anyone ever heard of, because Paul considered them family."

Simon, too, felt vulnerable when someone would criticize his behavior, because he didn't want to strike back. This was especially true when Ray Phiri, whom he had long championed, began making comments after leaving Paul's band in the early 1990s about being underpaid over the years—fueling the stereotype of Simon as the rich American who took advantage of the poor African musicians. The criticism didn't gain much traction, because other Africans in Simon's band—notably Bakithi Kumalo and guitarist Vincent Nguini—were on Simon's side when the matter came up. They—along with Joseph Shabalala—spoke passionately about all that Simon had done for them and for African music.

"*Graceland*, man, that record changed my life," said Kumalo, who has played bass with Simon for more than thirty years. "That was my passport to the world." Shabalala added, "That's why we gave Paul Simon the Zulu name *Vutlendela*: the one who opens the way." Nguini, who continued to tour with Simon in 2017 while battling cancer, said, "Paul has always been there for me—always. He even talks to my doctors to make sure I'm getting proper care."

More than simply a celebration of the album, Simon planned the entire Graceland tour as a salute to the full South African musical experience—a mix of music, culture, and even politics. Even if he avoided political statements as a songwriter, he wanted the tour to be a strong statement against apartheid. The journey, which would begin February 1 in Rotterdam, Netherlands, and go through Europe, Africa, and the United States, and then return to Europe, featured two dozen musicians and singers, including his key *Graceland* rhythm section and Ladysmith Black Mambazo. In addition, the tour showcased popular jazz trumpeter Hugh Masekela, a South African who had been living in exile for almost three decades because of his opposition to apartheid, and singer Miriam Makeba, who was known as Mother Africa because she was the first artist from Africa to popularize African music around the world. The highlight of the nearly three-month tour would be two outdoor concerts on February 14 and 15 in Harare, Zimbabwe, which was as close as Simon could take the tour to South Africa, around four hundred miles.

Five weeks before the opening concert, there was good news from the Grammys. *Graceland* was nominated for Best Album, Best Song (the title track), Best Male Vocal, and Best Producer (Simon). It was his fifth Best Album nomination. The awards would be announced in Los Angeles on February 24. Despite the nominations, Simon continued to be charged by a few musicians and activists with violating a 1980 UN ban on performing in South Africa, thus helping the racist regime. The criticism was largely beneath the radar of mainstream fans in the United States, but Simon tried to address it over the next few months by speaking to activist groups or students, including addressing forty African American students at Howard University in Washington, DC, in January 1987. He did receive some support at the meeting. "I saw this as a way for him to improve his own music and for the American public to find out about the great talents of black artists in South Africa," said a history major at Howard.

But most of the students were critical. "How can you justify taking over this music?" asked a sophomore pianist and music major. "For too long, artists have stolen African music. It happened with jazz. You're telling me the Gershwin story of Africa: 'I'll go there, I'll listen to the stuff, and I'll culturally diffuse it.' " In response, Simon said, "I went as a musician, and I interacted with other musicians. It's true there is another level to this story, but this is a beginning, a sincere beginning. I tried to introduce this music to people who never heard it before. Sincerity doesn't seem to be held in high regard. I'm here. I'm listening. I respond the best I can. At least I'm into dialogue. I have always intended that this music be used to serve the African people."

Simon was angry when the UN Special Committee Against Apartheid added his name to a list of artists who had broken the UN's cultural boycott against South Africa. He wrote a letter to the committee stating, "I write to you as an artist completely opposed to the apartheid system in South Africa. Like millions of people of conscience in that country and around the world who have contributed to the struggle to end the system, I am working in my field toward achieving this goal. As an artist who has refused to perform in South Africa, I reiterate and intend to maintain this position in the context of the UN cultural boycott." At a press conference the day before the tour was to start, Simon announced that the UN committee had removed his name from the boycott list, hoping, naïvely, that the action would end the controversy surrounding the shows.

At the concert the next day, Simon was nervous for the South African musicians. For most of them, this was their first time on the global concert circuit, and he went around to each one backstage before the show at the Ahoy Rotterdam arena. Even though most of the audience had surely heard some of *Graceland*, Simon worried that some fans might be restless listening to ten songs from the album plus guest numbers by Masekela, Makeba, and Ladysmith Black Mambazo. But the predominately white audience loved it. On the second night in Rotterdam, the audience gave the musicians a standing ovation after "Nkosi Sikelel' iAfrika," the unofficial African national anthem. "They started singing back to us, 'Oh, wey, oh, wey'—like a football chant," Masekela said. "We didn't know what it meant, but it lasted about ten minutes. We were in shock. It was amazing."

Two weeks later, the tour reached Harare, the emotional center of the journey.

"These are the days of miracle and wonder," Simon sang to twenty thousand cheering fans, hundreds of whom had driven north from South Africa to the February 14 concert at the Rufaro soccer stadium. To Simon, those lyrics from "The Boy in the Bubble" spoke of hope and dread. "That's the way I see the world," he said, "a balance between the two, but coming down on the side of hope."

Despite being dropped from the UN cultural boycott list, Simon continued to encounter pockets of criticism from various antiapartheid groups. On top of lingering resentment of his having gone to Johannesburg, many of the complaints were directed at the absence on the album of overt protest songs, the implication being that Simon was just using black South African musicians without having the courage or will to embrace their cause. The criticism erupted at a press conference the day before the weekend shows and in a guest column in the *Zimbabwe Herald* the morning of the first concert. The writer urged all politically conscious people to stay away.

Reading the piece backstage before a morning sound check, Simon thought the column had an incendiary edge. One of the reasons he had brought the tour to Zimbabwe rather than to one of the other neighboring countries was security; Zimbabwe offered the best guarantee against incidents. Still, security was a concern. He had hesitated in bringing his son, Harper, fourteen, but decided the experience was too valuable for him to miss. Throughout the day, members of the Zimbabwe army marched around the stadium grounds, carrying rifles.

"The reason I worked so hard to make my position clear was that it is a complex issue, and I thought that some people might be confused," Paul said. "But I realize now that there really isn't a misunderstanding anymore. We just have a disagreement over my role. To some, the album is of no value except as something to attack. So we'll just continue to disagree, because I'm not going to begin writing protest songs for them. I believe there are often political implications in cultural events, but I think it's important to maintain the integrity of art—and not let it be swept away by politics. Pop music is usually pretentious when it tries to be political. That's because it usually operates on the most naïve level. I've said it before: if your awareness of the world is based on pop music, you're probably not very aware."

Even with the tension at the start of the afternoon, the audience went away feeling good about more than just the music: the harmony between the races in the stadium was in itself inspiring. It was the biggest gathering by far of a racially mixed crowd in Zimbabwe since the country's independence ceremony in the same stadium seven years earlier. "The crowd was so beautiful," Makeba said. "I came out onstage and saw the stadium packed with black and white people, and it was a dream that I have carried around with me for years. The first thing I thought was, 'Why can't it be like this in South Africa?' And then I was filled with tears. I've got to think it will happen back home someday."

Nine days later, Simon was sitting in the Shrine Auditorium in Los Angeles at the twenty-ninth annual Grammy Awards ceremony. There was no clear favorite in the Best Album competition between Peter Gabriel's *So*, Janet Jackson's *Control*, Barbra Streisand's *The Broadway Album*, Steve Winwood's *Back in the High Life*, and *Graceland*, which led to all sorts of speculation over what might happen. Things didn't look good for Simon early in the ceremony, as he lost in the Best Producer category to Jimmy Jam and Terry Lewis for *Control*. Then "Graceland" lost in the Best Song category to "That's What Friends Are For," a paper-thin pop tune written by Burt Bacharach and Carole Bayer Sager. As Paul sat in the audience in a black tux, it looked as if his only appearance onstage was going to have been his performance of "Diamonds on the Soles of Her Shoes" with Ladysmith. But *Graceland* won for Best Album, and Paul was overjoyed. He used his acceptance speech to salute the South African musicians and all the other musical influences that had inspired him.

The Grammy victory contributed to the album's eventually selling five million copies in the United States, part of an estimated worldwide total of sixteen million. But Simon didn't have much time to celebrate. Three nights after the Grammys, he was onstage in San Francisco for the start of the US dates of the world tour, which would end with three shows in late April at New York's Radio City Music Hall.

When the tour reached London a few days before New York, the concerts were picketed by a few antiapartheid activists, and some prominent rock musicians, including Billy Bragg and Paul Weller, signed an open letter attacking Simon. At a press conference with Simon in London, where the tour played six nights at Royal Albert Hall, Joseph Shabalala, who had become a spokesman for the South African musicians, addressed the complaints:

"Those who criticize Paul Simon and say he did wrong in South Africa and do this thing, they themselves are now ashamed because so many people have said this is good—especially my group. This was a good opportunity to disclose our music all over the world because many people didn't know this kind of music."

Through it all, Dan Klores, the public relations adviser, was impressed by what he described as Simon's sensitivity. "Lots of pop stars would have just been celebrating the record's success and ignoring the protests because the protests were rather isolated, for the most part," he said. "But Paul wanted to reach out and go way beyond what I thought was necessary to explain himself, often in front of hostile audiences. I'd tell him, 'Paul, you don't have to do all this.' And he would say, 'Yes I do.' "

Amid the frenzy for tickets, especially on the US leg, Simon announced in early May that he was adding nine more dates, ending July 2 at Madison Square Garden. The new shows would all be benefits, with the money

1. Simon gave America its first taste of *Graceland* in May 1986, when South Africa's Ladysmith Black Mambazo joined him for a lively performance of "Diamonds on the Soles of Her Shoes" on *Saturday Night Live*.

2. Watching the Grammy Awards telecast in 1987, Lou and Belle Simon cheer as *Graceland* is named Album of the Year.

3. Before launching the Graceland world tour in 1987, Simon joined the show's large musical cast for a joyful "class photo."

4. If Elvis Presley was Simon's biggest rock hero, Mickey Mantle, the great New York Yankees center fielder, was his all-time baseball favorite, and Simon loved it when Mantle appeared in a 1988 video for "Me and Julio Down by the Schoolyard."

5. Another baseball dream came true for Simon when he sang "Mrs. Robinson" before more than fifty thousand people on Joe DiMaggio Day at Yankee Stadium.

6. Ten years after Simon and Garfunkel drew an estimated 500,000 people to a concert in New York's Central Park, Simon's solo concert in the park attracted, according to reports at the time, more than 750,000 fans. The event was saluted on the front page of the *New York Daily News*.

7. Simon warming up the pitcher during his days as a Little League coach.

8. After meeting her on the set of *Saturday Night Live* in 1988, Simon began a courtship with his future wife, Edie Brickell. Here, Paul visits Edie's hometown of Dallas, Texas, for the first time.

9. Simon fell in love with musically rich Louisiana after recording there, and he introduced Edie to the state's majestic Atchafalaya Swamp.

10. Simon goes over last-minute details with Lorne Michaels before singing "The Boxer" on the first *Saturday Night Live* broadcast after the terrorist attacks of 2001, a moving performance aimed at lifting the city's wounded spirit. Years later, Michaels declared, "Even after all this time, I think he's the only one who could have done it. He is as much a symbol of the show and of New York as there is."

11. On the emotional night when he was named the first recipient of the Library of Congress's Gershwin Prize for Popular Song, Simon hugs Ladysmith Black Mambazo leader Joseph Shabalala during a performance segment.

12. Simon trades guitar licks with Vincent Nguini, a native of Cameroon who was a key part of Simon's band for some three decades before he died of liver cancer in 2017 at age sixty-five.

13. Record producer Roy Halee, shown at his home in 2016, was such an essential part of the Simon and Garfunkel sound that industry insiders called the team Simon, Garfunkel, and Halee.

14. Simon and his oldest son, Harper, performing in 2000.

15. Lulu Simon in 2017.

16. Gabriel Simon in 2016.

17. Adrian Simon in 2017.

18. Paul and Edie renew their vows at their oceanfront home in Montauk, New York, in August of 2016.

going equally to three organizations: an antiapartheid campaign in South Africa to aid detained and imprisoned children, the United Negro College Fund, and various municipal "help" agencies in each city on the tour. In New York, the money would help provide medically equipped vans to serve homeless children. The latter charity, the Children's Health Fund, was founded earlier in the year by Simon and Dr. Irwin Redlener, a pediatrician and public health activist whom Simon met through the "We Are the World" project.

It was an issue close to Simon's heart because he had been touched by the plight of a homeless woman, Maria, who lived on the corner of Fifty-Fourth Street and Broadway, near the Hit Factory recording studio. He began giving her money and exchanging a few words with her, mostly casual things like the weather. Then she was gone, and Simon asked himself what he could have done to help her. He still had Maria on his mind when he and Dr. Redlener were given a tour of homeless facilities in New York by Gretchen Buchenholz, founder and executive director of the Association to Benefit Children. Seeing how little opportunity children had for medical care, Simon embraced Dr. Redlener's dream of providing that care via a mobile clinic, dubbed the "big blue bus." For Simon, the fund was part of a commitment to use his music to help social and charitable causes—a path that was inspired in large part by his *Graceland* experiences.

"It was *Graceland* that really put me into a world of people who were in need and were subjugated," Simon reflected years later. "I began to realize I could not only help through the music but in using music to raise money or lift people's awareness. It wasn't like a light went on in my head, like 'I've got to help people,' but just seeing problems and responding to them, one by one. When we talked about the vans, we weren't thinking of the ultimate remedy. We were concerned with something doable so that we could begin helping children right away. The vans did work, which is why the concept spread to other communities around the country and were even used eventually to help people during floods or other disaster situations."

When Dr. Redlener couldn't get public financing for the program, Simon put up $80,000 to buy a fully equipped mobile clinic. The Garden benefit raised another $50,000. By the end of the year, the first big blue bus was serving three thousand homeless children in Manhattan under a program affiliated with New York Hospital–Cornell Medical Center. To raise funds for a second mobile unit in Queens, Simon held a Madison Square Garden benefit on December 13 featuring most of his *Graceland* troupe, plus Lou Reed, Dion DiMucci, rapper Grandmaster Flash, and surprise guests Bruce Springsteen and Billy Joel. One of the highlights was when Simon, Springsteen, and Joel joined Dion on his doo-wop hit "A Teenager in Love," which Simon had loved since his teens. Near the end of the four-hour concert, Simon brought out Ladysmith Black Mambazo to sing "Diamonds on the Soles of Her Shoes" before bringing everyone back onstage to close the evening with Chuck Berry's "Rock & Roll Music."

Six days later, Simon hosted *Saturday Night Live* again, joined by musical guest Linda Ronstadt, who performed "Under African Skies" with him as a duet. Ronstadt, who sang the song on the album, was an outspoken champion of *Graceland* and defended Simon on the boycott issue. "It brought South African music onto the world stage and did a lot to enhance the political discussion," she said in 2017. The show got off to a humorous start with Paul and US senator Paul Simon of Illinois, complete with his trademark bow tie, walking onstage in a supposed booking mix-up, each pretending to think Michaels had told him that he was supposed to be hosting. "Look, this is very embarrassing," songwriter Paul Simon said. "I was sure they meant me. It's a comedy show and a music show, so it's got to be me." Replied Senator Paul Simon, "I just wish someone had told me earlier. I've been here rehearsing since Thursday."

Lorne Michaels saw that the *Graceland* success had a profound impact on Simon, helping restore his confidence after being written off by the music business and suffering through a second divorce. The general perception, too, was that he came away from *Graceland* a warmer, more generous person.

CHAPTER EIGHTEEN

How do you follow *Graceland*?

For much of 1987, Simon was torn between two challenging and time-consuming projects. Option A was writing a musical—not the easy, feel-good parade of old hits (like *Jersey Boys*) that would eventually become popular on Broadway, but a musical that was based on the story that had intrigued Simon for years: the 1959 tale of Salvador Agron, the sixteen-year-old gang member who stabbed two innocent youths to death. Option B was another album in the *Graceland* world music tradition, this time spotlighting musicians from Brazil and eastern Africa. Both ideas had potential danger signs.

If Simon had failed in Hollywood with *One-Trick Pony*, why did he think he could succeed in the even more treacherous waters of Broadway, where allegiance to long-standing industry rites and rituals—not one of Simon's strong suits—was strictly enforced? His proposed theme, too, was not likely to have theatergoers dancing in the aisles. The gang killings were all the more notorious because Agron showed no remorse. "I don't care if I burn," he told police in 1959. "My mother could watch me." From then on, Agron would be remembered as a savage killer, but Simon grew to see the story as one of redemption. The danger with a second world music–inspired album was that it could be dismissed as simply *Graceland II*.

After a few months, Simon decided on the world music album, thanks to three specific conversations, one of which was a long, philosophical talk with Quincy Jones. "Paul was so excited by the *Graceland* music that he didn't want to let go of it, and I told him not to worry, he was just getting started," Jones said. "There was a lot more music in Africa than what he found in South Africa, especially the marvelous drummers in the west, and his eyes just lit up."

That conversation coincided with what Grammy-winning Latin bandleader Eddie Palmieri told him about the great drumming tradition that had migrated over the years from Africa, to Brazil, to the Caribbean, and on to Cuba, where it found a new home. A third step came when Simon sang a duet with Brazilian singer-songwriter Milton Nascimento for his 1987 *Yauaretê* album, and Nascimento told him about the magical drummers in Brazil. That was enough. Simon made plans to go to Rio de Janeiro the following February.

Before he left, there was again good news from the Grammys. "Graceland," the single, was nominated for Best Record, alongside U2's "I Still Haven't Found What I'm Looking For," Los Lobos's "La Bamba," Suzanne Vega's "Luka," and Steve Winwood's "Back in the High Life Again." ("Graceland" was eligible in 1988 because the single had been released in a different qualifying period than the album.) Simon was too committed to Brazil, however, to attend the March 2 award ceremonies at Radio City Music Hall.

Recording in Brazil was a nightmare of red tape, much of which would have been impossible to overcome if Nascimento's record producer, Marco Mazzola, hadn't run interference. Mazzola not only booked time at studios for Simon and Phil Ramone (stepping in as engineer for the unavailable Halee) but also brought in the local musicians. After several days, Simon was eager to hear more, and Mazzola took him to the city of Salvador, where he heard Grupo Cultural Olodum, a cultural collective designed to both celebrate the region's African heritage and combat racial discrimination and economic oppression.

In his memoir, Ramone wrote that Olodum was eager to work with Simon because its leaders hoped the connection would bring worldwide attention to the group's objectives. The session was held in historic Pelourinho Square in the old part of Salvador, where the walls of the courtyard were painted a bright white. To record the performance, Ramone rented portable equipment and hung microphones from telephone poles. Once the tape began rolling, the group members injected their drumming with spectacular energy and spirit as they paraded around the square. Adding to the excitement, the single "Graceland" won the Grammy for Record of the Year. The album was nearing its eightieth week on the US chart, on its way to an eventual ninety-seven weeks. On the flight home, Simon decided to devote all his time to the new album, which would be titled *The Rhythm of the Saints*. He wanted it to be heavily percussion driven.

Think of all the hours Simon spent working on songs, especially with *Graceland* and subsequent albums, as a kid with dozens of building blocks—some of which consist of the instrumental tracks that served increasingly as the foundation of the music; others representing the musical refrains that have stayed with him since his teens; and the remaining blocks representing the new ideas inspired by all of the above. By the late 1980s, he had hundreds of such blocks. Simon may only use one or two of the old blocks, but they provide a crucial shading. No one is likely to think of Elvis Presley's recording of "Mystery Train" when listening to "Late in the Evening" or "Graceland," but it's there. For Simon, the link with some of those early, accessible musical passages helped keep his music connected to the sounds he loved as a boy.

After all this time, Paul continued to search for new ways to approach his art—looking, if you will, for more building blocks. He wanted to keep moving forward. "That's why a lot of Simon's contemporaries in the 1960s and 1970s eventually hit a dead end," Allen Toussaint suggested. "They stuck with one approach until they ran out of ideas. If Simon hadn't realized that he needed to develop new approaches and ideas after *Bridge Over Troubled Water*, he would have run out of ideas by the middle of the seventies, too."

As he spent time with the *Saints* tracks, Simon realized that he needed to approach them differently than the music from his Johannesburg sessions. "What I was trying to learn to do was to be able to write vernacular speech and then intersperse it with enriched language, and then go back to the vernacular," he explained. "So the thing would go along smoothly, and then some image would come out that was interesting, and then it would go back to this very smooth, conversational thing.

"By the time I got to *Graceland*, I was trying to let that kind of enriched language flow naturally, so that you wouldn't really notice it much. I think in *Hearts and Bones*, you could feel it, that it was coming . . . Whereas in *Graceland*, I tried to do it where you didn't notice it; where you sort of passed the line, and then it was over. And let the words tumble this way and that way. And sometimes I'd increase the rhythm of the words so that they would come by you so quickly that all you would get was a feeling. And so, I started to try and work with moving feelings around words." The result appeared almost effortless until you noticed the underlying complexity of the words and music.

During this period, Simon attended a reading by Derek Walcott, a poet from the Caribbean island of Saint Lucia who would win the Nobel Prize in Literature in 1992 and whose work was a source of immense pride in the region. Simon found a soulful nuance and deep compassion in Walcott's poems. After the reading, Simon invited the poet to his studio to learn more about the spirit and culture of the Caribbean people who were part of the Afro-Brazilian-Cuban drum trail. Walcott was flattered and wanted to know more about the man he called "America's greatest living songwriter."

"There is all this talk about lyrics being poetry, and certain songwriters are frequently cited in this regard, but there is very little poetry in songwriting," Walcott said years later in an interview at his home in Saint Lucia. "Mostly, songwriters try to be clever, and that's not the same as poetry." However, he felt that much of Simon's work contained the discipline, grace, and truthfulness of poetry, and he cited the opening lines of "Graceland" as evidence, describing them as "pure poetry, Whitmanesque." In "The Sound of Silence," he saw the same artistry that he admired in the work of Hart Crane, the American poet who, in turn, was greatly inspired by T. S. Eliot. After their meeting in New York, Simon sent lyrics of some of his new songs to Walcott. Among the images the poet liked especially were "cold coffee eyes" (from "She Moves On") and "the cross is in the ballpark" ("The Obvious Child").

Simon spent much of 1988 at his house in Montauk. He lived on an oceanfront cliff and enjoyed walking on the long stretch of beach below. He especially liked the house in the winter because the town was almost empty. When he wanted a break from writing, he sometimes ventured into Manhattan to spend time with Michaels and visit the *Saturday Night Live* set, which is how he happened to be there the night of November 5 when the musical guests caught his ear.

Edie Brickell, a twenty-two-year-old singer-songwriter from Dallas, had been majoring in art at Southern Methodist University until her life changed one night in a club. A friend who knew she was interested in singing coaxed her onstage with an instrumental group—the first time she had ever sung in public. She later explained that her first shot of Jack Daniel's that night helped her find the courage to step up to the microphone. Though the instrumental group cited Miles Davis and the Grateful Dead as influences, Brickell's taste leaned more to singer-songwriters like Elvis Costello and—wouldn't you know—Paul Simon. Whatever their differences, Edie Brickell & New Bohemians, as they eventually called themselves, clicked, and their distinctive musical blend—a bit folk, some quirky pop, just enough original vision—led to a contract with Geffen Records.

Thanks to an unusually inviting Top 10 single, "What I Am," and a terrific video, Brickell & New Bohemians found a big audience with the debut album *Shooting Rubberbands at the Stars*. It was already no. 65 (on its way to two and a half million in sales) the night of the *SNL* appearance.

Critics invariably compared Brickell and her songs to female artists such as Rickie Lee Jones, but the single would have been right at home in a Paul Simon songbook. It begins:

> *I'm not aware of too many things*
> *I know what I know, if you know what I mean*
> *Philosophy is the talk on a cereal box*
> *Religion is the smile on a dog*

Simon got so caught up in her performance that he accidently stepped in front of a camera, which momentarily threw Brickell off stride. "He made me forget how the song went when I looked at him," she told interviewers later. Paul wasn't just attracted to the music. In a *Los Angeles Times* review of her and New Bohemians at the Roxy in West Hollywood just two days later, Chris Willman described Brickell in a way that seemed tailor-made for an English major from Kew Gardens Hills:

"There's a kind of whimsicality to Brickell's demeanor—even during the more serious or passionate songs—that somehow never threatened to trivialize the material," he wrote. "This is the kind of woman college boys dream about meeting in English Lit class—one with long, wavy brown hair, who's fond of hats and dressing down, a sensitive-poet type." For Paul, it was love at first sight—the first time that had happened, he said, since Kathy Chitty.

Edie's arrival finally brought an end to Simon's relationship with Carrie Fisher. "He had been trying to end it, but we were just so compatibly incompatible that it was seductive, and we kept getting back together," Carrie said in 2016. "It was usually me who would go back to him, but he finally said we just couldn't see each other anymore, which meant I couldn't keep trying to get back into his life. I felt terrible that I had never been able to give him the peace that he wanted, and I respected his feelings." Carrie thought right away that Edie would be perfect for Paul, someone who could give him the comfort and family he wanted. "I met her right in the beginning and liked her," Carrie said. "She told me, 'I've always been jealous of you because you're so funny,' and I thought that was very sweet of her."

Looking back on her relationship with Paul a quarter century later, Carrie quoted these lines from the song Paul wrote about her, "Hearts and Bones"—the lines that begin with her asking a question:

And tell me why
Why won't you love me
For who I am
He said, "Cause that's not the way the world is, baby"

Sitting in the living room of her Beverly Hills home, which was next door to her mother's house, she repeated the last line. "That summed it up," she said, then paused. "What a great writer."

Paul and Edie started going out almost immediately. He went to see her perform with New Bohemians at the Bottom Line in Manhattan on November 18—the day Stephen Holden called her one of the year's brightest young songwriters in a *New York Times* feature—and they went to dinner between sets. Things moved along quickly enough, but after two failed marriages, he was nervous. At the same time, he had sacrificed so much of his personal life to his music that the idea of having a family again was deeply appealing.

The Rhythm of the Saints was an enormous undertaking. It had a larger cast of musicians and singers and a bigger budget than *Graceland*: an estimated $1 million versus $700,000. By the time he finished the album, Simon would have made four trips to Brazil and one to Paris in search of the right musicians, enlisting so many players and singers (nearly a hundred) that the LP credits ran as long as the scroll of names at the end of a movie.

As always, Simon trusted his instincts, which is why he held on to, rather than immediately discarded, what at first seemed odd or unrelated phrases. "Words would sometimes come with the melody, but sometimes they wouldn't come for a long time," he said. "I have a book of images and phrases that I keep. If there was a line that fit, I'd connect it up to whatever the story was, or begin the story with the line, almost like a skin graft."

Not everything made the cut as he mixed building blocks until the words fit the spirit of the music. This approach can be seen in the surrealistic images that are in "The Obvious Child," the song inspired by the music of Olodum in the public square. A reflection on aging and the uncertainties of life, the lyrics are tied together by the evocative image of "the cross is in the ballpark," which appears twice in the song. From Olodum's machine-gun-like drumming at the start through the striking synthesizer touches added by jazz saxophonist Michael Brecker in New York, the song demanded the listener's attention, and it was the "cross is in the ballpark" line that came through most vividly.

Even after he added the image to the song, Simon continued to wrestle with exactly what it meant. At first, he thought the image, which came to him while playing guitar over the instrumental track, referred to the practice of religious figures addressing the faithful in a stadium, like the three papal masses at Yankee Stadium. But then a more universal interpretation emerged, and he felt even better about the line: a reference to the crosses we bear in life and how they can be overcome. "The burdens that we carry are doable; they're in the ballpark," he said. This constant rethinking might leave some songwriters exhausted, but Simon delighted in it.

As 1989 drew to a close, Simon learned that he and Garfunkel had been voted into the Rock & Roll Hall of Fame along with Queens-mates Carole King and Gerry Goffin, among others. The news wasn't all that surprising—it was their first year of eligibility, and they were considered a shoo-in. Still, it felt wonderful. At the ceremony on January 17, 1990, at Manhattan's Waldorf-Astoria Hotel, he and Art tried gamely to hide the tension that had largely kept them apart since the Summer Evening tour in 1983, partially by making fun of their long-standing disagreements. At the podium that night, after being inducted by James Taylor, he said, "We can join those other happy couples—Ike and Tina Turner, the Everly Brothers, Mick and Keith . . . the Beatles. Maybe they'll have a separate wing for all of us . . . Probably be completed in time for the Eagles to be in it." Even after Garfunkel declared warmly that Simon was "the person who most enriched my life by putting those songs through me," Simon couldn't resist kidding, "Arthur and I agree about almost nothing. But it's true, I have enriched his life quite a bit."

Yet Simon could not let the moment at the microphone pass without saying how much music meant to him. Referring to his teenage days when he and Art first became intrigued with music, he said, "We were so taken with that idea. It became the dominant interest in our lives. To this day, it's still fascinating . . . the music, writing music, making records. I'm very grateful that for all this time, I've never been bored. It's been that thing that has sustained both of us. This was really a blessing for us." In line with the Hall of Fame custom of inductees performing at the ceremony, Simon and Garfunkel teamed up on "Bridge Over Troubled Water" and "The Boxer" before going back to their doo-wop days with a warm rendition of the Spaniels' 1954 hit "Goodnite, Sweetheart, Goodnite."

Simon and Garfunkel fans, once again, hoped that the signs of affection would lead to another reunion tour. But it didn't happen. Simon, minus Garfunkel, did, however, join Sting, Bruce Springsteen, Don Henley, and others onstage at a February 18 benefit at Carnegie Hall that generated more than $1 million to preserve the Amazon rain forest and to raise awareness within the entertainment community about environmental problems.

As the *Saints* recording sessions continued, Simon worked on a series of songs that would add greatly to the substance and appeal of the new album, the title of which was based on the traditional belief that the holy spirit was inside drums that were used in various religious rituals and rites in Africa and Brazil. Ultimately, the music would mirror Simon's growing belief in the importance of community and the shared faith in love, family, and the future. The sense of community was underscored by the way he blended an almost unwieldy bunch of musical traditions and instruments from the various American, Brazilian, African, and Caribbean music traditions.

Chief among the new songs was "The Cool, Cool River," which built

upon the optimism of "The Obvious Child." The spiritually edged track
tells of someone so poor he is reduced to living in his car in an age of battered dreams, anger, and metal detectors. Still, the song offers hope:

> *Moves like a fist through traffic*
> *Anger and no one can heal it*
> *Shoves a little bump into the momentum*
> *It's just a little lump*
> *But you feel it*
> *In the creases and the shadows*
> *With a rattling, deep emotion*
> *The cool, cool river*
> *Sweeps the wild, white ocean*
>
> *Yes, Boss—the government handshake*
> *Yes, Boss—the crusher of language*
> *Yes, Boss—Mr. Stillwater*
> *The face at the edge of the banquet*
> *The cool, the cool river*
> *The cool, the cool river*
>
> *I believe in the future*
> *I may live in my car*
> *My radio tuned to*
> *The voice of a star*
> *Song dogs barking at the break of dawn*
> *Lightning pushes the edge of a thunderstorm*
> *And these old hopes and fears*
> *Still at my side*
>
> *Anger and no one can heal it*
> *Slides through the metal detector*
> *Lives like a mole in a motel*
> *A slide in a slide projector*

The cool, cool river
Sweeps the wild, white ocean
The rage, the rage of love turns inward
To become prayers of devotion
And these prayers are
The constant road across the wilderness
These prayers are
These prayers are the memory of God
The memory of God

And I believe in the future
We shall suffer no more
Maybe not in my lifetime
But in yours, I feel sure
Song dogs barking at the break of dawn
Lightning pushes the edges of a thunderstorm
And these streets
Quiet as a sleeping army
Send their battered dreams to heaven, to heaven
For the mother's restless son
Who is a witness to, who is a warrior
Who denies his urge to break and run

Who says, "Hard times?
I'm used to them
The speeding planet burns
I'm used to that
My life's so common it disappears"
And sometimes even music
Cannot substitute for tears

The song was extremely personal for Simon. It was the first time, he noticed, that he had ever written in a song that he was going to die, and the final lines were an admission that not even music could always ease one's sorrows. The line was inspired in part by his father's health problems. On top of the heart issues, Lou Simon had been diagnosed with cancer in 1988. By the time the line was finished, however, Simon was thinking of social tragedies, from the Holocaust to the assassinations of President Kennedy and Dr. King. Yet the song was also a hopeful look at the future. When he wrote, *"We shall suffer no more / maybe not in my lifetime / but in yours,"* it was a nod to Harper and his generation. "You have to believe that some of the problems can be fixed, or you live in a state of such pessimism that you're immobilized," he said. "That's the hope of us all, isn't it? If the problems seem impossible now, well, maybe they'll be solved by the next generation." In the same upper echelon of Simon songs, "Born at the Right Time" contrasted the innocence and promise of a child with the realities awaiting her in an anxious time on an endangered planet. He wrote it around the time of the tearing down of the Berlin Wall in 1989, a time of hope in the world.

"Spirit Voices," another key song, described a trip Simon took along the Amazon River that had surprising repercussions. The journey began when Simon, who was increasingly curious about the spiritual beliefs of different cultures, heard about a *brujo*, or witch doctor, who lived in a nearby village. Simon saw him more as a spiritual teacher. "His function was that he was a doctor, but he was treating people with herbs and prayers and chants. It was traditional Indian medicine," he said. At the village, Simon said, the *brujo* sang a few lovely melodies, chanted over patients, and then handed out this drink, ayahuasca—a hallucinogenic made from herbs and roots. Simon drank the liquid but said he didn't have any physical ailments except a sore elbow. "And the *brujo* said, 'Oh, that's nothing'—like, 'Don't come here with an elbow problem; we're dealing with serious problems here.' " Still, Simon didn't return home with just a new song but also a continuing interest in ayahuasca, which he said gave him a liberating sense of bliss.

Taking a break from the album, Simon flew to Boston to join Stevie Wonder and Jackson Browne in a June 23 concert celebrating Nelson Mandela's first visit to the United States since the antiapartheid leader's release from prison in South Africa after twenty-seven years on various charges related to his activism. His freedom was a step toward the end of racial segregation in his country. During the six-hour event, which was attended by an estimated 260,000 people in a park on the banks of the Charles River, Mandela invited Simon to bring his music to his country. Simon replied that it was his dream to play South Africa. He also took another time out from his recording schedule in late August 1990 to do a benefit before around 10,000 people in Montauk at the first annual "Back at the Ranch" concert, raising $270,000 to help restore the local lighthouse. It was part of his lengthy association with the Back at the Ranch benefits.

While still fine-tuning the album, Simon was told by Warner Bros. that the label needed the CD right away if it was going to have a full-scale promotional campaign in place in time to release the album before the Grammy-eligibility deadline. Though he longed for an unprecedented fourth Best Album Grammy, Simon was still wrestling with details, chiefly sequencing, and he wouldn't sacrifice them for a possible award. The record eventually came out on October 16, 1990, fifteen days after the deadline. Given the album's eventual critical and commercial success, *Saints* would have probably been the favorite to win the award, which went to Quincy Jones's *Back on the Block*, a collection of tracks each showcasing a different artist, from Ella Fitzgerald to George Benson. As it turned out, *Saints* was nominated for Best Album the following year, but the delay took away much of its sizzle among Grammy voters, eliminating virtually any chance of a win.

As reviews for the album came in, most critics spoke about it in the context of *Graceland*, Simon's new standard of excellence. *Rolling Stone*'s John McAlley was dazzled by the album's daring but wondered if it wasn't too demanding for pop audiences. "Many of these 'art' songs are aggressively impressionistic and nonlinear—at times, to the point of opacity. The record requires several listenings before its abstract lines begin to emerge and take on flesh, but when Simon's literary gambles pay off—as they do to best effect on 'The Cool, Cool River'—the results are breathtakingly visceral." The album reached no. 4 on the US chart, which was within one of *Graceland*'s peak position, and it stayed on the charts for more than a year, selling more than two million copies. Decades later, Edie declared it her favorite of Paul's albums.

The next task for Simon was to transfer the range and ambition of *Saints* to the concert stage. He ended up with seventeen musicians, his largest band to date, a group that ranged from some of the New York regulars (notably Gadd, Tee, and Brecker), to various members of the *Graceland* and *Saints* lineups. The tour, titled Born at the Right Time, represented the longest continuous series of dates Simon had ever done. After opening January 2, 1991, at the Tacoma Dome in Washington, the stops stretched across the United States through April. Reviewing a stop at the Nassau Coliseum in the *New York Times*, Jon Pareles opened by declaring that Simon had discovered the glories of the big band, not "an Ellingtonian orchestra of saxophones and brass, but an African-style ensemble of percussion, guitars, singers, keyboards, and horns . . . In the past, Mr. Simon has often come across as a meticulous, painstaking craftsman. Now, with his craft intact, he also makes his music sound like fun."

In May the tour moved to Europe, where Simon reconnected with Kathy Chitty after almost a quarter century. Soon after *Graceland* was released, a friend from the old Brentwood Folk Club days had told Simon he knew where Kathy was living. Simon then asked the friend to forward a copy of the album and an accompanying letter to Chitty, but for some reason, the album didn't reach her until 1990, and the letter wasn't with it. Still, Kathy wrote back, updating him on her life. Paul subsequently invited Kathy, her longtime partner, Ken Harrison, and their three children to dinner the next time he came to London, which was for the Born at the Right Time concerts at London's Wembley Arena.

At dinner before the concert, Simon learned that Kathy, inadvertently, had recently become something of a cause célèbre in England because of the "Homeward Bound" plaque at the Widnes train station. To highlight the unveiling ceremony, someone came up with the idea of inviting Kathy to unveil it. But no one could find her. Never one to court attention, Kathy had simply faded from sight in the 1960s, never having spoken publicly about her time with Paul. In an otherwise slack news period, the media joined the search for—as one publication put it—"Kathy, Paul Simon's mysterious missing muse." The BBC News even got on board. Only one journalist managed to track her down in a remote village in North Wales, but Kathy turned him away. The resulting full-page article about the encounter in the *Mail on Sunday* was able to "reveal" only "the washing on the line testifying to an ordinary life." To add to the sideshow nature of the coverage, the reporter had been looking at a neighbor's clothesline.

The issue of Kathy was still news during the Wembley engagement. During a BBC interview that week, Simon was asked if he knew of Kathy's whereabouts. Realizing a "yes" would have led to further media speculation, he opted for her privacy and said no. Unknown to the Kathy searchers, she and Ken would also attend one of Simon's English stops on all his future tours.

After more dates in Europe, Simon and the band returned to the States for his second Central Park concert. When Garfunkel heard about the show, he hoped Simon would at least bring him onstage for a number or two as a guest artist. Simon did plan to bring on a guest, but it was Olodum. *New York Times* reporter Douglas Martin interviewed Garfunkel days before the concert, and Garfunkel didn't hide his disappointment. What made the week all the more excruciating for Garfunkel was that a few days earlier, Simon had invited him and his family (his second wife, former model Kathryn Cermak, and their eight-month-old son, James) to visit him and Edie in Montauk. Garfunkel assumed Paul was going to take advantage of the occasion to ask him to sing a couple of songs at Central Park—for old times' sake, if nothing else—but it didn't happen, and Art was so crushed that he didn't bring up the issue. There's no reason, he told the reporter, to ask a question if he already knew the answer. Instead, he said, "I'm not good enough to be invited. My guess is that it would hurt his sense of stature." Not that Garfunkel hadn't been burning his bridges by taking occasional jabs at Simon in the press. In the *New York Times* interview, for instance, he implied that Simon still relied on the old Simon and Garfunkel classics to give his concerts a winning edge. "He uses them as his aces," he said.

More than 750,000 people attended the concert on the Great Lawn of Central Park, which was broadcast live on HBO and on radio, followed by a live album, *Paul Simon's Concert in the Park*, released in November 1991. Unlike his nerves the first time at Central Park, he was fully relaxed. In fact, he said he became so comfortable in front of massive crowds that when he played years later before six hundred thousand fans outside the Colosseum in Rome, he looked up during the show at the apartments that overlooked the area and wondered about their real estate value. "I was still doing the show," he said, "but as I gazed up, I thought, 'I wonder what they get for those apartments.'"

Within a week, Simon was back on the road, doing shows around the United States in August and September, followed by shows in Japan, Australia, and South America before ending the trek on December 12 in Mexico City. Then, in January, he'd finally play South Africa.

Despite Simon's returning to South Africa with the approval of the African National Congress (ANC) and being hosted at a reception in his honor by Nelson Mandela, the opening week in Johannesburg proved more traumatic than his first visit to the country. Signs of controversy began days before he arrived on Tuesday, January 7, 1992. He was scheduled to play before an estimated sixty thousand fans over two weekend shows at Ellis Park Stadium, followed by three additional South African dates before ending the swing in neighboring Botswana.

While the powerful ANC was involved in formal negotiations with the government to end apartheid, two fringe black organizations, the Azanian People's Organization (AZAPO) and the Pan-Africanist Congress of Azania (PAC), took advantage of the Born at the Right Time tour to publicize their view that the ANC wasn't being aggressive enough. "It's not Paul Simon we're after," one PAC member told Scott Kraft of the *Los Angeles Times*. "He's just been caught in the realignment of political forces." That admission didn't soften the protest language. "We are convinced that Simon has offered himself as a pawn in the political chess board to undermine the cultural boycott, which is the weapon of struggle for the oppressed," said George Ngwenya, an officer of AZAPO's youth brigade. The remarks cast a cloud over the visit.

"We had these great hopes for the week," said Dan Klores, whose relationship with Simon had grown from his crisis management role to a broader advisory capacity. "Besides the concerts, we were going to hold music clinics in the townships and give concert tickets to young people who couldn't otherwise afford them, but the moment we arrived in Johannesburg, this Azanian youth group was protesting and warning of violence at the concerts."

A hand grenade exploded outside the office of the local concert promoter the night Simon arrived, and bomb threats forced them to change hotels at three in the morning. Police guard dogs were brought in to sniff for explosives. "Finally, I said to Paul, 'What do you want to do?' " Klores said. "It wasn't an easy decision because we had responsibility for the band and crew. He asked me what I thought, and I wasn't sure. He then looked me in the eye—and I'll never forget this—he said, 'Fuck that. We're staying.' "

The controversy was front-page news all week. The *Citizen*, a progovernment daily, praised Simon in an editorial for "putting black music on the world map," but other publications warned of possible violence at the shows. In recent weeks, five policemen in townships near Johannesburg had been murdered. To ease the nerves of the touring cast and crew, Simon took a break from rehearsal in a giant tent on a soccer field to schedule a five-on-five touch football game. Simon was the quarterback of one team, Klores the other. Afterward, Simon asked Klores to set up a meeting with leaders of a youth group opposing the concert.

"He wanted to meet with the protesters and settle it all, which meant we might have to give them money, because that's what I felt this could all be about," Klores said. "So Paul comes out of the meeting with a settlement. The group was going to stop the protesting, which was great if he had only left it there, but then Paul wanted to hold a press conference so the group could announce the end of the protest. Paul thought that would help calm the tension. My first reaction was these guys aren't reliable, they might get to the microphone and turn the whole thing around. But Paul insisted on going ahead with the plan. To me, it was a reaction to all the criticism over the *Graceland* recording. I think he was shaken by that and wanted the world to know there was no more protest."

Media from around the world attended the press conference, where Simon explained how he had made peace with the protesters. Then—to the dismay of Klores—he turned the microphone over to one of the protesters. Rather than confirm what Simon had said, the protester lashed out at Simon, claiming that everything he had just said was a lie. Simon was livid. He asked the youth group leaders to come to his hotel room, where he waited with Harper and Klores. Everyone stood around anxiously, Klores said, until Simon suddenly grabbed one of the leaders and pushed him hard against the wall and shouted, "Don't you ever make me into a fucking liar again!" Everyone froze. "I thought we might have to fight our way out of the room, but the youth group members just left," Klores said. "I had never seen Paul like that. The next day, he told me he had to do it for Harper. He wanted his son to know it was important to stand up for yourself."

Security at Saturday's opening concert was so tight it was described by one reporter as unprecedented. An estimated thousand police and security guards patrolled the area, and six tanks were stationed near the front of the stadium. Everyone who passed through the gates was searched. In the end, the protest was limited to a halfhearted march by sixty to seventy picketers with placards that said, "Simon Go Home," "Liberation First, Entertainment Second," and so on. Inside the stadium, the crowd was enchanted by the music and the first chance to see an international pop star after years of boycotts. The fans were especially loud when Simon hugged Joseph Shabalala. Paul had already announced that the South African shows were dedicated to Joseph's brother and fellow Ladysmith member Headman, who had been shot dead the previous December by an off-duty white security guard in what was widely believed in the black community to be a racially motivated crime. His mission complete, Simon looked forward to heading home.

Paul and Edie had been seeing each other for more than three years when they decided in the spring of 1992 to get married. True to their nature, there was no public announcement of the May 30, 1992, wedding at the house in Montauk. Equally media shy, the pair made a vow to each other to keep their personal life outside the spotlight. Except for a few special engagements, including a benefit in Miami's Joe Robbie Stadium on November 29 that raised $1.3 million for Hurricane Andrew victims, Simon was largely off the road the rest of 1992, spending time with Edie and writing songs for his Broadway musical. They welcomed the new year with their first child, Adrian Edward, who was born in December.

Steve Martin, the actor-comedian who has collaborated with Edie on two albums and two plays, including the critically admired 2016 Broadway production *Bright Star*, feels she adjusted easily to private family life. "I once called her when I was in New York and asked her to go to lunch, but she said she had to fix lunch for her kids. That's the way she was. She was devoted to the family."

Edie prized companionship and stability as much as Simon. She and New Bohemians were already on an indefinite hiatus by the time of the wedding, chiefly because she was unhappy with the lifestyle. "I was seeing people who were older who didn't create any kind of foundation in their lives, and it scared me to death," she said. "No matter how famous and established they were or however blessed they were with great songs or long careers, if they lived alone, they lived alone. That's not the way I wanted to live."

Edie did begin work, however, in 1992 on her first solo album, initially working with another producer before turning to Simon and Halee. "Paul knew what my taste was," she said. "He knew the records I love, the records I grew up on, and he knew how to get those sounds. He was the guy I ended up trusting the most and I felt the most relaxed with." Because of delays caused by Simon's schedule, the album, *Picture Perfect Morning*, wasn't ready for release until the summer of 1994. Though reviews were largely positive, the collection reached only no. 68, partially because Edie refused to tour. She didn't want to leave Adrian.

Simon resumed performing in a big way in 1993—with Art Garfunkel. The reunion started off as simply another one-off benefit concert on March 1 at the Dorothy Chandler Pavilion in Los Angeles to raise $1 million to help extend the Children's Health Fund mobile clinic program to Los Angeles County. This meant that the fleet of medical vans was now serving about 8 percent of the nation's estimated homeless children, Simon said proudly in an interview with Chuck Philips of the *Los Angeles Times.* Though he disliked protesting with his music, he felt free to comment outside of his lyrics. The *Graceland* experience had toughened him.

"Everybody agrees that little innocent kids should not have to suffer," he said. "At first, when I looked at how terrible the problem was, it seemed overwhelming. I thought, 'Well, why doesn't the government fix it, or the corporations or somebody else?' During the Reagan and Bush years, the country seemed to completely lose touch with the concept of idealism. Like the word *liberal*, people just made fun of it. We were seeing third world poverty right in the midst of extraordinary wealth, but for the longest time, nobody was measuring the damage to the nation. It wasn't like people were unaware of it. You couldn't miss it. There they were . . . homeless people . . . living right in front of us on the street. But nobody did anything."

At the Pavilion, Simon and Garfunkel not only teamed nicely but also joined Neil Young on backing vocals on his "Helpless" and "Only Love Can Break Your Heart," while Young later played electric guitar on "The Sound of Silence." The benefit went so well that Simon was open to doing more shows with Garfunkel, including a series of concerts in New York in October, that had, for Simon, the added benefit of promoting the late-September release by Warner Bros. of a three-CD boxed set that would salute his long career.

The concerts, a ten-night run at the 5,500-capacity Paramount Theater in the Madison Square Garden complex, were designed along the same retrospective lines as the boxed set. Because Garfunkel would again, in essence, be a special guest rather than a true costar, Simon called him personally to explain the concept of the shows, which were given the unusually grandiose name "Event of a Lifetime." The duo would open the show with a dozen or so songs; then Simon would take over for a longer set (joined variously by Ladysmith Black Mambazo and the gospel group Mighty Clouds of Joy) before Garfunkel returned to close the concert with "Bridge Over Troubled Water."

Things got off to a good start when the ten shows sold out so quickly that Simon and Garfunkel agreed to add eleven more nights at the Paramount and five stadium dates, including Toronto, Singapore, and Tokyo, which were redesigned to focus on the Simon and Garfunkel years. In his *New York Times* review of the opening-night show at the Paramount, critic Jon Pareles couldn't have been more praiseworthy—of Simon. "No other American songwriter of his generation," the review declared, "has so consistently renewed himself while still acting his age. He's the rare pop songwriter who admits to maturity while keeping his eyes and ears open."

The review was mostly dismissive of Garfunkel. Pareles wrote, "Mr. Garfunkel turned out to be just one of a large supporting cast of Mr. Simon's collaborators and fellow singers." According to Simon, Garfunkel was hurt and accused Simon of having encouraged Pareles to write a negative review.

The atmosphere backstage after that was hostile. Joseph Rascoff, Paul's business manager, literally had to position himself between Simon's and Garfunkel's dressing rooms to guard against trouble. "One or two times, I genuinely believed that if there had been a knife on the table, one of them would have used it," Rascoff said years later. "They never came to blows, but there was shoving, and I had to step between them. And this was in the middle of this great run of shows."

Simon recalled the incident that led to the backstage shoving. "During one song, I think it was 'The Boxer,' I made a mistake over when to come in, and it threw Artie off for a second," he said. "But it was an accident; it wasn't intentional. So later, we're singing 'Feelin' Groovy,' and suddenly Art just stops singing at the part that goes 'Life, I love you,' and I'm just left there by myself, trying to figure out what to do. I assumed it was another mistake—no big deal. But then at intermission, Art comes up to me and says, 'You tried to make me look like a fool on "The Boxer," ' and I said, 'No, Artie, it was a mistake. Mistakes happen, just like you forgot to do "Life, I love you." ' That's when he looked me in the eye and said, 'I didn't forget. I just wanted you to see what it feels like to be made a fool of.' "

That's when they went at each other. Simon described the incident as "ugly—the most vicious fight, verbally, at least, that I had in my life." Simon and Garfunkel managed to get through the tour, but they wouldn't tour again together for ten years. In fact, Simon wouldn't tour at all for six years. He was ready to write a musical of the story he had been thinking about for more than three decades.

CHAPTER NINETEEN

Unlike the ego-driven motivation behind *One-Trick Pony*, *The Capeman* was from the start a more heartfelt endeavor. It brought together several of Simon's passions, including Latin music, a message of redemption, and the challenge of testing himself on Broadway. When he shared his dream with friends, they virtually all warned him that theater audiences weren't likely to warm to the story of the brutal 1959 Capeman murders. But Simon wasn't about to stop now.

Salvador Agron, sixteen, was a member of the Vampires street gang, which was planning to attack a mostly Irish gang, the Norsemen, when they came across two teenagers they mistook for members of that gang. Agron stabbed the youths to death and raced away. The crimes came amid a growing outrage in the city over juvenile delinquency. Declaring a need for drastic action, the magistrate who arraigned Agron said it was getting "very monotonous when you see these young punks come before us. The rights of the people are being neglected. It's high time we all got together and did something quickly."

While the case was a natural for the tabloids, Agron's comments stood out even in the gray, normally unruffled pages of the *New York Times*. Waiting outside police headquarters on the way to court for arraignment, he was surrounded by reporters who wanted to know if he was sorry for the murders. "That's for me to know and you to find out," he responded. When a reporter asked Agron about the killing, the teenager snapped, "I feel like killing you; that's what I feel like."

While some notables, including former First Lady Eleanor Roosevelt, eventually pleaded for leniency, most of New York saw the youngster as evil incarnate and applauded when he was convicted on both counts of murder on July 21, 1960, making him the youngest person ever sentenced to death in New York State. As he headed to Sing Sing prison, most thought the case was closed. Yet the story didn't end there. In 1962, one week before Agron was to go to the electric chair, Governor Nelson Rockefeller commuted his sentence to life in prison. Fourteen years of good behavior later, New York governor Hugh Carey reduced the sentence, paving the way for a 1979 parole. Agron, who became a born-again Christian and earned a college degree, subsequently worked to combat juvenile delinquency. He died of pneumonia in 1986 at age forty-two.

Simon began seriously exploring the musical in late 1987 when he got together with Carlos Ortiz, the friend who, along with Bobby Susser, was an inspiration for "Me and Julio Down by the Schoolyard." Ortiz, who had made a documentary film about the Latin and black music scenes in New York, introduced Simon to people who knew Agron in prison. He also took Simon to Puerto Rico to meet Agron's mother, Esmeralda, who spoke of a dream about seeing her son enter heaven. Simon turned the story into a song, "Esmeralda's Dream," one of the musical's most memorable numbers. Ortiz and Simon also spent hours going through old Spanish-language newspapers to learn about the Latino perspective on the Capeman case, and they could be found several nights in New York clubs listening to some of the city's finest Latin musicians.

Absorbed, Simon set about writing songs, a process that continued, except for breaks for the Born at the Right Time and Event of a Lifetime tours, well into the next decade. The plan was to tell the story largely through songs, opening the musical with Agron's parole and then telling his early life through flashbacks, careful to include the context of the racial, economic, and judicial attitudes of the time.

By 1994, Simon was recruiting studio and club musicians to record the songs for the musical—a process that cost an estimated $1 million and stretched over nearly five years. Because of the massive amount of time involved, he used Andy Smith to engineer the album rather than Halee, who was still based in San Francisco and committed to projects there. Halee did eventually get involved with the album and was listed as coproducer, along with Oscar Hernandez, a pianist and arranger whose parents were from Puerto Rico. Hernandez, the show's musical director, and a few other musicians met almost daily with Simon in his home studio on Central Park West. They generally worked for eight hours, trying to build a musical base—or harmonic structures—as Simon had done for *Graceland* and *The Rhythm of the Saints*.

Then everything stopped for Simon.

On January 19, 1995, Lou Simon died in his sleep at his home in Englewood Cliffs, New Jersey. The cause was heart arrhythmia, but Paul would later say his father's whole body was a wreck—everything except "his extraordinary mind." Lou was seventy-nine. Simon, in Saint Lucia with Derek Walcott discussing *The Capeman*, chartered a flight home and went into a period of deep reflection.

"My father was a sympathetic character," Paul said twenty years later, still visibly emotional. "I think it was because he was hurt very young. My mother grew up in a family of six, and her parents lived into their eighties, but my father didn't have that sense of security. His father died when he was sixteen. When that happens, some people become bitter, but I think it gave my father this strong sense of empathy. I sometimes wonder if some of that didn't come from my grandfather's death. I have my grandfather's name and his genetic code, but I know nothing about him. I never got to go to the zoo with him or a baseball game. That's a big piece of my life missing. Who knows what it means? I was so close to my father, yet he never got the chance to say, 'Hey, Dad, this is your grandson.' My father was always reaching out to people who had problems; a really willing problem solver. I'm not sure I sensed it until years later, but I eventually began to see how he felt and how I shared those feelings."

Watching his father struggle against the heart problems and cancer gave Simon a perspective on death. "He was taking his weekly dialysis treatment at the hospital when he became unconscious, probably from the heart problems," Simon said. "The machines he was connected to immediately alerted the nurses, who gave him a shot of adrenaline, and he woke up. He said he didn't remember anything and was surprised to see everyone standing around him. If the nurses hadn't given him the shot, he would have died then—and what struck me is he had no fear of death. It was, he said, nothing."

Three months after saying goodbye to his father, Paul and Edie celebrated the birth of their second child, and they named her Lulu after Lou. For Paul, her arrival made his family all the more important to him. He loved being with Edie and the kids, though that didn't mean he lost his drive to make music. Hernandez was impressed that Simon wouldn't settle for something general in a Latin style, but asked about specific rhythms, such as *bomba* or *plena* or *aguinaldo*. As musicians built a base, Simon would sit with his guitar and try to find chord structures that led to a song. When Simon felt the songs were ready, he shifted to SIR Studios in Manhattan, where he and Hernandez worked with an eleven-piece band to flesh out the material that would then be transferred to the stage.

For Simon, the path to Broadway was a lot like his routine in the pop world, and that worked fine when he was recording the music for *The Capeman*, but his reluctance to share control in other aspects of the production would again prove to be a major problem. Rather than turn to experienced Broadway figures to assist him in developing the play, he pieced together his own team. Hernandez, for instance, had no Broadway experience—Simon hired him after admiring his production work on Eddie Torres's 1994 album *Dance City*, which blended smart jazz orchestration and classic Afro-Cuban music.

All this was in dramatic contrast to the normal way of doing business on Broadway, as Stephen J. Dubner chronicled in a detailed behind-the-scenes piece on the making of *The Capeman* that ran in the *New York Times Magazine* shortly before the show's Broadway opening in 1998. The problems, Dubner suggested, were with Simon's recordings of his songs for the musical. "These tapes became the armature for the Broadway show," wrote Dubner, who followed the production for two years. "Instead of delivering a script and a score for a director, Simon's plan was to essentially turn over a finished version of a musical, which a band and cast would then try to replicate. This was the first signal that Paul . . . felt no compunction to play by Broadway rules."

When Simon finally began interviewing potential directors, there was a sense of déjà vu for those who remembered the *One-Trick Pony* experience: big-name directors were wary because they feared the play would be governed by Simon's vision, not theirs. "At least," one of those familiar with the saga said wryly, "he didn't cast himself in the lead role again." Indeed, the show's casting proved—along with the music—to be one of the production's strong points. The lead character would be played by two talented stars of Latin music. Marc Anthony, a singer with family roots in Puerto Rico, would be the young Salvador Agron, while Ruben Blades, the widely respected singer-songwriter-activist who ran unsuccessfully for president in his native Panama in 1994, would assume the role of the older Salvador.

"I was a fan of Paul's as soon as I heard 'The Sound of Silence' as a boy," Blades said, "but the song that meant the most to me was 'Me and Julio Down by the Schoolyard,' because he used a Latino character in the song, which you almost never heard in popular music. I was so proud. It was like finally being welcomed to the party. My only concern about the musical was how Paul could turn that dark theme into a Broadway show."

Simon also enlisted his friend Derek Walcott, this time as a cowriter both for lyrics to individual songs and the book for the play. Walcott didn't have Broadway experience, but he at least had run his own theater workshop in Trinidad. The collaboration went through rocky periods, but their mutual respect kept them together—until they finally broke apart in the last, stressful stages of production. The final credits read, "Music by Paul

Simon. Lyrics and Book by Paul Simon and Derek Walcott." Walcott felt those credits were too generous because, he said, Simon had already written many of the songs and even much of the first draft of the play before he came on board. Years later, Walcott said about *The Capeman*, "My approach was he should have full rein to express himself, even if I didn't necessarily find the direction he was heading was right. It was his play, not mine. I did make a few suggestions—a word here, a word there—but I was more interested in the play than the music."

As time went on, Simon's failure to name a director caused alarm among the brain trust he had assembled to handle various production functions— most urgently fund-raising. The team included Dan Klores (who now operated his own firm, with a client list that included Simon and Lorne Michaels), Peter Parcher (Simon's longtime attorney and a top litigator), and Joseph Rascoff. In turn, they helped bring in James L. Nederlander Jr., the celebrated theater owner and producer; concert promoter Michael Cohl, who'd worked with the Rolling Stones and U2; and Brad Grey, a successful television producer and future president of Paramount Pictures. But these backers provided only a fraction of the funding needed. To help things move forward, Simon put up a chunk of his own money.

"For Paul, the whole thing was about the music," Rascoff said. "He never really thought about the staging and stuff. I kept saying to Paul, 'We need a director, and it would help if you had an experienced producer.' But he wouldn't give up one iota of control, which made it very difficult to raise money. If someone's going to write a check, they want to know who's in control, and if you tell them that the creator is in control, that's a danger sign."

The thing that kept everyone involved was a mixture of their faith in Simon and their unbending love of the show's music. "It's the best music you'd heard on Broadway in twenty to twenty-five years," said Parcher. "We were all just in such awe of what he was doing. We also saw all the resistance he ran into, and we wanted to help him get this music heard."

The music was indeed powerful, as Simon fused the fifties tradition of youthful doo-wop and various Latin street styles with a bold commentary. "Adios Hermanos" was one of the show's standouts, a sweeping panorama of emotions that showed young Agron reflecting on his troubled life while heading to the courthouse to be sentenced to death. It's an evocative mix of the innocence of doo-wop and the desperation of life in crisis.

> *Well, I entered the courtroom*
> *State of New York, County of New York*
> *Just some spic*
> *They scrubbled off the sidewalk*
> *Guilty by my dress*
> *Guilty in the press*

In tracing the story, Simon injected the music with sentiments that were tender, urgent, lustful, and combative—from youthful romanticism in "Satin Summer Nights" and "Quality," to a more forceful attitude in "The Vampires" to convey the reality of gang life. Before Agron's story ends, we meet others, from fellow inmates to prison guards, who debate his motives and his rights, but the most touching moment is "Can I Forgive Him?" Framed as a conversation between Esmeralda and the mothers of the two slain teenagers, Salvador's mother asks for understanding and forgiveness. In their responses, Simon presents a hard-line attitude and a more sympathetic one, representative of the divisions in society.

Finally, in the spring of 1996, Simon hired a director: not the experienced Broadway hand that his advisors wanted, but Susana Tubert, a native of Argentina who had directed Off-Broadway productions by Latino authors. The plan was that she'd work toward a ten-week workshop rehearsal at the Westbeth Theatre Center in New York in October, while Simon and Walcott continued to work on the troubled script. The musical would then open in Chicago in July 1997 and move to Broadway in the fall. Tubert lasted barely three months, during which there was tension between her and Simon and Walcott. "It was like somebody was going to take the project away from them and destroy it," she said. Next, the post went to Eric Simonson, a director from the Steppenwolf Theatre in Chicago, where he'd directed a musical featuring, of all people, Ladysmith Black Mambazo. But he, too, didn't last out the year.

The production budget, according to Rascoff, was $8 million, a high figure for Broadway at the time, and eventually soared to $13 million before being brought back to the $11 million range. By now, there was finger-pointing all around the inner circle. Relations between Simon and Rascoff became so strained that the business manager quit.

While he searched for a permanent director, Simon asked Mark Morris, the show's choreographer, to take over the director's role, though Morris, too, had no experience as a director. To save money, the Chicago performances, which could have helped address weak spots in the show, were cancelled. The play would roll the dice by going straight to Broadway. Previews were to start December 1, with the formal opening night on January 8, 1998. Simon was not pleased with the previews and, after consulting with director Mike Nichols and others, finally accepted an experienced Broadway director to help whip things into shape. He was four-time Tony Award winner Jerry Zaks, who agreed to work in "an unofficial capacity," leaving Morris as director in the show's official credits.

To give everyone more time, the play's formal opening was moved back to January 29. Zaks found the script "incoherent," he said years later, and was "horrified" when Walcott told him that he had always thought the play should have been about the mother. "It's no wonder the book was such a mess," Zaks said. "He and Paul weren't on the same page." It was shortly after that meeting that Walcott left *The Capeman*, feeling that Simon had essentially caved in to Broadway. Time was so short that Zaks had to focus on the musical's first act, trimming it by some thirty minutes, which speeded up things considerably and brought the production's total length under three hours. Privately, most of the brain trust was still in panic mode.

Adding to the pressures, relatives of murdered children were protesting all the attention being paid to a convicted murderer. Rose Lauria, whose daughter, Donna Lauria, was killed in the infamous Son of Sam murders two decades earlier, told reporters, "They don't know what we're feeling. It's been twenty-one years, and I'm still going through therapy. Why should people make money on something like this?"

In an interview with Bob Herbert, an op-ed columnist for the *New*

York Times, Simon defended himself. "I don't mean to brush aside the victims, or in any way suggest that the pain of their families is not immense and lifelong, and that they do not have a very powerful case," he said. "In fact, I am going to express their case as articulately and as touchingly and as beautifully as I can. Nevertheless, I want to bring your attention back to the possibility of redemption for this person. If, at the end of this play, a person comes out and says, 'I don't care, I still feel Salvador Agron was a worthless guy'—okay. But I insist upon—not that I can actually enforce this—but I insist upon an honest examination of the question. As unpopular as that is."

On the show's opening night at the Marquis Theatre on West Forty-Sixth Street, Simon was not optimistic. Neither was Zaks. "The story was very hard to follow," Zaks said. "Instead of a play, you had a concept album. When you add the lighting problems opening night, it would have been better if you had closed your eyes and listened to the music."

In the *New York Times*, Ben Brantley had good things to say about the music, as did most critics. "Intricately weaving Latin American rhythms and inflections with the doo-wop harmonies in vogue in the 1950s, these songs have a contemplative, sensuous elegance all their own and remain a pleasure to listen to," he wrote. On the larger question of the production itself, Brantley's remarks were about as dark as anyone could have imagined. "For those who regard theatergoing as blood sport, it promised to be the event of the season," he declared. "A budget of $11 million; a world-famous composer new to the Broadway musical and openly contemptuous of its traditions; a protracted period of previews replete with tales of desperate last-minute revisions; a parade of advice-dispensing show doctors: *The Capeman*, Paul Simon's pop-operatic retelling of a street-gang murder in 1959, seemed to have all the elements that make theater-disaster cultists drool."

That paragraph alone would have been enough to make most potential ticket buyers think twice. The following paragraph was, in effect, a death knell: "But it would take a hard-core sadist to derive pleasure from the sad, benumbed spectacle that finally opened last night at the Marquis Theatre, three weeks behind schedule. Although it may be unparalleled in its wholescale squandering of illustrious talents, *The Capeman* is no fun even as a target."

Ruben Blades was stunned by the harshness of the critical attacks. "It wasn't just that the critics didn't like the play, they took glee in twisting the knife over and over again," he said in 2016. "I felt so bad for Paul. I was so proud of him. It was like 'Me and Julio' all over again. He had brought a Latino story and Latino music to Broadway."

Simon was so nervous that, as usual, he didn't read the reviews. After the performance, he headed home with Edie, but he knew things were not good when he woke around ten the next morning. "I knew we got killed because nobody had called," he said. He returned to the theater that night to thank the cast. As the production limped on, everyone involved hoped that the public would step forward and miraculously embrace the musical—the ultimate Broadway happy ending. But it didn't happen. In late February Simon met with his *Capeman* business team to discuss the future of the musical. The recommendation was to close immediately. "Absolutely not," Simon replied. "We're going another month." When the decision was announced, much of the Broadway Establishment saw it as an ultimate ego move. Couldn't he see the play was doomed from the beginning? Why is he going to force the cast and crew to suffer through another month of the production?

But Oscar Hernandez scoffed at that view. He was proud of Simon. "He knew he was going to lose money keeping *The Capeman* going; maybe as much as an additional eight hundred thousand dollars, but he didn't care," Hernandez said. "He had this amazing cast that had worked so hard. He didn't want to tell them, 'Hey, it's over.' If he would have done that, everyone's heart would have been crushed. Instead, Paul wanted us all to be onstage with that wonderful music for a few more weeks."

Shortly after, Vincent Canby, the *New York Times* film-critic-turned-drama-critic, checked in with a second look at *The Capeman*. While the tone of the piece was much less hostile than Brantley's, the evaluation was again negative. "As a show, *The Capeman* is a great album," he wrote. Similarly, Greg Evans wrote in *Variety* that "the music ranks among the best Broadway scores of this or any recent season, an exquisite blend of salsa, 1950s American doo-wop, and Simon's own impeccable artistry." But he dismissed the book as "irredeemable." A positive spin came from an editorial in *El Diario*, New York's Spanish-language newspaper. Calling *The Capeman* the most important Broadway theatrical event ever for the city's Latino community, the editorial praised the musical for "denounc- ing the circumstances that surrounded the case of Salvador Agron— circumstances that still exist" and "capturing the essence of our culture. The teary Latino eyes we've seen at the end of each performance are the best evidence."

After sixty-eight performances, the end for the musical came on March 28, and the Broadway Establishment, which was offended by Si- mon's refusal to play by their rules, couldn't have been happier. "Normally in the theater community, people feel bad when they see someone whose production has just failed," declared Rocco Landesman, president of Ju- jamcyn Theaters and future chairman of the National Endowment for the Arts. "But I think there is a feeling about Paul Simon that it couldn't have happened to a nicer guy."

In the following weeks, all sorts of possibilities were floated, including plans for a cast album and a national concert tour featuring Simon singing selected songs from the play. But neither happened. The only spin-off was *Songs from The Capeman*, a Warner Bros. album featuring Simon sing- ing several songs from the show, but it didn't find an audience amid the negativity surrounding the production. When the Tony nominations were announced in May, *The Capeman* only picked up one mention: Simon and Walcott for Best Original Score. The Tony went to Stephen Flaherty and Lynn Ahrens for *Ragtime*.

The Capeman cost Simon around $6 million, but the emotional toll was far greater. Again, he took responsibility. "I thought it would be great to get Derek to work with me, but that premise was a mistake," he said. "What I really needed was someone who had experience in writing the book—the story—and Derek wasn't that guy. We ended up going in differ- ent directions. Then I made another major mistake in not bringing in an experienced director who could keep the story moving forward; a direc- tor who would tell us, 'That's a great song, but we can't use it because we already knew that piece of information. We need songs that keep the story moving for the audience.' Together, those mistakes were fatal."

High among them, he felt, was not showing proper respect for Broadway tradition. "When you go into a new neighborhood, say an Irish or Italian neighborhood, I learned as a kid that the first thing you do is show respect for the people in the neighborhood," Simon reflected. "You were a guest, you had to act properly—don't try to pick up the girls from that neighborhood or don't act like a wise guy, because you'll get beat up. When I went into Broadway, I didn't purposely try to offend anyone, but I just wasn't paying attention to what the neighborhood politics were."

PART SIX

Questions for
the Angels

CHAPTER TWENTY

Simon was fifty-six when *The Capeman* closed, making it a natural time to pause and think about the future. He had been a major recording artist for nearly thirty-four years. Most of the other great songwriters from the 1960s and early 1970s were either inactive or in serious creative decline. While working on *The Capeman*, Simon, too, had been thinking about a life without more albums and tours. If the musical had been a success, he told himself at one point, he would write another one. When *The Capeman* failed, he turned again to albums, though he knew it would take time to regain his confidence and direction.

"When you spend five years of your career on something, and it is trashed in one night, it takes a long time to regain your balance," he said. "For a while, you don't do anything because you can't. I wouldn't call it depression. I didn't throw a blanket over my head, but I needed time to heal. Not only did I lose my friendship with Derek, I lost my reputation for the moment. That doesn't mean I thought it was the end of my career. But it's like Steve Martin always used to say, 'You don't know that you're out of show business until five years after you're out.' Nobody tells you, 'Oh, I'm not calling you anymore,' but the phone stops ringing. When you have a flop, everybody leaves except your closest friends. One great thing was Gabriel was born just a month after the show closed."

Thanks to Edie and the kids, Simon was in a far different place in his personal life in 1998 than he had been in the aftermath of *One-Trick Pony*. "He would play with the kids for hours, and Edie grounded him," observed Bobby Susser. "She brought a strong element of common sense. She was his stability and his rock."

Simon's spirits were also lifted by ayahuasca, the hallucinogenic from South America that he had begun using in earnest during the final, stressful months of *The Capeman*. After the musical closed, he continued to consume the substance in a controlled fashion—not daily, like pot is often used, but every few weeks. Ayahuasca, which is made by mixing various plants and can either be eaten or brewed into a form of tea, can be traced to the sixteenth century, when Christian missionaries from Spain and Portugal came across it while exploring remote regions of South America. In recent years, it has been debated in medical circles, called both dangerous and a possible alternative to medical marijuana. It also has found favor in limited celebrity and Silicon Valley circles, leading to write-ups in mainstream publications, from the *New Yorker* to *Vogue*.

Simon tried to approach ayahuasca humbly as a spiritual experience. Initially, he would get up around five in the morning, eat the plant with a male friend, and say some prayers of thanks while waiting an hour for its effect. "The feeling was almost indescribable," Simon said. "You couldn't imagine feeling any better, and the afterglow would last for days. It also enabled me to hear new sounds in my head, which led to me being able to write songs much faster than before."

He described the calming qualities in the opening lines of "Quiet," a song that would be on his next album:

I am heading for a time of quiet
When my restlessness is past

And I can lie down on my blanket
And release my fists at last
I am heading for a time of solitude
Of peace without illusions
When the perfect circle
Marries all beginnings and conclusions

"The reference to releasing fists is in part about how people tend to get more peaceful with themselves as they get older," he said. "But the song is also about being on guard your whole life, being ready to compete or fight. It's a certain physical awareness I always had about people saying, 'You're not good enough.' It's something that seems to be going on more than ever on the internet. People are ripping each other apart all the time." Other new songs covered a wide thematic range, from the racial profiling commentary of "Pigs, Sheep and Wolves," to the philosophical questioning of "Señorita with a Necklace of Tears."

The new album's title number, "You're the One," was another love song, which opens with what had become a frequent element in Simon's writing—the self-questioning of the third line. The first verse:

May twelve angels guard you
While you sleep
Maybe that's a waste of angels, I don't know
I'd do anything to keep you safe
From the danger that surrounds us

"The twelve angels refer to the twelve gates to the city of Jerusalem, and it's what I meant, but then I look at the line and say, 'Maybe that's a waste of angels,' because it might be, but it's still what I wanted because that's how I felt," Simon explained. "That's something you find in several of my songs: a line and then a reaction to the line. It's something I find useful, but it's probably more a part of my later songwriting than the earlier."

Simon was still in this holding pattern in June 1998 when the Songwriters Hall of Fame saluted him with its most prestigious citation at a dinner in Manhattan. Named after the lyricist of songs such as "Blues in the Night" and "One for My Baby (and One More for the Road)," the Johnny Mercer Award had been given since 1981, but Simon, tellingly, was the first writer with rock 'n' roll ties to receive it.

Meanwhile, as Simon worked on songs for the new album, he knew he was going back to a much different music scene than in the days of *Graceland* and *Saints*. Where Madonna, Prince, and Michael Jackson were dominant new forces in the 1980s, the pop scene in the age of TV's *American Idol* welcomed a new crop of stars, most of whom leaned more toward entertainment and spectacle than the artful songwriting tradition of the 1960s and 1970s. If that sea change meant veterans like Simon would no longer be able to compete in the race for massive airplay and platinum sales, he could reach for listeners in the small but valuable radio format of Americana as well as speak to the body of fans who kept coming out to see him in concert. Above all, he still had his passion to make music.

Moving forward, Simon began putting together a new band and found two talented musicians who would remain with him for years: Mark Stewart, whom he spotted in a production of William Shakespeare's *Twelfth Night* at Lincoln Center, and Jamey Haddad, who was recommended by a friend. Simon was so impressed by Stewart's versatility (guitar, cello, wind instruments, and banjo were just the start) and his obsession with sound (he designed and built more than four hundred instruments) that he eventually named the Wisconsin native his bandleader. Haddad was a world-class percussionist from Ohio with a deep background in jazz and world music. He was playing the Arabic darbuka drum and Western trap drums at age four. Haddad, in turn, introduced Simon to a second percussionist, Steve Shehan, who also had been heavily influenced by world music. After bringing back drummer Steve Gadd to contribute traditional pop-rock elements to the African rhythms that had dominated his music in *Graceland* and *Saints*, Simon's plan was to make percussion the foundation of the new album. Over the next several months, he filled out the band with, among others, two more old favorites: guitarist Vincent Nguini and bassist Bakithi Kumalo.

During the fall of 1998 and the following spring, Simon's primary public presence was two essays for the *New York Times*'s op-ed pages. Just as he did in his songs, he wove pieces of his own experience and beliefs into the columns. But he didn't seem to have the same quality control in his prose as he had in his songwriting. For instance, the first column, in September, was in honor of the hundredth anniversary of the birth of composer George Gershwin, and some found it unseemly when Simon linked the struggles surrounding the original Broadway production of Gershwin's *Porgy and Bess* with those he faced with *Graceland*. His underlying point, however, was valid: the importance of artists stretching cultural boundaries. In a column the following March, he mourned the death of Joe DiMaggio for a tendency they both shared: the desire to keep their personal lives private.

Seven weeks after the DiMaggio column, Simon put on a Yankees cap and headed with his guitar to center field in Yankee Stadium to sing "Mrs. Robinson" before more than fifty thousand fans and a generous outpouring of former Yankees players. It was Joe DiMaggio Day, and the occasion meant so much to Simon that he kept a photo of himself waving to the crowd on his office wall for years. It was one of twenty baseball photos or pieces of memorabilia (including a Mickey Mantle bat and a photo of the Mick with his arm around Paul) in the office.

"I have performance anxiety in dreams a couple of weeks before I'm going on tour, where the microphones don't work, or I forget my guitar," Simon said. "But I rarely have butterflies in my stomach before a show. Except that day my heart was racing. I had thought about the song, and I realized everybody was waiting for the DiMaggio verse, but I couldn't just sing that. So I compromised by taking out one verse so I'd get to the line faster, and fortunately it worked well. I didn't make any mistakes. I was in tune. I was even invited to go with the family out to the unveiling of his monument in the stadium. It is one of my favorite memories."

By the time of DiMaggio Day, Simon and the band were working on new songs, including "Darling Lorraine," a six-and-a-half-minute reflection on a marriage in which neither party is sure what's holding them together. The song helped Simon regain his musical pulse. He had liked the title ever since hearing it in an old doo-wop record by a group called the Knockouts. As usual, he had no idea where the story would lead when he wrote the first line, which was about a young woman catching a guy's eye. He created the narrative line by line—an example of how he "discovers" the story and theme as he goes along. As usual, he came up with the line and then asked himself what that line suggested. He was as surprised as any listener when Lorraine suddenly dies. But that twist gave the song its touching edge. In "Darling Lorraine," the relationship rotates from infatuation, to regret, to affection, to resentment, to adoration, to the sudden loss and accompanying anguish, with Simon constantly pointing to moments of selfishness and delusion. The language is conversational, complete with deliberate clichés and overriding stereotypes to give the story a basic, everyman frame. Decades later, he would call it one of his favorite sets of lyrics.

The first time I saw her
I couldn't be sure
But the sin of impatience
Said, "She's just what you're looking for"
So I walked right up to her
And with the part of me that talks
I introduced myself as Frank
From New York, New York
She's so hot
She's so cool
I'm not
I'm just a fool in love with darling Lorraine

All my life I've been a wanderer
Not really, I mostly lived near my parents' home
Anyway, Lorraine and I got married
And the usual marriage stuff
Then one day she says to me

From out of the blue
She says, "Frank, I've had enough
Romance is a heartbreaker
I'm not meant to be a homemaker
And I'm tired of being darling Lorraine"

What—you don't love me anymore?
What—you're walking out the door?
What—you don't like the way I chew?
Hey, let me tell you
You're not the woman that I wed
You say you're depressed but you're not
You just like to stay in bed
I don't need you, darling Lorraine
Darling Lorraine
Lorraine
I long for your love

Financially speaking
I guess I'm a washout
Everybody's buy and sell
And sell and buy
And that's what the whole thing's all about

If it had not been for Lorraine
I'd have left here long ago
I should have been a musician
I love the piano
She's so light
She's so free
I'm tight, well, that's me
But I feel so good
With darling Lorraine

On Christmas morning Frank awakes
To find Lorraine has made a stack of pancakes
They watch the television, husband and wife
All afternoon, It's a Wonderful Life

What—you don't love me anymore?
What—you're walking out the door?
What—you don't like the way I chew?
Hey, let me tell you
You're not the woman that I wed
Gimme my robe, I'm going back to bed
I'm sick to death of you, Lorraine

Darling Lorraine
Lorraine
Her hands like wood
The doctor was smiling
But the news wasn't good

Darling Lorraine
Please don't leave me yet
I know you're in pain
Pain you can't forget
Your breathing is like an echo of our love
Maybe I'll go down to the corner store
And buy us something sweet
Here's an extra blanket honey
To wrap around your feet
All the trees were washed with April rain
And the moon in the meadow
Took darling Lorraine

"Once again, I was writing to a track we had already put together," Simon said. "I started off with this line, 'The first time I saw her, I couldn't be sure,' and I remembered a phrase in my notes, 'the sin of impatience,' and that seemed interesting. Where's this going? Then comes, 'She's just what you're looking for,' which shows the guy's making a hasty decision. So, I think about him walking right up to her and introducing himself 'with the part of him that talks,' which is just a funny way of saying it. I'm just having fun. I called him Frank because my doorman in New York was named Frank. He's 'Frank from New York, New York,' which is another joke because no one says they're from 'New York, New York.' If they are from Buffalo, they might add 'New York,' but not someone from New York City. They just say 'New York.' Then we throw in some songwriter clichés: 'She's so hot. She's so cool.' At this point, I still don't know where I'm going.

"Then I start off the second verse with, 'All my life I've been a wanderer,' which is another cliché—the way we romanticize about ourselves—and now I say to myself, 'Enough bullshit.' It was time to turn things around and get a little reality into the story, so I have the guy say, no, he's not really a wanderer at all. In fact, he still lives near his parents' home. And then, wham, they get married, which is like a big jump because he's just met her. They don't really even know each other, and, sure enough, Lorraine tells him one day that she's had enough. We're through with the clichés now. We're dealing with real emotions. She doesn't want to be married anymore. It's too hard.

"Frank is offended, and he fights back. 'Let me tell you, you're not the woman that I wed.' Before, he had been accepting; the fact is, Frank isn't frank at all. There's not much to him. He's a nonthinker. He says he doesn't need Lorraine, and then he realizes what he's said, and he longs for her love. It opens his heart, and he becomes defensive and quickly changes the subject to finances. He says he's a washout. By now, they've met, they got married, they have a big fight, he realizes he really does love her, and he admits he's not a successful guy. And the next part of the music, which again was written before the lyrics, was so sweet, almost saccharin sweet, so I write in a sweet scene: Christmas morning, with pancakes and watching *It's a Wonderful Life*.

"But they're soon fighting again, and suddenly he says, 'I'm sick to death of you, Lorraine.' As soon as I came up with that line, I stopped and took a deep breath. I thought, 'Oh, my God, she's going to die.' So we have the doctor smiling, but the news wasn't good. In my mind, it was cancer or something. It's all so sudden, and he realizes how much he does love Lorraine and how much he needs her. What can he do? The only thing he can think of is going to the store and buying something sweet for her. But first he takes out a blanket to wrap around her feet. He's helpless, and it's so devastating. He is left with the rain and the funeral images. Lorraine is gone."

While working on "Darling Lorraine" in the spring of 1999, Simon decided to reintroduce himself to live audiences with a summer arena tour. Uncertain about his drawing power after the *Capeman* publicity and wondering if he was up physically to a two-hour set after the seven-year break, he wanted to team up with another top artist, which meant he'd only have to be onstage just over an hour—and it turned out Bob Dylan was interested. It was a bold pairing that caught the imagination of the rock world. The *Los Angeles Times* declared it "the Heavyweight Summit." Despite the early rivalry, Simon and Dylan enjoyed going over ideas for the tour, including a possible segment where they would come out with acoustic guitars and just do folk songs like the old days in clubs. But they ended up doing more conventional sets and simply shared the microphone at one point on some mutual favorites.

At the June 20 stop at the Arrowhead Pond arena in Anaheim, California, the audience rose en masse as Simon walked onstage at the end of Dylan's seventy-five-minute opening set. The cheering grew even louder when Dylan began picking the opening notes of "The Sound of Silence" on his guitar. As Simon joined with his guitar, the performers stepped to the microphones to sing "Silence," followed by versions of Johnny Cash's "I Walk the Line," Elvis Presley's take on Bill Monroe's "Blue Moon of Kentucky," and Dylan's "Knockin' on Heaven's Door." In other cities, they substituted "The Boxer," Bob's "Forever Young," and Dion's old hit "The Wanderer." It was disarming to see these two largely private figures onstage together trying to find common ground after their sometimes prickly competition. The harmonies weren't pristine. Still, they enjoyed the experience, especially the night near the end of the tour when Dylan whispered to Simon near the end of "The Sound of Silence," "On a scale of ten, how do I compare to Artie?" Paul broke up laughing.

In mid-September Simon headed home from the tour with more than good memories. He thought he might have found a final player for the business team he had been putting together since *The Capeman*. He had originally met Jeff Kramer, who worked closely with Dylan, including overseeing his tours, through Edie, whose career Kramer had managed for years. But they didn't really get to know each other until this tour, and Simon was impressed by Kramer's perspective on his own career.

As wary of all-powerful managers as he was of big-name directors, Simon had largely managed himself after ending his relationship with Mort Lewis soon after the break with Garfunkel. He then depended on a parade of advisors, from Michael Tannen to the triumvirate of Klores, Parcher, and Rascoff, and they mostly served him well. But he had been through some unsettling rough spots—particularly his relationship with Ian Hoblyn, who'd worked for him in various capacities for some twenty years. Though sometimes described in the press as Simon's manager or business manager, the Irishman was more a personal assistant or aide-de-camp. Whatever the official role, Simon put his trust in Hoblyn. They were so close that Simon once described Ian and Lorne Michaels as his two best friends. But the relationship unraveled in the early 1990s, when an audit of Simon's finances turned up troubling discrepancies, including a series of loans from Simon to Hoblyn that Simon said he didn't make. In a related search, Joseph Rascoff's accounting firm, RZO, found several unauthorized checks by Hoblyn on Simon's account.

More than the money (reportedly between $6 million and $7 million), Simon felt betrayed and fired Hoblyn in March 1993. "This wasn't just anybody," he said. "This was my confidant. He's the guy I had dinner with almost every night we were on the road. I was really shaken, but Edie helped me move past it. She said, 'You will make the money back. Don't let this make you a cynical person. That would really be a loss.' " Simon didn't press criminal complaints, but he never spoke again to Hoblyn, who died of cancer in 2012 at the age of seventy-four.

The episode made Simon want to examine his whole business operation, but he was too busy with *The Capeman* to address it until he was finished with that. By the time he did take inventory, Rascoff had left amid the *Capeman* tensions, and Klores told Simon that he wanted to make documentary films. The regulars Simon still had at that point in his lineup, so to speak, included C. Vaughn Hazell, who joined Simon part-time in 1984 to organize his tape archives and became a personal assistant in 1992, and Juanita DeSilva, who started as a temp answering the office phone in 1995 and soon evolved into a personal assistant to both Paul and Eddie.

To review his business affairs, Simon turned to Eddie, who was smart, a quick learner, and fiercely loyal. Simon's brother was also an experienced businessman. After a brief attempt at trying to establish himself as a record producer and performer, Eddie had opened the Guitar Study Center in New York City, offering classes in various styles, from folk and rock to jazz and classical. The center had about four hundred students the first year, 1973, and grew to more than two thousand, but Eddie wanted a new challenge. In 1983 he began running a radio station that he bought with Simon and Lorne Michaels on Long Island. It was WWHB-FM, and it featured imaginative and eclectic programming that included music and comedy, from the Beatles to Lenny Bruce. The station's signal was so weak that it reached only the eastern tip of Long Island, but it was enough of a success that the trio was able to sell it after a few years for a profit. Now Eddie immersed himself in his brother's business operations with the same intensity he had brought to his earlier pursuits.

The more Simon learned about Kramer, the more he wanted to add him to his team. Kramer was born in Brooklyn and had been in the music business as agent or manager since he was seventeen. He didn't have clients—he had passions. Simon also liked the fact that Kramer was a private person. He wasn't one of those managers who loved to see his own name in print. Eddie, too, was impressed by Kramer, and he welcomed his practical experience in the music world. The pairing worked so well as comanagers that Eddie was soon calling Kramer "family."

Simon was pleased with the new album, *You're the One*. To promote it, he sat for a series of interviews in the fall of 2000 that were as warmly upbeat as the music. Asked about the tone, he told the *Los Angeles Times*, "It's the first time I ever had domestic bliss." It was a remarkable statement from a man who had long tended to back away from acknowledging any hint of happiness in his personal life. Asked whether he thought he'd found the right person or if he was a better partner, he said the answer was both, adding, "I'm really fortunate."

One thing Simon didn't mention in the interview was his reliance on ayahuasca, because he went through a bad period with the substance around the time he finished the album; one that lasted for months. "It was frightening and confusing, and it was all my fault," he said years later. "I started misusing the plant. When I started out, I was very careful about my diet and respectful of its spiritual purpose. But I started using it for selfish purposes. I started taking it more frequently to help my songwriting, and it eventually turned against me. I had this voice inside that said, 'You're a liar, you're a fake. You didn't even write these songs. They were given to you.' I was used to believing in my inner voice, because I've found over the years that it is helpful and accurate. But now I was also hearing this negative voice."

The result was a debate between the negative and positive voices that drained Simon and left him tense and unsettled. The breakthrough came when he visited an acupuncturist to ease pain in one of his hands, which was caused by carpal tunnel syndrome. He mentioned his problem with ayahuasca, and the acupuncturist referred him to a former psychiatrist in Baltimore who had helped people with the problem. Simon phoned the man, expecting to fly to Baltimore for a session, but the man said he could advise him over the phone. What you need to do, he said, was to demean the negative voice, to take away its power. One way to do that, he continued, was to imagine the negative force speaking in the comic voice of Bugs Bunny or Donald Duck and imagine the voice was coming from under the sole of his shoe. Simon followed the advice, and it worked. "I didn't use the cartoon voices, but I did, over time, get rid of the negative voice." He also stopped using ayahuasca.

Privately, Simon worried about how fans would respond to the album. "I thought *You're the One* was very, very interesting in terms of color and other things, and it had very interesting lyrics—funny lyrics—but I didn't know if it was hooky enough," he said years later. He also wondered if ayahuasca had led his mind to go from sound to sound in ways that would elude listeners. Simon tried to build interest with a two-month tour of Europe and the United States and by appearing on *Saturday Night Live* on November 4. But none of it helped. Released the first week in October 2000, the package reached no. 19 and qualified for a gold album, but that was closer to the sales of *Hearts and Bones* than *Graceland* or *The Rhythm of the Saints*.

One problem was that veteran artists like Simon, who were longshots for mainstream radio airplay anyway, really needed a blockbuster single to gain attention, and—despite such outstanding songs as "Darling Lorraine" and "Señorita with a Necklace of Tears"—no track cried out for radio attention. The critical response didn't help, either. Despite praise in the *Los Angeles Times, Rolling Stone,* and other mainstream publications, the album failed to make the Top 75 in *Village Voice*'s annual poll of hundreds of music critics. It was the same poll in which *Graceland* and *The Rhythm of the Saints* had finished first and seventh, respectively. The low showing wasn't because critics trashed the album but because many didn't even bother writing about it. They had given up on Simon after *The Capeman.*

The promotional tour was also frustrating. Besides still struggling with the fallout from the ayahuasca, Simon had trouble transferring the musical arrangements from the album to the live show. "Paul really believed in these songs, and he just couldn't get them the way he wanted onstage," a member of the tour said. "It wasn't a happy time for him, and he even called the band together at one point to apologize for being so testy."

When the tour reached London in the fall, Simon took a break to visit

George Harrison at Friar Park, the ex-Beatle's massive estate in Henley-on-Thames, about forty miles northwest of London. What Simon loved about the place was its thirty-five acres of spectacular gardens and lakes. He knew George from their *Saturday Night Live* appearance, but this was the first time he got to spend any quality time with him. It was soon after George had been stabbed by an intruder in his home. "There was this spiritual calm about him," Simon said. "We walked around the property, and I thought about how peaceful it was, too. It made me think about getting some place outside of New York where you could feel like you were living in the country."

The tour ended the second week in December with three nights at the Beacon Theater in New York, just in time for Paul to spend the holidays with Edie and the kids and think about what came next. He didn't have to wait long. In early January the Grammy nominations were announced, and *You're the One*, to considerable surprise, was up for Album of the Year, but it lost eventually to Steely Dan's *Two Against Nature*.

A month later, Simon was back onstage—this time at the sixteenth annual Rock & Roll Hall of Fame induction dinner in New York, as he became one of the few artists at that point to be inducted for his work in a group or duo and then for his solo achievements. The others included Lennon and McCartney, Eric Clapton, Curtis Mayfield, Neil Young, and Michael Jackson. He gave a ten-minute speech devoted to key influences in his life, from his father and Elvis Presley, to Quincy Jones and Ladysmith Black Mambazo. After an enjoyable summer tour, with Brian Wilson as the opening act, Simon again looked forward to being off the road for most of the rest of the year.

Then came the terror of 9/11.

"Like most people in New York, we were afraid, but also proud because the city stood up," Simon said years later. "It was a mixture of emotions, and it took months to absorb what really happened. I guess that's why I couldn't write a long piece when the *New York Times* asked me to write something about the tragedy. When I turned it in, they called and said they needed another nine hundred words, but I said, 'I don't have anything more to say.' They told me I had to give them more words, or they'd have this big empty space in the paper because what I wrote wouldn't fill the space they had laid out for it. They finally went ahead and ran it, and, sure enough, there was this big, awkward white space. I was sorry, but I had said everything I wanted to say. It was such a shattering experience that I just wanted to be with the family."

Simon was finally experiencing balance in his life, something he'd rarely considered earlier. "I wasn't aware of the importance of balance for a long time," he said. "I was immature. I wasn't thinking about how you do this or how you do that in a relationship. I thought everything just sort of came naturally, like it did with my parents. After two marriages and two divorces, I wasn't especially looking to get married again, but then I met Edie, and the balance came naturally. We had three children, and it was at a later stage in life. Edie was also stable, so that gave the marriage stability."

Except for a three-week series of shows in Europe in July and two award ceremonies, Simon was out of action for two years. He was in no rush. He enjoyed being with the family on the estate they purchased in New Canaan, Connecticut, in 2002, chiefly to allow the kids to be raised in a quiet, country setting. "I first looked for a place closer in [than Montauk] on Long Island; a place that had enough land for you to feel you were in the country yet close enough to drive into the city in an hour," Simon said. "But we had trouble finding a place with enough land, so a Realtor found this place in Connecticut. I wasn't sure about it at first—not the place, but Connecticut. If you grew up in New York, you're not a big fan of Connecticut, with its image of trimmed lawns and hedges. But it turned out to be fine."

In December 2002, Simon was one of five recipients of the prestigious Kennedy Center Honors, which recognize lifetime contributions to American culture through the performing arts. Since its launch in the late 1970s, the organization has saluted A-level members of the arts such as Katharine Hepburn, Aaron Copland, Tennessee Williams, Frank Sinatra, and Bob Dylan. Simon was toasted along with Elizabeth Taylor, James Earl Jones, Chita Rivera, and conductor-composer James Levine. The nationally televised program unfolded every December, in a series of events in the nation's capital, including a reception at the White House and a black-tie ceremony at the Kennedy Center Opera House, usually attended by the president and the First Lady.

For the musical salute that night, event sponsors wanted Aretha Franklin to sing "Bridge Over Troubled Water," but she wasn't available, and the task fell to Alicia Keys, a gifted young neo-soul/R&B singer whose 2001 debut album, *Songs in A Minor*, won five Grammys. But Keys failed to connect with the emotional heart of the song. Elizabeth Taylor, sitting next to Simon, leaned over and asked, "Tell me, Paul, does it upset you when somebody fucks up one of your songs?" The rest of the tribute went more smoothly, especially James Taylor and Alison Krauss's rendition of "The Boxer."

A few days later, Simon was touched when he received a letter from his old high school baseball coach, Chester (Chet) Gusick, who had watched the ceremony on television. In the note, Gusick referred to Simon's greatest baseball feat fifty-four years earlier: "Dear Paul: The old coach and his wife viewed, with much pleasure, the honors that were bestowed upon you at the Kennedy Center . . . For a brief moment in time, you stole home again."

CHAPTER TWENTY-ONE

When Simon and Garfunkel were honored in February 2003 for lifetime achievement during the Grammy telecast at Madison Square Garden, the evening would have far greater consequence than another plaque for the trophy case. The reunion was such a coup for the show's organizers that the duo was given the opening spot: just the two of them on a small stage on the arena floor, surrounded by fans. Their performance of "The Sound of Silence" was so moving that Ken Ehrlich, who produced the Grammy telecast for decades, called it one of the most thrilling in all his years with the event. He wasn't alone in that view.

Seeing them together again, concert promoters around the world offered the duo $1 million or more a night if they would go on tour. Surprisingly, Simon agreed. It was partly a business decision: a way to play before huge crowds again and be paid handsomely for it. But sentiment was also involved. Simon remembered how George Harrison, who'd died of cancer in 2001, had mentioned during their meeting at Friar's Park that he had gone through lots of tension with Paul McCartney but eventually put it aside to reconnect with his old friend. About the reunion, Simon said, "The way I looked at it was, how long are we going to live? Am I going to dic without making up with this guy who I've known since I was eleven? I finally called Artie and said, 'Let's fix it.' "

For all the good intentions, issues arose as soon as Simon and Garfunkel met to discuss the tour. "It was all 'You did this' and 'I did that,' and I could see where we were headed," Simon said. "I finally told Art, 'If we go down this road, nothing will happen. Let's talk about the music. Who do we want in the band, and what songs do we want to do?' And that got us going. That's when the Everly Brothers came up. We both thought how great it would be to have them on the tour, and everyone said, 'It'll never happen. They've broken up. They don't even talk to each other.' " True enough, Don and Phil, who called it quits in 1973, had a more turbulent relationship than even Paul and Art. The pair did get back together for three albums in the 1980s, but they never regained their initial success. Yet when Simon asked them to join the tour, they agreed to get on board.

The Old Friends tour started in mid-October 2003 in Wilkes-Barre, Pennsylvania, and continued throughout North America and Europe before ending July 31, 2004, with a free concert attended by six hundred thousand fans in Rome. Night after night, the audience sensed a genuine warmth between the headliners. On most nights, the show opened with the pair singing "Old Friends," and the audience certainly picked up on the line "How terribly strange to be seventy." Simon and Garfunkel were still eight years from seventy, but they were awfully close to it in rock 'n' roll time, which added to the poignant undercurrents of the tour. The song selection consisted chiefly of their early material, but the band updated the tunes with such vigorous rhythms that they were probably a touch jolting to some fans. They even found time to sneak in a playful rendition of "Hey, Schoolgirl" and to join the Everlys on "Bye Bye Love." The old issues were set aside. It was a joy to be making music together again.

As the tour reached London in July 2004, it had been more than four years since Simon finished *You're the One*, and he still didn't have any plans for a new album. That changed when he met the British musician

Brian Eno at a party thrown for him by Melissa North, a longtime friend who often hosted stylish gatherings for Simon and Lorne Michaels that featured some of England's leading poets and artists. Eno shared Simon's endless desire for new and enticing sounds, as evidenced by his credits, which ranged from early membership in the art-rock band Roxy Music to a series of solo albums steeped in ambient and electronic music soundscapes, to producing or coproducing albums for U2, David Bowie, and Talking Heads. Simon went to Eno's studio in England and was intrigued by his soundscapes. He returned to London after the tour to spend a week in Eno's studio, the first of four recording sessions there.

Early in the process, Simon got an urgent call from Lorne Michaels. Dick Ebersol, the NBC executive who had helped launch *Saturday Night Live* and gone on to become a major force in TV sports programming, wanted to know if Simon would sing a song at a memorial for his fourteen-year-old son, Teddy, who was killed in a November 28 plane crash in Colorado. Ebersol, who was also injured seriously, was reaching out because Teddy's favorite song was Simon's "Citizen of the Planet," a statement of shared global birthright that Simon wrote in the early 1980s and sang on some dates on the Old Friends tour. Ebersol used the song to close the telecast of the 2004 Summer Olympics in Athens. Simon sang "Citizen of the Planet" at the two-hour service at St. Anthony of Padua Catholic Church in Litchfield, Connecticut, and he broke into tears, unable to finish the number. He couldn't imagine the anguish of losing a child. When Simon and his son Harper went through a period of estrangement, Simon called it one of his darkest periods.

A singer-songwriter himself, Harper has had a varied career in music. He studied at the Berklee College of Music and played or shared the bill with an eclectic group of musicians, including Yoko Ono, Sean Lennon, Rufus Wainwright, and Jon Brion. His first album, 2009's *Harper Simon*, was coproduced by the same Bob Johnston who had worked with Simon and Garfunkel, and the record was lauded by *Rolling Stone* as "a gorgeous collection of vintage-sounding country-folk tunes." Three of the songs were cowritten by Paul. The most engaging was written by Harper alone. An ode titled "Berkeley Girl," it includes the tender, grateful line,

She is crinoline and satin
She is leopard skin and lace
Hard to believe that she believed in me
When I was such a hopeless case

Harper's second album, *Division Street*, in 2013, was coproduced by Tom Rothrock, who had worked with highly regarded singer-songwriters such as Elliott Smith and Beck, and it drew even stronger praise. Michael Hann's review in the Guardian declared, "Two albums into a solo career, and Harper Simon is staking a claim for the title—not that hotly contested, if we're honest—of most talented child of a major artist." Neither album made much of a dent commercially.

As mum on his personal life as his dad is, Harper rarely mentioned his experiences with drugs, though he did open up in an interview with *Purple Diary* magazine to promote his second album. Asked if he was off the radar or a party fixture as a teenager, he responded, "I'm still off the radar. When I was in my early teens, I went to hardcore matinees at CBGBs on Sunday. Nowhere else would let me in. I was vaguely aware that the punk movement was coming to a close, and I'm glad to have caught the tail end before the Pixies, Beastie Boys, and Sonic Youth set the stage for the next great era. Those years were spent floating around on some hippie drug. I was drunk a lot and thrown out of schools. And I discovered LSD." When asked if he had tried other drugs, Harper replied, "Yeah, around twenty-one, I began to like the hard stuff." But he added that he had been sober for five years.

About Harper, Simon said in 2017, "Again, I don't want to talk about my children except to say I love them all. There have been times, especially after a difficult day, when I picture their faces, and it helped me finally go to sleep."

After the Ebersol funeral, Simon returned to Eno's London studio to work on the next album, which he titled *Surprise*. He played pieces that he had recorded in New York with a few musicians—no cast of thousands this time. Eno added his own electronic touches, resulting in a partnership that was conveyed in the album credit: "Produced by Paul Simon/Sonic Landscape by Brian Eno." Except for three numbers with Eno, Simon wrote all the songs. One of the strongest, "Father and Daughter," was a holdover—a ballad Simon wrote for his daughter, Lulu, and appeared in the 2002 animated children's film *The Wild Thornberrys Movie*. It was one of the few times he knew the theme of a song before he started writing it and the first time he had written on guitar since *Hearts and Bones*. The song was nominated for an Academy Award but lost to Eminem's "Lose Yourself." Simon redesigned the arrangement for *Surprise*. The lyrics were among his sweetest and most straightforward. A key verse:

I'm gonna watch you shine
Gonna watch you grow
Gonna paint a sign
So you always know
As long as one and one is two
There could never be a father
Love his daughter more than I love you

To make the track on *Surprise* even more personal, Simon had his son Adrian sing a background vocal—an idea that came to him when Adrian, then ten, started singing along to a CD of the song that Simon played in the car. Another standout was "How Can You Live in the Northeast?," which addressed the outspoken anti-Northeast attitude of the George W. Bush administration. Simon also dipped into social issues, with "Wartime Prayers," a meditation on the hawkish mentality during the ongoing Iraq and Afghanistan battles.

Simon realized early that *Surprise* might be too abstract for a mass audience. "It may be, as with Brian's own work, that it's meant to speak to a specific group of listeners, and that group may not number in the millions," he said. "They might number in the thousands. That doesn't mean that you shouldn't do it. It just means you have to accept that you're going to be talking to a smaller group of people."

The album received mixed reviews when it was released in the spring of 2006. The main complaint was that Simon's and Eno's styles didn't quite mesh. In the *Los Angeles Times*, Richard Cromelin commented, "The idea of Simon's erudite folk pop meeting Eno's elegance and experimentation holds a lot of promise, but the connection between the two is faulty." Once again, Simon failed to make the Top 75 of the *Village Voice*'s year-end national critics' poll. Sales were also disappointing. Just when the music world seemed to be writing him off again, Simon headed out on tour, including a May 7 stop in New Orleans that he would call one of his most emotional gigs ever.

Quint Davis, a Louisiana native, is the visionary force behind one of America's musical treasures, the annual New Orleans Jazz & Heritage Festival, its stages having been graced since the early 1970s by hundreds of musicians linked to the rich diversity of the New Orleans music scene. The festival offered such a warm, embracing spirit that it lured fans from all over the country. Not only have such Louisiana-bred artists as Professor Longhair, Wynton and Branford Marsalis, Fats Domino, and Allen Toussaint headlined the festival's numerous stages, but leading artists from outside the state have also contributed to its vitality and spirit, from Bob Dylan and Miles Davis, to Aretha Franklin and Al Green. Quint Davis first brought Simon and his band to the festival in 1991. He had fallen in love with the way *Graceland* blended contemporary American music with traditional African sounds, and he said Simon hit the festival audience like a lightning bolt.

Davis thought of Simon again when he put together the lineup for the first festival after Hurricane Katrina's catastrophic damage to the region in August 2005. Levee breaks contributed to massive flooding, hundreds of thousands of residents were displaced, and the ensuing damage was estimated at more than $100 billion. It was the sixth time New Orleans had been flooded, but once again the residents of the city started rebuilding, and Davis wanted the May 2006 festival to toast the region's resilience and future. Again, he said, the impact of Simon and the band was phenomenal. "Paul and the music meant so much to everyone that there were a hundred thousand hands in the air and a hundred thousand eyes crying," Davis said. "The highlight was when he brought out Allen Toussaint and Irma Thomas to join him on 'Bridge Over Troubled Water.' It was the most emotional moment that we've ever had at the festival. He wasn't just a musician. He was a hero."

During the same week, Simon was named by *Time* magazine as "one of the 100 men and women whose power, talent, or moral example was transforming our world." Significantly, he was placed in the section of the list devoted to "heroes and pioneers," not "entertainers and celebrities." At a ceremony for the honorees, Simon met Peter Singer, an Australian moral philosopher known for his writing and advocacy of animal rights and human altruism. Simon was interested in Singer's ideas on how to most efficiently give money to charity, and it led him to performing occasional living-room concerts in sponsors' homes to raise money for specific causes. Simon also credits his growing philanthropic impulses to his conversations with Gelek Rimpoche, a Tibetan Buddhist lama whom he met through Philip Glass.

Equally important, Simon performed at the TED conference in Monterey, California, in early May 2007 and was intrigued by biologist Edward O. Wilson's belief that man had a chance to stop destroying the planet and turn it into a paradise by the twenty-second century. The concept stayed with Simon, and he would write a short piece in 2016 for the *New York Times* endorsing Wilson's book *Half-Earth: Our Planet's Fight for Life.*

All this was part of Simon's awakening to passions beyond music: first, his family, but also his philanthropy and concerns about the environment. All three would have a bearing on Simon's ultimate decision about his career and how he wanted to spend the rest of his life. The same week as the TED conference, the Library of Congress announced a new musical award, the Gershwin Prize for Popular Song, which was designed basically to honor contemporary songwriters who best upheld the grand tradition of the Great American Songbook. Its first choice for the prize was Simon, and the significance of the honor would be underscored by the list of subsequent honorees, including Stevie Wonder, Paul McCartney, the team of Burt Bacharach and Hal David, and Carole King. The ceremony on May 23 at the Warner Theatre in Washington, DC, closed with an eloquent piano version of "The Sound of Silence" by Philip Glass.

It was around this time that Simon met someone else outside of music who would become a lasting friend: Thomas Friedman, the *New York Times* op-ed columnist and best-selling author. Born in Minneapolis, Minnesota, in 1953, Friedman is an intellectual whose writing focuses chiefly on foreign affairs, the Middle East, and the environment. The three-time Pulitzer Prize winner was also blessed with a marvelous wit and sense of storytelling, which made him an ideal companion for occasional lunches and Yankees games. "We talk about family, kids, parenting, songs, lyrics, and politics," Friedman said. "Paul is an intellectual omnivore. He is interested in or is capable of being interested in almost anything. He is always up for a serious conversation and always eager to learn about almost anything. The last thing Paul likes to talk about is his last concert. It is what he does and has been doing for half a century. He knows exactly how to do it, and while he puts his heart into each one, the act itself doesn't interest him to talk about. He much prefers to talk about what is going on outside the concert hall."

Then Simon lost his mother. Belle died on June 16, 2007, in the Bronx at the age of ninety-seven. She had been at the Hebrew Home for the Aged to be near her doctor after having lived for years near Paul and Edie in Connecticut. C. Vaughn Hazell, Simon's longtime personal assistant, remembered the day Paul and members of his band played a mini-concert for Belle and other residents of the home. "Belle was dancing in the middle of the room and going around telling everyone else to get up and dance too," Hazell said. "It was thrilling to see her so energized."

Belle's love was constant and deep. "Whenever I did anything," Simon said, "my mother would go, 'Look at what he did: this is my son and he wrote this song or made this record.' She was my biggest fan. When Clive Davis said leaving Simon and Garfunkel was going to be my biggest mistake, she would say, 'Who cares what he says? You know what you're going to do. You're going to be bigger than Simon and Garfunkel.' That's how my mother would react. She was strong; stronger than my dad."

As Bobby Susser saw it, Lou was Paul's role model. Lou challenged him to live up to his potential as a man and as a musician, but Belle was the one who constantly told him he could reach his goals. If you took away either one, he maintained, Paul would not have been the person he is.

Simon's worry about his parents had already crept into his writing. He was thinking about his father's struggle with cancer when he wrote these lines in "Further to Fly" on *The Rhythm of the Saints*:

> *There may come a time*
> *When I will lose you*
> *Lose you as I lose my light*

Simon was also imagining a world without Belle in "That's Me," which appeared on *Surprise*. When he referred to beauty and sorrow in the song, the beauty was Edie and the sorrow was eventually losing Belle. There is also a lot in that song about Simon himself, which explains why he even includes the word *biography*:

> *Well, I'll just skip the boring parts*
> *Chapters one, two, three*
> *And get to the place*
> *Where you can read my face and my biography*
> *Here I am, I'm eleven months old, dangling from my daddy's knee*
> *There I go, it's my graduation*
> *I'm picking up a bogus degree*
> *That's me*
> *Early me. That's me*
>
> *Well, I never cared much for the money*
> *And money never cared for me*
> *I was more like a landlocked sailor*

Searching for the emerald sea
Just searching for the emerald sea, boys, searching for the sea

Oh, my God
First love opens like a flower
A black bear running through the forest light
Holds me in her sight and her power
But tricky skies, your eyes are true
The future is beauty and sorrow
Still, I wish that we could run away and live the life we used to
If just for tonight and tomorrow

I am walking up the face of the mountain
Counting every step I climb
Remembering the names of the constellations
Forgotten is a long, long time
That's me
I'm in the valley of twilight
Now I'm on the continental shelf
That's me—
I'm answering a question I am asking of myself
That's me
That's me

Toward the end of 2007, Simon's spirits were lifted when his old friend and advisor Dan Klores suggested bringing back the *Capeman* music in the form of a concert at the Brooklyn Academy of Music (BAM), the home of progressive, cutting-edge performances. The plan was to hold a three-week residency the following April with the first week dedicated to the music from *The Capeman*, the second week to *Graceland* and *The Rhythm of the Saints*, and the third to earlier work. The series title would be "Love in Hard Times: The Music of Paul Simon," a twist on a song he had been working on, "Love and Hard Times." The first week proved closest to his heart as *The Capeman* music was performed with a cast that included the Spanish Harlem Orchestra, led by Oscar Hernandez. "It was an emotional time," Hernandez said. "I remember rushing up to Paul after the first night with tears in my eyes and told him, 'This is redemption.' " To make the evening even sweeter, Derek Walcott accepted Simon's offer to attend, and they hugged backstage.

In writing about the series, the *New York Times*'s Jon Pareles sought to put to rest any lingering charges of cultural colonialism against *Graceland*. "Those arguments can seem quaint now that the world's music cruises the internet and countless songs are built by cut-and-paste," he wrote. "The decades proved Mr. Simon's instincts were right . . . [He] has turned out not to be a carpetbagger, but a connoisseur, and, at best, an alchemist." Energized by BAM, Simon headed to Europe in July for a month of shows that were built around snippets from his career.

When he returned home, Simon wrote another essay for the *New York Times*, this one marking the tearing down of Yankee Stadium to pave the way for a new $1.2 billion home for the team—a move that was accompanied by a sense of deep loss by millions of Yankee fans. Increasingly, Simon was feeling comfortable expressing himself outside of music. In the column, he touched on his own memories, again sharing a piece of his private world by citing his love for the man who had introduced him to baseball. Recounting his history with the Yankees, he mentioned the time he sat with his father and listened to his first Yankees game, then riding the subway to Yankee Stadium, where he sat in the left field bleachers as Joe DiMaggio hit a home run. "My youngest son always says that his favorite moment is when you're just coming out from under the stands and you see the players on the field," Simon wrote in closing. "I know that pleasure will still be there in the new stadium, but for those of us lucky enough to have known the House That Ruth Built, something has passed. So, so long, Scooter, so long, Joe, so long, Mick, and since I never got the chance to say it, so long, Dad."

Thinking back on the column, Simon said, "I remember going to that game with my dad so clearly. It was my first time at Yankee Stadium, and when DiMaggio hit that home run, I couldn't see a thing because I was just a kid, and everyone stood up in front of me. But the moment stayed with me forever: being there with my dad." Simon would pass his love of baseball to his children, especially Gabriel, whose Little League team Simon helped coach for parts of three summers.

On October 30, Simon performed at the Rock & Roll Hall of Fame's twenty-fifth anniversary celebration at Madison Square Garden, where he brought some of his old doo-wop heroes onstage: Little Anthony & the Imperials and Dion DiMucci. The highlight was when Garfunkel joined him for "Bridge Over Troubled Water" and "The Sound of Silence." The lesson was clear: all Simon needed to do to fill venues for as long as his health held up was to go back on the road and play the oldies, with or without Art. He didn't have to keep spending years writing and recording new songs. But Simon wasn't finished. Despite the lessened impact of the last two albums, he felt he was making progress. Again, there was no special strategy. He just tried to make the best music he could. Though he would not put it this way, he was also fighting to reaffirm his place in the contemporary music world—and the only way he knew to do that was to continue to move forward, not retrace.

The path to his new album, which would be his twelfth solo studio collection, dated back to the early months of 2007 when Simon, having enjoyed writing "Father and Daughter" on guitar, again started writing as he had done before *Graceland*: the song before the instrumental track. The song was "Love and Hard Times," which was inspired by his relationship with Edie, and it didn't come to him in a day or two like the songs he wrote for *You're the One*. The lyrics, in part:

> *I loved her the first time I saw her*
> *I know that's an old songwriting cliché*
> *Loved you the first time I saw you*
> *Can't describe it any other way*
> *Any other way*
> *The light of her beauty was warm as a summer day*

Simon began working on "Love and Hard Times" in the studio in his Central Park West residence, but he shifted in the spring of 2009 to a studio he built in what was formerly a guest cottage on the New Canaan property. He was assisted by sound engineer Andy Smith, who had begun working with Simon since *Songs from The Capeman* and had earlier worked with Edie on *Picture Perfect Morning*.

The new album was also propelled by a Christmas present from Brian Eno. *Goodbye, Babylon* was a six-disc boxed set (the CDs were actually packaged in a wooden box) devoted to the grass roots of gospel music, both black and white. It contained 135 songs by artists as famous as the Carter Family and bluesman Robert Johnson and as obscure to pop audiences as the Dinwiddie Colored Quartet. The boxed set's final disc contained 25 sermons by African American preachers. For Simon, the collection was a playground of sound, and he listened to it all. What caught his ear most was the opening sermon on the last disc.

Titled "Gettin' Ready for Christmas Day," the sermon was delivered by the Reverend J. M. Gates in an Atlanta hotel in the fall of 1941. Gates, who recorded more than two hundred songs and sermons, was so popular that his funeral is said to have drawn the biggest crowd of any memorial service in Atlanta prior to that of Dr. Martin Luther King Jr. In the sermon, Gates urged his listeners to use Christmas Day to make sure they had their spiritual house in order because Santa Claus wasn't the only one waiting. If you were living a life of sin, the undertaker and the jailer were also waiting. Simon was especially drawn to the call and response between Gates and the congregation.

"It made me want to do a foot-stomping thing, like we used to do in the late fifties and early sixties—something like Dion did on 'Runaround Sue,' " Simon said. "You set a box on the floor in the studio and just stomp, stomp, and that's the beat. Then we put a guitar thing against it, and we had a really great groove, so I thought about putting the sermon right there, and it sounded great, so I wrote a song around it. It was a great start to the album."

Though planning to produce the album himself, Simon ran into Phil Ramone at a New Canaan supermarket and invited him into the studio to hear some of the new music. Phil, who lived in the area, loved it, and Simon asked him to coproduce. Work on the new album stopped for a month in 2009 when the Old Friends tour resumed in Japan and Australia. Things continued to go so well that Simon and Garfunkel planned yet another leg of the tour the following summer.

CHAPTER TWENTY-TWO

Fifty-three years after "Hey, Schoolgirl," the Simon and Garfunkel relationship broke for what Simon vowed was the final time at the scene of two of his greatest triumphs: the New Orleans Jazz & Heritage Festival. To the thousands of fans on the festival grounds on Saturday, April 24, 2010, the main concern was the weather. Monsoon rains swept through the region Friday, and forecasts warned of more heavy precipitation. By midafternoon, however, the sun had broken through the clouds.

Arriving onstage with a local brass band, Simon and Garfunkel opened with "A Hazy Shade of Winter," and then followed with more of their early material, including "I Am a Rock" and "America." It was soon apparent that Garfunkel was having trouble with his voice, a point he acknowledged finally when he asked the crowd to bear with him. The problem was so severe, according to Keith Spera's review in the *New Orleans Times-Picayune*, that Garfunkel's voice "seemed on the edge of evaporating completely" by the sixth number. After leaving the stage during some

Graceland tunes, Garfunkel returned to struggle on gamely. At the end of the set, Spera wrote, Paul and Art "exchanged warm smiles, clasped hands, and embraced, relieved."

John Scher, who managed Garfunkel for nineteen years before severing ties with him in 2013, traced the singer's throat problems to a trip he took to Central America earlier in 2010 to perform at a private function. "Art caught some kind of bug, and it really destroyed him," said Scher. "I got him the best doctors, and the prognosis was that one of his vocal cords was slightly paralyzed. They recommended vocal therapy. They said if he worked hard at it for six months, maybe a year, he'd be okay. The problem is Art didn't follow through. He went to a voice therapist once or twice, but he thought he could take care of it himself. Meanwhile, he kept telling Paul that things would be fine, not to worry."

But there was plenty of worry in April when Simon and Garfunkel held rehearsals before flying to New Orleans. Again, Garfunkel assured Simon that it wasn't a big deal and that he'd be ready for Jazz Fest and the monthlong Canadian-US tour that was to follow. Quint Davis recalled there was so much concern the night before the duo's set that they scheduled a rare early-morning sound check on the festival grounds. What they found was that Garfunkel's voice was fine on the high and low ends, but he had trouble—lots of trouble—with the midrange. "It was like a strange *Twilight Zone* thing, watching Art, at eight o'clock, going through the different songs with the band to see where his voice would go and where it would stop and where it would pick up again," Davis said. "It was almost like a race car driver going into the Daytona 500 with his left foot broken and his right hand broken, trying to figure out how to do the clutch and accelerator with one foot and then shift and steer with the other hand."

At this point, Scher said, Simon was supportive. He believed it when Garfunkel said the problem was temporary, and he also felt badly for his old friend. "I think to some degree that both of these guys really loved each other," Scher continued. "That's what made the Old Friends tour so special. There was this deep, deep feeling for the audience and for each other." With Jazz Fest behind them, the remaining tour dates were pushed back to July to give Garfunkel's vocal cords time to rest. But by mid-June, it was obvious the shows would have to be cancelled again. At that time, Simon decided Garfunkel had been underplaying the vocal problem all along—and he was angry.

In an interview with the *Los Angeles Times* in 2012, Garfunkel gave his side of the story:

"When I flew home [from the Nicaragua concert], something about that gig caused me to start having vocal cord trouble . . . My midrange, which is my life, suddenly became crude and unmanageable . . . and I went into a state of tragedy—me and my voice have been best friends since I was five," he said. "I didn't know who I am without the voice. I have to figure who I am besides a loving husband and a loving father. And then I noticed slowly, slowly it is improving. On frequent visits to the doctor, pictures of the throat show that it is mending, but boy, is it slow . . . I underestimated how long the mending process was, something I'm sure Paul did not enjoy."

Simon and Garfunkel had to pay nearly $1 million each in cancellation fees, but it wasn't the money that upset Simon. He was disappointed over what he felt was the lack of candor, reminding him of the final days of Simon and Garfunkel when he believed Garfunkel had betrayed him by accepting a second movie role without telling him. "He could have said he couldn't do this after New Orleans, but he didn't," Simon said. "There was all this denial. He let us all down. I was tired of all the drama. I didn't feel I could trust him anymore."

Because Simon had come around before, Garfunkel likely held on to the belief that Paul would change his mind and they'd tour together again as soon as Garfunkel regained his vocal strength. He spent much of the coming decade chasing that dream. Meanwhile, Simon moved on with his career. The break was complete—personally and professionally.

With "Love and Hard Times" and "Getting Ready for Christmas Day" already finished, he concentrated on the song that would be the new collection's centerpiece: "Questions for the Angels," a quintessential expression of his overriding empathy and social ideals, especially the environmental concerns that he so admired in the work of Edward O. Wilson.

A pilgrim on a pilgrimage
Walked across the Brooklyn Bridge
His sneakers torn
In the hour when the homeless
Move their cardboard blankets
And the new day is born
Folded in his backpack pocket
The questions that he copied from his heart
Who am I in this lonely world?
Where will I make my bed tonight?
When twilight turns to dark

Questions for the angels
Who believes in angels?
Fools do
Fools and pilgrims all over the world

If you shop for love in a bargain store
And you don't get what you bargained for
Can you get your money back?
If an empty train in a railway station
Calls you to its destination
Can you choose another track?
Will I wake up from these violent dreams
With my hair as white as the morning moon?

Questions for the angels
Who believes in angels?
I do
Fools and pilgrims all over the world

Downtown Brooklyn
The pilgrim is passing a billboard
That catches his eyes
It's Jay-Z
He's got a kid on each knee
He's wearing clothes that he wants us to try
If every human on the planet
And all the buildings on it
Should disappear
Would a zebra grazing in the African savannah
Care enough to shed one zebra tear?

Questions for the angels

"I wrote the song on a Gibson Byrdland electric guitar, which I played through an amp with the top end rolled off so it sounded like an old jazz guitar from the fifties," Simon said. "After I recorded the guitar part, I played it over and over as I drove around in my car, taking the kids to school or heading into the city. When I'm driving, you wouldn't want to be on the same road, because I'm basically just listening to the latest song I'm working on. I'm often trying to figure out what words go with the music. Eventually I came up with a phrase that fit the rhythm, the one about a pilgrim on a pilgrimage and walking across the Brooklyn Bridge. That line came from the time when the Brooklyn Academy of Music was presenting three weeks of my music. I'd go over to Brooklyn every day, and on the Brooklyn side of the bridge there was a billboard with a photo of Jay-Z. He was selling something, as I recall, and that became part of the story.

"Occasionally going into Brooklyn, I'd see homeless people and think about them sleeping on cardboard and struggling to just get through the day: *A pilgrim on a pilgrimage / Walked across the Brooklyn Bridge / His sneakers torn / In the hour when the homeless / Move their cardboard blankets / And the new day is born.* Now I have a character and a story about someone traveling, seeking something. I like writing about journeys. It gets things moving. In the song, the pilgrim asks himself some questions about who he is and where he'll make his bed at night, and that enables me to use this title I've had in my head for a while, 'Questions for the Angels.' That's when the song starts to form. Then I ask myself, who believes in angels—and my first response is 'Fools do,' which is what a lot of people think; then I add 'and pilgrims all over the world.'

"Then there's the verse about the bargain store: *If you shop for love in a bargain store / And you don't get what you bargained for / Can you get your money back?* Well, it's kind of a funny line, but it's also talking about making choices, including the right and wrong choices when looking for someone to love. Next we come to the line about the train: *If an empty train in a railway station / Calls you to its destination / Can you choose another track?* That's asking are we predestined to our fate. It's time now to ask the question again: *Who believes in angels?* But this time, I say, *I do.* That changes things, but I still don't know where the song is taking me.

"That's why the last verse is the payoff, the final question for the angels: *If every human on the planet / And all the buildings on it / Should disappear / Would a zebra grazing in the African savannah / Care enough to shed one zebra tear?*"

Another song that Simon favored was "Rewrite," which is about a burned-out Vietnam vet who is trying to write a screenplay that reimagines his life with a happy ending. In the story, the vet eliminates the pages about having a breakdown and leaving his family. Instead, he's going to be a superhero who's in car chases and races across rooftops to save children. "It's a very touching story to me," Simon said. "It's a generational story, and when I later played it in concert, I played it before 'America,' and I realized the kid who gets on the Trailways bus in Pittsburgh is the old guy at the car wash. That guy is some version of me, my generation, the ones damaged in Vietnam. I was going backward in the song, like the [Harold] Pinter play *Betrayal.* It started with the old guy, and going back to the bus trip in 'America.' "

> *I've been working on my rewrite, that's right*
> *I'm gonna change the ending*

Gonna throw away my title
And toss it in the trash
Every minute after midnight
All the time I'm spending
Is just for working on my rewrite
Gonna turn it into cash

I've been working at the car wash
I consider it my day job
Cause it's really not a pay job
But that's where I am
Everybody says the old guy working at the car wash
Hasn't got a brain cell left
Since Vietnam

But I say
Help me, help me
Help me, help me
Whoa! Thank you!
I'd no idea
That you were there

When I said help me, help me
Help me, help me
Thank you
For listening to my prayer

I'm working on my rewrite, that's right
I'm gonna change the ending
Gonna throw away my title
And toss it in the trash
Every minute after midnight
All the time I'm spending
Is just for working on my rewrite, that's right

I'm gonna turn it into cash
I'll eliminate the pages
Where the father has a breakdown
And he has to leave the family
But he really meant no harm
Gonna substitute a car chase
And a race across the rooftops
When the father saves the children
And he holds them in his arms

And I say
Help me, help me
Help me, help me
Thank you!
I'd no idea
That you were there
When I said help me, help me
Help me, help me
Whoa! Thank you
For listening to my prayer

Simon was in the final stages on the album in the summer of 2010 when *The Capeman* was reprised again. Twelve years after his original, damning review, the *New York Times*'s Ben Brantley saw a "radically streamlined" ninety-minute treatment of the musical at the Delacorte Theater in Central Park. He called the show "an organic part of a New York tradition of tale-telling, of how accounts of tragic events in an overcrowded city are passed around and passed down until they become urban legends." Brantley went on to say the score, again under the musical direction of Oscar Hernandez, "seemed truly to emanate from the city itself in a way it hadn't at the Marquis. The sirens from the streets, the barking dogs, the planes overhead: these all melded into a scrappy, percussive counterpoint to Mr. Simon's summoning of a city that is always an unexpected symphony of fractured calls and responses."

Brantley's words were all the more gratifying because Simon was feeling good about his new album. He was so protective of it, in fact, he didn't want to leave its fate up to Warner Bros. It wasn't the same label he had signed with in 1978. Mo Ostin and Lenny Waronker had both left in 1996 after a regime change. "I didn't feel the label understood what I was doing anymore," Paul said. "I think I still owed them one album, but they agreed to let me go, and Jeff started taking *So Beautiful* around to other companies. We weren't looking for the biggest deal. We were looking for a company that would be really behind it."

The search ended with the Concord Records Group, an outgrowth of a jazz label that had taken on a more aggressive and wider focus after being purchased in 1999 by, among others, television producer Norman Lear. The new ownership's early successes were Ray Charles's *Genius Loves Company*, his final studio album, which won eight Grammys, including Album of the Year, and rights to the global distribution of Paul McCartney's solo and Wings catalogs. "I am a huge Paul Simon fan, and I felt he was moving forward again with *So Beautiful or So What*," said Robert Smith, senior A&R executive at Concord at the time. "Jeff Kramer brought it by to play for me, and about two-thirds of the way through, I couldn't wait any longer. I said, 'I think this is the best thing Paul has done since *Graceland*. We've got to have this record.' "

In the album, Simon employed samples from blues and gospel recordings and verbal touches from old doo-wop and rock tunes, and then filled out the arrangements with African and Indian percussion as well as segments of recordings made by Edie during a family trip to Kenya in 2009. Simon was also writing with renewed passion about many of the same themes that had interested him ever since his early songwriting days in England, including love, faith, and mortality.

Critics cheered. The *New York Times*'s Jon Pareles placed it second in his year-end Top 10, noting, "Questions of mortality, faith, and the meaning of life fill an album that's never weighed down by its serious-ness. Simon, who turned 70 this year, tucked his philosophical rumina-tions amid light-fingered guitars, deceptively casual vocals, and intricately effervescent rhythms with global underpinnings (and some hip-hop-style sampling). His musings arrive with punch lines, not pretensions." Robert Christgau added to the chorus for *So Beautiful or So What*. In his Con-sumer Guide style, he wrote, in part, "A good bet to turn 70 before year's end, the patient craftsman surrounds a 96-second acoustic guitar moment with nine four-minute songs about eternity. The mood is melancholy, yet suffused with gratitude—for his wife's love, first of all, but even more for God's gifts, with the Divinity Himself an actor in several lyrics and close by in most of the others. A."

Concord Records's publicist, Joel Amsterdam, also loved the album, and he was thrilled by how eager Simon was to help promote it. "After the *Capeman* stuff, I think the public did sour a bit on Paul, but I had a sense the public was thirsty for his music again, and I got the sense Paul was hungry to matter again." Amsterdam drafted an ambitious promo-tion schedule built around National Public Radio and the internet, which helped introduce Simon to a new audience and reminded critics of his relevance. On a wave of glowing reviews, Simon rebounded to no. 14 in the national critics' poll. He was deemed relevant again.

The album sold three hundred thousand copies in the United States, an impressive figure for the time. Simon spent much of the year on the road, starting in Seattle on April 15, 2011, and ending up in the Miami area in early December. In between, he celebrated his seventieth birthday with a party on October 13 at the Waverly Inn in New York, joined by seventy-five relatives and friends. As he had said after the success of *Graceland*, Simon denied any master plan behind *So Beautiful*. In both cases, he had just continued to work hard. "I think a lot of people gave up on *You're the One* and *Surprise* because of all the negativity surrounding *The Capeman*, but I couldn't have gotten to *So Beautiful* without things I learned on those albums."

To Roy Halee, the lesson in those three albums is that Simon didn't blink. "He didn't let the debate surrounding *You're the One* and *Surprise*"—or the declining sales—"make him change course," the producer said. "He didn't try to think of some new way to get the public's attention. He just kept going where the music led, and people eventually caught up with him again."

Regarding his musical path, Simon said, "I don't really have a whole lot of choice about what it is I do because my mind keeps writing another song. That's what I am, and if the work is valued in any way, that's great. If it isn't, then someone else will make that donation. The public will always find the artists it needs. I'm just an artist because that's my personality trait, a characteristic of how my brain works. I can't figure out a lot of things; I'm not a computer scientist. This is who I am. This is what I do. I make up songs, and I try to make them as interesting as possible. Stand back and just let me get on with it."

The key stop on the So Beautiful tour was a concert in Johannesburg in July that would be documented in an album celebrating the twenty-fifth anniversary of *Graceland*. Despite having left Warner Bros., Simon reteamed with his former label for a lavish boxed set that included a new documentary. Directed by Joe Berlinger, *Under African Skies* used Paul's return to Johannesburg to examine many of the musical, cultural, and political issues surrounding the original recording sessions through interviews with principals involved. In one of the documentary's most dramatic sequences, Simon sat down with Dali Tambo, son of the late African National Congress leader Oliver Tambo and an outspoken opponent of Simon's original visit to Johannesburg. Though their conversation was polite, it was clear that neither Simon nor Tambo had changed his views.

When Berlinger asked another opponent of the 1985 sessions—Steven Van Zandt, the leading force behind the *Sun City* album—to look back on his decision, Van Zandt refused after learning that Simon hadn't apologized for recording in South Africa. In a 2016 interview, Van Zandt was still sharply critical. Though he called Simon "one of the greatest songwriters of all time," Van Zandt said he found it "extraordinarily arrogant of him to think he's smarter than the UN and smarter than the people in South Africa who chose Mandela as their leader." Asked again about the boycott, Simon said the album and the reaction over the years speak for themselves.

"What the ANC said to me was, 'You didn't do anything wrong by recording in South Africa. What you did wrong was you didn't ask our permission,' " Simon said. "And I said, 'Oh, is that the kind of government you're going to be? You're going to decide who musicians can record with and where. Are you going to check the lyrics, too?' The ANC is a political party, like the Democratic Party or the Republican Party. And my position was they can't tell me 'You can't record with South African musicians.' That was never in the boycott. No one envisioned it. Even the idea of that is an insult to musicians. That's what the fight was. I don't care if people disagree with my views about artists having more say about their art and their politics. I believe in the artists." The anniversary tour lineup included the return of Ray Phiri.

In the months after *So Beautiful* was released, Simon waited anxiously for the Grammy nominations to be announced in December. He knew the awards were an imperfect measure of the year in music, but he welcomed the chance to pick up an unprecedented fourth Album of the Year award. Though Simon said he never set out to write a hit, once a recording was finished, his competitive instincts kicked in, and he very much wanted a hit or recognition, which is why he was crushed when he saw the nominations. He not only failed to get a nomination in the Best Album category, but also he failed to receive any nomination—not Best Song, not Male Vocal, not Pop Album, not Producer. He again felt a long way from the music business. Still, he began work on a new album.

Simon took a break from the sessions in April 2012 for a rare foray into jazz when he joined Wynton Marsalis and the Jazz at Lincoln Center Orchestra for three concerts at the 1,100-seat Rose Theater in New York. The program offered bold reinterpretations of his songs over the years—from "The Sound of Silence" and "The Boxer" all the way through "Late in the

Evening" and "Diamonds on the Soles of Her Shoes." Marsalis and Simon became friends. "What has always impressed me about Paul is that his artistic objectives have always been greater than his commercial objectives," Marsalis said. "You don't find a lot of that in popular music. He serves the right master."

Simon devoted most of the year to the new album, which meant he was constantly looking for inspiration. One place he found it was in the musical ideas of the late Harry Partch, an American composer and music theorist who rejected the accepted notion that there are only twelve notes in a musical octave. Partch was nicknamed the "Hobo composer" because he spent part of his early life riding the rails and working in fields much like a character from a John Steinbeck novel. But it wasn't Partch's lifestyle that interested Simon, it was his ideas about music, which maintained there should be as many as forty-three notes in an octave. Partch had even built numerous instruments to utilize these microtones.

Eager to explore this approach, Simon went with Mark Stewart, who had a deep understanding of Partch's work, to Montclair State College in New Jersey to meet with Dean Drummond, a composer and musician who is credited with saving and restoring Partch's custom instruments. The trio spent an afternoon going through the massive collection, a piece of which Simon bought and placed in his cottage studio: an upright keyboard that allows you to play in microtones. Simon relied on some of Partch's concepts when writing the music for the first song on the new album, again on guitar. When he played it for Edie, she said it sounded like a lullaby, which surprised him because he thought the music was too restless for that. "Well," he thought to himself, "if it is a lullaby, it's got to be an insomniac's lullaby," and that led to the lyrics, which included these lines:

Soft as a rose
The light from the East
As if all is forgiven
And wolves become sheep
We are who we are
Or we're not

But at least
We'll eventually all fall asleep
Eventually all fall asleep

In the song, Simon was trying to imagine what might go through a person's mind while lying awake most of the night. Gradually the song moved from random thoughts to a specific issue that seems fitting at the end of a long, restless night: mortality. Simon was now seventy-two.

CHAPTER TWENTY-THREE

After the successful tour with Bob Dylan, Simon wanted to team up again with another top artist to help guarantee sellouts in arenas around the world. The question was who could add the star power and still be a compatible, fully involved musical partner. He found the answer when he performed at a benefit in May 2013 in New York for the Robin Hood foundation's campaign to combat poverty in the city. On a bill with Elton John, Bono, and Mary J. Blige, Simon and Sting stole the show when they teamed on acoustic versions of "The Boxer" and Sting's "Fields of Gold." During their miniset, Sting, joked, "We've started a new band. It's called Simon and Stingfunkel." The joke was corny, but the idea was planted.

Simon and Sting had a lot in common; smart men and demanding songwriters with an eagerness to explore world music textures. They also shared the courage to take chances (both had tried movies and Broadway), and they triumphed after leaving hugely successful teams. They'd also both been described as arrogant and aloof. "Paul is very sensitive," said Sting, who had gained stardom with the rock trio the Police. "He probably takes criticism very deeply. But neither of us show our emotions that easily. It's a mask, if you like. It sometimes looks like arrogance, but it's really not." Sting, who was born ten years after Simon, had been a fan since "The Sound of Silence" because he found the songs so literate. "He was the kind of songwriter I wanted to be," he said. "I was inspired by all his changes because I have the same gadfly instincts. I'm not interested in just plowing the same piece of land."

While the tour was being planned, Simon continued to show interest in expressing himself outside the traditional boundaries of music—he was no longer content with merely writing an occasional column in the *New York Times*. The forum this time was the 2013 Richard Ellmann Lectures in Modern Literature presentation in late September at Atlanta's Emory University. Over the three-day event, Simon gave a concert, but, more significant, he also delivered two lectures and talked about poetry and songwriting with former US poet laureate Billy Collins. The most thoughtful and revealing moment was his second lecture, titled "View from a Cloud: The Solitary Artist in a Collaborative Culture." In it, Simon went well beyond the topic of songwriting to touch on an issue that had become a growing focus of his writing: the competing worlds of science and faith. But it was also another defense of what he saw as the integrity of artistic pursuit, this one framed more gracefully than the *Porgy and Bess* column in the *New York Times*. The lecture included these thoughts:

> W. H. Auden said, "When I find myself in the company of scientists, I feel like a shabby curate who has strayed by mistake into a drawing room full of dukes." At first, I empathized with his feelings. To be in the presence of gifted people capable of exploring the universe, mapping the human genome, finding a cure for cancer, perhaps vanquishing death itself—that would be a humbling experience. But the more I read the Auden quote, the more I began to wonder if I hadn't been played by the esteemed poet with a bit of false modesty. After all, he didn't write, "When I find myself in the company of scientists, I feel like a worm in a dish of pasta primavera." No, he was a "shabby curate," an assistant to

the vicar, who "strayed in by mistake" . . . uninvited, he implies. Into what? A scientist's convention? No, "a drawing room full of dukes."

The description of Auden's discomfort is vivid and a beautifully apt metaphor for the feelings of insignificance we all experience when confronted by life's great mysteries; our universes, external and internal; the countless galaxies of the heavens and the atomically microscopic neurotransmitters in our bodies are awe inspiring. Yet it's the elegance and concision of a poet's language that made those feelings palpable.

An MRI will help a doctor chemically analyze our brains. Elation: dopamine breaking down into opioids. Anger: components of adrenaline and testosterone. Sadness: the command for prolactin to be secreted to help cope with the suffering, et cetera. But people have spiritual questions and doubts that persist despite chemical explanations. Who are we as human beings? Why are we here? Is there a difference between the brain and the mind? The mind and the soul? What is existence? Where does it go when we die? Science, for the most part, says the brain is the mind. The soul doesn't exist scientifically. It can't be seen; its energy cannot be measured. But what does a feeling of awe look like on an MRI? What color is it? It's a chicken-and-egg question. Do the chemicals produce the feeling or vice versa?

Scientists are only beginning to understand the whole wondrous bundle of unanswered, and possibly unanswerable, questions that mankind has been pondering for the millennia. These thoughts are as enticing as a mountain stream, and science has an unquenchable thirst, but to understand the mind and the soul, if such a thing exists, we will need the help of Auden's "shabby curate": the artist.

Looking back on *So Beautiful or So What* and even earlier albums, you could see Simon wrestling with issues of science and faith, nowhere more so than in "Questions for the Angels."

In November 2013 Paul Simon and Sting: On Stage Together was announced. The tour's opening leg would include twenty-two shows in North

America, from February 8, 2014, in Houston to March 16, 2014, in Orlando, Florida. When Simon and Sting began rehearsing for the tour, the pairing proved solid. "I saw that Paul really wanted to experiment—with his music and with my music," Sting said. "That meant I had to keep on my toes. I'd be singing songs like 'The Boxer,' but he was doing them differently. He had changed his phrasing, and the melody had evolved slightly, so I'm standing next to him onstage trying to guess where he's going with each song, and it would change every night. The remarkable thing was he didn't stop with his own songs during rehearsal. He took my songs and messed with the rhythm, in a good sense, and he was really singing them as stories. He was investing more meaning than I was into my own songs. I had been taking some of them for granted."

In line with the equal billing, Simon and Sting came out together each night to open the show, generally to perform Sting's "Brand New Day" and "Fields of Gold" and Simon's "The Boy in the Bubble." They would then each take the stage for individual sets, broken up by their occasionally reteaming on such songs as "Fragile," "Mother and Child Reunion," and "The Boxer." The approach injected the evening with a winning sense of surprise, both in the way the members of Sting's and Simon's bands interacted and in the new arrangements of many of the songs. For the end, on most nights, Simon and Sting teamed again on "Every Breath You Take," "Late in the Evening," and a stirring interpretation of "Bridge Over Troubled Water" that helped restore character to the ballad after decades of overexposure had drained it of some of its emotional power.

Early in the tour, Garfunkel resurfaced in *Rolling Stone* to declare he had recovered 96 percent of his voice and to outline his long, lonely road back from the vocal collapse four years earlier at Jazz Fest. After fearing for months that he might never be able to sing again professionally, Garfunkel said he started singing to himself. Then, in 2011, he booked a small theater in New York, where he worked with a sound engineer on trying to push his voice further—a concert, he said, without an audience. His voice improved enough to do a few shows before a sympathetic crowd in 2012 at the Blue Door, an art gallery in Yonkers, New York. As his voice strengthened, Garfunkel did a few more under-the-radar shows in the Northeast, eventually playing to two hundred to three hundred people.

In the magazine Q&A by Andy Greene, Garfunkel was so optimistic that he answered yes when asked whether he thought he and Simon would ever tour again. When Greene requested specifics, however, Garfunkel appeared testy. "It takes two to tango. I don't want to be a blushing bride waiting for Paul Simon to walk down the aisle. If he's too busy to work with me, I guess the real answer to your question is, 'I'm too busy to work with him.' I think that's the only answer I can give you for pride's sake."

Garfunkel returned a year later in an interview with Nigel Farndale of the *Sunday Telegraph* in England in which he was asked whether Paul might have a Napoléon complex; was there a height thing between them? Rather than dodge the insensitive question, Garfunkel used it as a platform to demean his old partner. "I think you're on to something," he said. "I would say so, yes." He added that he felt sorry for Paul at school because of his height, and he'd offered him love and friendship as a compensation— "and that compensation gesture has created a monster." In earlier times, the interview would have slipped by relatively unnoticed, but in the age of the internet, it was circulated worldwide. It was subsequently picked up by news outlets ranging from the *Times of Israel* to the *Huffington Post* and *Rolling Stone*. Asked about the remarks, Simon said, "I don't even read them anymore. Artie's just working out his demons."

Simon was energized when he got home from the first leg of the tour and threw himself back into songs for a new album. In the nine months before the tour resumed in New Zealand, he was assisted greatly by his band members, whose international backgrounds and fondness for exotic musical touches made them a virtual repertory company as well as musical detectives. When Simon mentioned his fondness for flamenco music, Jamey Haddad told him about a group of Spanish flamenco players in Boston. Simon brought four of them to New York to put down grooves with Haddad that were incorporated into four tracks. Similarly, Simon was impressed by *Tayi Bebba*, an electronic dance album by Cristiano Crisci, an Italian DJ/producer who goes by the stage name Clap! Clap! Simon learned about the DJ through his son Adrian, who was now twenty-one and a composer himself. He loved the way Clap! Clap! took African sound samples and placed digital dance strains behind them. He arranged to meet with Crisci, who then sent Simon some overdubs that he could use.

On a visit to a New York music store, Music Inn, Simon purchased a gopichand, an Indian one-stringed instrument attached to a gourd. Playing around with it one day in the cottage studio, he produced an eerie tone that sounded to Simon like the howl of a werewolf. He added it to the beginning of an instrumental track that had been sitting around for months and liked the results enough to begin writing a song about a modern werewolf. Eventually the song turned into a warning of dangerous forces of all kinds that are at work in a world of greed and environmental destruction.

Elsewhere in the album, which would be titled *Stranger to Stranger*, Simon reflected on subjects ranging from social inequality ("Wristband") to baseball heroes ("Cool Papa Bell") to families of war victims ("The Riverbank") to mentally disturbed, homeless people ("Street Angel"). One of these, "Wristband," started out as a rather playful gripe about a musician being locked out of his own show, but it led to a more substantial reflection on social injustice—a statement that was all the more biting in the middle of a presidential election dominated by outcries against the growing gap between the haves and the have-nots in America.

I stepped outside the backstage door
To breathe some nicotine
And maybe check my mailbox
See if I can read the screen
Then I heard a click
The stage door lock
I knew just what that meant
I'm gonna have to walk around the block
If I wanna get it in a . . .

Wristband, my man
You got to have a wristband
If you don't have a wristband, my man
You don't get through the door
Wristband, my man
You got to have a wristband
And if you don't have a wristband
You don't get through the door

I can't explain it
I don't know why my heart beats like a fist
When I meet some dude with an attitude
Saying, "Hey, you can't do that . . . or this"
And the man was large
A well-dressed six-foot-eight
And he's acting like Saint Peter
Standing guard at the Pearly . . .

Wristband, my man
You've got to have a wristband
If you don't have a wristband
You don't get through the door
And I said, "Wristband? I don't need a wristband
My axe is on the bandstand
My band is on the floor"
I mean it's just . . .
(Wristband)
(Wristband) . . .

The riots started slowly
With the homeless and the lowly
Then they spread into the heartland
Towns that never get a wristband
Kids that can't afford the cool brand

Whose anger is a shorthand
For you'll never get a wristband
And if you don't have a wristband
Then you can't get through the door
No, you can't get through the door
No, you can't get through the door
Say you can't get through the door, no

Before starting the international leg of the tour with Sting in late January 2015, Simon agreed to appear on the fortieth-anniversary *Saturday Night Live* TV special even though he'd have to take a nineteen-hour flight from Australia to New York to do the show on February 15, and then return to Australia to resume the tour. To make matters worse, Simon had a tooth-ache on the flight home. In an email to a friend, he said, "If I didn't love Lorne . . ." The three-and-a-half-hour broadcast featured comedians, musi-cians, and other celebrities who had been closely identified with the show over the years, including Steve Martin, Alec Baldwin, and Chris Rock. Simon joined Paul McCartney in a duet of the Beatles' "I've Just Seen a Face." Lorne saved the closing spot for Simon, whose "Still Crazy After All These Years" was a poignant anthem for the telecast—not just a toast to his own generation but also to *SNL*'s legacy. At the end of the number, Simon, having admired the *SNL* band for decades, asked the audience to give the musicians a standing ovation. It was his favorite moment of the night.

Back on the tour, Simon was looking forward to England, especially April 15 and 16 at the twenty-thousand-plus O2 Arena in London. In Manchester two nights before London, he told the audience that he didn't know "when I'll see you again." After the flight that night from Manchester to London, Simon was still in a nostalgic mood. On the way into town, he asked his van driver to go by his old apartment in Hampstead. "This is a very emotional time for me," he said. "It may be the last time I ever tour England." The following evening, Simon had dinner with Kathy Chitty and Ken.

Neither Simon nor Sting cared for large postshow greeting sessions, but

Simon invited a dozen or so of his longtime British friends backstage after the second London show, including Kathy, Lynne McCausland, Beverley Martyn, and Melissa North. At the end of the evening, he slowly circled the room and gave everyone a long, strong hug. At his hotel in Amsterdam the following afternoon, he was still thinking about England. "These last few days, particularly, have been something special to me," he said. "There was a friendship and support here long before anyone else cared about my music, and I still feel that friendship and support when I step onstage here. That is something I'll miss."

On Sunday, April 19, Simon returned home, expecting to continue working on the album, which was only months from being completed. But his world was shaken six nights later by an incident in the New Canaan cottage that made headlines around the world, including this siren blast from the *New York Post*: "Paul Simon, Wife, Suffered Injuries During Fight."

The 911 line in the New Canaan police station rang shortly after eight o'clock on Saturday night, April 26, but the caller hung up. The police phone system registered the number and, under department regulations, dispatched a car to the scene. According to police reports, the car arrived at Simon's cottage at eight twenty. Brickell told the police that she went from the main house to the cottage to confront Simon on "something which he'd done that broke my heart," but there was no indication of what that might have been. She admitted she slapped Simon, who then reportedly shoved her. After determining the situation was under control, the police left the grounds. Two days later, the couple appeared in Norwalk Superior Court to respond to charges of misdemeanor disorderly conduct. Holding hands, they assured the judge that they weren't a threat to each other or anyone else. Leaving the building, Simon told reporters, "This was very atypical of us."

Less than forty-eight hours later, Paul and Edie released a gentle acoustic ballad, "Like to Get to Know You," on her SoundCloud page. There was no indication whether it was a new or old song, but the duet's message was about recapturing a relationship. Adrian soon tweeted, "Everything

AOK." Lulu, who was nineteen, also tweeted, "We are more than the worst thing that's ever happened to us." For his part, Simon released a statement on Friday through his attorney labeling reports that Edie was to blame for the disagreement "totally unfair." He added, "I got what I deserved." Two months later, the court case was officially dismissed.

Asked during an interview in 2017 to discuss the incident, Simon declined, even after it was pointed out that millions of people would likely think of that night whenever his marriage was brought up. He said, in essence, so be it.

"As in any relationship, there have been good times and difficult times, and the worst time was that night," he said. "My job and responsibility is writing songs and making records and stepping onstage. That's my public world, and I love that part of my life. That's what I want to share. I feel blessed for that. But I also feel blessed in my personal life, and I don't ever want to take on the unnecessary strain of making it part of fame and celebrity. Edie has been the greatest love of my life, and I'm nuts about the kids, but I've seen what celebrity and gossip can do to people, especially people in show business, and Edie and I have tried to make sure our children had the chance to grow up outside of all that."

Simon spent the rest of the year finishing the new album. He completed work on "In a Parade," which continued the story of "Street Angel," finding the character in even darker times. Simon also recorded two guitar pieces, "The Clock" and "In the Garden of Edie," that he'd written for a play, John Patrick Shanley's *Prodigal Son*. He was mainly concentrating on "Stranger to Stranger," the song that not only gave the album its title but its emotional center. It's another example of what the Library of Congress had in mind when it awarded Simon the Gershwin Prize: a ballad that Bing Crosby, Frank Sinatra, or any of the great pop vocalists of the 1930s, 1940s, and 1950s would have embraced. Part of the love song's strength is that it doesn't come at the theme head-on. Instead, it asks what might happen if longtime lovers might by chance meet again for the first time. Would they still fall in love? For the listener, it sounded like Simon was again straddling the line between memoir and imagination. In fact, the song was written in the months after the police incident in New Canaan, a tender time for both him and Edie. With that in mind, the lyrics become even more memorable. They include these lines:

Stranger to stranger
If we met for the first time
This time
Could you imagine us
Falling in love again

Still believing
That love endures
All the carnage
And the useless detours
Oh I love you, I love you, I love you
I love you, I love you, I love you . . .

Coming on the heels of *So Beautiful or So What*, the new album led to a widespread reassessment of Simon's post-*Capeman* career. The *Guardian* gave the album its top five-star rating, declaring, "His tenacious pursuit of new sounds, such as the unique microtonal instruments of composer Harry Partch on 'Insomniac's Lullaby,' and juxtapositions such as the gnarled blues guitar (played by Simon) and cello on 'The Riverbank,' make this album as rewarding as anything he's done." The *Boston Globe* liked it even more than *So Beautiful*, calling it his "richest, most instantly appealing collection since *Graceland*."

Stranger to Stranger, released by Concord Records, was a Top 10 hit in both the United States and the United Kingdom. When tickets for the shows sold out quickly, even Simon felt something special was going on. "It's like a lot of people suddenly are realizing that a lot of us—artists who have been around most of their lives—won't be doing shows forever," he said. "I think there's some of that in the air."

CHAPTER TWENTY-FOUR

Longevity wasn't all that unusual in other areas of music where artists routinely continued into their sixties and beyond. Most memorably, Roy Acuff, one of country music's most beloved stars, moved into a small house on the Opryland grounds in his eighties and continued to perform daily on the Grand Ole Opry stage in Nashville. Blues great B. B. King did a farewell tour in 2006, but kept doing occasional shows until his death three years later at eighty-nine. Tony Bennett was still filling concert halls in his nineties. Yet rock was so youth obsessed that it did feel strange as its aging stars, including Bob Dylan and the Rolling Stones, refused to leave the stage, and the question Simon faced in almost every interview during his promotional rounds for the new album was "How long are you going to keep making records and touring?" He answered the question in different ways on different days because, in truth, he still hadn't decided if he was ready to call it quits. Writing remained as natural to him as breathing, and he was still breathing just fine, thank you.

"Part of the answer to longevity has to do with music being more important than anything else in your life, and that's not easy," said Randy Newman, who also has continued to write at a high level for a half century. "When I commit a year to making a record, I'm not only unhappy most of the time myself but I'm so involved in the writing that everybody and everything else around me suffers. When I first started making records, I used to say in interviews what a drag songwriting was, and I finally realized I was being such a jerk by complaining about a job where I just sit at the piano all day. So I sort of stopped telling the truth about it in interviews."

Simon certainly didn't look like a man slowing down as he and his band gathered in a Connecticut rehearsal studio in early March 2016 to prepare for the North American dates that would stretch from late April to a pair of shows, starting June 30, at his old neighborhood's Forest Hills Stadium. Even more than concerts, the rehearsals demonstrated the care Simon still put into exploring the ever-changing character and nuance of his songs. This version of his band was well equipped to follow him through the various musical styles he had embraced over the years, from R&B to rockabilly, from pop to world music. Besides Stewart, Kumalo, Nguini, and Haddad, the lineup included keyboardist Mick Rossi, guitarist-drummer Jim Oblon, saxophonist Andy Snitzer, and trumpet player C. J. Camerieri—all world class. Even newcomer Joel Guzman was a Grammy-winning accordionist and guitarist who was a superstar in the world of Texas alt-country and Tejano music. The relationships worked because the musicians had enough respect for Simon to bend their individual styles to fit his vision—as time consuming as that could be.

During the sometimes three-hour rehearsals, Simon frequently conferred with individual musicians to explain what he wanted. The work was demanding, and it didn't stop once the tour began. While afternoon sound checks are casual affairs for many musicians, Simon's were so serious that they amounted to a second show—which is why his crew members referred to them as "the matinee." "On some nights, we'll do a version of a song so well you can't imagine it being any better," bandleader Mark Stewart said. "But on the way out of the venue, Paul will say, 'We've got to work on that song some more tomorrow. I've got an idea I want to try.' "

As the tour progressed, Simon was constantly being urged—by friends, fans, and the media—not to retire. At the same time, he didn't want to keep on making records and touring simply because it was expected or because he didn't know how to stop. With the children in college or on their own, he and Edie were now empty nesters, as they called themselves, and they liked to travel, so he wanted to leave time for that. As he thought about options, one attractive possibility emerged.

Simon had been moved when three of his early songs reappeared in prominent public roles in recent months: First, U2 performing "Mother and Child Reunion" on its worldwide Innocence + Experience tour. (Simon joined the band onstage during the song on July 30, 2015, at Madison Square Garden.) Second, "America" was adopted as the theme song of Senator Bernie Sanders's campaign for the Democratic Party's presidential nomination. And finally, "The Sound of Silence" was a hit all over again after being recorded by the heavy-metal band Disturbed.

More than sales charts, he began to see that the real measure of a song's impact is whether it enters the cultural consciousness, a test that can be determined only over time. This led Simon to think about revisiting some of his favorite compositions that weren't hits and giving them new arrangements—and therefore a second chance at catching the public's ear. He even began making an informal list, singling out tunes such as, "Questions for the Angels," "Darling Lorraine," "Some Folks' Lives Roll Easy," and "René and Georgette Magritte with Their Dog After the War." Rather than spending three or four years writing and then recording songs for a new album, this concept of giving songs a second chance was something he felt was manageable and enjoyable. He could record these relatively quickly, leaving ample time for whatever else might arise, especially aiding social causes—such as biologist Edward O. Wilson's visionary conservation plan to designate half of the Earth's land a human-free natural reserve to preserve biodiversity. Simon had recently reconnected with Wilson, and he wanted to do some benefit concerts for the Half-Earth campaign.

As the US leg of the tour headed to its final dates at Forest Hills Stadium, the question of Simon's future remained a subtheme. Then, suddenly, it became *the* theme. Jim Dwyer, a Pulitzer Prize–winning journalist who wrote the About New York column for the *New York Times*, learned long ago to trust his own instincts about what could be a good story—and those instincts led him to Simon. When Dwyer heard about the tour, he remembered that a former neighbor of his—percussionist Jamey Haddad—had told him years ago about how Simon rehearsed every day that he was on tour. Dwyer had long been intrigued by people who maintain their drive their entire life—"runners," he once wrote, "who race through the tape at the finish line and keep going." He arranged to interview Simon for a column that would appear just before the Forest Hills shows.

Eager to report on what kept Simon going, Dwyer watched in fascination as Simon led the band through a typically long sound check at the Wolf Trap performing arts center in Virginia. During the subsequent interview, the conversation drifted into other areas, including what Simon might want to do beyond music—and it was his answers that made news two days before the first of the Forest Hills concerts, under the provocative headline "After Six Decades of Making Music, Embracing the Sound of Silence." Especially attention grabbing was the cross-reference to the story on page A1 that declared: "There Goes Rhymin' Simon: After 61 Years of Making Music, Paul Simon Says He's Ready to Call It a Career."

The words hit Simon fans with tabloid-like shock. "Showbiz doesn't hold any interest for me," Simon was quoted as saying in the June 28 column. "None." He also spoke about the question that he had been thinking about for months: the possibility that there would be something heroic in quitting music. "It's an act of courage," he said to Dwyer. "I'm going to see what happens if I let go. Then I'm going to see, who am I? Or am I just this person that was defined by what I did. And if that's gone, if you have to make up yourself, who are you?" The quotes were provocative, but Simon later said he was speaking hypothetically about the time he would retire. Even Dwyer wrote a few words of caution: "Yet nothing—not a moment—

about a day with Paul Simon suggests a man ready to withdraw from the pursuits that have absorbed his life."

Chuck Close, a celebrated American painter known for often strikingly large abstract portraits, phoned Simon as soon as he read the column to encourage his old friend to keep working. "Artists don't retire," he said. "Don't deny yourself this late stage, because late stages can be very interesting. You know everybody hated late de Kooning, but it turned out to be great stuff. Late Picasso, nobody liked it, and it turned out to be great. Had Matisse not done the cutouts [late in life], a lot of people wouldn't know who he was." Close, who continued painting after he was confined to a wheelchair following a spinal artery failure in 1988, had known Simon for years, and they enjoyed talking about the creative process, often with Philip Glass during semiannual meals. His belief was that hard work was at the bottom of most great art. "Talent is a dime a dozen," he said in 2016. "But some of the most talented people never accomplish anything. Sometimes the person with far less talent far outperforms the talented person because he's hungrier, he wants it more."

When Simon told Close that he was tired of the recording-and-touring cycle, the painter responded, "Then stop touring. You've earned the right to work the way you want to work." He also told Simon that he didn't have to commit himself to months in the studio to make an album; simply record one song at a time. "That's what I do," he said. "I finish a painting, then I do eleven more, and I eventually have a show. But I do each painting separately. I don't paint them all at once. It takes a lot of pressure off. The only pressure you feel is the making of one painting." Simon also received calls from others offering encouragement and advice. All this public attention added a touch of urgency to Simon's thoughts about the future. Even the band members were wondering how much longer he'd be calling on them.

The Forest Hills Stadium concerts had a strong homecoming aura, both in the audience, where fans talked about how much Simon meant to the area, and backstage, where Edie waited with him in his dressing room during a half-hour downpour that interrupted the concert. Back onstage, Simon playfully acknowledged the hometown locale. "It's kind of a time warp," he said. "I'm trying to get over whether it's strange or some beautiful dream."

When he returned for the encore, he made a couple of changes in his usual closing selections: going back sixty years to play "That's All Right," the Elvis record he heard in the parking lot of the Grand Union supermarket, and then back forty years for a song from *There Goes Rhymin' Simon* that Adrian and Gabriel had asked him to play, "One Man's Ceiling Is Another Man's Floor." Simon followed "Ceiling" with a song that was almost always part of his encores: the song about a musical journey that began only blocks from where he was standing, "The Boxer."

If Simon was ready to say goodbye to touring, this would have been a memorable ending. But he still had nearly two dozen European dates, including six shows in England, where the talk about farewell would be even more intense. As soon as the tour began, in Prague, Czech Republic, on October 17, fans began checking the internet for reports about Simon's future, but there was no word from any of the cities en route to London.

The café area of London's Royal Albert Hall was filled before the show on November 7 with fans who both reminisced and speculated on the future. The concert itself was another lovefest. Seeing the enthusiasm from the audience, Simon joked early in the set, "I'm so happy to be here, but obviously not as happy as you are." Afterward, he hosted a small group of friends, including Lynne and Jonty McCausland, Melissa North, Dream Academy's Nick Laird-Clowes, and, of course, Kathy Chitty and Ken, along with their two daughters, Rachel and Rhiannon, and son, Jim. Simon invited Kathy and Ken to bring their three-year-old granddaughter, Lola, to the following day's sound check, where Lola and her mother, Rachel, danced in an aisle of the largely empty hall during some of the numbers. When Simon went over to say hello, Lola greeted him with "Hi, Uncle Paul."

The feeling at the second Albert Hall concert was equally warm. Early in the set, Simon dedicated "Mrs. Robinson" to the US election, the results of which wouldn't be known for several hours. Besides allowing Bernie Sanders to use "America" in TV ads, Simon later supported the eventual Democratic nominee, Hillary Clinton, by singing "Bridge Over Troubled

Water" during the Democratic National Convention in July. To close the Albert Hall concert, he again turned to the song.

As in New York, numerous English critics used the London engagement to reflect on Simon's career. The *London Times*'s review began, "Paul Simon really is the godfather of world music. Bob Dylan had the prophet's vision and Neil Young the hippy heaviness, yet it was Simon who looked beyond the music of his own country and found a way to utilize styles from all over the world in a way that made them palatable to rock audiences." The *Financial Times* review also paid Simon a compliment by noting the rarity of a veteran artist's new material being among his strongest: "Usually at gigs when [rock veterans] unveil their latest material, punters find an urgent excuse to go to the bar. Here it was a minor disappointment that only three tracks [from his new album] were played."

After the second London concert, Simon was up all night watching the US election results, and he was still trying to come to grips in his hotel room the following night with Donald Trump's stunning victory. "The election put a pall on everything," he said, looking exhausted as he sat in a chair. As he spoke, however, it was clear that his fatigue went further than election disappointment. He was drained by the tour. It was like he had come full circle. With a word change here or there, the road-weary lyrics of "Homeward Bound" applied again. He could definitely see an end to touring, he said. He was even thinking, he acknowledged, of a farewell tour in 2018. In his spare time on the road, Simon had continued to revise the lineup of songs for the "revisit" album. He enjoyed this exercise because there had often been a disconnect between the songs of his that he favored and the ones that were embraced by the public.

As the hours went on that night, Simon was increasingly relaxed. It was as if he could see the end of one period in his life and the beginning of another. He even agreed to name his favorite ten compositions ever, though he warned the list could change depending on his mood. In considering the possibilities, he mentioned more than fifty songs. (Most are listed in the Notes.) The favorite ten, chronologically, were "The Sound of Silence,"

"The Boxer," "Bridge Over Troubled Water," "Me and Julio Down by the Schoolyard," "Still Crazy After All These Years," "Graceland," "Diamonds on the Soles of Her Shoes," "The Cool, Cool River," "Darling Lorraine," and "Questions for the Angels." Simon has favorites from *Stranger to Stranger*, including the title song and "Insomniac's Lullaby," but he wanted to live with them longer before a final judgment.

When Simon later told Chuck Close about the revisit project, his friend scoffed. "He'll never finish that album," he said privately. "It won't be challenging enough. At some point, he'll think of a new melody or new lyric, and he'll be back to writing songs." Informed of Close's comments, Simon reaffirmed his interest in the project. "It's a joy when people accept one of your songs," he said. "That's not the same as starting off to write a hit; you must always write what you feel, knowing fully that no one else may care about the song. But when people do respond, it is very gratifying, and I think it would be extremely gratifying if the new album caused even one or two of these songs to gain that wider acceptance."

Thirteen nights later, the tour ended triumphantly before nearly ten thousand fans at the 3 Arena in Dublin. Simon headed home on the following day with Edie, who had joined the tour in Madrid four days earlier. As the charter jet left the Dublin airport, the flight was in many ways a bookend to the Air India flight he had taken from London a half century earlier. Where his big-time music career was just beginning in 1965, it was now winding down. "Actually," Simon said, "when I completed the *Stranger to Stranger* album, I told myself, 'I'm finished.' I've just been waiting to say anything to make sure about it." He now planned to go to Hawaii with Edie and the kids for a monthlong vacation and try to figure out if he could really walk away. Whatever; he felt blessed. Only three months before, he and Edie had renewed their vows overlooking the ocean at their home in Montauk.

EPILOGUE

Whether or not he never writes another song, Simon's body of work has guaranteed him a place on the list of the greatest American songwriters—a list that goes all the way back to Stephen Foster, the father of American music. Indeed, he has qualified for a place in that list several times over.

If you considered only the songs he wrote during the Simon and Garfunkel years—including "The Sound of Silence," "The Boxer," "Mrs. Robinson," and "Bridge Over Troubled Water," for starters—Simon would be on the list of great American songwriters.

If you considered only the songs he wrote in the 1970s—including "Me and Julio Down by the Schoolyard," "American Tune," "Something So Right," and "Still Crazy After All These Years"—Simon would also be on that list.

If you considered only the songs he wrote in the 1980s and 1990s—including "Hearts and Bones," "Graceland," "The Boy in the Bubble," "The

Obvious Child"—Simon would still be viewed as one of the great American songwriters.

When you put all three periods together, Simon isn't just on the short list, he's high on it.

Add to that Simon's remarkable fourth phase, the post-*Capeman* albums that Kelefa Sanneh, a former *New York Times* pop critic, saluted in a 2016 essay in the *New Yorker*, offering a fresh look at *You're the One* and *Surprise.* "Starting in 2000 with *You're the One*, Simon has turned out a series of clever, quietly audacious albums, containing some songs that are as good as anything he has made," Sanneh wrote. "He has earned plenty of gravitas over the years, but he seems too restless to spend it, embarking instead on a series of experiments in rhythm and texture, and honing in his lyrics a shrugging acceptance of an imperfect world . . . More than any other musician of his age or stature—more than Bob Dylan or Aretha Franklin or Mick Jagger, more than Paul McCartney or Joni Mitchell—he seems unburdened by the years, and by his own reputation. He has managed to become neither a wizened oracle nor an oldies act, and his best songs convey the appealing sensation of listening to a guy who is still trying to figure out what he's doing."

Simon's friend Thomas Friedman certainly believes he will write more songs at some point. "I can't imagine him not writing," he said. "While he might not always be interested in songwriting, songwriting is always interested in him. Every once in a while, we will be talking, and he will say something. And I will either say out loud or think to myself, 'That's a song lyric.' Lyrics are part of his DNA. He can't help himself. The zeitgeist flows through him in a way that it doesn't with other people, which is why so many of his lyrics have penetrated so deeply and stayed so long. Just think about the last album. He was working on that two years before the 2016 presidential election. Yet somewhere he pulled out of the atmosphere 'the werewolf's coming.' And then Trump got elected."

Even so, the months of soul-searching about his future convinced Simon that he wanted the freedom to explore other avenues and passions. For all the immense rewards of a life in music, the pressures, self-imposed and external, to live up to expectations can be staggering. In the days after returning from Hawaii, he was able to say he finally felt fully free.

"I didn't do anything special," he said of Hawaii. "I was tired. I looked around a little bit. I read a little bit. Edie and I walked on the beach, did some yoga. We went to different islands, and we're even looking for a place there to spend the winter. The kids were with us, and it was great. In fact, we were all together last night. It was Lulu's twenty-second birthday, and it was so nice because she wanted to have dinner with just the family."

Home from Hawaii, where he later bought a house, Simon hit the ground running. He joined Edward O. Wilson at a "Biodiversity Days" program at Duke University to promote awareness of the Half-Earth campaign and he finalized details for a June tour, which would raise funds for that cause. He also planned to spend a day at his home studio with jazz guitarist Bill Frisell to readdress "Questions for the Angels" for his album project and attend the opening of a Simon exhibit at the Skirball Cultural Center in Los Angeles, where he would be joined by Lorne and Mo, among other longtime friends. In the midst of it all, he and Edie snuck away to Norway for a few days to see the northern lights.

Looming above everything musically was his decision to commit to a lengthy 2018 farewell tour which, too, could help raise awareness for Half-Earth. "The important thing is to spread the word that this isn't just some horrific, intellectual idea that the planet is headed toward extinction," Simon said, talking Half-Earth with the urgency normally reserved for his songwriting. "Extinction is so enormous that the first thing you do is go into denial and say, 'Well, that's not going to happen.' Wilson's message is that it can happen, but there are things we can do about it. But the word has to get out to more people, and that's where I feel a responsibility.

"As I get older, I understand more and more the powerful effect that songs have, far more powerful than just being hits. After the 9/11 *Saturday Night Live* appearance with Lorne and the program devoted to the tenth anniversary of the World Trade Center attack, I could see this power exists, and I want to use that power whenever I can. It makes me feel I'm doing some good and exercising my responsibility as a grown-up to my children and to the planet. It's a bit of an answer for me when I ask myself, 'What am I doing out here onstage?' which I do ask myself sometimes on tour. I can say, 'What you are doing is raising millions of dollars for a cause you believe in.' It's saying thank you for all I have been given." He also started looking into how to set up a foundation to leave much of his fortune (now estimated between $200 million and $400 million) that could continue to fund causes important to him.

Yet there was sobering news. On March 17, Derek Walcott, who had remained Simon's friend throughout their *Capeman* differences, died at his home in Saint Lucia at the age of eighty-seven. Nine months later, on December 8, there would be further heartbreaking news: Simon's longtime guitarist, Vincent Nguini, would succumb to liver cancer at age sixty-five.

Asked late in the year if he would care to reflect on his life in music— not just the rewards but also the sacrifices—Simon considered the proposition before ultimately declining. "That's too big a subject, and I don't think in terms of that," he said. "That's the reason I'm not writing a memoir. I'm not drawn to making big observations about it. Basically, I feel that I have had a very, very fortunate life. I've had a tendency to slip into some form of depression, but it has been mild, not chronic—part of my personality since adolescence. I haven't had any terrible tragedy. There was the death of my parents, but that came the way it should, chronologically. Sure, you pay a price for fame, but I'm not inclined to calculate it. I really have no complaints. Mostly, I've been lucky. I've been able to spend my whole life in music, and I have the love of Edie and the children, and I have some wonderful friends."

Pausing briefly, Simon, who told an interviewer in the 1980s that he found it hard to acknowledge the good times in his life, showed no reluctance adding, "I'm grateful for my life."

Bobby Susser, who knew Simon longer than anyone outside his family, said he has heard Simon express gratitude in the past, but he believed his friend had indeed entered a new phase of peacefulness and contentment— one rooted, he felt, in the failures of the past: the confidence gained in bouncing back from despair with *Graceland* and then realizing after *The Capeman* that no matter what happened, he still had his songs and his family.

"As he matured and became easier on himself," Susser said, "I could see that he's grown into the man he wanted to be and the one that Lou knew he'd be. I once told Paul, after seeing him lead his band, 'You remind me of Lou up there,' and he got this Lou-like glow on his face when he said, 'Thanks. I hope so.'"

ACKNOWLEDGMENTS

Before I started writing books, I felt writers could save readers a lot of time and a few trees by thanking people important to the book with flowers, a box of chocolates, or a good bottle of wine rather than in an acknowledgment. But I now understand the need for authors to publicly express appreciation to those who aided and accompanied them during the years they spent on a book.

First, I want to thank Paul Simon. After decades of not speaking to any potential biographer, he not only agreed to talk to me about his life and music but also encouraged those close to him to do so. The plan was to meet for five hours a day on one day a month for a year, which would have given us sixty hours of tape, but the talks ended up stretching over three years and easily totaled more than one hundred hours.

Despite this unprecedented access, Simon agreed that I would have full editorial control over the book's contents. We met numerous times in his recording studio/cottage in Connecticut and in his office in Manhattan, as well as in hotel rooms when he was on tour. He was patient, gracious, and unrelentingly thoughtful. The empathy in his songs is no accident. I liked him. But there were difficult moments.

Interviewing Simon over the years for the *Los Angeles Times*, I found him to be one of the most articulate people I met in pop music. But we were focusing in those days on his new music, a subject that he is always interested in. With the book, he wasn't as eager early on to talk about his private life and sometimes bristled when a touchy subject came up, leading occasionally to heated discussions.

There were even times when I feared the project was close to breaking down. In the end, however, Simon was a man of his word. He never challenged my final control. When he saw we were at an impasse over something, 'he would simply shrug, wave his hand, and say, "It's your book," and we'd move on. Gradually, he began speaking about his personal life with the same eloquence and detail he exhibited when talking about music. The bottom line was that he, too, wanted a complete and objective account.

I'm also grateful to those around Simon, from his brother, Eddie (who comanages him and guards his back with the tenacity of one of my English bulldogs), to Bobby Susser, his pal since childhood (who was quick to answer more than seventy-five emails I sent asking about moments in Simon's life). Thanks as well to Simon's band members for their generous assistance, and to his office staff—Juanita DeSilva, C. Vaughn Hazell, Cristina Miranda, Selwyn Rogers, and Martia Gordon. The glue in the project was Jeff Kramer, who believed in the book from the start and offered valuable counsel.

Thanks to everyone listed under the Interviews headings in the Notes section, but especially to a group of people that reaches back to grade-school classmate Helene Schwartz Kenvin and the 1960s English crowd that includes Ken Harrison and Jonty and Lynne McCausland, and that ultimately includes Roy Halee, Mort Lewis, Peggy Harper, Carrie Fisher, Lorne Michaels, Dan Klores, Clive J. Davis, Mo Ostin (whose reflections were especially appreciated because he has done so few interviews over the years), Lenny Waronker, Quincy Jones, Allen Toussaint, Michael

Tannen, Wynton Marsalis, Chuck Close, Philip Glass, Ruben Blades, Oscar Hernandez, Joe Rascoff, Derek Walcott, Paul Zollo, and Thomas Friedman.

In my professional world, my thanks begin with Luke Janklow, a visionary agent who is forever insightful and supportive. Also, Claire Dippel. At Simon & Schuster, the views of president and publisher Jonathan Karp and executive editor Jofie Ferrari-Adler were wise and helpful. Ferarri-Adler, my editor, has a warmth that makes him feel like a friend you've known for years and a calmness that is helpful in moments of uncertainty or doubt. The S&S team also includes Jessica Breen, Rachel DeCesario, Paul Dippolito, Lisa Erwin, Sabrina Evans, Cary Goldstein, Julianna Haubner, Benjamin Holmes, Kristen Lemire, Jennifer Lopes, Anne Tate Pearce, and Richard Rhorer. Also, thanks to Mona Houck and Philip Bashe.

As always, I want to express my gratitude to a series of editors at the *Los Angeles Times* who gave me unending encouragement and freedom over the years: Charles Champlin, Irv Letofsky, Shelby Coffey, John Lindsay, John Carroll, and Dean Baquet.

Then there's my family, whose love is the foundation of it all: Alice Marie and John through my first wife, Ruthann Snijders, and our children, Kathy Morris and Rob Hilburn, on to my son-in-law, Ronald Morris, and daughter-in-law, Sarah Coley-Hilburn, and my wife Kathi's children, Keith and Kate Bond—and the wonderful grandchildren, Chris and Lindsey Morris and Genevieve and Grant Hilburn. Extra thanks to Rob, Kathy, and Chris, who assisted me in various ways over the last three years.

Finally, it is a blessing for a writer to have friends that he can bounce ideas off and even share parts of the manuscript with, and no one served that role better for me than Bret Israel, who was another of my editors at the *Los Angeles Times* and remains a smart and trusted friend. And my wife, Kathi, who read the book at every stage and was quick to point out when I ventured off the track and to praise when things suddenly came alive. The flowers, the chocolate, and the wine will follow.

BIBLIOGRAPHY

Except for the quotes cited after each chapter below, all quotes in the book are from interviews I conducted with Paul Simon between late 2014 and late 2017. The same is true for the remarks of the more than a hundred others that were interviewed for the book.

INTERVIEWS

Lou Adler, Wally Amos, Joel Amsterdam, Vic Anesini, Burt Bacharach, Jeff Barry, Glenn Berger, Ruben Blades, Hal Blaine, Bono, Ariel Bruce, Martin Carthy, Robert Christgau, Chuck Close, Marty Cooper, Father "Jay" Cunnane, Clive Davis, Quint Davis, Ron Delsener, Freddy DeMann, Juanita DeSilva, Dion DiMucci, Dick Ebersol, Ken Ehrlich, Don Everly, Patti Everly, Carrie Fisher, Thomas Friedman, Jack Froggatt, David Geffen, Philip Glass, Henry Goldrich, Al Gorgoni, Dr. Rod Gorney (no psychological assessment), Charles Grodin, Joel Guzman, Jamey Haddad, Roy Halee, Ken Harrison, C. Vaughn Hazell, Anthony Heilbut, Oscar Hernandez, Patrick Humphries, Jimmy Iovine, Quincy Jones, Denise Kaufman, Helene Schwartz Kenvin, Carole King, Victoria Kingston, Dan Klores, Glenn Korman, Barry Kornfeld, Jeff Kramer, Bakithi Kumalo, Nick Laird-Clowes, Jon Landau, Dickie Landry, Mort Lewis, Michael Lindsay-

Hogg, Wynton Marsalis, Steve Martin, Beverley Martyn, Jonty McCausland, Lynne McCausland, Charlie McCoy, Lorne Michaels, Cristina Miranda, Chris Morris, Sigrid Nama, Randy Newman, Vincent Nguini, Melissa North, Jim Oblon, Mo Ostin, Rob Oudshoorn, Brad Paisley, Peter Parcher, Joe Rascoff, Dr. Irwin Redlener, Lou Robin, Terre Roche, Linda Ronstadt, Mick Rossi, John Scher, Iris Schneider, Mitch Schneider, Chris Sherwen, Eddie Simon, John Simon, Peggy Simon, Andy Smith, Robert Smith, Geoff Speed, Pam Speed, Roger Steffens, Chris Stern, Al Stewart, Mark Stewart, Sting, Dick Summer, Bobby Susser, Michael Tannen, Benmont Tench, Russ Titelman, Allen Toussaint, Steven Van Zandt, Derek Walcott, Beverly Wax, Guy Webster, Jann Wenner, Jack White, Paul Zollo, and Ali J. Ahmed and Sonny T. Hung of the Queens College Comparative Literature Department.

BOOKS

Abbott, Jim. *Jackson C. Frank: The Clear, Hard Light of Genius*. Brooklyn: Ba Da Bing, 2014.

Bean, J. P. *Singing from the Floor: A History of British Folk Clubs*. London: Faber & Faber, 2014.

Bennighof, James. *The Words and Music of Paul Simon*. Westport, CT: Praeger, 2007.

Berger, Glenn. *Never Say No to a Rock Star*. Tucson, AZ: Schaffner Press, 2016.

Bonca, Cornel. *Paul Simon: An American Tune*. Lanham, MD: Rowman & Littlefield, 2015.

Brackett, Nathan, with Christian Hoard, eds. *The New Rolling Stone Album Guide*. New York: Fireside, 2004.

Browne, David. *Fire and Rain: . . . The Lost Story of 1970*. Cambridge, MA: Da Capo Press, 2011.

Carlin, Peter Ames. *Homeward Bound: The Life of Paul Simon*. New York: Henry Holt, 2016.

Castle, Alison. *Saturday Night Live: The Book*. New York: Taschen, 2015.

Christgau, Robert. *Christgau's Record Guide: Rock Albums of the 1970s*. New York: New Haven: Ticknor & Fields, 1981.

———. *Christgau's Record Guide: The '80s*. New York: Pantheon, 1990.

Cornyn, Stan, with Paul Scanlon. *Exploding: The Highs, Hits . . . and Hustlers of the Warner Music Group*. New York: Harper Collins, 2002.

Costello, Elvis. *Unfaithful Music & Disappearing Ink*. New York: Blue Rider Press, 2015.

Davis, Clive, with Anthony DeCurtis. *Clive Davis: The Soundtrack of My Life*. New York: Simon & Schuster, 2012.

DeCurtis, Anthony. *In Other Words: Artists Talk About their Life and Work*. Milwaukee: Hal Leonard, 2005.

Eliot, Marc. *Paul Simon: A Life*. Hoboken, NJ: John Wiley & Sons, 2010.

Evanger, David. *Woody: The Biography*. New York: St. Martin's Press, 2015.

Fisher, Carrie. *Postcards from the Edge*. New York: Simon & Schuster, 1987.

——. *Shockaholic*, New York: Simon & Schuster, 2011.

——. *Surrender the Pink*. New York: Simon & Schuster, 1990.

——. *Wishful Drinking*. New York: Simon & Schuster, 2008.

Flanagan, Bill. *Written in My Soul*. Chicago: Contemporary Books, 1986.

Fornatale, Pete. *Simon & Garfunkel's Bookends*. New York: Rodale, 2007.

Garfunkel, Art. *What Is It All but Luminous: Notes from an Underground Man*. New York: Alfred A. Knopf, 2017.

George-Warren, Holly, ed. *Paul Simon: Words & Music-Exhibition Guide*. Cleveland: Rock & Roll Hall of Fame and Museum, 2014.

Granade, S. Andrew. *Harry Partch: Hobo Composer*. Rochester, NY: University of Rochester Press, 2014.

Grodin, Charles. *It Would Be So Nice If You Weren't Here*. New York: William Morrow, 1989.

——. *We're Ready for You Mr. Grodin*. New York: Charles Scribner's Sons, 1994.

Hagan, Joe. *Sticky Fingers: The Life and Times of Jann Wenner and Rolling Stone Magazine*. New York: Alfred A. Knopf, 2017.

Harper, Colin. *Dazzling Stranger: Bert Jansch and the British Folk and Blues Revival*. London: Bloomsbury, 2006.

Harris, Mark. *Pictures at a Revolution: Five Movies and the Birth of the New Hollywood*. New York: Penguin, 2009.

Heilbut, Anthony. *The Fan Who Knew Too Much*. New York: Alfred A. Knopf, 2012.

Hill, Doug, and Jeff Weingrad. *Saturday Night: A Backstage History of Saturday Night Live*. San Francisco: Untweed Reads, 2014.

Humphries, Patrick. *The Boy in the Bubble*. London: Sidgwick & Jackson, 1988.

——. *Lonnie Donegan and the Birth of British Rock & Roll*. London: Robson Press, 2012.

Jackson, Laura. *Paul Simon: The Definitive Biography of the Legendary Singer/Songwriter*. New York: Citadel Press, 2002.

King, Carole. *A Natural Woman*. New York: Grand Central, 2012.

Kingston, Victoria. *Simon & Garfunkel: The Biography*. London: Sidgwick & Jackson, 1996.

Kooper, Al. *Backstage Passes & Backstabbing Bastards*. New York: Backbeat Books, 2008.

Laing, Dave, and Richard Newman, eds. *Thirty Years of the Cambridge Folk Festival*. Ely, UK: Music Maker, 1994.

Leigh, Spencer. *Simon & Garfunkel: Together Alone*. Carmarthen, UK: McNidder & Grace, 2016.

Lindsay-Hogg, Michael. *Luck and Circumstance*. New York: Alfred A. Knopf, 2011.

Luftig, Stacey. *The Paul Simon Compilation: Four Decades of Commentary*. New York: Schirmer Books, 1997.

Marmorstein, Gary. *The Label: The Story of Columbia Records*. New York: Thunder's Mouth Press, 2007.

Martyn, Beverley. *Sweet Honesty*. Guildford, UK: Grosvenor House, 2011.

Morella, Joseph, and Barey, Patricia. *Simon and Garfunkel: Old Friends*. New York: Birch Lane Press, 1991.

Morris, Chris. *Los Lobos: Dream in Blue*. Austin: University of Texas Press, 2015.

Olsen, Eric, with Paul Verna and Carlo Wolff. *The Encyclopedia of Record Producers*. New York: Billboard Books, 1999.

O'Neil, Thomas. *The Grammys*. New York: Perigee, 1993.

Pang, May, and Henry Edwards. *Loving John*. New York: Warner Books, 1983.

Passman, Donald S. *All You Need to Know About the Music Business*. New York: Simon & Schuster, 2015.

Petrus, Stephen, and Ronald D. Cohen. *Folk City: New York and the American Folk Music Revival*. New York: Oxford University Press, 2015.

Ramone, Phil, with Charles L. Granata. *Making Records: The Scenes Behind the Music*. New York: Hyperion, 2007.

Redlener, Irwin. *Americans at Risk*. New York: Alfred A. Knopf, 2006.

Roche, Terre. *Blabbermouth: A Memoir*. Self-published, 2013.

Rodgers, Jeffrey Pepper. *Rock Troubadours*. San Raphael, CA: String Letter, 2000.

Shelton, Robert. *No Direction Home: The Life and Music of Bob Dylan*. New York: Beech Tree Books, 1986.

Simon, Paul. *Paul Simon Lyrics 1964–2011*. New York: Simon & Schuster, 2008.

Spera, Keith. *Groove Interrupted: Loss, Renewal and the Music of New Orleans*. New York: Picador, 2011.

Sting. *Broken Music: A Memoir*. New York: Dial Press, 2003.

Van Ronk, Dave, with Elijah Wald. *The Mayor of MacDougal Street: A Memoir*. Cambridge, MA: Da Capo Press, 2006.

Warner, Jay. *The Billboard Book of American Singing Groups: A History 1940–1990*. New York: Billboard Books, 1992.

Warwick, Neil, Jon Kutner, and Tony Brown. *The Complete Book of the British Charts*. London: Omnibus Press, 2004.

Webb, Jimmy. *The Cake and the Rain*. New York: St. Martin's Press, 2017.

———. *Tunesmith*. New York: Hachette, 1998.

Whitburn, Joel. *The Billboard Albums*. Menomonee Falls, WI: Record Research, 2006.

———. *Billboard Pop Charts 1955–1959*. Menomonee Falls, WI: Record Research, 1992.

———. *Hot 100 Charts The Sixties*. Menomonee Falls, WI: Record Research, 1990.

———. *Hot 100 Charts The Seventies*. Menomonee Falls, WI: Record Research, 1990.

———. *Pop Memories, 1890–1954: The History of American Popular Music*. Menomonee Falls, WI: Record Research, 1986.

———. *Top Pop Singles 1955–2015*. Menomonee Falls, WI: Record Research, 2016.

Wilentz, Sean. *360 Sound: The Columbia Records Story*. San Francisco: Chronicle Books, 2012.

Williams, Paul, ed. *The Crawdaddy! Book*. Milwaukee: Hal Leonard, 2002.

Willis, Ellen. *Out of the Vinyl Deeps: Ellen Willis on Rock Music.* Edited by Nona Willis Aronowitz. Minneapolis: University of Minnesota Press, 2011.

Wilson, Edward O. *Half-Earth: Our Planet's Fight for Life.* New York: Liveright, 2016.

Woliver, Robbie. *Bringing It All Back Home: Twenty-Five Years of American Music at Folk City.* New York: Pantheon Books, 1986.

Woodward, Bob. *Wired: The Short Life & Fast Times of John Belushi.* New York: Simon & Schuster, 1986.

Yagoda, Ben. *B-Side: The Death of Tin Pan Alley and the Rebirth of the Great American Song.* New York: Riverhead Books, 2015.

Yetnikoff, Walter, with David Ritz. *Howling at the Moon: The Odyssey of a Monstrous Music Mogul in an Age of Excess.* New York: Broadway, 2004.

Zollo, Paul. *Songwriters on Songwriting.* Cambridge, MA: Da Capo Press, 2003.

———. *More Songwriters on Songwriting.* Cambridge, MA: Da Capo Press, 2016.

NOTES

PROLOGUE

INTERVIEWS
---- Lorne Michaels, Paul Simon.

QUOTES
---- Belle Simon's comments here and throughout the book are from unpublished reflections on her life. The scene in chapter 4 about Paul playing "The Sound of Silence" for his father and the one in chapter 9 about watching Paul with Peggy at
Royal Albert Hall, among others, are from those reflections.

ARTICLES
---- Richard Green, "Because Pop Lyrics Are So Banal," *New Musical Express*, February 21, 1970.

RECORDINGS AND DVDS
---- *America: A Tribute to Heroes*, a two-disc album showcasing the September 21,
2001, telethon, Interscope Records. The DVD is from Warner/Reprise Video.

WEBSITES
---- Paul Simon's post-9/11 performance of "The Boxer" on *Saturday Night Live* can be
seen on YouTube and other websites.

CHAPTER 1

INTERVIEWS

---- Helene Schwartz Kenvin, George Schulman, Eddie Simon, Paul Simon, Bobby Susser, Beverly Wax.

WEBSITES

---- See Elvis's first appearance—September 9, 1956—on *The Ed Sullivan Show* on You-Tube.

CHAPTER 2

SIDELIGHTS

---- All of Dick Clark's *American Bandstand* episodes have been preserved—except for Paul and Art's appearance on November 22, 1957. The original Tom & Jerry recording of "Hey, Schoolgirl" can be heard on YouTube and found on the box set, *Paul Simon 1964/1993*.

INTERVIEWS

---- Burt Bacharach, Carole King, Mort Lewis, Eddie Simon, Paul Simon, Bobby Susser, Allen Toussaint.

QUOTES

---- "Our manager was always looking," Al Contera to Marc Eliot in *Paul Simon: A Life* (Hoboken, NJ: John Wiley & Sons, 2010).

RECORDINGS

---- There are several unauthorized albums featuring music from the Tom & Jerry days, the Jerry Landis singles, and the demo exercises, including a three-disc series titled *Paul Simon aka Jerry Landis*, on Bonus Records.

CHAPTER 3

INTERVIEWS

---- Dr. Ali J. Ahmed, Marty Cooper, Freddy DeMann, Sonny T. Hung, Jonty McCausland, Lynne McCausland, Eddie Simon, Paul Simon, Bobby Susser.

CHAPTER 4

INTERVIEWS

---- Wally Amos, Martin Carthy, David Geffen, Roy Halee, Patrick Humphries, Victoria Kingston, Barry Kornfeld, Jonty McCausland, Lynne McCausland, Eddie Simon, Paul Simon, Bobby Susser.

QUOTES

---- "It was a phenomenon," Wally Whyton to Victoria Kingston in *Simon & Garfunkel: The Biography*.

ARTICLES

---- Ann Geracimos, "A Record Producer Is a Psychoanalyst with Rhythm," *New York Times Magazine*, September 29, 1968.
---- Michael Hall, "The Greatest Music Producer You've Never Heard of Is . . . ," *Texas Monthly*, January 6, 2014.

CHAPTER 5

SIDELIGHTS

---- The other guests on the July 23, 1965, episode of *Ready Steady Go!* included Marianne Faithfull, the Moody Blues, P. J. Proby, and the Pretty Things.
---- On a tape of Paul's performing at a club in Exeter in 1965, he introduced "I Am a Rock" by referring to the television appearance. "The [British] record company said, 'Well, all right, if you're doing [the show], let's get a single out,' [and] they looked through all the tracks that I've been doing for this LP that I am working on, and they picked unquestionably my most neurotic song."
---- Also on the Exeter tape, Paul introduced "Kathy's Song" with these words: "When I left England last time to go back to New York, there was a lot of people I had become very friendly with, you know. I missed them very much, and I missed England very much when I was back home. So I wrote this song to sort of remind me of people and places I have been."
---- The English folk club owners in the Widnes area each had lots of Paul memories, a sign of the impact he made on them in 1965 and, most likely, the hundreds of times they have been asked about those days by Simon fans. Jack Froggatt, of the Minor Bird club, delighted in showing the receipt Paul signed on September 8 for his £12 payment.

INTERVIEWS

---- Jack Froggatt, Al Gorgoni, Victoria Kingston, Paul Simon, Mort Lewis, Michael Lindsay-Hogg, Quincy Jones, Lynne McCausland, Rob Oudshoorn, George Schulman, Chris Sherwin, Paul Simon, Geoff Speed, Pam Speed, Al Stewart, Dick Summer, Bobby Susser.

QUOTES

---- "Nobody there knew what to do," Judith Piepe to Patrick Humphries in *The Boy in the Bubble*.

---- "Paul was a very lovable person," ibid.

---- Joan Bata's recollection about Paul bringing home doughnuts is from Laura Jackson, *Paul Simon: The Definitive Biography of the Legendary Singer/Songwriter*.

---- "Kathy used to get a bit sulky because she felt that Paul was neglecting her," Joan Bata to Laura Jackson in *Paul Simon: The Definitive Biography of the Legendary Singer/Songwriter*.

RECORDINGS

---- *Song Book* was released briefly in America in 1969, and then rereleased at various points, including as part of *Paul Simon: The Complete Albums Collection* in 2012.

CHAPTER 6

SIDELIGHTS

---- Paul Williams's review of the debut album appeared in the February 7, 1966, issue of *Crawdaddy* magazine and is reprinted in *The Crawdaddy! Book*.

---- Shortly after Paul read the *Crawdaddy* review, he phoned Paul Williams at his college dorm and told him it was the first "intelligent" thing that had been written about Simon and Garfunkel's music. He also invited Williams to one of the duo's concerts.

---- The Simon and Garfunkel concert fees noted in this and other chapters are from Mort Lewis's notebook.

INTERVIEWS

---- Clive Davis, Roy Halee, Peggy Harper, Denise Kaufman, Mort Lewis, Paul Simon, Bobby Susser, Guy Webster, Jann Wenner.

QUOTES

---- "I never forget, and I never forgive," Garfunkel in *What Is It All But Luminous: Notes from an Underground Man*.

ARTICLES

---- Altham, Keith, "Paul Simon: Now They All Want Paul Simon Songs," *New Musical Express*, April 22, 1966.

CHAPTER 7

SIDELIGHTS

---- The set list for Paul and Art at the Monterey Pop Festival performance was "Homeward Bound," "At the Zoo," "The 59th Street Bridge Song," "For Emily, Whenever I May Find Her," "The Sound of Silence," "Benedictus," and "Punky's Dilemma."

---- If Paul knew what he wanted to do in life at age thirteen, Peggy looked back on her life in 2016 regretting she never had a dream about the future as a teen in rural Tennessee. "Later on, in New York, I took art classes, photography, and developed all these interests, and I always wished I had [embraced] them earlier, but the only goal the girls and guys had when I went to high school was getting married, and most of them were married by eighteen and never left the area. That would have been me, too, except for Mrs. Sweeten. God bless her."

INTERVIEWS

---- Lou Adler, Robert Christgau, Clive Davis, Roy Halee, Peggy Harper, Quincy Jones, Jon Landau, Mort Lewis, Beverley Kutner Martyn, Mitch Schneider, Eddie Simon, John Simon, Paul Simon.

ARTICLES

---- Schwartz, Tony, "Playboy Interview: Paul Simon," *Playboy*, February 1984.
---- Stevenson, James, "Simon and Garfunkel," *New Yorker*, September 2, 1967.

CHAPTER 8

INTERVIEWS

---- Hal Blaine, Father Jarlath "Jay" Cunnane, Clive Davis, Ron Delsener, Roy Halee, Peggy Harper, Quincy Jones, Mort Lewis, Charlie McCoy, Lou Robin, Eddie Simon, Paul Simon, Bobby Susser, Michael Tannen, Derek Walcott.

QUOTES

---- The account of Art Garfunkel hitchhiking to Boston was from an interview with Mort Lewis.
---- "For Art Garfunkel to be a little bit," Garfunkel to Paul Zollo in *SongTalk* magazine, the journal of the National Academy of Songwriters.
---- "Mike held me in Mexico," ibid.

ARTICLES

---- Greenfield, Josh, "For Simon And Garfunkel: All Is Groovy," *New York Times*, October 13, 1968.

CHAPTER 9

SIDELIGHTS

---- "Mary Don't You Weep" is a spiritual that can be traced to pre–Civil War days. The first recording of the song is believed to be by the Fisk Jubilee Singers in 1915. Besides the Swan Silvertones' 1959 recording, the song was also recorded by the Caravans gospel group in 1958. Aretha Franklin later included it on her *Amazing*

Grace album. The Silvertones' version was inducted into the Library of Congress's National Recording Registry in 2015.

INTERVIEWS

---- Hal Blaine, Clive Davis, Charles Grodin, Roy Halee, Peggy Harper, Quincy Jones, Mort Lewis, Terre Roche, Eddie Simon, Paul Simon, Bobby Susser, Michael Tannen.

QUOTES

---- "[It] has a very tender thing about it," Garfunkel to Zollo, *SongTalk*.
---- "He felt it was his best song," Garfunkel told *Rolling Stone* in 1973.

ARTICLES

---- Alterman, Lorraine, "Paul Simon," *Rolling Stone*, May 28, 1970.

RECORDINGS

---- The Simon and Garfunkel TV special, *Songs of America*, is part of the fortieth anniversary edition of the *Bridge Over Troubled Water* album.

CHAPTER 10

INTERVIEWS

---- Robert Christgau, Clive Davis, Roy Halee, Peggy Harper, Anthony Heilbut, Jon Landau, Paul Simon, Bobby Susser.

QUOTES

---- "I like other kinds of music," Simon told Jon Landau in a 1972 *Rolling Stone* article.
---- "I'm neurotically driven," Simon said to author in 1973 for the *Los Angeles Times*.
---- "I am really happy to be by myself now," he said to the *New York Times*'s Don Heckman.
---- "I think it's impressive," Simon to Landau, *Rolling Stone*.

ARTICLES

---- Landau, Jon, "Paul Simon: The Rolling Stone Interview," *Rolling Stone*, July 20, 1972.

RECORDINGS

---- The deluxe edition of *The Harder They Come* album is Hip-O; the DVD is part of the Criterion film series.

WEBSITES
---- The Paragons' recording of "Florence" can be heard on YouTube.

CHAPTER 11

SIDELIGHTS
---- During one of my interviews with Paul for the *Los Angeles Times*, he spoke about how amusing it was when headline writers frequently used "Still Crazy After All These Years" and "Bridge Over Troubled Water" in articles about him. "They'll do some take-off on it . . . like 'Still *This* After All These Years' or 'Still *That* After All These Years.' "

INTERVIEWS
---- Clive Davis, Roy Halee, Peggy Harper, Quincy Jones, Terre Roche, Paul Simon, Allen Toussaint.

QUOTES
---- "Paul was flabbergasted that it took us so little time," Barry Beckett in Phil Ramone's memoir, *Making Records: The Scenes Behind the Music*.
---- "Barry . . . by every indication," ibid.
---- "When I first wrote that melody," Simon to the author for the *Los Angeles Times* in 1973.
---- "The reason I wanted to do this tour now," ibid.

RECORDINGS AND DVDS
---- "Liquidator" by the Harry J. All Stars is available on YouTube.
---- Paul's gospel-heavy version of "Bridge Over Troubled Water" with the Jessy Dixon Singers is on the *Live Rhymin'* album on Columbia Records. A video can be found on YouTube.

CHAPTER 12

INTERVIEWS
---- Peggy Harper, Jimmy Iovine, Eddie Simon, Paul Simon, Michael Tannen.

QUOTES
---- "Most people look at me and wonder," Simon to Tony Schwartz in *Playboy* magazine in 1984.
---- May Pang's comments about John Lennon's irritation with Simon during the Harry Nilsson recording sessions are from her memoir, *Loving John*.
---- "Look, I'm working," Eddie Simon, quoted in Joseph Morella and Patricia Barey biography, *Simon and Garfunkel: Old Friends*.

RECORDINGS
---- The oldies album John Lennon recorded with producer Phil Spector, *Rock 'n' Roll*, was released in 1975 by Apple Records.

CHAPTER 13

INTERVIEWS
---- Dick Ebersol, Lorne Michaels, Paul Simon, Michael Tannen, Jann Wenner.

ARTICLES
---- Maureen Orr, "Simon Says," *Newsweek*, December 15, 1975.

CHAPTER 14

INTERVIEWS
---- Ariel Bruce, Carrie Fisher, Charles Grodin, Nick Laird-Clowes, Mort Lewis, Lorne Michaels, Mo Ostin, Paul Simon, Michael Tannen.

QUOTES
---- "I never liked the way Paul left Art," Walter Yetnikoff in his memoir *Howling at the Moon: The Odyssey of a Monstrous Music Mogul in an Age of Excess*.
---- "teeny, tiny little squirt," ibid.
---- "Just like in one of his songs," Shelley Duvall in 1980 interview in *Mademoiselle* magazine.
---- "If Carrie hadn't come along," Duvall in 1981 to *Cosmopolitan* magazine.
---- "My father was extremely unavailable," Carrie Fisher quoted in Eddie Fisher's autobiography *Been There, Done That*.
---- "As a teen, I *loved* this man's lyrics," Carrie Fisher in her memoir *Wishful Drinking*.

ARTICLES
---- Dave Marsh, "What to Do When You're Not a Kid Anymore . . . ," *Rolling Stone*, October 30, 1980.
---- Tony Schwartz, "Playboy Interview, Paul Simon," *Playboy*, February 1984.

RECORDINGS
---- The Dream Academy's "Life in a Northern Town" is on the group's *The Dream Academy* album on Warner Bros. Records.

CHAPTER 15

SIDELIGHTS
---- When asked in a 1983 interview with the author about how he approached the reunion album concept with Art, Simon said, "With great trepidation."

INTERVIEWS
---- Ron Delsener, Carrie Fisher, David Geffen, Roy Halee, Mort Lewis, Lorne Michaels, Mo Ostin, Paul Simon, Russ Titelman, Lenny Waronker, Jack White.

QUOTES
---- "I didn't want to do a film about music that I couldn't believe in," Simon said to the author for the *Los Angeles Times* article in 1980.
---- The detailed account of Simon's visits with Dr. Rod Gorney is based on an interview Simon gave to Tony Schwartz for *Playboy* in 1984.
---- "We just sort of got swept away," Simon to author in 1983 interview for *Los Angeles Times*.
---- "We had grown apart," Simon in BBC interview in the 1980s.
---- "Who told you to fall in love with an actress?" Eddie Fisher, in his autobiography *Been There, Done That*.
---- "I was told [about the disorder]," Carrie Fisher to *People* magazine in 1983.
---- "Anybody as bright as her in the biggest movie," Simon to *People* magazine in 1983.
---- Art Garfunkel's quote, "Well, how would you feel if you just found out you'd been erased from an entire album?" is from Arlen Roth's interview for *Analog Planet* in 2010.

RECORDINGS
---- Simon and Garfunkel, *The Concert in Central Park* is a CD-DVD deluxe edition from Sony Legacy.

CHAPTER 16

SIDELIGHTS
---- Carrie Fisher's *Wishful Drinking* was based on a stage production of the same name that ran at the Geffen Playhouse in Los Angeles in 2006. It subsequently was filmed for an HBO special and released later by HBO Documentary Films.

INTERVIEWS
---- Heidi Berg, Carrie Fisher, Philip Glass, Roy Halee, Bakithi Kumalo, Dickie Landry, Lorne Michaels, Randy Newman, Mo Ostin, Paul Simon, Roger Steffens, Lenny Waronker.

QUOTES

---- "I thought it was an excellent idea," Harry Belafonte to the author for the *Los Angeles Times* in 1987.

---- "It was definitely a risk," Koloi Lebona said in the documentary *Under African Skies*.

---- "I was very conscious of not wanting," Simon in a booklet for the twenty-fifth anniversary edition of the *Graceland* album.

---- "We were able to get a really great sound," ibid.

---- "When I first [heard South African music], it all seemed familiar to me," ibid.

---- "Another new thing was working," ibid.

---- "I like Paul Simon. . . . He's a musician," Joseph Shabalala to Patrick Humphries in *The Boy in the Bubble*.

---- Los Lobos' Steve Berlin's recounting of the group's dealings with Simon on the track that became "The Myth of Fingerprints" is from Berlin's comments in music journalist-critic Chris Morris's biography *Los Lobos: Dream in Blue*.

CHAPTER 17

SIDELIGHTS

---- In a frequently stormy press conference in Harare, nothing epitomized what Simon called the "political heckling" of the questioning more than one somewhat fuzzy question that went something like this: How—after recording an album with black musicians—could Paul be so insensitive as to name the record after Elvis Presley's home, Graceland, a name that reflects the slave-owner tradition of the American South? First, Paul explained that the song is not about Presley's home. It's a metaphor representing a search for inner peace. Besides, he continued, Presley's home wasn't some antebellum plantation. It was built in 1939 by a chiropractor who named the house in honor of his wife, Grace.

---- At the time of the concert in Zimbabwe, *Graceland* had been the best-selling album at Singalong Record Shop in downtown Harare since Christmas. Everest Chitagu, the shop manager, said the album had encouraged many white buyers for the first time to check out some of the black groups from the area. "We have whites coming in and asking for Ladysmith Black Mambazo and other musicians on the album. It's a real breakthrough."

---- I wrote the *Los Angeles Times* review of *Graceland* and did the interview with Paul in Zimbabwe.

---- Despite the boycott column, the *Herald*'s review of the concert was a rave. "Graceland Concert Holds Crowd Spellbound," the headline on David Masunda's review declared.

INTERVIEWS

---- Robert Christgau, Roy Halee, Dan Klores, Jeff Kramer, Dickie Landry, Miriam Makeba, Hugh Masekela, Lorne Michaels, Chris Morris, Vincent Nguini, Dr. Irwin Redlener, Linda Ronstadt, Paul Simon, Steven Van Zandt, Lenny Waronker.

QUOTES

---- The exchange between Simon and students at Howard University is drawn from James C. McBridge's 1987 report in the *Washington Post*.

---- "That's the way I see the world," Simon to David Fricke in 1987 for *Rolling Stone*.

---- "The reason I worked so hard," Simon to the author in 1987 for the *Los Angeles Times*.

---- "The crowd was so beautiful," ibid.

---- "Those who criticize," Joseph Shabalala to Patrick Humphries in *The Boy in the Bubble*.

RECORDINGS AND DVDS

---- Paul Simon's *Graceland: The African Concert*, Warner Reprise Video, 1987. Directed by Michael Lindsay-Hogg, who had also directed Paul's appearance on *Ready Steady Go!* The ninety-minute disc includes both Paul's *Graceland* tunes as well as South African music.

---- Paul's performance with Ladysmith Black Mambazo on *Saturday Night Live* can be found on YouTube.

CHAPTER 18

INTERVIEWS

---- Carrie Fisher, Quincy Jones, Dan Klores, Jeff Kramer, Steve Martin, Lorne Michaels, Mo Ostin, Joseph Rascoff, Paul Simon, Allen Toussaint, Derek Walcott.

QUOTES

---- "Words would sometimes come with the melody," Simon to Wayne Robins of *Newsday*.

---- "The burdens that we carry are doable; they're in the ballpark," Simon to Jay Cocks of *Time*.

---- "I was seeing people who were older," Edie Brickell to Andy Langer of the *Austin Chronicle* in 2000.

---- "Paul knew what my taste was," Brickell to Larry Katz in 1994 and now found on the Katz Tapes website.

ARTICLES

---- Scott Kraft, "Simon's Troubled Water," *Los Angeles Times*, January 10, 1992.

---- Christopher Wren, "Paul Simon Brings South Africa Concerts," *New York Times*, January 13, 1992.

---- Nicholas Wroe, "The Laureate of St. Lucia," *Guardian*, September 2, 2000.

RECORDINGS

---- *Paul Simon's Concert in the Park* is a two-disc set on Warner Bros. Records.

CHAPTER 19

SIDELIGHTS

---- In the post-9/11 essay in the *New York Times*, Simon encouraged artists in all fields to look beyond commerce. "Our notions of profit and value could be adjusted to allow for a greater degree of artistic questioning without an implication that such actions would automatically have adverse economic consequences," he wrote, in part. "Artists could hold themselves to a higher standard of honesty. Corporate America should allow more voices to reach our ears. We are saturated with music and videos that have no relationship to anything but the bottom line. We should encourage the compassion and generosity that flowed reflexively to victims' families and communities in the last week to permeate our everyday lives."

INTERVIEWS

---- Ruben Blades, Roy Halee, Oscar Hernandez, Dan Klores, Peter Parcher, Joseph Rascoff, Paul Simon, Andy Smith, Bobby Susser, Derek Walcott, Jerry Zaks.

QUOTES

---- "It was like somebody was going to take," Susana Tubert to William Grimes in 1997 for the *New York Times*.

ARTICLES

---- Stephen J. Dubner, "The Pop Perfectionist on a Crowded Stage," *New York Times*, November 9, 1997.

CHAPTER 20

SIDELIGHTS

---- Both DeSilva and Hazell were tireless, loyal, and had an easy way with people. DeSilva, who was born in Guam, worked in a public relations firm when she met Paul in 1995. She prided herself in never saying that something can't be done and somehow managed to answer emails within thirty seconds regardless of the time of day or night. A New York City native who grew up around music, Hazell was raised by a family whose son, Bobby Tucker, played piano for Billie Holiday. It was the legendary singer who gave Vaughn his first dog, a boxer named Mister. He accompanied Paul on tour and special events. When they arrived, Selwyn Rogers, gracious and dedicated, was already Paul's financial controller. His team also includes personal assistant Martia Gordon and archives specialist Cristina Miranda.

INTERVIEWS

---- Juanita DeSilva, Jamey Haddad, Roy Halee, C. Vaughn Hazell, Jeff Kramer, Bakithi Kumalo, Lorne Michaels, Cristina Miranda, Vincent Nguini, Mo Ostin, Selwyn Rogers, Eddie Simon, Paul Simon, Andy Smith, Mark Stewart, Bobby Susser.

QUOTES

---- "It's the first time," Simon to the author for the *Los Angeles Times* in 2000.

ARTICLES

---- Alec Wilkinson, "An Instrumental Man," *New Yorker*, May 12, 2003.

CHAPTER 21

SIDELIGHTS

---- Everything about "Love and Hard Times" took time, and Paul eventually reached out to his friend Philip Glass to discuss challenging aspects of it. "Philip is like Google," Paul told Paul Zollo, smiling. "You ask Philip, you pretty much get a quick answer. Unless he decides it's better for me to just work it out, in which case he says, 'Hmmm, I don't know.' He knows [*laughs*]."

---- To underscore Simon's love of information and discovery, Thomas Friedman told this story: "I was once going to the GE labs in upstate New York for research for my last book, and I invited Paul along. I had to change the schedule at the last minute, and he could not shift his, but he was totally up for hearing about 3-D printing, and the GE folks were so excited that Paul Simon was coming to their lab. Once I brought a pollster, Craig Charney, to our lunch to talk about the work he had been doing overseas."

INTERVIEWS

---- Quint Davis, Dion DiMucci, Dick Ebersol, Ken Ehrlich, Don Everly, Thomas Friedman, C. Vaughn Hazell, Oscar Hernandez, Dan Klores, Lorne Michaels, Melissa North, Paul Simon.

QUOTES

---- "It may be, as with Brian's own work, that it's meant," Simon to Alan Light for the *New York Times*.

DVD

---- *Paul Simon and Friends*, released in 2009 by Shout! Factory, shows the night Paul was honored with the Library of Congress's Gershwin Prize for Popular Song. Among the artists performing Paul's songs: Art Garfunkel, Ladysmith Black Mambazo, Alison Krauss, Stevie Wonder, and James Taylor.

CHAPTER 22

INTERVIEWS

---- Joel Amsterdam, Quint Davis, Roy Halee, Oscar Hernandez, Jeff Kramer, Wynton Marsalis, John Scher, Paul Simon, Robert Smith, Mark Stewart, Steve Van Zandt.

QUOTES

---- "When I flew home," Garfunkel to Irene Lacher in the *Los Angeles Times* in 2012.

---- "I don't really have a whole lot of choice," Simon to Allen Jones in *Uncut* magazine in 2011.

ARTICLES

---- E. E. Bradman, "After All These Years," *Bass Player*, October 2016.

DVD

---- *Under African Skies*, the documentary of Paul's *Graceland* experience, including the Zimbabwe concert, was released in 2012 by Sony Legacy. The disc is also included in the *Graceland 25th Anniversary Collector's Edition Box Set* released by Sony Legacy the same year.

CHAPTER 23

SIDELIGHTS

---- Like Simon, Sting has long wrestled with the issue of fame and its impact on artistry. "I think people feel they know you through the media and therefore make judgments about what you are doing, which really doesn't help, but then, on the other hand, would anybody be listening to you if you weren't known?" he said. "It's a price to be paid or a balance to be achieved."

---- During Simon's conversation with poet Billy Collins at Emory University, Collins asked Paul if he ever wrote poetry aside from his music, and Paul replied, "Yeah, a few times. It wasn't that good."

INTERVIEWS

---- C. Vaughn Hazell, Bakithi Kumalo, Lorne Michaels, Paul Simon, Mark Stewart, Sting.

QUOTES

---- The 911 coverage is drawn largely from reporting by the *New Canaan News*, the *New Canaan Advertiser*, CNN, and Associated Press.

CHAPTER 24

SIDELIGHTS

---- On the issue of longevity, Mark Stewart, the bandleader who has worked with Paul for two decades, said he sees Paul more in the tradition of poets and composers than pop artists. "While you can certainly say he is a writer of popular music, he is also a poet in a tradition of fine poets, and Paul is a composer in a tradition of fine composers . . . and I have more experience in those traditions than I do in popular music. In both, they continue to listen, they continue to write, they continue to create."

---- A portion of Chuck Close's painting of Simon was used as the cover of the *Stranger to Stranger* album.

---- Here are more of Simon's fifty favorite songs—at least they were on one evening in 2016: "Adios Hermanos," "America," "American Tune," "The Boy in the Bubble," "Can I Forgive Him?," "The Coast," "Dazzling Blue," "Duncan," "Esmeralda's Dream," "Father and Daughter," "50 Ways to Leave Your Lover," "Further to Fly," "Getting Ready for Christmas Day," "Hearts and Bones," "Homeward Bound," "How the Heart Approaches What It Yearns," "Insomniac's Lullaby," "Kodachrome," "The Late Great Johnny Ace," "Late in the Evening," "Love," "Love and Hard Times," "Loves Me Like a Rock," "Mother and Child Reunion," "Mrs. Robinson," "Night Game," "The Obvious Child," "Old Friends," "Peace Like a River," "René and Georgette Magritte with Their Dog After the War," "Rewrite," "Señorita with a Necklace of Tears," "Slip Slidin' Away," "Some Folks' Lives Roll Easy," "Something So Right," "Spirit Voices," "Stranger to Stranger," "Train in the Distance," and "You Can Call Me Al."

During a break from drafting his Top 10 song list, Paul selected his all-time Yankees team, at least from those players he saw personally at Yankee Stadium: C Yogi Berra. RHP David Cone, Allie Reynolds, Vic Raschi, and Don Larsen. LHP Whitey Ford. RP Mariano Rivera and Goose Gossage. 1B Don Mattingly. 2B Robinson Cano. SS Derek Jeter. 3B Alex Rodriguez and Graig Nettles. LF Brett Gardner, Gene Woodling, and Lou Piniella. CF Mickey Mantle and Joe DiMaggio. RF Reggie Jackson. DH Bernie Williams.

INTERVIEWS

---- Chuck Close, Joel Guzman, Jamey Haddad, Bakithi Kumalo, Jonty McCausland, Lynne McCausland, Randy Newman, Vincent Nguini, Jim Oblon, Mick Rossi, Paul Simon, Chris Stern, Mark Stewart.

EPILOGUE

INTERVIEWS

---- Thomas Friedman, C. Vaughn Hazell, Quincy Jones, Jon Landau, Wynton Marsalis, Eddie Simon, Paul Simon, Bobby Susser.

PHOTO CREDITS

INDEX

Abbey Road Studios, London, 269
Academy Awards, 121, 343
Ace of Cups, 98
Acuff, Roy, 379
Ade, King Sunny, 252
"Adios Hermanos" (Simon), 312–13, 415n
Adler, Lou, 108, 111
Agora Ballroom, Cleveland, Ohio, 224–25
Agron, Salvador. See Capeman, The
Ahrens, Lynn, 317
Albert, Marv, 206
"All Around the World" (Simon), 276–77
Allen, Mel, 9
Allen, Woody, 210–11, 213
"Allergies" (Simon), 228, 229, 236, 246
"All Through the Night" (Mystics), 37
Alterman, Loraine, 153, 154
Altman, Robert, 211, 213
"America" (Simon and Garfunkel), 5, 125,
    353, 358, 381, 415n
America: A Tribute to Heroes LP, 2, 401n
American Bandstand (TV show), 26–30, 402n
"American Tune" (Simon), 5, 182–84, 186,
    266, 387, 415n
Amigo Studios, 261
Amos, Wally, 61
Amsterdam, Joel, 362
Amy Records, 41, 42–43, 45, 46, 47
Anderson, Laurie, 261
Angel Clare LP (Garfunkel), 186, 198
"Angi" (Graham), 86, 87
Anka, Paul, 131
"Anna Belle" (Simon), 36
Annie Hall (film), 210–11, 213

Another Side of Bob Dylan LP (Dylan), 71
Ansen, David, 225
Anthony, Marc, 311
Apollo Records, 21
Apple Music, 194, 408n
"April Come She Will" (Simon), 87, 113
Association, The, 111
At Folsom Prison LP (Cash), 86
At San Quentin LP (Cash), 86
"At Seventeen" (Joplin), 132
"At the Zoo" (Simon and Garfunkel), 104–5,
    111, 404n
Auden, W. H., 368–69
Avalon, Frankie, 32
ayahuasca, 296, 322, 333, 334
Aykroyd, Dan, 204, 213, 224

"Baby Driver" (Simon), 145
Bacall, Lauren, 193
Bacharach, Burt, 32, 38, 281, 346
Bachelors, 97
"Back in the High Life Again" (Winwood),
    286
Back in the High Life LP (Winwood), 281
Back on the Block LP (Jones), 297
Baez, Joan, 43, 47, 76, 139, 238
Baker, Arthur, 272
Baker, LaVern, 30
Baldwin, Alec, 374
Bancroft, Anne, 107, 122
baseball, 9–11, 19–20, 26, 27, 35, 203–4, 244,
    325, 349, 415n
    "Night Game" and, 200
Baskin, Edie, 204–5

Bata, Joan, 76, 79

BBC, 66, 69–70

Beach Boys, 104, 108, 163

Beastie Boys, 194

Beatles, 35, 38, 62, 88, 104, 111, 127, 128, 130, 138, 139, 145, 153, 157, 159, 164, 269.
    See also specific songs

Beatty, Warren, 172, 195

Beck, 342

Beckett, Barry, 178, 197

Belafonte, Harry, 252–53

Bell, Al, 177

Bell, Vinnie, 74

Bellport, Long Island, 27

Beltone recording studio, 28

Belushi, John, 224

"Benedictus" (Simon), 61, 66, 405n

Bennett, Tony, 379

Berea College, Kentucky, 89

Berg, Heidi, 250–51, 252

"Berkeley Girl" (Harper Simon), 341–42

Berlin, Steve, 261, 277

Berlinger, Joe, 363

Bernstein, Leonard, 128, 193

Berry, Chuck, 26, 33, 40, 259, 284

Beverly (Beverly Kutner), 108–11

"Big, Bright Green Pleasure Machine, The"
    (Simon), 100

Big Brother and the Holding Company, 108

Big Hits LP (Rolling Stones), 87

Big Records, 28, 30–31, 36, 129

Billboard
    Graduate soundtrack album and, 122, 124
    review of Forest Hills concert, 157
    Simon and Garfunkel releases and, 68, 75, 85, 93, 103, 122
    Simon solo LP and, 245

Blades, Ruben, 311, 316

Blaine, Hal, 87, 134, 145, 170, 199

"Bleecker Street" (Simon), 48, 60

"Blessed" (Simon), 87

Blige, Mary J., 367

Blonde on Blonde LP (Dylan), 86

Blood on the Tracks LP (Dylan), 205

"Blue Jay Way" (Beatles), 145

"Blue Moon of Kentucky" (Monroe), 330

Blues Brothers, The (film), 224

"Blues in the Night" (Mercer), 324

"Blues Run the Game" (Frank), 72, 87

"Bob Dylan's Dream" (Dylan), 64

Bono, 272, 367

Bookends LP (Simon and Garfunkel), 104, 109–10, 115, 117–18, 124–31, 138, 158

Booker T and the MG's, 162, 177

Borge, Victor, 123

"Born at the Right Time" (Simon), 296

Born in the U.S.A. LP (Springsteen), 261

Boston Globe, Stranger to Stranger review, 377

Boulez, Pierre, 44

Bowie, David, 112, 222, 276, 341

"Boxer, The" (Simon), 131–36, 139, 144–45, 147, 153, 168, 199, 208, 258, 260, 266, 336, 386, 387
    covers, 139, 337
    Garfunkel's part in, 135
    performances, 4–5, 6, 173, 206, 224, 234, 293, 305, 330, 337, 364, 367, 370, 384, 402n
    "wild track," 135

"Boy in the Bubble, The" (Simon), 5, 256, 263–66, 269, 273, 276, 280, 370, 387, 415n

Boyoyo Boys, 252

"Brand New Day" (Sting), 370

Brando, Marlon, 23, 41

Brantley, Ben, 315, 360–61

Breakaway LP (Garfunkel), 199, 207

Brecker, Michael, 198, 292, 298

Brentwood Folk Club, England, 47, 54, 63, 65, 76, 298

Brewer, Teresa, 28

Brickell, Edie (wife), 3, 77, 197, 289–91, 297, 299, 316, 331, 347, 351, 361, 365, 383
    altercation in news (2015), 375–76, 377
    children born, 303, 310, 322
    on Hoblyn, 331–32
    marriage to Simon, 302–3, 322, 333, 335, 336, 350, 381, 386, 389
    solo album, 303

Brickman, Marshall, 213

"Bridge Over Troubled Water" (Simon and Garfunkel), 2, 139, 141–49, 151–53, 159, 174, 209, 229, 245, 384–86, 387, 407n
    covers of, 153, 213, 337
    performances, 150, 173, 184, 293, 304, 345, 350, 370, 407n

Bridge Over Troubled Water LP (Simon and Garfunkel), 145–48, 150, 151, 153, 158, 159, 163, 173, 287–88, 406n
Simon's solo, "Song for the Asking," 148
Bright Star (Broadway musical), 303
Brill Building, NYC, 28, 102, 131, 227, 250
Bringing It All Back Home LP (Dylan), 94
Brion, Jon, 341
Broadway Album LP (Streisand), 281
Brooklyn Academy of Music (BAM), 348–49, 357
Brooks, Albert, 207
"Brother, Can You Spare a Dime?" (Gorney), 228
Brothers Four, 60, 74, 88, 89, 90
Brown, Blair, 226
Brown, Hux, 164
Browne, Jackson, 296
Brubeck, Dave, 88, 92
Bruce, Lenny, 35, 71, 88, 98, 101–2, 128
Bruno of Hollywood, 41
Bryant, Felice and Boudleaux, 27
Buchenholz, Gretchen, 283
Burke, Michael, 144
Bush, George W., 3, 343
"Bye Bye Love" (Everly Brothers), 25–26, 150, 173, 340
Byrds, 74, 75, 87, 93, 134
Byrne, David, 261
By the Time I Get to Phoenix LP (Campbell), 138

Cage, John, 44
Cajun music/zydeco, 180, 257, 258, 276
Camerieri, C. J., 380
Camp, Bob (Hamilton), 61
Campbell, Glen, 87, 138
Campbell, Ian, 57
Canadian American records, 40
Canby, Vincent, 316–17
"Can I Forgive Him?" (Simon), 313, 415n
Capeman, The (Simon), 3, 285–86, 307–18, 321, 332, 334, 362, 390
concert at BAM, 348–49
NYT Magazine pieces on, 311
reprisal (2010), 360–61
Cardozo, Benjamin Nathan, 41
Carlin, George, 206
"Carlos Dominguez" (Simon), 48

Carmichael, Hoagy, 163
Carnal Knowledge (film), 151, 157
Carr, Pete, 178
Carter, Fred, Jr., 87, 134, 149
Carter, Ron, 170
Carthy, Martin, 64, 65, 76
Cash, Johnny, 86, 153, 255, 330
Cash Box, 83
Catch-22 (film), 129–30, 134, 137–39, 144, 150, 157
Cauble, Rebecca, 59
CBS, 149, 152
TV special, 150, 151, 218, 406n
"Cecilia" (Simon), 145–46, 151, 173
Cermak, Kathryn, 299
Chaplin, Charlie, 116
Charles, Ray, 2, 361
Charms, 21
Charney, Craig, 413n
Chase, Chevy, 206, 274, 275
Chenier, Clifton, 180
Children's Health Fund, 283–84, 303–4
Chitty, Kathy, 63–64, 71, 78, 79, 83, 94–95, 109, 114, 220, 290, 298–99, 374, 384
Chords, 21
Christgau, Robert, 171, 276, 362
Christie, Lou, 88
"Citizen of the Planet" (Simon), 341
Clapton, Eric, 238, 335
Clark, Dick, 29
Cliff, Jimmy, 164, 177, 212
Clinton, Hillary, 384–85
"Clock, The" (Simon), 376
Close, Chuck, 383, 386, 415n
"Cloudy" (Simon), 99
Clovers, 21
"Coast, The" (Simon), 415n
Coasters, 33
Coffee and Confusion, North Beach, California, 98
Cohl, Michael, 312
Collins, Billy, 368, 414n
Collyer, David Sorin, 194
Columbia Records, 54, 55, 59, 85, 185
annual convention, 74, 101, 186
Bookends LP, 104, 109–10, 115, 125–27, 129
"The Boxer" and, 134–36
Bridge Over Troubled Water LP, 145
CBS Records in London, Simon and, 69–70

Columbia Records (*cont.*)
  The Concert in Central Park LP, 232–33
  Dylan and, 54, 55, 57, 59, 73–74, 85, 86
  The Graduate LP, 122, 124, 127–28
  most singles sold in one week, 101
  "My Little Town" release, 205–6
  Nashville recording studio, 134–36
  Parsley, Sage, Rosemary and Thyme LP,
    99–103
  Paul Simon: Live Rhymin' LP, 192
  Simon and Garfunkel at, 55–56, 59–62, 85,
    117, 127
  Simon and Garfunkel reunion, 198, 205–6
  Simon and Garfunkel's Greatest Hits LP, 173
  Simon as solo artist, 158, 161, 185, 210,
    215–20, 222
  Simon's suit against, 219
  "The Sound of Silence," 56–59, 73, 74–75,
    82–83
  Sounds of Silence LP, 83, 85–87
  Studio A, 55, 60, 61, 86, 104
  Yetnikoff takeover at, 215–18
Concert in Central Park, The LP (Simon and
  Garfunkel), 232–33, 235, 409n
concerts: Simon and Garfunkel
  Berkeley, California, 98
  Carnegie Hall, 122, 123, 148, 151, 155
  Central Park reunion (1981), 229, 231–35,
    409n
  closing months of 1968, 130–31
  college venues, 92, 95, 96, 98–99
  Convention Hall, Philadelphia, 122, 123
  earnings, 92, 96, 103, 131, 404n
  final appearances before split, 155–57
  first touring cycle, 95–96
  Forest Hills Stadium, 101, 155–57
  Hollywood Bowl, 115
  Melodyland, California, 98
  Monterey Pop, 108–11, 116, 404–5n
  number of (1967), 109
  Old Friends tours (2003, 2009), 339–41,
    352
  Philharmonic Hall, NYC, 105
  recordings of, 149
  reunion fund-raiser (1972), 170
  reunion tour (1993), 303–6
  Royal Albert Hall, 124, 155
  Summer Evening reunion tour, 234–45,
    292

  Symphony Hall, Boston, 122, 123–24
  ten-city tour (1969), 146, 148–49
concerts: Simon as solo artist
  "Back at the Ranch" concert, 297
  benefit, Children's Health Fund, 283–84
  benefit, Half-Earth campaign, 381
  benefit, Hurricane Andrew, 303
  benefit, Mandela's US visit, 296–97
  benefit, McGovern campaign, 172–73
  benefit, "No Nukes," 224
  benefit, Robin Hood foundation, 367
  benefit, Save the Amazon Rain Forest,
    293
  Bread & Roses Festival, 238
  Central Park (1991), 299–300
  Europe tour, 349
  farewell tour (2018), 385, 389
  first solo tour, 184–85
  Forest Hills Stadium, 379, 382–84
  Graceland tour, 278–83, 410n
  jazz concerts, 364–65
  New Orleans Jazz & Heritage Festival
    (1991, 2006), 344–45, 353–54
  One-Trick Pony tour, 225
  Paul Simon and Dylan, 330–31, 367
  Paul Simon and Sting, 367–71, 374–75
  Paul Simon: Live Rhymin' tour, 192
  refusal to tour (1972), 172
  Saints tour, 298–300
  Saratoga Springs, New York, 252
  So Beautiful or So What tour, 362, 363–64
  South Africa concert, 300–302
  Still Crazy tour, 207–8
  Stranger to Stranger tour, 377
  Summer Festival for Peace (1970), 158
  summer tour (2001), 335
  summer tour (2016), 379–80, 382, 384–86
  Surprise tour, 344–45
  There Goes Rhymin' Simon tour, 184
  You're the One tour, 334–35
Concord Records Group, 361, 362, 377
"Congratulations" (Simon), 171, 172
Contera, Al, 37
Control LP (Jam and Lewis), 281
Cooke, Sam, 200
"Cool, Cool River, The" (Simon), 293–97, 386
"Cool Papa Bell" (Simon), 372
Cooper, Marty, 41–42
Costello, Elvis, 289

Crane, Hart, 289

Crawdaddy magazine, 94, 404n

"Crazy Love, Vol. II" (Simon), 256

Crew-Cuts, 21

Crisci, Cristiano "Clap! Clap!," 372

Cromelin, Richard, 344

Cross, Christopher, 226

Crowley, Louisiana, 257, 258

Crows, 11–12, 28

"Crying in the Chapel" (Sonny Til and the Orioles), 141

Cunnane, Father Jarlath "Jay," 124

Cyrkle, 97, 101

Dance City LP (Torres), 310

"Dancing Wild" (Simon), 28

"Dangling Conversation, The" (Simon), 100, 103, 104

Daniels, William, 107–8

Darin, Bobby, 26

"Darling Lorraine" (Simon), 325–30, 334, 381, 386

David, Hal, 32, 38, 346

Davis, Clive, 85–86, 101, 109, 117, 122, 124, 127, 151, 158, 161, 171, 184, 185, 210, 215, 346

Davis, Gordon J., 231

Davis, Miles, 273, 289, 344

Davis, Quint, 344, 345, 354

"Dazzling Blue" (Simon), 415n

Dazzling Stranger (Harper), 76

Dean, James, 23

Delsener, Ron, 123, 231

DeMann, Freddy, 42–43

Denny, Sandy, 69

Deram Records, 109

DeSilva, Juanita, 332, 412–13n

Diamond, Neil, 222

"Diamonds on the Soles of Her Shoes" (Simon), 272, 275–76, 282, 284, 364, 386, 415n

DiMaggio, Joe, 126–27, 138, 325, 349

DiMucci, Dion, 284, 330, 350, 351

Division Street LP (Harper Simon), 342

Dixie Hummingbirds, 173, 176, 179

Domino, Fats, 164

Donegan, Lonnie, 64

Donovan, 76, 109

"Don't Think Twice, It's All Right" (Dylan), 59

doo-wop, 12, 20–21, 34, 37, 41, 284, 293, 312, 317, 326, 350

Dream Academy, 227, 384, 408n

Drifters, 21

Drummond, Dean, 365

Dubner, Stephen J., 311

"Duncan" (Simon), 168–70, 172, 415n

Dunn, Donald "Duck," 162

Duvall, Shelley, 211, 212, 213, 220, 245

Dwyer, Jim, 382

Dylan, Bob, 33, 35, 43–46, 54, 55, 57, 59, 67, 73–74, 85, 86, 94, 102, 111, 112, 131, 139, 162, 208, 252, 272, 344, 379, 385, 388

covers of, by Simon and Garfunkel, 57, 59

guitar-playing of, 64

as songwriter, 161

tour with Simon (1990), 330–31, 365

Eagles, 61

"Earth Angel" (Penguins), 12

Ebersol, Dick, 204, 341

Eclectic Music, 56

Edie Brickell & New Bohemians, 289–91, 303

Edward B. Marks Music Company, 47–48, 54, 56

Ehrlich, Ken, 339

Einstein, Albert, 116

Eisenhower, Dwight D., 35

"El Condor Pasa (If I Could)" (Simon), 146, 168, 252

Eliot, T. S., 289

Emerson, Ken, 208, 209

Eminem, 343

Emory University, Richard Ellmann Lectures in Modern Literature, 368–69

Eno, Brian, 340–44, 351

Ephron, Nora, 137

Epstein, Brian, 97

"Esmeralda's Dream" (Simon), 308, 415n

Evans, Greg, 316–17

"Eve of Destruction" (McGuire), 75

Everly Brothers, 25, 26, 340

"Everybody's Talkin' " (Nilsson), 193

"Every Breath You Take" (Sting), 370

Faithfull, Marianne, 403n

"Fakin' It" (Simon), 109, 110

Farndale, Nigel, 371

"Father and Daughter" (Simon), 343, 350, 415n
Feiffer, Jules, 151
"Fever" (Little Willie John), 47
"Fields of Gold" (Sting), 370
Fifth International Popular Song Festival, 162
"50 Ways to Leave Your Lover" (Simon), 199, 209, 415n
"59th Street Bridge Song, The" (Simon and Garfunkel), 102–3, 236, 305, 404n
Financial Times, Simon review (2016), 385
"Fire and Rain" (Taylor), 153, 159
Fisher, Carrie, 195, 213, 220–25, 228, 229, 233–35, 239, 243, 244, 259, 266, 290–91
   marriage to Simon, 244–45, 249–50
   Wishful Drinking, 250, 409n
Fisher, Eddie, 220, 221, 222, 224, 244
Flaherty, Stephen, 317
Flamingo Club, London, 66
Fleetwoods, 42
"Florence" (Paragons), 164, 407n
folk music, 5, 36, 43, 128, 131, 208
   British folk scene, 46–47, 53–54, 62, 63–65, 68, 72, 75–82, 403n
   in Greenwich Village, 5, 43, 45–46, 57, 60–61, 71, 132
   guitar-playing and, 43, 64, 65
   record labels, 54
folk rock, 74, 75, 85, 87, 112, 170, 208
"For Emily, Whenever I May Find Her" (Simon and Garfunkel), 105, 171, 404–5n
"Forever Young" (Dylan), 330
"For No One" (Beatles), 62
Four Seasons, 88
"Fragile" (Sting), 370
Frame, Pete, 76–77
Francis, Connie, 38
Frank, Jackson C., 72, 87
Franklin, Aretha, 153, 337, 344, 388, 406n
Freed, Alan, 12, 26, 29
Freeman, Ernie, 148, 159
Freewheelin' Bob Dylan, The LP (Dylan), 45, 46, 71
   liner notes, 46, 64–65
Friedman, Thomas, 346, 388, 413n
Frisell, Bill, 389
Froggatt, Jack, 403n
"Further to Fly" (Simon), 347, 415n

Gabriel, Peter, 281
Gadd, Steve, 199, 207, 223, 298, 324
Gale, Eric, 223
Gardner, Herb, 212
Garfunkel, Art, 61
   architecture study and, 31, 128, 144
   awards and accolades, 339
   childhood and background, 12–13, 20
   at Columbia University, 31, 48, 68, 97
   Dakota apartment bidding and, 193
   decision to pursue a film career, 129–30, 134, 137–39, 144, 151, 157
   early singing with Simon, 21, 26
   earnings, 92, 93, 96, 103, 131
   fame, success, and, 91, 124
   girlfriend, Penny Marshall, 225
   hitchhiking, 123–24
   homes/apartments of, 128, 145
   hurt and resentment of, 31, 129
   marriage to Kathryn Cermak, 299
   marriage to Linda Grossman, 193
   performing as Artie Garr, 48
   Rock & Roll Hall of Fame and, 292–93
   Simon as childhood friend, 2, 12–13, 18–19, 340
   Simon as partner, 31, 96, 124, 129, 130, 139, 143, 153–55, 182, 191–92, 199, 209, 232–34, 292–93, 413–14n
   Simon-Fisher wedding and, 244
   Simon's songs about, 144–45
   Tom & Jerry days, 28–30, 402n
   vocal ability, 18–19
   vocal collapse, 353–55, 370–71
   walking trips, 175
Garfunkel, Art, as group "Simon and Garfunkel"
   "America" arrangement and, 125
   Big Records and first recording, 28–30
   Bookends LP, 104, 109–10, 115, 122, 125–27, 131
   "The Boxer" recording sessions, 134–36
   breakup (1958), 30–31
   breakup (1970), 2, 150–54, 156–59
   breakup (1993), 303–6
   breakup (2010), 353–55
   "Bridge Over Troubled Water," 147, 149, 152
   Bridge Over Troubled Water LP, 145–48, 150
   Columbia recordings, 54–62, 67–68, 85–87

The Graduate and, 113, 138–39
group begins again (1962), 48
group's image and, 105, 112
Hearts and Bones LP and, 236–38, 241–44
Lennon's *Pussy Cats* LP and, 193–94
in London with Simon (1964), 66
manager Mort Lewis, 88–93, 95–96
Parsley, Sage, Rosemary and Thyme LP
    recording sessions, 99–103
performances (1968), 109
performing in Greenwich Village, 60–61
as record producer, 104, 109
reunion performances and recordings,
    172–73, 198–99, 205–6, 218, 232–45,
    276, 339–41, 350, 352, 354, 409n
as songwriter, 21–22, 27
"The Sound of Silence," 57–58, 61, 73–75,
    83
three albums in the Top 6 and, 128
touring, college venues, 92, 95, 96, 98–99
TV special (1969), 149–51, 218, 406n
"Voices of Old People" and, 127
"Wednesday Morning, 3 A.M.," 60
Wednesday Morning, 3 A.M. LP, 55–62,
    67–68
See also concerts: Simon and Garfunkel;
    specific songs; specific LPs
Garfunkel, Art, as solo artist
Angel Clare LP, 175, 186, 198
barbs at Simon, 371
Breakaway solo album, 199, 207
manager for, Scher, 354
Simon and "My Little Town," 198–99
on *SNL*, 1, 206–7, 276
Garfunkel, Jack and Rose, 13, 28, 31
Garfunkel, James, 299
Gates, Rev. J. M., 351
"Gee" (Crows), 11–12, 20, 23, 28
Geffen, David, 61, 232
Geffen Records, 232, 233, 289
Gelek Rimpoche, 345
Genius Loves Company LP (Charles), 361
"Geordie" (Baez), 47
"Georgy Girl" (Seekers), 97
Gerde's Folk City, NYC, 60–61, 71
Gershwin, Ira and George, 163, 325
"Getting Ready for Christmas Day" (Simon),
    355, 415n
"Get Up & Do the Wobble" (Simon), 42

Getz, Stan, 163
Getz/Gilberto LP, 163, 177
Gibbs, Jake, 144
Gibson, Bob, 61
"Girl for Me, The" (Simon), 21
"Girl from the North Country" (Dylan), 45,
    59, 65
Giuliani, Rudy, 2, 4
Glass, Philip, 260–61, 264, 345, 383, 412n
Gleason, Ralph J., 98, 102, 111
Goffin, Gerry, 34, 292
Goldsboro, Bobby, 138
"Gone at Last" (Simon), 199, 206
Goodbye, Babylon LP (Eno), 351
Goodman, Andrew, 66
"Goodnite, Sweetheart, Goodnite" (Spaniels),
    21, 293
Good Rockin' Dopsie and the Twisters, 257
"Good Vibrations" (Beach Boys), 163
Gordon, Martia, 413n
Gorgoni, Al, 74–75
Gorney, Jay, 228
Gorney, Rod, 228–29
gospel music, 141–42, 147, 173–74, 184, 351,
    405–6n, 407n
    concert, Radio City Music Hall, 173–74
Gospel Sound, The (Heilbut), 173
"Go Tell It on the Mountain" (spiritual), 61
"Gotta Get a Girl" (Bacharach), 32
Gould, Elliott, 194
"Graceland" (Simon), 23, 256, 258–59, 262,
    266–69, 286, 287, 289, 386, 387
Graceland LP (Simon), 2, 251–88, 291, 304,
    309, 324, 325, 344, 377, 390, 410n
    anniversary boxed set and documentary,
        363–64, 414n
    BAM's series and, 348, 349
    Los Lobos and, 261–62, 276
    Louisiana recording sessions, 257–58, 276
    reviews, 276
    sales, 275, 282, 287, 297, 334
    South African boycott and, 273–75,
        278–81, 284, 301, 363–64, 410n
    South Africa recording sessions, 252–56
    tour for, 278–83, 410n
Graceland: The African Concert LP (Simon),
    411n
Graduate, The (film), 107–9, 113, 115, 121–22,
    138

Graduate, The LP, 122, 124, 127–28, 235
Graham, Davy, 64, 86
Grammy Awards, 138–39, 155, 159, 172, 190,
    192, 209, 226, 270, 278–79, 281–82, 286,
    287, 297, 335, 364
    Simon and Garfunkel lifetime achievement,
    339
Grandmaster Flash, 284
Granta (literary journal), 40
Grappelli, Stephane, 170
Grateful Dead, 108, 111, 113, 289
Greatest Hits, Etc. LP (Simon), 217–18
Great McGinty, The (film), 170
Greene, Andy, 370–71
Greenfield, Josh, 128
"Greenfields" (Brothers Four), 60, 88
Grennen, Winston, 164
Grey, Brad, 312
Gribble, Jim, 34, 37
Grodin, Charles, 150, 218, 223, 244
Grossman, Albert, 71, 73–74, 88
Grossman, Linda, 193
Grossman, Stefan, 170
Grupo Cultural Olodum, 287, 292, 299
Grusin, David, 122, 138
Guardian, Stranger to Stranger review, 377
"Gumboots" (Simon), 256
Gumboots: Accordion Jive Hits, Vol. II LP, 251
Gusick, Chester (Chet), 10, 336
Guzman, Joel, 380

Haddad, Jamey, 324, 371, 380, 382
Hagan, Joe, 210
Halee, Roy, 59–60, 62, 74, 86, 87, 99–100, 104,
    117, 125, 144, 155, 159, 177
    "The Boxer" and, 133–36
    Brickell album and, 303
    "Bridge Over Troubled Water" and, 144,
    147, 148
    Bridge Over Troubled Water LP and, 145–46
    The Capeman and, 309
    Central Park (1981) concert and, 232, 233
    Columbia studio, Bay Area, 162
    concert recordings by, 149
    Garfunkel's first solo album and, 175–76
    Graceland LP and, 251, 253–70
    Hearts and Bones LP and, 238, 242, 245
    "Living Boy," "Frank Lloyd Wright," and,
    145

"Mother and Child Reunion" and, 164–65
Paul Simon LP and, 162, 170–72
    on Simon and Jamaican ska/reggae, 164
    Simon as solo artist and, 162
    Simon breaks with, 175–76
    on Simon's post-*Capeman* LPs, 362–63
    sixteen-track recordings and, 135–36
Half-Earth (Wilson), 345
Hammerstein, Oscar, 163
Hammond, John, 55
Hann, Michael, 342
Harder They Come, The (film), 164, 211–12,
    406n
"Hard Rain's A-Gonna Fall, A" (Dylan), 45
Harper, Colin, *Dazzling Stranger*, 76
Harper, Peggy (ex-wife), 89, 220, 273, 405n
    Dakota apartment, 193
    marriage to Mort Lewis, 88, 89–90, 110
    as Simon's girlfriend/wife, 114, 118, 145,
    147, 151, 154–56, 162, 189–90, 244
    "Something So Right" and, 180–82
    son Harper James born, 176
    "Train in the Distance" and, 239
Harpers Bizarre, 103, 236
Harper Simon LP (Harper Simon), 341
"Harper Valley P.T.A." (Riley), 138
Harris, Richard, 148
Harrison, George, 130, 145, 153, 212–13, 335,
    339–40
Harrison, Ken, 298, 299, 374, 384
Harrison, Wilbert, 33
Harry J. All Stars, 178
Hart, Lorenz, 163
Haskell, Jimmie, 159
Hawkins, Connie, 206
Hawkins, Roger, 178
Hazell, C. Vaughn, 332, 346, 412–13n
"Hazy Shade of Winter, A" (Simon and
    Garfunkel), 102, 103, 353
"Heartbreak Hotel" (Presley), 23
"Hearts and Bones" (Simon), 227, 239–41,
    291, 387, 415n
Hearts and Bones LP (Simon), 236–46, 249,
    251, 254, 261, 288, 334, 343, 409n
"Hearts of Stone" (Charms), 21
Heckman, Don, 172–73
Heilbut, Anthony, 173–74, 179
    The Gospel Sound, 173
Heilbut, Wilbred, 173

Heller, Joseph, 129
"Hello, Dolly" (Bachelors), 97
"Helpless" (Young), 304
Hendrix, Jimi, 108, 111
Henley, Don, 293
Henry, Buck, 221
Hentoff, Nat, 46, 64–65
Herb Alpert & the Tijuana Brass, 128
Herbert, Bob, 314–15
"Here, There and Everywhere" (Beatles), 62
"Here Comes the Sun" (Beatles), 213
Hernandez, Oscar, 309, 310, 316, 349, 360
"He Was My Brother" (Simon and Garfunkel),
    45, 47, 48, 55, 56, 60, 66, 68, 72, 105
"Hey, Schoolgirl" (Tom & Jerry), 27, 28–30,
    42, 43, 340, 353, 402n
"Hey Jude" (Beatles), 138, 139
Hidalgo, David, 261, 262
Highway 61 Revisited LP (Dylan), 86
Hoblyn, Ian, 331–32
"Hobo's Blues" (Simon), 170
Hoffman, Dustin, 107, 109, 122
Holden, Stephen, 184, 186, 245, 291
Holiday, Billie, 413n
Holly, Buddy, 26, 30, 40
"Homeless" (Simon), 269, 272
"Homeward Bound" (Simon and Garfunkel),
    79–82, 87, 93, 96, 105, 111, 112, 213, 233,
    298, 385, 404n, 415n
"Honey" (Goldsboro), 138
"Honey Love" (Drifters), 21
Hood, David, 178
Horovitz, Adam, 194
Horovitz, Israel, 194
"Hound Dog" (Presley), 24
Houston, Cissy, 165
Howard J. Rubinstein company, 274
"How Can You Live in the Northeast?"
    (Simon), 343
Howling at the Moon (Yetnikoff), 216
"How the Heart Approaches What It Yearns"
    (Simon), 415n
How Will the Wolf Survive? LP (Los Lobos),
    261
Hullabaloo (TV show), 96
"Hushabye" (Mystics), 37

"I Am a Rock" (Simon and Garfunkel), 65, 72,
    78, 87, 93, 100–101, 110, 353, 403n

"I'd Like to Be" (Simon), 38
"I Do It for Your Love" (Simon), 199–200
"I Hear a Symphony" (Supremes), 82
"I Know What I Know" (Simon), 256
"I'll Take You There" (Staple Singers), 177
"I'm Lonely" (Simon), 40
"In a Parade" (Simon), 376
Indestructible Beat of Soweto, The LP
    (Earthworks/Shanachie Records), 273
"In My Life" (Beatles), 62
"In My Room" (Beach Boys), 163
Innervisions LP (Wonder), 190, 192
"Insomniac's Lullaby" (Simon), 365–66, 377,
    386, 415n
Interscope Records, 194
"In the Garden of Edie" (Simon), 376
Ionesco, Eugène, 44
Iovine, Jimmy, 194
Irish Rovers, 60
Israels, Chuck, 194
"I Still Haven't Found What I'm Looking For"
    (U2), 286
"I've Just Seen a Face" (Beatles), 374
"I Walk the Line" (Cash), 330
"I Wish I Weren't in Love" (Simon), 40

Jackson, Mahalia, 61
Jackson, Michael, 216, 249, 252, 324, 335
Jagger, Mick, 222, 388
"Jailhouse Rock" (Presley), 30, 33
Jam, Jimmy, 281
Jamaican ska and reggae, 146, 163–65, 177,
    211–12
    "Mother and Child Reunion" and, 163–66
    "Take Me to the Mardi Gras" and, 178
James, Bob, 226
Jansch, Bert, 64, 76
Jefferson Airplane, 108
Jessy Dixon Singers, 173, 184, 207, 407n
Jeter, Claude, 142, 174, 178
Jobim, Antonio Carolos, 163
Joel, Billy, 216, 244, 284
Johannesburg, South Africa, 250–52
    Graceland and, 253–56, 363–64
    Ovation Studios, 254
    So Beautiful or So What concert in,
        363–64
John, Elton, 99, 170, 222, 253, 367
Johnson, Jimmy, 178

Johnson, Pete, 115, 129
Johnston, Bob, 86–87, 99, 104, 109
Jones, Quincy, 79, 112–13, 126, 158, 159, 172, 179, 182, 226, 253, 286, 297, 335
Jones, Rickie Lee, 290
Joplin, Janis, 108, 111
Juluka, 252
Just Arrived LP (Pilgrims), 67, 68
"Just to Be with You" (Passions), 34

Kalfin, Marvin, 34
"Kansas City" (Harrison), 33
"Kathy's Song" (Simon), 72, 87
Kaufman, Andy, 206
Kaufman, Denise, 98–99
Keaton, Diane, 211
"Keep the Customer Satisfied" (Simon), 146
Kennedy, John F., 6, 35, 48–49, 53, 172, 296
Kennedy, Robert F., 172
Kennedy Center Honors for Lifetime Achievement, 336–37
Kenton, Stan, 88, 92
Kenvin, Helene Schwartz, 17, 18
Kerouac, Jack, 46
Kew Gardens Hills, Queens, 12–14, 16, 244
Keys, Alicia, 337
Khumalo, Vusi, 254, 255, 258
King, B. B., 379
King, Carole, 34, 145, 172, 292, 346
King, Martin Luther Jr., 49, 127, 296, 351
Kingston Trio, 36, 61
Klores, Dan, 274–75, 282, 301–2, 312, 331, 332, 347
Knechtel, Larry, 145, 147, 152, 159, 165
"Knockin' on Heaven's Door" (Dylan), 330
Knockouts, 326
"Kodachrome" (Simon), 178–79, 184, 186, 415n
Kong, Leslie, 164
Kornfeld, Barry, 56, 58
Kraft, Scott, 300
Kraft Music Hall (TV show), 123
Kramer, Jeff, 277, 331–33, 361
Krauss, Alison, 336, 413–14n
Kubrick, Stanley, 211
Kumalo, Bakithi, 254–55, 262, 278, 324, 380

"La Bamba" (Los Lobos), 286
Ladysmith Black Mambazo, 1, 252, 255–56, 269, 270, 272, 273, 275–76, 278, 280, 282, 284, 302, 304, 313, 335, 411n, 413–14n
Laing, Denzil, 164
Laird-Clowes, Nick, 226–28, 384, 408n
Lamont, Rosette (Rose) C., 39, 44, 46
Landau, Jon, 158–59, 171, 172
Landesman, Rocco, 317
Landry, Dickie, 257, 275
Lanin, Lester, 15
"Last Night I Had the Strangest Dream" (McCurdy), 57
"Late, Great Johnny Ace, The" (Simon), 233, 261, 276, 415n
"Late in the Evening" (Simon), 23, 226, 234, 287, 364, 370, 415n
Latin music, 166, 226, 286, 310, 311, 312
Afro-Brazilian-Cuban drum trail, 288
See also Capeman, The; specific songs
Lear, Norman, 361
"Leaves That Are Green" (Simon), 66, 87
Lebona, Koloi, 252, 253, 256
Lee, Bill, 56–57
Lefkowitz, Nat, 91
Leiber, Jerry, 33
Lennon, John, 24, 33, 38, 64, 112, 161, 162, 193–94, 233–34, 335, 408n
Lennon, Sean, 341
Les Cousins, London, 76, 109
"Let It Be" (Beatles), 153, 159
Levin, Tony, 199, 207, 223
Levine, Joseph E., 121
Levy's Recording Studio, London, 69–70, 72
Lewis, Jerry Lee, 26, 29, 40
Lewis, Mort, 34, 74, 88–93, 95–96, 98, 101, 110, 118, 122–23, 155, 156, 191, 233
"The Boxer" recording sessions and, 134
Catch-22 and, 129–30
Simon-Garfunkel split and, 157
Simon in Central Park and, 229, 231
Simon's generosity and, 237
Simon's LSD trip and, 114
Lewis, Smiley, 164
Lewis, Terry, 281
Library of Congress, Gershwin Prize for Popular Song, 345–46, 376, 413–14n
Lieberson, Goddard, 56, 67, 88, 95

"Life in a Northern Town" (Laird-Clowes), 227, 408n

"Like a Rolling Stone" (Dylan), 75

"Lily of the West, The" (Baez), 47

Lindsay-Hogg, Michael, 78, 79, 411n

"Lion Sleeps Tonight, The" (Tokens), 42

"Liquidator" (Harry J. All Stars), 178, 407n

"Lipstick on Your Collar" (Francis), 38

Little Anthony and the Imperials, 350

"Little Green Apples" (Russell), 138

Little Richard, 27, 30

Little Willie John, 47

Live from New York City, 1967 LP (Simon and Garfunkel), 105

London Times, review of Simon's career, 385

"Loneliness" (Simon), 36

"Lone Teen Ranger, The" (Simon), 42

Long Island Press, "Simon Steals Home," 11

"Lord Franklin" (traditional song), 64

Los Angeles Times
    Garfunkel on his vocal problems, 355
    on Simon and Dylan tour, 330
    Simon and Garfunkel benefit (1993), 304
    Simon interviews, 115, 129, 242
    Simon's South Africa concert and, 300
    Surprise review, 344
    Willman on Brickell, 290
    You're the One and, 333, 334

"Lose Yourself" (Eminem), 343

Los Incas, 146, 168, 184

Los Lobos, 261–62, 276–77, 286

"Love" (Simon), 415n

"Love and Hard Times" (Simon), 348–51, 355, 412n, 415n

"Love Me Tender" (Presley), 24

"Loves Me Like a Rock" (Simon), 179, 186, 200, 415n

Lowe, David, 71

Lucas, George, 244

"Luka" (Vega), 286

Lydon, Michael, 111

Lymon, Frankie, 26

"MacArthur Park" (Harris), 148

Mack, Joe, 74

Macklow, Joseph, 44

Madison Records, 41

Madonna, 249, 271, 324

Makeba, Miriam, 278, 280, 281

Mamas & the Papas, 101, 108, 111

Mandela, Nelson, 296–97, 300, 364

"Man of Constant Sorrow" (Dylan), 47

Mantle, Mickey, 35, 325

Marley, Bob, 164

Marsalis, Wynton, 344, 364–65

Marshall, Penny, 225, 244, 245

Martin, Douglas, 299

Martin, George, 62

Martin, Steve, 303, 322, 374

Martyn, Beverly, 374

Martyn, John, 110

Masekela, Hugh, 278, 280

Mathis, Johnny, 85

Matthews, David, 232

May, Elaine, 107–8

"Maybellene" (Berry), 33

Mayfield, Curtis, 335

Mazzola, Marco, 286–87

McAlley, John, 297

McCartney, Paul, 2, 24, 33, 157, 161, 162, 170, 194, 335, 340, 345, 361, 374, 388

McCausland, Dave, 47, 53, 63

McCausland, Jonty, 47, 53–54, 384

McCausland, Lynne, 54, 78, 83, 374, 384

McCoy, Charley, 87, 134, 170

McCracken, Hugh, 199, 207

McCurdy, Ed, 57

McGovern, George, 172

McGuire, Barry, 75

"Me and Julio Down by the Schoolyard" (Simon), 166–68, 170–72, 177, 206, 226, 308, 311, 316, 386, 387

"Memphis" (Berry), 259

Mercer, Johnny, 163, 324

Merenstein, Charlie, 21

MGM Records, 36

Michaels, Lorne, 201, 203–5, 210, 212–13, 221, 222, 244, 245, 289, 312, 331, 341, 374, 389
    Central Park concert (1981) and, 232
    Graceland and, 274, 284
    Simon in Louisiana and, 257–58
    Simon TV special and, 213, 218
    SNL and, 2–5, 204, 207, 250, 270, 272, 284
    WWHB-FM and, 332

Midler, Bette, 199, 204, 222

Mighty Clouds of Joy, 304
Milchberg, Jorge, 146
Miller, Mitch, 59
Minnelli, Liza, 253
Miranda, Cristina, 413n
Mitchell, Joni, 61, 145, 172, 388
Monroe, Bill, 330
Montauk, Long Island, 250, 258, 259, 289, 299, 336, 386
    "Back at the Ranch" concert, 297
    Simon-Brickell wedding at, 302–3
Monterey Pop Festival, 108–13, 116, 404–5n
Moody Blues, 403n
Moog, Robert and synthesizer, 117–18
Moonglows, 12
Moreira, Airto, 170
Morris, Mark, 314
"Most Peculiar Man, A" (Simon), 87
"Mother and Child Reunion" (Simon), 162, 163–66, 170–73, 254, 370, 415n
    covered by U2, 381
Mothers of Invention, 74
Motloheloa, Forere, 254, 255
"Mrs. Robinson" (Simon and Garfunkel), 5, 104, 113, 121–28, 131, 138–39, 144, 153, 165, 387, 415n
    performances, 173, 233, 325, 384
"Mr. Tambourine Man" (Dylan), 74
Mtshali, Isaac, 255
MTV, 216, 249, 275
Mulate's, Breaux Bridge, Louisiana, 257–58
Muscle Shoals Rhythm Section, 178–79, 197–98, 277
"My Little Town" (Simon), 198–99, 205–7, 209
"Mystery Train" (Presley), 23, 287
Mystics, 37
"My Sweet Lord" (Harrison), 153
"My Way" (Sinatra), 131

Nascimento, Milton, 286
NBC, 146, 149–50, 204, 213, 218. See also Saturday Night Live
Nederlander, James L. Jr., 312
Neil, Fred, 194
New Canaan, Connecticut, 336, 346, 351, 375–76, 377
    Simon's studio at, 351, 375
Newhart, Bob, 137

New Hope, Pennsylvania, 118, 153, 155
Newman, Randy, 162–63, 186, 200, 236, 244, 251, 379
New Orleans Jazz & Heritage Festival, 344–45, 353–54
New Show, The (TV show), 250
Newsweek, 111, 209, 218, 225
New Yorker
    Simon interview (1968), 115–16
    on Simon's post-Capeman LPs, 388
    Willis column, 112
New York Times
    on BAM's Simon series, 349
    "Bridge Over Troubled Water" review, 151–52
    Capeman articles and reviews, 311, 314–16, 360–61
    Dwyer on Simon's musical longevity, 382
    Emerson on Simon, 208
    Ephron piece on Catch-22 filming, 137
    on Garfunkel's being snubbed, 299
    Greenfield profile of Simon and Garfunkel, 128
    Hearts and Bones review, 245
    Heckman on McGovern fund-raiser, 172–73
    Holden on Brickell, 291
    O'Connor on Simon on SNL, 207
    Rockwell on Simon, 207–8
    Shelton on Simon and Garfunkel, 102
    Shelton reviews Simon, 96
    Simon and Garfunkel concerts, 105, 305
    Simon's op-ed pieces, 325, 349, 368, 412n
    on Simon's Saints tour, 298
    So Beautiful or So What review, 361–62
New York University, 154
Nguini, Vincent, 278, 324, 380, 390
Ngwenya, George, 300
Nichols, Mike, 107, 109, 113, 121, 129–30, 151, 212, 314
Nicholson, Jack, 211
"Night Game" (Simon), 195, 200, 415n
Nilsson, Harry, 193
9/11 telethon, 2, 401n
Nirvana, 61
Nixon, Richard M., 172
No Direction Home (Shelton), 71
North, Melissa, 341, 374, 384
Norton, Daniel (Sonny), 11
"Norwegian Wood" (Beatles), 62

Oak Ridge Boys, 217
"Ob-La-Di, Ob-La-Da" (Beatles), 164
Oblon, Jim, 380
"Obvious Child, The" (Simon), 289, 292, 294, 387–88, 415n
O'Connor, John L., 207
"Oh Mary Don't You Weep" (traditional), 141–42, 405–6n
"Old Friends" (Simon), 127, 340, 415n
Olympics, 42
"One for My Baby" (Mercer), 324
"One Man's Ceiling Is Another Man's Floor" (Simon), 384
One-Trick Pony (film), 3, 222–26, 232, 235, 246, 285, 307, 311, 322
"Only Living Boy in New York, The" (Simon), 144, 145
"Only Love Can Break Your Heart" (Young), 304
Ono, Yoko, 193, 194, 341
On the Road (Kerouac), 46
Onward Brass Band, 178
Orenstein, Harold, 90–91
Orth, Maureen, 209
Ortiz, Carlos, 168, 308
Osborn, Joe, 134, 145
Ostin, Mo, 216–17, 223, 225–27, 233, 236, 238, 243, 246, 251, 271, 361, 389
    Simon signs with Warner and, 217, 219
"Overs" (Simon), 110, 113, 115, 128
Oxenberg, Catherine, 270

Paine, John, 89
Palmieri, Eddie, 286
Pang, May, 194
Paragons, 164, 407n
"Paranoia Blues" (Simon), 170
Parcher, Peter, 312, 331
Pareles, Jon, 298, 305, 349, 361
Parsley, Sage, Rosemary and Thyme LP (Simon and Garfunkel), 93, 99–103, 109, 117, 124, 171
Partch, Harry, 365, 377
Passions, 34
"Patterns" (Simon), 99
Paul Simon: The Complete Albums Collection LP (Simon), 404n
Paul Simon: Live Rhymin' LP (Simon), 192, 407n

Paul Simon 1964/1993 LP (Simon), 402n
Paul Simon aka Jerry Landis LP (Simon), 402n
Paul Simon and Friends LP (Simon), 413–14n
Paul Simon LP (Simon), 162–73
Paul Simon's Concert in the Park LP (Simon), 300, 412n
Paul Simon Song Book, The LP (Simon), 69–72, 86, 87, 99, 101, 219, 404n
payola, 29, 185
"Peace Like a River" (Simon), 170, 415n
"Peggy-O" (traditional folk song), 61
"Peggy Sue" (Holly), 30
Penguins, 12
People magazine, 235, 243, 244
Pet Sounds LP (Beach Boys), 104
Petty, Tom, 112
Philips, Chuck, 303–4
Phillips, John, 101, 108
Phillips, Sam, 23
Phiri, Chikapa "Ray," 255, 258, 260, 262, 277, 364
Picture Perfect Morning LP (Brickell), 303, 351
Piepe, Judith, 66–67, 69–70, 72, 76, 79, 80
"Pigs, Sheep and Wolves" (Simon), 323
Pilgrims, 55, 56, 67
Playboy, Simon interview (1984), 112
"Poem on the Underground Wall, A" (Simon), 100
Porgy and Bess (Gershwin), 325
Presley, Elvis, 2, 22–24, 27, 30, 33, 35, 40, 131, 153, 211, 212, 213, 221, 255, 258, 259, 287, 330, 335, 402n
Pretty Things, 403n
Price, Lloyd, 200
Prince, 225, 249, 261, 271, 324
Proby, P. J., 403n
Prodigal Son (Shanley), 376
Prosen, Sid, 28, 29, 30–31, 129
Pryor, Richard, 204
"Punky's Dilemma" (Simon and Garfunkel), 109, 113, 118, 405n
Purple Diary, Harper Simon interview, 342
Purple Rain (film), 225
Purple Rain LP (Prince), 261

"Quality" (Simon), 313
Queen, 253

Queens College, 11, 31–32, 34, 35, 38–40, 48, 66, 75, 173
"Questions for the Angels" (Simon), 355–58, 381, 386, 389
"Quiet" (Simon), 322–23

R&B, 12, 21, 30, 33, 164, 176, 177, 178, 179, 200, 380
Ragtime (Broadway musical), 317
Raitt, Bonnie, 273
Ramone, Phil, 177, 226, 232
　　The Rhythm of the Saints LP and, 286–87
　　So Beautiful or So What LP and, 351–52
　　"Still Crazy After All These Years" and, 197–98
　　Still Crazy After All These Years LP and, 199–200
　　There Goes Rhymin' Simon LP and, 177, 178, 180
Rascoff, Joseph, 305, 312, 314, 331, 332
Rawls, Lou, 111
Ready Steady Go! (BBC), 78–79, 403n, 411n
Redding, Otis, 111, 177
Redlener, Irwin, 283–84
"Red Rubber Ball" (Simon), 97, 101
Reed, Lou, 284
Renbourn, John, 64, 76
"René and Georgette Magritte with Their Dog After the War" (Simon), 238–39, 381, 415n
"Rewrite" (Simon), 358–60, 415n
Reynolds, Debbie, 213, 220–22, 224, 235, 244, 291
Rhinoceros (Ionesco), 44
Rhythm of the Saints, The LP (Simon), 286–300, 309, 324, 334, 347, 348
"Richard Cory" (Simon and Garfunkel), 87
Righteous Brothers, 147
Riley, Jeannie C., 138
"Riverbank, The" (Simon), 372, 377
Rivers, Johnny, 111
Rizzuto, Phil, 10
Robin, Lou, 123
Roche, Maggie and Terre, 154–55, 179
Rock, Chris, 374
Rock & Roll Hall of Fame, 292–93, 335, 350
"Rock & Roll Music" (Berry), 284
rockabilly, 30, 42, 86, 258, 380
"Rock Island Line" (traditional song), 64

rock 'n' roll, 5, 11–12, 20, 29–30, 36, 38, 40, 41, 63, 79, 85, 94, 95, 108, 128, 200, 211, 262, 340
　　Brooklyn Paramount concerts, 26
　　cultural change and, 111–13, 152–53, 221
　　Johnny Mercer Award and, 324
Rock 'n' Roll LP (Lennon), 408n
Rockwell, John, 207–8
Rodgers, Richard, 163
Rogers, Selwyn, 413n
Rolling Stone magazine, 94, 99, 102, 111, 172
　　"American Tune" as song of the year, 186
　　Bookends LP review, 128
　　Garfunkel on his vocal problems, 370–71
　　interviews with Simon, 153, 154, 172
　　Paul Simon LP review, 171
　　Saints LP review, 297
　　There Goes Rhymin' Simon LP review, 184
　　You're the One LP review, 334
Rolling Stones, 62, 87, 111, 312, 379
Ronstadt, Linda, 273, 284
Rosas, Cesar, 262
Roseland Ballroom, NYC, 15, 166
Rosenthal, Hilton, 251–52, 253, 256
Ross, Diana, 222
Rossi, Mick, 380
Rostova, Mira, 223
Roth, Arlen, 245
Rothrock, Tom, 342
Roxy Music, 341
Rubin, Alton Jay "Dopsie," 257, 276
"Runaround Sue" (Dion), 351
Russell, Bobby, 138

Sager, Carole Baer, 281
St. Judy, Robert, 180
"St. Judy's Comet" (Simon), 179–80
Saltzman, Buddy, 74
Sanders, Bernie, 381, 384
Sanders Recording Studio, 28
San Francisco Chronicle, Gleason's review of Simon and Garfunkel, 98
Sanneh, Kelefa, 388
"Satin Summer Nights" (Simon), 313
Saturday Night Live (SNL), 1, 206–7, 210, 212–13, 228, 250
　　Brickell on, 289
　　Garfunkel on, 1, 206–7, 276

Simon and, 1, 3, 205–7, 220, 270, 272, 274–76, 284, 334, 335, 389

Simon and fortieth anniversary, 374, 411n

Simon's post-9/11 performance, 1–5, 385, 402n

"Save the Life of My Child" (Simon), 117

"Scarborough Fair" (Simon), 65

"Scarborough Fair/Canticle" (Simon), 100, 101, 113, 122, 206

Schantz, Bobby, 10

Scher, John, 354

Schlosser, Herb, 204

Schneider, Mitch, 112

Sears, Big Al, 26

Seeger, Pete, 57

Seekers, 97, 99

Segelstein, Irwin, 215, 218

"Señorita with a Necklace of Tears" (Simon), 323, 334, 415n

"7 O'Clock News/Silent Night" (Simon), 100–102

Sgt. Pepper's Lonely Hearts Club Band LP (Beatles), 104

Shabalala, Joseph, 256, 269–70, 272, 278, 302

Shaka Zulu LP (Ladysmith Black Mambazo), 270

Shampoo (film), 195, 200, 213

Shanley, John Patrick, 376

"Sh-Boom" (Chords, Crew-Cuts), 21

Shehan, Steve, 324

Shelton, Robert, 71, 96, 102, 105, 111
   No Direction Home, 71

"She Moves On" (Simon), 289

Sherwood, Bob, 205–6

Shirelles, 34

Shooting Rubberbands at the Stars LP (Brickell), 289

Shulman, Ettie Marcus (grandmother), 15

Shulman, George (cousin), 77

Shulman, Jerry (cousin), 12, 13

Shulman, Lee (uncle), 12

Shulman, Samuel (grandfather), 9, 15

"Side of a Hill, The" (Simon), 48, 101

Simon, Adrian (son), 3, 303, 343, 375–76, 384

Simon, Belle Shulman (mother), 6, 12–18, 41, 94, 116, 155, 244, 309, 346

Simon, Edward "Eddie" (brother), 13, 14, 16, 18, 20, 26, 53, 118, 137, 144–45, 244, 332
   Guitar Study Center and, 332
   "Still Crazy After All These Years" and, 196
   WWHB-FM and, 332

Simon, Gabriel (son), 322, 350, 384

Simon, Harper James (son), 176, 179–80, 189, 193, 210, 244, 259, 280–81, 296, 301, 341–42

Simon, John, 110, 117, 125

Simon, Lou (father), 9, 11, 12–16, 18, 28, 31, 46, 77, 137, 155, 224, 244, 296, 309, 335
   Paul's music and, 21–22, 25–26, 31, 33, 53
   Paul's relationship with, 22, 46, 77, 116, 309–10, 347, 349–50

Simon, Lulu (daughter), 3, 310, 343, 376, 389

Simon, Paul
   acting lessons, 223
   advisor, Klores, 274, 282, 301–2, 331, 347
   appearance and height, 10, 20, 37–38, 41, 191–92, 371
   awards and accolades, 2, 276, 292–93, 323–24, 336, 339, 345–46, 376 (*see also* Grammy Awards)
   bands of, 148–49, 225, 254, 277–78, 298, 310, 324, 325, 340, 344, 346, 367, 370, 371, 380–83, 391
   baseball and, 9–11, 19–20, 26, 27, 144, 200, 203–4, 244, 325, 336, 349, 415n
   business manager, 305, 312, 314, 331, 332
   cars owned, 36–37, 65, 156
   character and personality, 14, 17, 20, 37, 40–41, 43, 58, 76–78, 79, 83, 97, 116, 137, 143–44, 155–57, 177, 191, 205, 220, 223–24, 227, 275, 282, 284, 304, 325
   children of, 3, 176, 193, 210, 259, 280–81, 296, 301, 303, 310, 322, 341–43, 350, 375–76, 389
   competitive drive of, 20, 24, 42, 45, 77, 79, 154, 163, 217, 251, 310, 382
   critics and reviews, 94, 96, 98, 128, 151–52, 171, 184, 207–8, 218, 225, 276, 297, 298, 305, 334, 361–62, 377
   critics' reassessment of post-*Capeman* career, 377
   cultural change and, 6, 111–13, 246, 249, 275, 276

Simon, Paul (*cont.*)
  depression and anxiety, 13, 72, 116, 131,
    153, 161, 165, 190, 195, 200, 205, 226,
    228, 232, 251, 252, 321, 325, 390
  drug use, 6, 113–14, 250, 296, 322, 333–34
  ego, 6, 131, 216, 307, 316
  Emory University concert and lecture
    series, 368–69
  in England (2015), nostalgia and, 374–75
  fame, success, and, 6, 91, 97–98, 116, 124,
    153, 190, 213, 390
  films and, 3, 116, 195, 200, 210–13, 217,
    219, 222–26, 343 (*see also One-Trick
    Pony; specific films*)
  friendships (*See* Michaels, Lorne; Susser,
    Bobby; *specific people*)
  generosity and philanthropy, 174, 237, 253,
    277–78, 283–84, 303–4, 345–46, 381,
    389–90
  gopichand (instrument) and, 372
  Grammy Awards, 138–39, 155, 159, 172,
    190, 192, 209, 226, 270, 278–79, 281–82,
    286, 287, 297, 335, 339, 364
  guitars of, 12, 43, 47, 65, 134, 357
  homes/apartments of, 13–14, 97–98, 118,
    128–29, 141, 153, 155, 162, 190, 193, 205,
    211, 250, 258, 289, 299, 302–3, 336, 351,
    374, 375, 377, 386
  key influences in his life, 335
  lawyers for, 90–91, 139, 217, 219–20, 222,
    312, 331
  longevity of his music, 379–86, 415n
  manager, Jeff Kramer, 331, 332–33
  manager, Mort Lewis, 87, 88–93, 95–96
  mentoring by, 226–28
  musical education, 16, 194, 200, 260
  musical path of, 363
  9/11 terrorist attacks and, 1–5, 335–36
  obsession with his music, 79, 126, 156, 189,
    224
  as perfectionist or controlling, 31, 79, 88,
    136, 222, 310, 312
  as performer, 18, 80
  personal team for, 331–33, 412–13n
  polarized view of, 76–78, 317
  as record producer, 99–100, 104, 109, 134–36,
    148, 165, 178, 255, 269–70, 303, 343
  relationship with Kathy Chitty, 63–64, 71, 78,
    79, 83, 94–95, 109, 114, 298–99, 374, 384

  relationship with Shelley Duvall, 211, 212,
    213, 220
  relationship with Carrie Fisher, 215,
    220–25, 228–29, 233–35, 239, 243–45,
    249–50, 259, 266, 290–91
  relationship with Peggy Harper, 89–90,
    110, 114, 118, 145, 147, 151, 154–56, 162,
    189–91, 195–96, 199–200, 244, 273
  relationship with his father, 21–22, 33, 46,
    53, 77, 137, 309–10, 347, 349–50
  relationship with his mother, 346–47
  relationship with wife, Edie Brickell,
    289–91, 299, 302–3, 316, 322, 333,
    335–36, 347, 350, 375–77, 381, 383, 386,
    389
  religion and spirituality, 18, 94
  seventieth birthday, 362
  singing voice, 200–201, 208
  wealth, 6, 34, 116, 131, 237, 390
  work ethic, 20
  Zulu name for, 278
Simon, Paul, early years
  Amy Records, 41, 42–43, 45, 46, 47
  Big Records and Garfunkel, 28–30, 36, 129
  birth of, 12
  CBS Records, London, and *Paul Simon
    Song Book* LP, 69–72
  childhood and background, 2, 9–24, 168
  demos and, early, 32–33, 34
  draft status, 36
  dreams, violent, and, 13
  earliest songs, recordings, 25–38
  early search for a record label, 21–22,
    27–28, 32
  E. B. Marks Music Company and, 47–48,
    54, 56
  Eclectic Music and, 56
  education, 11, 16–18, 21 (*see also* Queens
    College)
  first recording, MGM Records, 36
  first recordings, home tape recorder, 21, 26
  folk scenes and, England and Greenwich
    Village, 5, 36, 43, 46–47, 53–54, 62–65,
    68, 72, 75–82
  Garfunkel as childhood friend, 2, 12–13,
    18–19, 340
  heroes of his teenage years, 35, 48–49, 88
  hitchhiking cross-country (1962), 46
  law school and, 49, 67, 68

Madison Records and, 41
music as a career (1958–60), 31–38
parents and, 11, 14–18, 25–26, 31
Paris trip with Redd Sullivan (1964), 66–67
Piepe and BBC, 66, 69–70, 72, 80
performing as Paul Kane, 48
performing as True Taylor, 31
at Queens College, 31–32, 34, 35, 38–40, 75
as singer with the Mystics, 37
sketch of himself (1965), 75–76
as songwriter for other groups, 41–42, 97
songwriting, starts own company, 56
Tom & Jerry days/Jerry Landis singles,
    28–30, 31, 36, 38, 40, 42, 132, 402n
touring, Europe (1965), 82
Tribute Records and, 48
Warwick Records and, 38
Simon, Paul, as group "Simon and Garfunkel"
    Bookends LP (1968), 104, 109–10, 115,
        117–18, 124–31, 138, 158
    breakup (1958), 30–31
    breakup (1970), 2, 150–54, 156–59
    breakup (1993) and shoving incident,
        303–6
    breakup (2010), 353–55
    Bridge Over Troubled Water LP (1970),
        145–51, 153, 158, 159, 163, 173, 287–88,
        406n
    Catch-22 and, 129–30
    Columbia Records and Wednesday
        Morning, 3 A.M. LP (1964), 54–62,
        67–68, 85–87
    concerts (see concerts: Simon and
        Garfunkel)
    famous/favorite songs by (see "Boxer, The";
        "Bridge Over Troubled Water";
        "Mrs. Robinson"; "Sound of Silence";
        specific songs)
    Garfunkel and, 21, 26, 28–30, 48, 155, 276,
        292–93
    Garfunkel and conflict, 31, 96, 124, 129,
        130, 139, 143, 194, 199, 209, 232
    The Graduate and, 107–9, 113, 115, 121–22
    group begins (1962), 48
    group's image and, 105, 112
    Lennon's Pussy Cats LP and, 193–94
    LP focus of, 103–4
    Parsley, Sage, Rosemary and Thyme LP
        (1966), 99–103

performances, number of (1968), 109
performing in Greenwich Village,
    60–61
reunion performances and recordings,
    172–73, 198–99, 205–6, 218, 232–45,
    276, 339–41, 350, 352, 354, 409n
sales, first three LPs, 103
in San Francisco (1966), 98–99
Sounds of Silence LP (1966), 83, 85–87, 93,
    96, 124
three albums in the Top 6 and, 128
touring, college venues, 92, 95, 98–99
touring, early earnings, 92, 93, 96, 103
TV special (1969), 149–51, 218, 406n
See also specific LPs; specific songs
Simon, Paul, as solo artist, 2, 30–40, 41,
    157–59, 161–62, 170–71, 175–76, 186,
    198–99, 209–10
    The Capeman (1998), 3, 285–86, 307–18
    Columbia Records and, 158, 161, 210,
        215–20, 222
    concerts (see concerts: Simon as solo artist)
    Graceland LP (1986) and South Africa
        boycott controversy, 2, 251–88, 291, 297,
        301, 304, 309, 324, 325, 334, 344, 348,
        349, 363–64, 377, 390, 410n, 414n
    Greatest Hits, Etc. LP (1977), 217–18
    Hearts and Bones LP (1983), 236–46, 249,
        251, 254, 261, 288, 334, 343, 409n
    Paul Simon LP (1972), 162–72
    Rhythm of the Saints, The LP (1990),
        286–300, 309, 324, 334, 347, 348
    So Beautiful or So What LP (2011), 350,
        355–64, 369, 377
    Still Crazy After All These Years LP (1975),
        198–200, 205–9, 217
    Stranger to Stranger LP (2016), 364, 365,
        371–77, 386, 415n
    Surprise LP (2006), 340–44, 347, 362–63,
        388
    There Goes Rhymin' Simon LP (1973), 173,
        175–84, 198–99
    TV special, CBS, 218
    Warner Bros. Records and, 219, 226,
        232–33, 237–38, 243, 245–46,
        271–72
    You're the One LP (2000), 5, 322–37, 350,
        362, 388
    See also specific songs

Simon, Paul, as songwriter
approaches to creating a song, 44, 115,
125–27, 129, 131–32, 141, 165, 254,
260–63, 266–67, 287–88, 291–92, 309,
326, 328–30, 343, 350, 357–58 (*see also*
specific songs)
Cajun music/zydeco and, 257, 258
concept of writing, 99
confidence and, 5–6, 43, 115, 130–31, 246
Davis's belief in his artistry, 161
doo-wop and, 12, 20–21, 34, 37, 41, 44, 284,
293, 312, 317, 326, 350, 361
enduring themes of, 45, 131–32, 143, 168,
170, 171, 234, 238–39, 269, 311, 326, 343,
361, 372, 376–77
evolution of, 108–13, 125–26, 170–71, 185,
260, 262–63, 284, 287–88, 321, 324, 368
father's career as musician and, 16
favorite songs written by, 386, 415n
favorite songwriters, 162–63
"flow" and, 143
folk music and, 5, 36, 43–47, 53–54, 57,
60–65, 68, 71, 72, 75–82, 128, 131–32,
208, 403n
four periods of, 387–88
generic teen pop and, 33, 38, 40, 45
gospel music and, 141–42, 173–74, 184,
351, 361
influence of Harry Partch, 365
influence of songwriters and performers,
22–28, 33, 44–45, 46, 62–63, 161, 186,
200
Jamaican ska/reggae and, 146, 163–68, 177,
178, 211–12
literary influences, 39–40, 43, 44
lyrics are not facts and, 90
piano pieces, 197
poetry of lyrics, 17, 64, 288–89
quintessential qualities of, 7
R&B and, 12, 21, 30, 33, 164, 176, 177, 178,
179, 200, 361
rearrangements of favorite songs, 381, 389
recognition as American great, 210,
387–88 (*see also* awards and accolades)
rockabilly and, 30, 42, 86, 258, 380
rock 'n' roll and, 5, 11–12, 20, 26, 29–30, 36,
38, 40, 41, 63, 79, 85, 94, 95, 108, 111–13,
128, 152–53, 200, 211, 221, 262, 324,
340, 361

singers of gentle songs and, 200–201
slowness of, 117, 163, 228, 263, 269, 308–9,
412n
song royalties and, 34, 38
songwriting credit disputes and, 276–77
South African music and, 250–56, 272–73,
278–80, 282, 284, 344
spirituality of lyrics, 18
teaching at NYU, 154–55
"trigger" for work of, 38, 39–40, 44–45
universality of the music, 234, 235
world music and, 42, 102, 146, 162, 168,
250–72, 285–97, 361
writer's block, 163, 189, 194, 228
See also specific albums; specific songs
Simon, Paul (US senator), 284
Simon, Pinkas (grandfather), 14–15, 46, 309
Simon and Garfunkel's Greatest Hits LP
(Simon and Garfunkel), 173
Simonson, Eric, 313
"Simple Desultory Philippic" (Simon), 71,
99–100
Sinatra, Frank, 2, 148, 253, 336
"Sincerely" (Moonglows), 12
Singer, Peter, 345
SIR Studios, NYC, 310
skiffle, 64
Skirball Cultural Center, Simon exhibit,
389
"Slip Slidin' Away" (Simon), 217, 415n
Sloan, P. F., 75
Smith, Andy, 309, 351
Smith, Elliott, 342
Smith, Robert, 361
Smokey Robinson and the Miracles, 88
Smoky Mountain Music Festival, 156
Snitzer, Andy, 380
Snow, Phoebe, 199
Snyder, Tom, 213
So Beautiful or So What LP (Simon), 350,
355–64, 369, 377
"So Long, Frank Lloyd Wright" (Simon), 144,
145
So LP (Gabriel), 281
"Someday, One Day" (Simon), 97
"Some Folks' Lives Roll Easy" (Simon), 381,
415n
"Something So Right" (Simon), 180–84, 387,
415n

"Somewhere They Can't Find Me" (Simon and Garfunkel), 86
Sondheim, Stephen, 163
"Song for the Asking" (Simon), 148
Songs from Liquid Days LP (Glass), 261
Songs from The Capeman LP (Simon), 351
Songs in A Minor LP (Keys), 337
Songwriters Hall of Fame, Johnny Mercer Award, 324
Sonny Til and the Orioles, 141
Soul Brothers, 253
"Sound of Silence, The" (Simon and Garfunkel), 6, 34, 53–54, 56–59, 61, 72–75, 80, 82–83, 85, 88, 91, 113, 131, 289, 311, 386, 387, 405n
    covers of, 97, 381
    performances, 66, 73, 184, 224, 234, 304, 330, 331, 339, 346, 350, 364
Sounds of Silence LP (Simon and Garfunkel), 83, 85–87, 93, 96, 124
South, Joe, 87
South African music, 250–56, 272–73, 278–80, 282, 284, 344
    South Africa concert (1992), 300–302
    See also Graceland LP
Spaniels, 21, 293
Spanish Harlem Orchestra, 349
"Sparrow" (Simon), 48, 61
Spector, Phil, 134, 147, 408n
Speed, Geoff, 80
Speed, Pam, 80
Spera, Keith, 353
"Spirit Voices" (Simon), 296, 415n
Springsteen, Bruce, 112, 171, 216, 225, 252, 261, 272, 284, 293
"Stagger Lee" (Price), 200
Stanhope Hotel, NYC, 190, 193
Stanley, Owsley III, 113
Staple Singers, 177
Star Is Born, A (film), 223
Starr, Ringo, 194–95
Stax Records, 177
Steely Dan, 335
Steffens, Roger, 252, 256
Stern, Isaac, 59
Stevens, Cat, 69, 109, 204
Stevenson, James, 115
Stewart, Al, 69, 72–73, 80–81
Stewart, Mark, 324, 365, 380–81, 415n

Stewart, Rod, 222
"Still Crazy After All These Years" (Simon), 190, 195–98, 200, 206, 213, 374, 386, 387, 407n
Still Crazy After All These Years LP (Simon), 198–200, 205–9, 217
    Simon and Garfunkel reunion track, 198, 205–6
Stimela, 255
Sting, 293, 367–71, 374–75, 414n
Stoller, Mike, 33
"Stranded in a Limousine" (Simon), 217–18
"Stranger to Stranger" (Simon), 376–77, 386, 415n
Stranger to Stranger LP (Simon), 364, 365, 371–77, 386, 415n
"Street Angel" (Simon), 372, 376
Streisand, Barbra, 2, 59, 85, 93, 172, 222, 232, 281
Sturges, Preston, 170
Sullivan, Redd, 65
Summer, Dick, 73
"Sun City" (Van Zandt), 272–73
"Sun Is Burning, The" (Campbell), 57
Sun Records, 23, 255, 258
Supremes, 82
Surprise LP (Simon), 340–44, 347, 362–63, 388
Susser, Bobby, 11, 16, 19–20, 22, 36–37, 40, 46, 83, 91, 155, 168, 205, 244, 308, 322, 346, 390–91
Swan Silvertones, 141–42, 406n

"Take Me to the Mardi Gras" (Simon), 178
Talking Heads, 261, 341
Tambo, Dali and Oliver, 363
Tannen, Michael, 139, 155, 193, 217, 219–20, 225, 331
Tao Ea Matsekha, 254
Tayi Bebba LP (Crisci), 372
Taylor, Derek, 157
Taylor, Elizabeth, 336, 337
Taylor, James, 99, 145, 153, 159, 172, 204, 217, 292, 336, 413–14n
Tee, Richard, 199, 207, 223, 232, 298
"Teenage Fool" (Simon), 30
"Teenager in Love, A" (DiMucci), 284
"Tenderness" (Simon), 176–79

"That's All Right" (Presley), 22–23, 384
"That's Me" (Simon), 347–48
"That's What Friends Are For" (Bacharach and Sager), 281
"That Was Your Mother" (Simon), 258, 276
There Goes Rhymin' Simon LP (Simon), 175–84, 186, 190–92, 197–99, 205, 275, 384
Thousand Clowns, A (film), 212
Thriller LP (Jackson), 216, 249
Tico and the Triumphs, 41
"Till I Waltz Again with You" (Brewer), 28
Time magazine, 345
"Times They Are A-Changing, The" (Dylan), 57, 59
Titelman, Russ, 238, 263, 264
Tokens, 42
Too Late at 20 LP (Laird-Clowes), 227
Toots and the Maytals, 164
Top 40 radio, 104
Tormé, Mel, 200
Torre, Joe, 20
Torres, Eddie, 310
Toussaint, Allen, 38, 176–77, 287–88, 344, 345
"Train in the Distance" (Simon), 90, 239, 415n
Travis, Merle, 43
Tribute Records, 48
Troubadour club, London, 63
Troxel, Gary, 42
"True or False" (Simon), 30
Tubert, Susana, 313
"Tutti-Frutti" (Little Richard), 27
"Tweedle Dee" (Baker), 30
Two Against Nature LP (Steely Dan), 335

U2, 2, 225, 286, 312, 341
Innocence + Experience tour, 381
Under African Skies (documentary), 363–64, 414n
"Under African Skies" (Simon), 260, 284
Urubamba, 184

"Vampires, The" (Simon), 313
Van Zandt, Steven, 272, 273, 363–64
Varèse, Joseph, 44
Variety, The Capeman review, 316–17
Vega, Suzanne, 286
Velvet Underground, 74

Verve/MGM Records, 74
"Vietnam" (Cliff), 164
Village Voice
    Graceland review, 276
    Surprise ranking, 344
    You're the One ranking, 334
Vipers, 65
"Voices of Old People" (Simon and Garfunkel), 127

WAAT radio, 13
Wainwright, Rufus, 341
Waits, Tom, 112
"Wake Up Little Susie" (Everly Brothers), 27, 28
Walcott, Derek, 125, 288–89, 309, 311–12, 314, 317, 321, 349, 390
"Wanderer, The" (Dion), 330
Warner Bros. Records, 216, 219, 227, 236, 252, 261
    Concert in Central Park LP, 232–33, 237
    Graceland anniversary boxed set and documentary, 363–64
    Graceland LP, 271–72
    Hearts and Bones LP, 238, 243, 245–46
    Shaka Zulu LP (Ladysmith Black Mambazo), 270
    The Rhythm of the Saints LP, 297
    Simon leaves, 361
    Simon's *One-Trick Pony* and, 226, 237
    Simon signs with, 217, 219
Warner Bros. Studios, 222–23, 225
Waronker, Lenny, 103, 236–38, 243, 251, 252, 261, 263–64, 271, 273, 277, 361
"Wartime Prayers" (Simon), 343
Warwick Records, 38
"Was a Sunny Day" (Simon), 179
Wasserman, Paul, 220
Wax, Beverly, 14, 17
Wax, Harold, 14
WBZ radio, 73
"We Are the World" project, 252–53, 283
Weavers, 57
Webb, Charles, 107
Webb, Jimmy, 148, 186
Webster, Guy, 87
Webster, Paul Francis, 87
"Wednesday Morning, 3 A.M." (Simon and Garfunkel), 60, 86

Wednesday Morning, 3 A.M. LP (Simon and Garfunkel), 55–62, 67–68, 93
  "He Was My Brother" on, 66
Weis, Gary, 274
Wenner, Jane, 210
Wenner, Jann, 99, 111–12, 210, 362
"Western Movies" (Olympics), 42
"We've Got a Groovy Thing Goin' " (Simon and Garfunkel), 86
"What Have They Done to the Rain" (Baez), 47
"What I Am" (Brickell), 289, 290
"When I'm Sixty-Four" (Beatles), 127
White, Jack, 234
White Swan Club, Romford, England, 47, 63
Who, 108, 111
"Who Else But You" (Avalon), 32
Who's Afraid of Virginia Woolf? (film), 107
"Why Don't You Write Me" (Simon), 146
Whyton, Wally, 65
"Wichita Lineman" (Campbell), 138
Widnes, England, 79–80, 298, 403n
"Wildflower" (Simon), 42
Wild One, The (film), 23, 41
Wild Thornberrys Movie, The (film), 343
William Morris Agency, 61, 88, 91, 93
Williams, Andy, 85
Williams, Marion, 173
Williams, Paul, 94, 404n
Willis, Ellen, 112
Willman, Chris, 290
"Will You Love Me Tomorrow" (Shirelles), 34
Wilson, Brian, 163, 335
Wilson, Edward O., 345, 356, 381, 389
  Half-Earth, 345
Wilson, John S., 151–52
Wilson, Tom, 54–58, 60, 62, 67, 69, 73–75, 86, 88, 101
Windsor Folk Club, Widnes, England, 80

WINS radio, 11, 12
Winwood, Steve, 238, 281, 286
Wired (Woodward), 224
Wishful Drinking (Fisher), 250, 409n
Wonder, Stevie, 64, 153, 170, 190, 194, 296, 345, 413–14n
Woodley, Bruce, 97, 99
Woodstock (1969), 108
Woodward, Bob, *Wired*, 224
WOR radio, 13
"Wristband" (Simon), 372–74
WWHB-FM, 332

"Yakety Yak" (Coasters), 33
Yale, Arthur, 42, 46
Yardbirds, 88
Yauaretê LP (Nascimento), 286
"Year of the Cat" (Stewart), 73
"Yesterday" (Beatles), 62
Yetnikoff, Walter, 215–20
  Howling at the Moon, 216
"You Can Call Me Al" (Simon), 255, 256, 260, 273–75, 415n
"You Can Tell the World" (Gibson and Camp), 61
Young, Neil, 112, 304, 335
Young, Robert M., 223, 225
"Your Cash Ain't Nothin' but Trash" (Clovers), 21
"You're Kind" (Simon), 199, 200
"You're the One" (Simon), 323
You're the One LP (Simon), 5, 322–37, 350, 362, 388
"You've Lost That Lovin' Feelin' " (Righteous Brothers), 147

Zaks, Jerry, 314, 315
Zappa, Frank, 44
Zollo, Paul, 130, 412n

ABOUT THE AUTHOR

Robert Hilburn was the chief pop music critic for the *Los Angeles Times* for more than three decades, during which he reported extensively on many of pop music's most significant figures, including Bob Dylan, John Lennon, Stevie Wonder, Joni Mitchell, Michael Jackson, Bruce Springsteen, and U2. He is also the author of two bestselling books: *Corn Flakes with John Lennon: And Other Tales from a Rock 'n' Roll Life* (a memoir) and *Johnny Cash: The Life*. He lives in Los Angeles.